HISTORY
OF RUSSIA

Sergei Mikhailovich Soloviev

The Academic International Press Edition of Sergei M. Soloviev's History of Russia From Earliest Times. *Peter von Wahlde, General Editor.*

Contributing Editors:

HUGH F. GRAHAM

JOHN D. WINDHAUSEN

ALEXANDER V. MULLER

K.A. PAPMEHL

RICHARD HANTULA

WALTER J. GLEASON JR.

WILLIAM H. HILL

G. EDWARD ORCHARD

LINDSEY A.J. HUGHES

NICKOLAS LUPININ

GEORGE E. MUNRO

SERGEI M. SOLOVIEV

History of Russia

Volume 48

The Rule of Catherine the Great

War, Diplomacy and Domestic Affairs, 1772 – 1774

Edited, Translated and With an
Introduction by

George E. Munro

Academic International Press

1991

The Academic International Press Edition of S.M. Soloviev's
History of Russia from Earliest Times in fifty volumes.

Volume 48. *The Rule of Catherine the Great, 1772–1774*. Unabridged translation of the text of Chapter IV of Volume 28 and
Chapters I and II of Volume 29 of S.M. Soloviev's *Istoriia Rossii s
drevneishikh vremen* as found in Volumes XIV and XV of this work
published in Moscow in 1963, with added annotation by George E.
Munro.

Library of Congress Card Number: 75–11085
ISBN: 0-87569-122-6

Composition by Janice Frye and Iris Knoebl

Printed in the United States of America

A list of Academic International Press publications is found at the
end of this volume.

ACADEMIC INTERNATIONAL PRESS
Box 1111 Gulf Breeze FL 32562

CONTENTS

The War With Turkey and Unsuccessful Peace Talks—The
Crimean Issue—Austria Agrees to Partition Poland—Final Ne-
gotiations on the Polish Partition—The Reaction in Poland—
The View from France—Upheaval in Swedish Politics—The
Reaction in Petersburg and Berlin—The Danish Revolution—
England's Reaction to the Events of 1772—The Significance of
the Polish Partition

Collapse of the Bucharest Congress—The Russian Offensive
of 1773—Rumiantsev's Retreat—The Second Russian Campaign—Activity of the Russian Navy—Shagin-Girey's Ouster
from the Crimea—Stanislaw and Poland's Proposed Constitution—Poland's Reaction to the Partition—The Diet Meets—
Interference from the King—Negotiations with the Delegation
of the Diet—The Dissidents—The Rights of the King—Frederick's View of Russian Options—Austrian Perspectives—The
View from France—The Crisis Subsides in Sweden—Denmark
Draws Closer to Russia—Russian-English Relations—The
Military Situation in the Balkans—War Brings Peace—Unresolved Problems in the Crimea—Order Restored in Poland—
Frederick II Intervenes—Some Observations

Illustrations

WEIGHTS AND MEASURES

Linear Measure

Verst: 500 sazhen, 1166 yards and 2 feet, .663 miles, 1.0668 km.
Sazhen: 3 arshins, 7 feet, 2.133 m
Arshin: 16 vershoks, 28in. (diuims) 72.12 cm
Chetvert: 1/4 arshin
Fut: 12 diuims, 1 foot, 30.48 cm
Vershok: 1.75 in., 4.445 cm, 1/16 arshin
Diuim: 1 inch, 2.54 cm
Desiatina: 2400 square sazhens, 2.7 acres, 1.0925 hectare
Chetvert (quarter): 1/2 desiatine, 1.35 acre (sometimes 1.5 desiatinas or ca. 4.1 acres)

Liquid Measure

Stof: Kruzhka (cup), 1/10 vedro, ca. 1.3 quarts, 1.23 liters
Kufa: 30 stofy
Vedro (paid): 3.25 gallons, 12.3 liters, 10 stofy
Bochka (barrel): 40 vedros, 121 gallons, 492 liters
Chetvert (quarter): 1.4 bochka, 32.5 gallons

Weights

Berkovets: 361 olbs., 10 puds
Pud: 40 funts, 36,113 lbs. (US), 40 lbs. (Russian), 16.38 kg
Funt: 96 zolotniks, .903 lb., 14.4 ozs., 408.24 grams
Grivenka: 205 grams
Korob (basket): 7 puds, 252 lbs.
Rad: 14 puds, 505.58 lbs
Chetvert (grain measure): 1/4 rad, 3.5 puds, 126.39 lbs., ca. 8 bushels
Chetverik (grain measure dating from 16th century): 1/8 chetvert, 15.8 lbs.
Zolotnik: 1/96 lb., 4.26 grams

Money

Chervonets (chervonny): A gold coin minted in the first half of the 18th century worth
    about 3 rubles
Muscovite Denga: 200 equals 1 ruble
Novgorod Denga: 100 equals 1 ruble
Ruble: 100 copecks, 200 dengas
Altyn: 6 Muscovite dengas, 3 copecks
Grivna: 20 Muscovite dengas, 100 grivnas equals 1 ruble, 10 copecks
Poltina (Poltinnik): 50 copecks, 100 dengas
Polupoltina (-nik): 25 copecks, 50 dengas
Poltora: 1 1/2 rubles
Peniaz: 10 equals one grosh (Lithuania)
Kopa grosh: 60 groshas, one Muscovite poltina
Chetvertak: silver coin equal to 25 copecks or 1/4 rubles (18-19th centuries)
Copeck: two Muscovite dengas
Foreign Denominations: 1 efimok or 1 thaler (Joachimsthaler)-about 1 ruble, 1 chervonets
    or chervonnyi—a ducat, about 3 rubles
Levok—Dutch silver lion dollar

Note: Weights and measures often changed values over time and sometimes held more than
    one value at the same time. For details consult Sergei G. Pushkarev, *Dictionary of
    Russian Historical Terms from the Eleventh Century to 1917* (Yale, 1970).

PREFACE

This book is an unabridged translation of Volume 28, Chapter 4, and Volume 29, Chapters 1-2, which are pp. 538-612 and 7-162 in Volumes XIV and XV of the multi-volume edition of Soloviev's *Istoriia Rossii s drevneishikh vremen* (History of Russia From Earliest Times, 29 vols., St. Petersburg, 1851-1879) published from 1962 through 1966 in Moscow.

The present translation endeavors to render the text and Soloviev's thought as accurately as possible. No attempt has been made to reproduce his style and text word for word for this would have yielded a bizarre Russianized text. The main consideration has been to make his history as readable as possible consistent with accuracy, while retaining at least something of the flavor of the language of the era. An effort has been made to find English-language equivalents for all technical terms Soloviev employs (ranks, offices, titles, legal, administrative and so forth) in the belief that English is no less rich in such terms than other languages. This is intended to smooth the flow of the narrative for the reader and to avoid marring the pages with annoying untranslated words. The exception involves Russian and other non-English words which have become common in English—boyar, tsar, cossack. Soloviev often underlined the literary flavor of a non-Russian source by quoting the key word, phrase or clause in the original tongue (usually French) and this has been retained. In all of this the translator remains painfully aware of the inevitable shortcomings that may remain.

Soloviev's pages are featureless and interminable, one long and complex sentence marching after the last. To make the text easier to follow for today's readers, long paragraphs and sentences have been broken into shorter ones. Most of the subtitles are based on the descriptive topic headings clustered at the beginnings of the chapters in the Russian edition. These headings have been moved into the body of the text as subtitles to mark and ease for the reader the transition from one subject to another. In some cases, to even the frequency of breaks in the text or to show topics not listed by Soloviev at the beginning of chapters, new subtitles have been added. Soloviev's arrangement of the material has been followed strictly.

Brief explanatory or interpretive materials have been inserted into the text enclosed in brackets, or added as footnotes to each chapter at the end of the book. All material enclosed in brackets has been added by the present editor and all material in parentheses is the author's. Emphasized words or phrases in italics are the author's.

The general policy followed in annotating has been to identify prominent personalities at first mention, and to give explanation and elucidations of less common or obscure terms and passages, assuming the typical reader to have relatively little familiarity with Russian history. If brief, these have been included in the text in brackets; otherwise they appear as numbered footnotes at the back of the book by chapters. Most of the author's own notes are not included because their highly specialized archival, documentary and bibliographic nature is of value solely to specialists who, in any case, will prefer to consult the original Russian text. In addition, most of the notes added by the editors of the edition published in the Soviet Union which also are technical in nature—fuller bibliographic citations than those in Soloviev's notes—have not been included. When the author's notes and those of the Soviet editors are included, they are so designated. All other notes are those of the present editor.

Russian personal names are preserved in their Russian form except for Alexander, Alexis, Michael, Nicholas, Catherine and Peter, which English usage has made familiar with respect to Russian historical figures, and for important ecclesiastics whose names have been recast into Latin or Greek equivalents, especially for the earlier period of Russian history. This applies to prominent individuals; Russian forms usually are used for the less prominent. Certain other names and terms have been anglicized for the sake of clarity and because they are used widely— Casimir, Sophia, Dantzig, boyar, rubles, versts, Dnieper river, and others.

The editors of the edition published in the USSR frequently have added patronymics and other names, and these have been retained without brackets; patronymics appearing in the original edition have also been included. Plural forms for names and terms which might be confusing have been anglicized—VolVolians rather than Vologzhane, Voguls and not Vogulichi, the Dolgorukys not Dolgorukie, and so forth. Even so, in a few cases the Russian plural form is used when this form is common. Most Slavic surnames show gender, and this has been preserved. Since an "a" at the word end usually signifies a female, Golovkin would have a wife or daughter Golovkina. The final "iia" in feminine personal names has been shortened to "ia"—"Maria" and "Evdokia" instead of "Mariia" and "Evdokiia".

Non-Russian names, locations, terms, ranks and so on are spelled according to the language native to the person or particular to the city, region or culture when this can be determined. Confusion arises at times because the text is not clear about nationalities. An excruciating example is Lithuania where at least three languages intermingle. In such cases the context is the guide used and as a last resort the Russian spelling in the text is accepted. Individuals whose names were once non-Russian but had been in Russian service for generations are named by the original spelling of the family name. Turkish, Tatar, Persian and other names and terms are spelled in the original according to accepted forms in scholarly books. In some instances, if not otherwise ascertainable they are translated from the Russian as given by Soloviev. The names of geographical locations conform to commonly accepted English usage—Podolia, Moscow, Copenhagen, Saxony and so forth.

Finally, with respect to transliteration, this translation follows a modified Library of Congress system omitting diacritical marks and ligatures, and rendering the initial "ia" and "iu" as "ya" and "yu" ("Yasnaia" and "Yury"), the suffixes "ii", "skii", "skaia" and "skoe" as "Dmitry Poliansky", "Polianskaia", "Polianskoe", and the form "oi" has been replaced by "oy" ("Donskoy" not "Donskoi") for certain family names familiar in this form in English. In some cases "i" has been inserted in place of hard and soft signs, or apostrophes indicating these signs. Hence Soloviev, not Solov'ev. The soft sign is not indicated by an apostrophe, as in some transliteration systems, but is dropped completely.

All dates, as in the original, except where otherwise specified, are according to the Julian calendar ("Old Style"); that is, for the seventeenth century, ten days and for the eighteenth century eleven days behind the Gregorian used in the West. A table of weights and measures is included at the front of this volume for the convenience of the reader.

I owe thanks to Harriet Meetz, Miranda Cooper, Betty Leviner, Laverne Elliott, and Wanda P. Clary for their help in typing the various stages of the manuscript. Special gratitude is due John T. Alexander for his careful reading of the entire manuscript and his helpful criticism. Whatever errors remain are mine. And I ask the forgiveness of my wife Sue and daughter Emily for the time the translation took away from them; they have been most understanding of the amount of work involved in "just a translation."

George E. Munro

INTRODUCTION

Sergei Mikhailovich Soloviev, from 1847 until his death in 1879 professor of history at Moscow University, is one of the greatest figures in Russian historiography. His principal legacy, the *History of Russia From Earliest Times* in twenty-nine volumes, is not only the most comprehensive and detailed pre-revolutionary interpretation of Russian history, but also one of the first histories of Russia utilizing the methodologies of the modern historical profession. All subsequent students of Russia's past have had to go back to Soloviev to acquire a full picture of Russian historiography, for he was a pioneer in stressing the utmost importance of sources and documentation in constructing historical interpretations. The *History of Russia* reaches only the mid-1770s; thus the present volume comprises the three concluding chapters of Soloviev's monumental opus. Soloviev did write elsewhere about the years following 1774, where this volume ends, but those essays are mere sketches when compared with the completed canvas of the *History*. Soloviev died with the final century of Russian history to his time unwritten by his hand.

In composing his vast overview of Russian history, Soloviev painstakingly assembled masses of documentation. He belonged to that group of nineteenth-century historians who believed that the sources could speak for themselves. Were one to collect all the evidence pertinent to an event and arrange it in the proper order, one would be able to understand the event sufficiently. Consequently Soloviev hesitated to impose his own organization on the sources, preferring to treat them in chronological or sequential order rather than use them as support for a framework of his own invention. The result is often visible as a lengthy compilation of passages drawn from the sources and quoted either directly or in paraphrase. Soloviev interjects himself from time to time (more than he would perhaps like to think) but is satisfied, to utilize the modern sports vernacular, with providing a play-by-play presentation and color instead of analyzing the action.

The tale thus told sometimes is confusing, introducing the reader to situations without adequate preparation to understand the context. The patient reader is rewarded in the end, for Soloviev eventually fills in the background, sometimes in his own words but more often through the sources. Despite his reluctance to judge his sources, Soloviev does reveal a distinctive interpretation of Russian history.

Soloviev considered the reign of Peter the Great critical in Russia's development, for he believed that Russia entered a new age at the beginning of the eighteenth century. This conviction was not his alone; the controversies over westernization and Peter's reforms were raging long before Soloviev's time. The new age was exemplified for Soloviev by Russia's altered relationships with other European nations. With Peter's victory in the Great Northern War (1700-1721) Russia pushed its way into the first rank of European states. While this rise was a military reality, diplomatic recognition of Russia's great power status was more difficult to achieve.

It should be noted that throughout the *History* Soloviev devoted particular attention to Russia's foreign affairs, seeking to define Russia's place in the European world. The problem was magnified by Russia's late entrance onto the international stage. The dominant states in Europe—Spain, France, Austria and England—had developed a system of alliances with a precarious balance. The injection of a new power could only upset the balance. For Russia, the principal adversary was France. Soloviev speaks through his sources on this issue. Thus Count Nikita Ivanovich Panin in a long instruction to the Russian envoy to France, Prince Ivan Sergeevich Bariatinsky, summarized Russo-French relations during the first decade of Catherine's reign, concluding that France was an implacable enemy because it could not endure the challenge of another state for primacy among Europe's kingdoms.

Prussia was in a similar position to Russia, for it also emerged as a claimant to major power status during the eighteenth century. At the time of the Seven Years War (1756-1763) Prussia and Russia were enemies, but this quickly changed after Peter III mounted the throne. The reversal of policy in his short reign in 1762, abandoning an Austrian ally for a Prussian, held for the first decade and more of Catherine's reign; indeed, the Prusso-Russian alliance was crucial for the execution of the first partition of Poland in 1772-1774.

Like the other major powers of Europe, Russia cultivated client states during the eighteenth century, among them Poland, Sweden, and Denmark. But rival factions in each of them owed allegiance to or attempted to coordinate actions with other powers, principally France and sometimes Turkey. Consequently, it was not always easy for Russia to exert its patronage over smaller states.

Two of the three chapters in this volume are concerned with foreign affairs. The first long chapter focuses on the year 1772 and touches on Russia's relationship with most European states. The second chapter, even lengthier, does the same for 1773 and the first half of 1774. Together these chapters deal with two significant episodes in Russia's expansion of its borders during Catherine's reign, the many-sided negotiations leading to the first partition of Poland and the protracted diplomacy of Russia's war with Turkey from 1768-1774.

Soloviev attributes the partition of Poland primarily to Frederick the Great of Prussia. Frederick's desire to flesh out his kingdom by attaching East Prussia territorially to Prussia proper underlay his machinations to divide Polish territory among its neighbors. In Nikita Panin, the leading official in Russia's College of Foreign Affairs, he found a willing ally. Panin, in Soloviev's view, was at times little more than a mouthpiece for Frederick. Under his leadership Russia consented to forsake acquisitions from Turkey in the valley of the lower Danube for gains from Poland in Belorussia (White Russia). With this bilateral partition worked out, the issue was compounded by Austria's sudden claim to a fair share in order to maintain the balance among the major powers of Eastern Europe. More than a year was consumed before the three states forged an agreement on the boundaries of their shares. In fact, it appeared for a time, when Austria wished an additional strategic gain and Frederick desired Dantzig and Thorn, as if Poland might disappear entirely. Soloviev condemned both Prussia and Austria for making unjust acquisitions, but Russia's incorporation of White Russia he saw as the just fulfillment of an historical destiny begun during the seventeenth century, although he conceded that in appearance the acquisition was besmirched by its company.

Once the partition had been agreed upon, it remained to persuade the Poles to accept it. Here the structure of Polish government came into play. Poland was dominated internally by the Czartoryski family and externally by Russia. Ostensibly a republic with an elective king, an oligarchic Senate and a Diet (Sejm) to which any member of the gentry (szliachta) might belong simply by attending its sessions, Poland was in reality ruled by bribe and intimidation. Most landowners lived in penury, a condition which made them particularly susceptible to bribes, which were proffered freely. Thus the three allies could expect to buy consent to the partition. But there were numerous pitfalls before the goal could be achieved. The powerful senators had to be neutralized, the king's inflammatory oratory had to be calmed, and the fears of an intensely Catholic gentry that religious dissidents might gain powerful political positions, had to be allayed. It is no wonder that Catherine wanted to celebrate when the partition was approved fully and finally.

That there was a direct connection between affairs in Poland and the Russo-Turkish war Soloviev had no doubt. To begin with, Turkey declared war because of Russian violations of its border while pursuing Polish guerillas fighting against Russian occupation of Poland. But more significantly for Soloviev it was obvious that snags in Poland were reflected in Turkish attitudes toward negotiations. Only as the settlement of the Polish question was hammered out did Turkey respond to Russia's peace efforts. Soloviev attributed the winning of peace largely to the efforts of three men, Field Marshal Peter Alexandrovich Rumiantsev, Aleksei Mikhailovich Obreskov, and Count Grigory Grigorevich Orlov. The latter two presented Russia's views, which constituted the basis of the peace, at the initial negotiations in Focsani (July-August 1772) and Bucharest (October 1772-March 1773). Rumiantsev, commander of Russia's First Army in the Danube basin, eventually won the peace through the successes of his spring campaign in 1774. By examining his correspondence with Catherine, Soloviev found that Rumiantsev was embittered by political opposition at court and wavering in his will to press the fight to the Turks because of his endless bouts with fevers brought on by the mosquito-plagued climate in the area where his army was encamped. Catherine dealt with him firmly and dispassionately; ultimately he justified her confidence in him.

The greatest barrier to the conclusion of peace from 1772 to 1774 was Russian insistence on independence for the Crimea. This was not one of Russia's initial war aims, but tactical and strategic considerations soon raised it to primary importance. The Crimea nominally was ruled by a khan of the Girey family, but his powers were severely limited. In practice the various Tatar hordes, or tribes, kept their own counsel. In war the khan did assume command and was treated by the Ottoman Porte as the moral and political leader of his people. Because of its geographical position the Crimea increasingly became a pawn between Russia and Turkey. Both large powers had their factions and supporters. Russia, which long was the prey of marauding bands of Tatars, seized upon the opportunity presented by the war with Turkey to neutralize the Tatar threat. In 1770 Russia struck an agreement with the Nogay Horde by which the Nogays agreed to move from the Bug river area to the steppes of the Kuban, some three hundred miles further east, in exchange for Russian guarantees of their independence of the Crimean khanate under the Gireys. Meanwhile Russia negotiated with the khan regarding independence for the entire khanate. When these talks proved barren Russia invaded and occupied the Crimea, thereupon initiating the agreement with the Nogays in favor of an independent khanate comprising all the hordes. Turkey hardly could be expected to accede to this loss of territory; it redoubled its resolve to fight to extinction if necessary rather than yield. Soloviev believed that Russia made a grave error by insisting on Crimean independence, citing it as the single most troublesome clause in the subsequent Treaty of Kuchuk-Kainardji with Turkey in July 1774.

The year 1772 was important in determining Russia's future relations with Poland and Turkey. That year also witnessed significant developments in Russia's relationships with Sweden and Denmark, for both countries underwent revolutions, as Soloviev terms them, or to be more precise, coups.

King Gustavus III inherited the Swedish throne in 1771. He chafed at the close confines on royal power imposed by the constitution of 1720, adopted under the guaranty of Russia, Prussia and Denmark. Whereas he retained the trappings of royalty, the constitution gave effective control over affairs of state to the nobility, the strongest of the four estates in the Riksdag and the source of members of the royal council and the Senate. King Gustavus's coup in August 1772 upset the harmony with Russia for, by implication if not overtly, France had encouraged him. Russia regarded the coup as a threatening gesture and might have attacked Sweden and restored the former constitution had its army not been bogged down against Turkey. Gustavus's repeated assurances that Sweden had no intention of fighting an irredentist war over Finland restored Russia's trust and the crisis passed.

Almost simultaneously a coup in Denmark deposed Queen Matilda and her lover Doctor Struensee and their supporters. Russia approved of this overthrow and used it to restore to power the party clearly supportive of Russia's interests. Soloviev reveals Russian disapproval of the justice meted out to Struensee and Colonel Brandt, quoting Catherine's views as expressed in her correspondence. Her reaction to the events in Denmark is highly revealing of her awareness of the similarity between the Danish situation in 1772 and her own coup against her husband Peter III a decade earlier.

Underlying Russia's problems with Poland, Turkey, Sweden, and Denmark and its misunderstandings with Austria and England was the fundamental antagonism with France. In both chapters on foreign relations Soloviev is careful to establish that their relationship was proper but cool. He quotes at length from conversations between the Russian ambassadors and the French foreign minister. By way of introduction to this relationship Soloviev provides a succinct summary of the development of Russo-French antagonism. Attributing responsibility to France's unwillingness to accept Russia as an equal power, he unhesitatingly points to the Duke de Choiseul as the chief villain. Soloviev's hostility to France decreases with the replacement of Choiseul by the Duke d'Aiguillon, but the ineptitude of the latter, in Soloviev's view, did not result in an effective reorientation of French foreign policy.

Austria figures in the tale not as an initiator of policy but as a state reacting to the initiatives of others. Indecisiveness is its hallmark, the result of a three-cornered difference of opinion among Prince Kaunitz, Maria Theresa, and her son Joseph II. Soloviev portrays Austria's gradual estrangement from Turkey and France and warming to Russia as a consequence of a promise of territorial acquisition. By the same token, Russia's reorientation from a Prussian to an Austrian axis was the inevitable outcome of Frederick's effrontery and Austria's responsiveness during the crises of 1772-1774. Although the Prussian treaty remained in effect for several more years, Russian attention was drawn ever closer to the southwest and the commonality of Russian and Austrian interests towards Turkey.

Only after exploring the significance of foreign affairs does Soloviev turn to Russia's domestic situation during these years. The final chapter is organized around the effects of the Turkish war on life in Russia and focuses on several problems. Most prominent among them was the difficulty of providing enlightened, efficient administration. Soloviev approaches the issue from the dual standpoints of the central government and the local administration. His examination of the Senate's activities in particular reveals the difficulty of accomplishing administrative tasks effectively and expeditiously. Matters initiated in the late 1760s still had not been settled several years into the 1770s despite a flood of instructions, reproofs, and admonitions. On at least one occasion Catherine ordered a prisoner to be released on the grounds that his appeal was not heard within a reasonable time.

In the provinces the task was even greater. Local officials often bullied the people under their jurisdiction into obedience, frequently incurring the wrath of central government offices in the process. Soloviev cites numerous instances when innocent people were coerced into signing confessions by police torture. Religious superstition was widespread, its influence documented amply through several illustrations.

Soloviev did not make gentry-serf relations a focal point of his history but several pages are found here reciting a "doleful list" of crimes committed against serfs, usually murder by their landlords. His explanation of the widespread distribution and frequency of such crimes rests on his conception of the nature of the gentry. Soloviev believed that Peter III's decree of 1762 emancipating the gentry from state service in peacetime was responsible for a large proportion of the crimes because the gentry had not been prepared for its transformation from servant of the state to lord of the manor. In the countryside the untrammeled power of the gentry resulted in an abuse of power by many landowners, the younger in particular, who were intoxicated by their new freedom from following orders and their license to issue them. Soloviev notes that women often turned out to be less humane masters than men, attributing this fact to their lesser degree of preparation and greater emotional susceptibilities.

The administration of Russia's towns is summarized in a few pages, stressing the high incidence of riot and disorder. Soloviev devotes a substantial portion of the chapter to a single episode in Moscow, the great riot of 1771, which is treated as an unfortunate but largely fortuitous event, the result of natural calamity as much as human error or shortcomings.

A second theme Soloviev nurtures in these pages is that of the fates of competing factions for power and influence at court. During these years the struggle involved the Panin party and the Orlov party. At the conclusion of the first chapter Soloviev summarizes Catherine's relationship with Nikita Panin as inexorably deteriorating, doomed because of Panin's insistence on the primacy of the Prussian alliance. But Catherine's relationship with Panin was never intimate; Panin did not enter her boudoir. As everyone knows, Grigory Orlov did. In the third chapter Soloviev chronicles his fall from influence and favor. Orlov dreamed of military laurels, but his ambition was thwarted by Field Marshal Rumiantsev, whom Catherine preferred to lead her troops. Orlov went to Moscow to restore order following the great riot in anticipation of parlaying this position of prominence in domestic affairs into a major military command. In fact, his assignment to Moscow presaged his eventual dismissal from court. Soloviev believed that Catherine began to reevaluate her relationship with Orlov even before his departure, citing her correspondence with Frau Bielcke as evidence that Catherine no longer was blinded to Orlov's faults by his proximity. Their relationship was never the same following his return. Soon he was sent to Focsani as chief negotiator, but after his failure to achieve peace Catherine refused to grant him an audience on his return to the capital. Thus the great competition between the rival factions led by the Panins and the Orlovs ended in victory for neither side. The ultimate victor was an ambitious general with Rumiantsev's army in Wallachia, Grigory Potemkin. Soloviev provides a thumbnail evaluation of Potemkin's character in the last pages of the volume, a sketch he undoubtedly hoped to flesh out in subsequent chapters.

Although the first two chapters of this final volume of the *History* end on the positive notes of the successful partition of Poland and the conclusion of the peace of Kuchuk-Kainardji, the chapter on domestic affairs ends on a quite different note. Indeed, the picture of Russia's domestic conditions is bleak: superstition gripping the minds of the peasants and government officials alike; riots in the major cities; bestial treatment of serfs by their owners; conspiracies in the guards against the crown—and Soloviev did not live to write the most lurid and depressing part of the final chapter, the story of the Pugachev rebellion (1773-1774). He referred to it in earlier chapters and apparently intended to end this chapter with its narration. Unfortunately death claimed him before he could complete the task.

The present account undeniably would have been enhanced by the history of the Pugachev rebellion. Soloviev was well aware of the great irony in the fact that the most embarrassing moments for Catherine domestically—and the most tragic for Russian society in her reign—came precisely at the moment when her foreign policy was achieving notable goals. Even without Pugachev it is clear that in Soloviev's mind the period 1772-1774 marked the first large turning point in Catherine's reign, domestically as well as internationally. It is here that the first shifts in advisors, policies, and goals are observed. With Soloviev, then, let us examine these changes.

DIPLOMATS MENTIONED IN THE TEXT
(dates in office when known)

In Russian Service

Foreign Minister:
Nikita Ivanovich Panin (1763-1780)

To Austria:
Dmitry Mikhailovich Golitsyn (1764-1792)

To the Crimea:
Peter Petrovich Veselitsky (1772-1775)

To Denmark:
Ivan Ivanovich Mestmakher (1770-1772)
Ivan Matveevich Simolin (1772-1775)

To England:
Aleksei Semenovich Musin-Pushkin (1765-1768)
Ivan Grigorevich Chernyshev (1768-1769)
Aleksei Semenovich Musin-Pushkin (1769-1779)

To France:
Nikolai Konstantinovich Khotinsky (1767-1773)
Ivan Sergeevich Bariatinsky (1773-1783)

To Poland:
Nikolai Vasilevich Repnin (1764-1769)
Mikhail Nikitich Volkonsky (1769-1771)
Caspar von Saldern (1771- 1772)
Otto Magnus von Stackelberg (1772-1790)

To Prussia:
Vladimir Sergeevich Dolgoruky (1762-1786)

To Sweden:
Ivan Andreevich Ostermann (1760-1774)
Alexander Stakhievich Stakhiev (1774-1775)

To Turkey:
Aleksei Mikhailovich Obreskov (1751-1768)
Nikolai Vasilevich Repnin (1774-1776)

In Austrian Service

Foreign Minister:
Wenzel Anton von Kaunitz-Reitberg (1753-1780)

To France:
Francis Florimond Claude Mercy-Argenteau (1766-1790)

To Poland:
Karl Emerich Rewiczki

To Prussia:
Godefroy van Swieten (1768-1776)

To Russia:
Joseph Maria Karl von Lobkowitz (1764-1777)

To Turkey:
Franz Maria von Thugut (1769-1774)

In Danish Service

Foreign Minister:
Johann Hartwig Bernstorff (1751-1772)
Andreas Peter Bernstorff (1773-1780)

In English Service

To Austria:
Robert Murray Keith (1772-1789)

To Denmark:
Robert Murray Keith (1772)

To Prussia:
Robert Gunning (1771-1772)

To Russia:
Charles Schaw, Lord Cathcart
(1768-1771)
Robert Gunning (1772-1775)

To Sweden:
John Goodricke

In French Service

Foreign Minister:
Etienne François, Duke de Choiseul
(1758-1770)
Emmanuel-Armand de Vigneret,
Duke d'Aiguillon (1771-1774)
Charles Gravier, Count of Vergen-
nes (1774-83)

To Austria:
François Michel Durand de Distroff (1770-1772)
Louis-René-Edouard de Rohan
(1772-1774)

To Denmark:
Paul Blosset (1766-1774)

To Poland:
Charles-François de Broglie (1752-
1773)

To Russia:
Honoré Auguste Sabatier de Cabre
(1772)
François Michel Durand de Distroff (1772-1775)

To Sweden:
Charles Gravier, Count of Vergennes (1771-1774)

In Polish Service

Special envoy to Russia:
Frantizsek-Ksavery Branicki (1772,
1774)

Special envoy to France:
Frantizsek-Ksavery Branicki (1773-
1774)

In Prussian Service

To Austria:
Edelheim

To Denmark:
Joachim Erdmann von Arnim

To France:
Wilhelm Bernhard von Goltz
(1772-1792)

To Poland:
Benoit (1758-)

To Russia:
Victor Friedrich Solms (1762-
1779)

To Sweden:
Count Denhoff

To Turkey:
J.C. von Zegelin (1765-1776)

In Swedish Service

To Russia:
Baron Ribbing

To Turkey:
Zelzang

Russo-Turkish War, 1772–1774

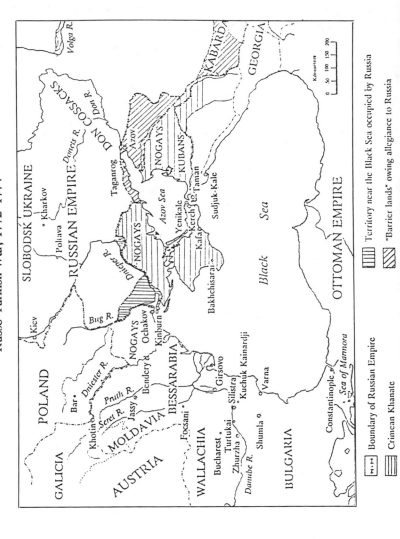

GALICIA

POLAND

SLOBODSK UKRAJNE

Volga R.

o Kiev

o Poltava

o Kharkov

Bug R.

Dnieper R.

DON COSSACKS

Donets R.

Don R.

RUSSIAN EMPIRE

NOGAYS

NOGAYS

Taganrog

KABARDA

GEORGIA

Bar •

Dniester R.

Khotin

Seret R.

Pruth R.

Jassy o

Bender o

NOGAYS

Ochakov

Kinburn

Azov

Azov Sea

Yenikale

Kerch o Taman

Kafa

Sudjuk-Kale

KUBANS

MOLDAVIA

BESSARABIA

Focşani •

Girsovo

Silistra

Kuchuk Kainardji

Bakhchisarai

Black Sea

WALLACHIA

Bucharest o

Turtukai

Zhurzha o

Danube R.

Shumla o

o Varna

Constantinople o

Sea of Marmora

AUSTRIA

BULGARIA

OTTOMAN EMPIRE

Kilometers

0   50   100   150   200

- - - Boundary of Russian Empire

|||||| Crimean Khanate

|||||| Territory near the Black Sea occupied by Russia

//// 'Barrier lands' owing allegiance to Russia

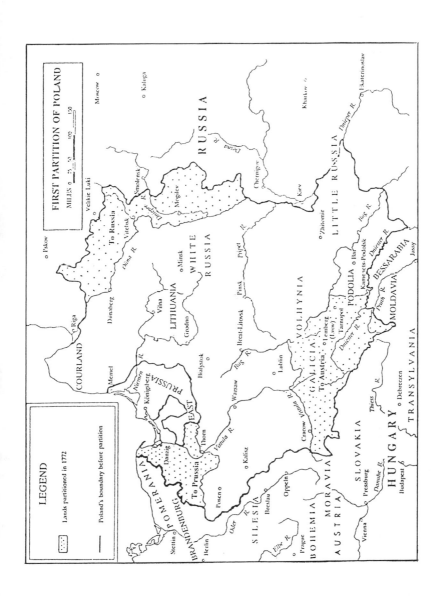

LEGEND

Lands partitioned in 1772

Poland's boundary before partition

FIRST PARTITION OF POLAND

MILES 0 25 50 100 150

History of Russia

Volume 48

The Rule of Catherine the Great

War, Diplomacy and Domestic Affairs

1772 – 1774

I

FOREIGN RELATIONS, 1772

THE WAR WITH TURKEY AND UNSUCCESSFUL PEACE TALKS[1]

It seemed that the hopes for peace that greeted 1772 would vanish at the very beginning of the year. On January 21 Count Nikita Ivanovich Panin, Russia's leading minister, informed the Council of disturbing news from Berlin.[2] Prince Wenzel Anton von Kaunitz, the Austrian chancellor, seemed doubtful that the Ottoman Porte would accept the latest Russian terms.[3] Furthermore, Frederick II had reported that the rumored alliance between Austria and Turkey was authentic.[4] The Council agreed to conceal its own knowledge of the treaty's existence until it had sized up the matter once and for all. Two days later, on the twenty-third, Count Grigory Grigorevich Orlov[5] revealed that Catherine wanted the Council to reach a final decision whether an expedition to Constantinople was practical or would assure peace in 1772, and to decide who should lead it, Count Peter Alexandrovich Rumiantsev or someone in Petersburg.[6] (The members of the Council must have guessed that Orlov himself desired the appointment.) Catherine directed the Council to hold a special session in her presence to discuss these matters. Not wanting to delay, they arranged a meeting for the next day, January 24.

Count Zakhar Grigorevich Chernyshev opened the debate with the opinion that it would be impossible to dispatch troops against Constantinople before June. Although only 350 versts separated the Danube and Constantinople, he argued that the march would require at least three months because the army would have to carry all its provisions and supplies. Otherwise, crossing the Balkans presented no insuperable difficulties. Because of the disorder of the Turkish army, Chernyshev expected the Russians to win any skirmishes that took place.

Having heard this opinion, the empress again put the first two questions to the Council: would the march of troops against Constantinople promote peace, and would the enterprise be practical? The members of the Council answered affirmatively, but added that success likewise would depend on unforeseeable circumstances. Count Orlov expressed the view that a campaign to Constantinople would encounter the fewest logistical problems and maintain the best security if it proceeded by way of Varna. Some of the regiments could travel down the Danube by boat, for which reason he suggested building as many more transport craft there as possible and also using part of the Azov flotilla. The two frigates being outfitted on the Don might serve to protect the transports and clear the Black Sea of enemy ships. Strong naval armaments would have to be built as a further demonstration of Russian power. The Council also decided the third issue, concerning the command of the operation, by stating that Catherine should name the commander, but that overall direction should be entrusted to Field Marshal Rumiantsev.

Catherine then expressed her desire that the Austrians reveal their plans more quickly, to enable her government to develop its measures accordingly.[7] Count Panin interjected that in the event of an Austrian entry into Wallachia it would be necessary to ravage that province hastily in order to impede the movement of the Austrian troops. Since a lasting peace with the Turks would never be possible, in the event of Austrian intervention in Poland Russia could achieve peace for the present by razing Moldavia and Wallachia and evacuating all inhabitants by force. Thereby Russia might remain safe from the Turks so long as peace endured. The Azov flotilla would suffice to protect the Crimea. Thus secure from the Turks, Russia could use its entire army to expel the Austrians from Poland and restore calm there. But all this should be a last resort, were the Porte not to agree to send plenipotentiaries to conclude peace.

The alarm over Austria's unknown intentions subsided when the favorable news arrived from Vienna that the anxiety in the Austrian capital aroused by the difference of opinion between Emperor Joseph II and Kaunitz had abated.[8]

The chancellor had raised the question of whether Austria should take its share of territory from Turkey, or Poland, or both.[9] The study of the relevant maps was leading Kaunitz again to the idea that the acquisition of Polish districts, no matter how large, would not be advantageous, for they would not be in natural communication with the other parts of the monarchy, separated as they would be by the Carpathian mountains. In this most important respect the shares of Prussia and Russia would be much more advantageous. Kaunitz was returning to his favorite idea: let

Frederick take whatever he wanted from Poland, as long as he returned Silesia to Austria.[10] But if Frederick would not give up Silesia, would it not be more advantageous for Austria to demand from him German lands, the margravates of Ansbach and Bayreuth? Should Prussia in the end not agree even to this, it would be both more advantageous and more natural for Austria to find an outlet for expansion in the south along the Danube, the empire's main river, downstream toward the Black Sea, by taking Wallachia and the seacoast of Bessarabia and Moldavia. Austria might give the remainder of Bessarabia and Moldavia to Poland as a compensation for the land the latter would lose to Prussia and Russia. This arrangement seemed particularly desirable to Kaunitz because Turkey could agree to it too without war. Or one might take Russia's view and seize much more Turkish territory. But in that case it would be necessary to make war on Turkey jointly with Russia, which Vienna did not at all want to do. Besides, in that case it would be necessary to share the gains with Russia and increase the latter's power.

Kaunitz's opinion that Austria should receive territories here and there solely to uphold the balance among the powers astounded Emperor Joseph. The empire would gain nothing of substance but would risk gaining much less than Russia and Prussia, if not in the size of the acquisitions then in their significance in the general composition of the empire. Joseph opposed the chancellor's proposals for partition, favoring instead a naked acquisition by Austria alone. To bring his plan to fruition, Joseph thought it necessary to prolong the conflict between Russia and Turkey. Whereas it was improbable that military fortune would swing toward the Turks and allow them to drive the Russians out of the occupied Turkish districts, it was equally unlikely that Russia would deal Turkey a serious enough blow in the next campaign to shake its foundations. Austria stood to lose nothing from a continuation of the war; on the contrary, it stood to gain much. It might profit not only from the vicissitudes of war, but coincidentally the weakening of both belligerents would lend Austria the opportunity to demand greater advantages than it had been able to stipulate up to then.

Moreover, the king of Prussia would continue to pour money into subsidies for his ally.[11] Perhaps he would fall out with Russia, whose expectation of more aid would be frustrated. The ensuing quarrel would force the king into Austria's arms in the hope of attaining his aims with its help. Austria could not enter the fray now; but a year hence, in 1773, it would be in a position to exert pressure on a weaker country in greater need of peace. It was immaterial whether the Porte regarded its convention with Austria as binding. If it did, Austria would be rewarded richly for its military expenditures. Should it not, Austria would be free to move against Turkey, seizing whatever territories it desired. Consequently Austria must bend every effort to persuade the Porte to reject the Russian offers and the truce. Frederick must be convinced that Austria would pursue resolutely a policy in Poland congruent with his. Meanwhile, Austria must occupy Cracow, Sandomierz, Lwow, and Czestochowa. At the same time Austria must announce its intention to maintain the king of Poland on his throne and to restore all Polish districts occupied by Austrian troops should Russia and Prussia do the same. In this way, even if it should prove impossible to induce Turkey to continue the war, Austria would be holding a strong security for acquisitions in Poland.

But the wily old chancellor, Kaunitz, victoriously challenged the emperor's view. It would be strange to expect Russia not to receive significant gains from this latest war, which would not constitute great loss for Austria. Russia, Prussia, and the Porte all seriously desired peace. Turkey's obstinacy merely signalled the hope that Austrian interference might gain it advantageous terms. Were Vienna now to oppose peace, it might well be concluded without Austrian participation. Austria's show of force and strong language had forced Prussia and Russia to consider its wishes and agree to divide with Vienna the gains they had won. But a show of force now could not gain anything further, for the Porte was even more beleaguered while Prussia and Russia were in total agreement. Military preparations, besides wasting much money, would lead merely to Turkey and Prussia winning at Austrian expense. Russia would propose the most advantageous terms to the Turks if only to thwart Austrian intentions, and at the same time would be forced to draw even closer to the king of Prussia and offer him similar, most advantageous terms. The deliberate behavior of Frederick II was designed perfectly to this end; he would be delighted should Austria decide to continue its already quite untimely demonstrations without striking an agreement with either side. By obstructing the conclusion of peace, Austria would incur the hatred of the other powers and would stand apart as a mere spectator while Russia and Prussia extracted all possible advantages from their alliance. But by facilitating the consummation of an armistice Austria might hope to participate in the peace congress and to turn its negotiations in its favor.[12]

Joseph confessed that he was won over by what he called the "mathematical" calculations of the chancellor. "The question remains," he wrote his mother, "which of Prince Kaunitz's many suggestions we must take. In military, political, and administrative terms Silesia is the most advantageous territory; Bayreuth and Ansbach are not worth much. But if the return of Silesia is impossible, which unfortunately seems to be the case, the most profitable acquisition would be Belgrade and the part of Bosnia extending to the gulf of the Drina. Itself remote from the enemy, this region would buffer the districts of Karlstadt and Lower Austria from any possible Turkish attack."[13]

Maria Theresa was delighted that Joseph and Kaunitz agreed on the necessity of facilitating the start of peace negotiations between Russia and Turkey. But because she recognized that this action alone would not lead to peace, she was quick to protest about everything that had been done against her desires. "It is now impossible," she wrote her son, "to recover from the false steps made since November 1770, when we decided to remove troops from Italy and the Netherlands and to make the unfortunate convention with the Turks. We used an overly harsh tone towards Russia and dealt secretly with allies and enemies alike in order to use the war between Russia and the Porte to extend our borders, to gain advantages that we had not thought about before the war. We wanted to act like Prussians while preserving the appearance of honesty.

"Perhaps I delude myself and these events are more favorable than I think. Yet although they might win us Wallachia and even Belgrade, it is my opinion that all these acquisitions will cost our honor, the glory of the monarchy, our good faith, and our religion too dearly. Since the beginning of our unfortunate reign we have tried at least to uphold justice in everything, to observe moderation and fidelity in our obligations. This brought us the confidence, I dare say, the astonishment of Europe, the respect of enemies. But in a single year all this has been lost. Nothing on earth can grieve me so much as the loss of our reputation. We deserved this, and I want the matter set right by abandoning the principle of exploiting these troubles. We must think of a way to extricate ourselves quickly from this unfortunate dilemma and concern ourselves less with acquisitions than with the restoration of our reputation and good faith and the possible preservation of political equilibrium."[14]

Thugut, Austria's envoy in Constantinople, was instructed to cooperate in starting peace negotiations.[15] He was to inform the Turkish ministry directly that the Porte's terrible mismanagement of the war was the primary reason Austria now demanded the opening of negotiations. He was to explain further that it had become known that Frederick had pledged in Petersburg to attack Austria were it to raise arms against Russia. True, Austria had concluded a convention with the Porte; but Vienna's obligation was solely that of gaining a respectable peace for the sultan[16] either by force of arms or by peace negotiations. Austria faithfully had sought to fulfill this pledge by moving troops from Italy and the Netherlands at great expense and placing its regiments on a war footing. Toward Russia and Prussia, Austria had employed harsh language and had succeeded in persuading Russia to renounce the Danubian principalities. To do more was impossible for Austria without placing itself in the greatest danger. Vienna had used every means to convince the Prussian monarch that an untoward strengthening of Russia represented a danger to him too. Had it been possible to convince him to remain a peaceful spectator Austria would not have hesitated to raise arms against Russia in support of an honorable peace for the Porte. But Vienna had never intended to rush into war with both Russia and Prussia over the Turkish question. Were Austria to declare war on Russia under the present circumstances, the interests and relief of the Ottoman empire scarcely would be served.

The Porte hesitated until the end of May before answering Thugut's message. The sultan had heard it with deep sorrow, for Austrian assistance heretofore had been the touchstone of his every hope. As he did not want to insist that Vienna do what it clearly could not, he was renouncing voluntarily all benefits the convention had promised him. Should the assistance of Austria inspire a peace at the congress that would return the Danubian principalities and the Tatars to the sultan's rule, and should the Porte receive the support pledged in the fifth article of the convention, the sultan would consider himself obligated to fulfill the provisions without exception. If, however, Russia was not inclined to accept peace on these terms, the convention would be abrogated and the sultan would not demand the return of the subsidy of three million piasters given earlier to Austria.

On February 1 Count Panin informed the Council of good news from Vienna.[17] The Austrian court, pleased by Catherine's consent to return Moldavia and Wallachia to the Porte, had instructed its minister in Constantinople to cooperate with Prussia's ambassador in persuading the Porte to send plenipotentiaries as quickly as possible to a peace congress to conclude an armistice. Count Orlov noted that this sharp turn in Vienna's policy might permit Russia to argue for an independent Moldavia and Wallachia. Panin objected that, having agreed to return these principalities, it would be inappropriate to renew the earlier demand for their independence. However, the guarantees of Vienna and Berlin might allow the restoration of the system of government the Turks had destroyed.

Not before March 12 could Panin lay before the Council the message from Vienna that the Porte had agreed to negotiate an armistice and to dispatch plenipotentiaries to a congress to be held in Bucharest. At this point Catherine gave the Council the following "sanction": "Despite the present hopes for peace, greater than ever before, I want you to keep under consideration a plan for a future campaign, for the latest word from Tsargrad [Constantinople] indicates that the Turks are preparing single-mindedly for a fourth campaign. That indeed is quite likely.[18] For this reason we must not let time pass. We must now duly consider what to do: so far we have conducted three campaigns with considerable success. Consequently in this campaign too, which we hope will be the last, we shall sustain the name of Russian arms. Therefore I ask that this campaign be conceived for the gain and glory of the empire. Spring is not far off; it has even begun in places."

Count Panin cautioned the Council to await responses from Vienna and Constantinople inasmuch as the Council could arrive at the most suitable decision only if it knew Austria's true intentions. Catherine replied that should a rift develop between the Austrians and the Turks she did not wish the Austrians to act in concert with the Russians, but that each conduct the war separately. Shifting the discussion into a new direction, Chernyshev pointed out that the army would be supplied with all necessary materiel for the forthcoming campaign and now was deployed in such a way as to carry out fully whatever mission it was given. But the empress persevered, asking: "Does the Council think it would be useful at present to build ships on the Danube and send a corps beyond the river if peace is not soon concluded?" The Council found this absolutely necessary and Count Orlov added that he considered the dispatch of a corps the sole remaining means for achieving a timely and lasting peace.

Meanwhile Rumiantsev, in command of the troops on the Danube, wrote Panin on March 22: "Your excellency surely knows what a great number of recruits is required, for several regiments must be supplied with a thousand each, and virtually every regiment requires half that many. But the replacements necessary to make up the army's losses are still a long way from their units. When do you suppose there will be time to make soldiers of them? Several detachments of recruits assigned to distant regiments who have come this far are obviously totally exhausted already.

It is the same as when some had to stay behind from the last levy, so as to be toughened for service. The cavalry, despite the zealous efforts of its colonels and its sparing use, can purchase horses neither near nor far because there are none to buy. Instead of the reinforcement of my command with the additional troops promised for this year I foresee the opposite, that its fighting capacity will be reduced from last year's."

At the end of March came news that the Porte had named its plenipotentiaries to the congress. The Russians did not want the congress to take place in Bucharest, the capital of Wallachia, for it was full of intrigues. The Russians preferred Ismail but the Turks balked at the suggestion, pointing out that Ismail suffered from excessive humidity and swarms of mosquitoes. Their actual reason was that the mosques there had been transformed into Russian churches and storehouses. Finally the two parties agreed to meet in Focsani and to begin the sessions in June. The Russian envoys were Count Grigory Grigorevich Orlov and the former ambassador to Constantinople, Aleksei Mikhailovich Obreskov, recently released from Turkish confinement.[19]

Orlov and Obreskov's instructions read: "Our declaration renouncing all demands concerning the principalities of Moldavia and Wallachia has removed Vienna's doubts and vacillations, has gained its full consent to our proposals for peace negotiations and all our other demands, and has brought us at the same time the good services of Austria at the Porte in bending it to the congress. This will prove useful to us in future negotiations, as the Turks are growing fearful, observing the participation of Austria in discussions with us and our ally, the king of Prussia, about partitioning several of Poland's provinces.[20] The grounds for negotiations consist of the following three articles: (1) to decrease the ability of the Porte to attack Russia in the future; (2) to acquire sufficient compensation for the losses in the war, begun by Turkey without provocation; and (3) to free commerce and navigation.

"Under the first article, our demands include: (1) that both Great and Little Kabarda[21] be ceded to us; (2) that the boundary remain as before from the Kabardas through the Kuban steppes to Azov ; (3) that Azov and the territory around it be ceded to us; (4) that all Tatar hordes living within and without the Crimean peninsula be declared free and independent; (5) that all lands in the Caucasus taken by Russian arms be ceded to the rulers of Georgia; that the Georgians and all other Christian peoples participating in the war be granted full amnesty; and that in the future the Porte provide greater protection for Christian churches in its territories. The Turks are least likely to accept the fourth demand. To bring them around to this concession you may, besides withdrawing claims to Moldavia and Wallachia, also yield on the article concerning the rulers of Georgia, agreeing merely to restore Georgian borders as they were before the war, provided that Georgia forever be relieved of the inhuman levy of Christian maidens exacted by the Turkish pashas.[22] You may agree further to leave Great and Little Kabarda as delineated by the treaty of 1739, which accorded only Russia the freedom to establish and build towns and settlements on its own lands in that vicinity.[23]

"Under the second article we had in mind demanding reparations for our military expenses, but you may concede this demand too, in whole or in part, in order to gain independence for the Tatars. Under the third article we are demanding free trade and navigation on the Black Sea, and from this we cannot retreat." The instructions were signed April 21 and on the 25th Orlov left Tsarskoe Selo.

In a letter from Catherine to Frau Bielcke[24] on June 25 we find the following curious passage dealing with Orlov: "My angels of peace are now, I think, face to face with those vile bearded Turks. Count Orlov, who without exaggeration is the handsomest man alive, must seem an absolute angel to those peasants. He has a brilliant and select retinue, and my ambassador does not disdain brilliance and splendor. Yet I am prepared to wager that Orlov's looks will demolish everyone around him. He is a remarkable man; nature was unusually generous to him in looks, mind, heart, and soul. None of these attributes had to be acquired; everything is natural, and what is very important, it is all good. But Mother Nature also spoiled him, because the most difficult thing for him to do is apply himself diligently. For thirty years nothing has been able to hold his attention for very long. It is truly remarkable how much he knows, and his mind is so sharp that, hearing about some topic for the first time, he is able in a minute to grasp its strong and weak points and leave in his dust the one who informed him about it."[25]

The Focsani congress began at the end of July because of the belated arrival of the Turkish delegates Osman-effendi and Yassin-zade-effendi, who were accompanied from Constantinople by the Austrian and Prussian ministers.[25] On August 6 Obreskov wrote Panin about the behavior of these two ministers: "The one from Berlin seems to deal sincerely on all questions and supports our aims on the principal issue, the independence of the Tatars. The one from Vienna, in contrast, not only displays coolness on this point, but has all but encouraged the Turks to be obstinate. Perhaps he is doing so in anticipation of a resolution of Polish affairs. In any event, his interpreter visits the Turkish ministers daily. Sometimes he goes too and remains with them quite a while. He tells us nothing. When he speaks at all, it is to strengthen Turkish obstinacy on the Tatar question. The matter has not begun to move forward yet; we can make neither progress nor even soften things up. The Turks, as is their wont, link matters to Muslim law, asserting that the sultan alone is unable of deciding.[27] There is no subtlety, as they call it—to us dastardliness and baseness—to which they will not stoop. All this we observe with contempt and hold to our instruction."

On August 19 Obreskov wrote that the subject of Tatar independence was meeting insurmountable difficulties and that the Turkish plenipotentiaries were preparing to leave. They had consented for the Crimean khans to be chosen by their own people, but demanded that the newly chosen khan receive confirmation from the sultan. Because the Russian plenipotentiaries did not agree to this, the congress broke up on August 28. On September 7 Rumiantsev received a letter from the grand vizier suggesting that the congress be reconvened in Bucharest and that the armistice continue for six months. He claimed that the Focsani congress broke up because Count Orlov had departed. Rumiantsev, taking the present circumstances into consideration, particularly the revolution in Sweden, realized that it was in Russia's interest not to allow this opportunity to renew negotiations to slip from its hands. Instead of six months, he stated that Russia was prepared to continue the armistice until October 20, in order in the interval to communicate with Petersburg.

Petersburg was deeply alarmed by the collapse of the Focsani congress. To the strong desire for peace now was added the danger of war with Sweden following the change of government effected by King Gustavus III.[28] At the August 27 session of the Council Panin read his letter to Orlov and Obreskov advising them not to linger too long on the single point about the Tatars but to move on to the others. At the meeting on September 1 the dispatch of August 18 from Orlov and Obreskov was read, stating that the Turkish plenipotentiaries had decided to depart Focsani. Panin proposed that Rumiantsev be directed to write the grand vizier with an expression of regret that the Turkish plenipotentiaries had ruptured the congress and suggesting renewal of the talks. At the same time he should be instructed to try to inflict a new blow on the enemy by landing at least a small force onto the right bank of the Danube. "If these measures do not lead to peace and a war starts with Sweden," Panin concluded, " we must adopt the extreme measure which I proposed earlier; that is, ravaging Moldavia and Wallachia and evacuating all their inhabitants to Russia." The Council concurred.

Count Orlov was sent a rescript permitting him to exercise his own judgment, if he was still in Jassy with the field marshal, whether to proceed with the negotiations upon their resumption, but meanwhile to make himself useful in the army under Rumiantsev's leadership. This, of course, referred to the "new blow" against the Turks by crossing the Danube. But Orlov had left for Petersburg. Later the empress wrote that the failure of the congress "by no means" was attributable to Count Orlov.

It suited Panin, however, to repeat the Turkish accusation, writing to Obreskov on September 4: "I am truly grieved, my good friend, by your present circumstance, realizing from your last dispatches that your senior colleague's newly conceived madness and raving have spoiled everything. In these deplorable and vexing circumstances at least I can bring you this consolation, swearing to you by my honor and esteeming you as a true friend, that this unhappy development has brought no shadow on your name. On the contrary, her imperial majesty knows within her heart that it was impossible under the circumstances for you to do anything other than what you did. Believe me, my friend, you are being vindicated and your earlier service has not been besmirched by the unruliness of your colleague.

"In fact, any outsider must marvel that the foremost men of both states, sent on such a high mission, could meet as if for a single word and, having spoken it, simply leave. But it does not amaze me at all, knowing well the circumstances familiar to you as well as other information you have not yet heard. Oh, how the breakup of the congress and the destruction of hopes for a general peace torment my heart and insult me as a minister and as a man who loves his fatherland with all his soul. As you easily can imagine, the collapse of the peace talks places us in the most critical position of renewing an old war while accelerating towards a new one, which has begun to threaten us.

"You would do well to deliver the nation from such a serious crisis. Although you may surmise, from the rescript sent you, that your former colleague will remain with you, I nonetheless trust that you alone will be left in charge while he gallops hither. Should he remain there, contrary to my hope, you no longer will need to respect his pipe dreams as before, for his previous favor at court has vanished utterly. Thus it will no longer be necessary to interrupt his unbridled opinions and judgments with your enlightened understanding and reasonable inclinations. You may adhere safely to your own views with greater tenacity and bend him to them. In those cases when you disagree with him, you may write me candidly."

Panin proposed that Obreskov not begin the negotiations, as at Focsani, with the most difficult point of Tatar independence, but to lay out individually all of Russia's particular demands, one by one, so that a concession on one would facilitate the winning of another. He suggested that it might be necessary to agree to the sultan's investiture of a newly chosen khan, but in return to demand the cession of Kerch and Yenikale.[29] Doubtless, only terrible enmity towards Orlov drove Panin to blame him for the collapse of the Focsani congress; it was overly naive for him to suppose that a reversal of the order of articles might bring success in the negotiations when the Porte, supported by Austria, had decided to reject absolutely independence for the Tatars. The subsequent failure of the Bucharest congress served to exonerate Orlov's actions at Focsani, for Obreskov conducted the negotiations alone. Furthermore, the instability of the Treaty of Kuchuk-Kainardji resulted wholly from the article about the independence of the Tatars, which Constantinople in no way could digest.[30]

Notwithstanding the fact that his task had been eased by assent to investiture of the khan, Obreskov on leaving for Bucharest wrote Panin: "I take the liberty of reporting that due to the Turks' stupid (in my opinion) and obviously boundless disgust at seeing any Black Sea fortress in Russian hands, the winning of Yenikale and Kerch will meet, it appears, insuperable difficulties, particularly should the Porte not be allowed to retain garrisons in other fortresses in the Crimea. Furthermore, access to the Black Sea is not as easy to obtain as it might seem to someone who is not at the negotiations on account of the same Turkish bias. I know these things from diverse experiences; indeed many, if not all, of the interested parties are laying obstacles in our way on this point."

On this occasion Catherine wrote: "If the peace treaty fails to win independence for the Tatars, navigation on the Black Sea, and fortresses on the Gulf of Azov and Black Sea, it can be said in truth that all the victories over the Turks have not won us two copecks and I will be the first to say that, under the circumstances, such a peace would be as shameful as those of the Pruth and Belgrade."[31] Her note was read to the Council on October 25.

Four days later the congress opened in Bucharest and the truce was extended until March 9 of the following year. At the end of 1772 the talks remained snagged on the issue of the Crimean towns which Russia demanded.[32] Petersburg feared a shameful peace similar to the Pruth and Belgrade settlements and likewise dreaded continuing the war. Russia wanted free hands in the south, concerned as it was about events in Sweden that threatened war in the north. Yet Rumiantsev still sang the same old song about the deplorable condition of the First Army and therefore the need to end the war, "which is frightful and onerous not primarily for the might and quality of the enemy, but because of the pernicious diseases inseparable from it. The truth of this observation," continued the field marshal, "we felt when the pestilential distemper reached the heart of our country.[33] It has begun belching its poison again in the towns just across the Polish border. The command which was formerly in Focsani has been infected and is now suffering from it, which causes me the greatest embarrassment. As our strength is exhausted, other infectious diseases, and especially strange types of fevers, have become in truth the inevitable consequences of staying here so long. They are so general and widespread that they have reduced virtually all the generals and colonels,continually suffering tortuous attacks, to sheer and extreme exhaustion. From this you can judge for yourself the number of sick officers and soldiers. You can see that all measures we have employed to benefit and treat them have been powerless to prevent our losing a great number of dead. We have such a great lack of doctors that seeing and treating the sick almost exceeds their strength, inasmuch as the greater part of them have offered up their lives to the same diseases."

Even as Rumiantsev complained about the shortage of troops in the First Army he suddenly received an order from Petersburg to send eight infantry regiments to Pskov in the event of war with Sweden. This order was the more insulting for the field marshal in that he did not receive it in an imperial rescript, as was customary. Rumiantsev expressed to Panin his astonishment that at the very moment when the Bucharest congress was beginning to come to some sort of agreement he was directed to reduce the field army's strength. Not only would this feed the obstinacy of the Turks, it also might encourage them to break off negotiations altogether. Rumiantsev expressed his regret and embarrassment that, in case of extreme need, Petersburg had decided to blow up the fortresses and evacuate Moldavia and Wallachia. The field marshal complained about this decision without knowing that it was based on Panin's proposal, ascribing it instead to Count Orlov.

THE CRIMEAN ISSUE

The settlement of the Crimean question met with profound difficulties at the congress and in the Crimea itself. The final arrangement of matters with Khan Sahib-Girey[34] was entrusted to General Evdokim Alexeevich Shcherbinin, who was supposed to go to Bakhchisarai.[35] Before his departure copies of letters from the Crimeans to the Porte and to the pasha of Ochakov fell into his hands. From them he learned how disloyal to Russia the Tatars really were; on no account could their promises be relied upon, for their actions were governed solely by insidiousness and deception. On the basis of this new information about the hidden intentions of the Tatars, Shcherbinin found it necessary to proceed to the Crimea with at least 1500 troops. Encamped outside Bakhchisarai, he received the khan's officials and tried to clarify Catherine's intention of guaranteeing their eternal freedom and prosperity under her protection.

The Crimeans asked: "If a truce has been concluded with the Turks and we have become your allies, why did Major General Alexander Alexandrovich Prozorovsky enter the Crimea with troops?".

"He came prior to the armistice," answered Shcherbinin. "It was necessary to increase Russian troop strength for your own safety and because, I have discovered, your government with nefarious intent instructed the local princes to assemble and conceal soldiers."

The Crimeans asked for the identity of the Tatars who so had informed him. Shcherbinin, hesitant to tell them, answered that copies of the letters had been received directly from Constantinople. Thereupon the Tatars desired to know why Prince Prozorovsky continued to move closer to Bakhchisarai, and asked that he be halted. Shcherbinin responded that his movements continued because of scanty provisions and grass, but that he had informed Prozorovsky that he should come no closer nor disturb the inhabitants. To the question why Shcherbinin's own retinue was so numerous, he replied that it suited the dignity of a triumphal embassy. Finally, the Tatars sought to discover when Russian soldiers would leave the Crimea and were told that time alone would provide the answer.

When Shcherbinin raised the subject of the ceremonial audience with the khan, an official told him that the khan would not accept the empress's presents in public and would not stand during the presentation of the imperial patent. Shcherbinin answered that this would violate the spirit of gratitude obligatory towards the khan's great benefactress, and that these actions merely served to cast doubt upon his intentions. "Everything clearly indicates," wrote Shcherbinin, "that Russian garrisons are wanted by no means in the Crimea nor is the protection of her majesty. When I suggested that they face danger from the Turks even after peace is concluded, they retorted that they had nothing to fear from the Turks. It seems that when peace is made and the Russian troops depart the Crimeans will turn again to the Turks, to whom they are absolutely devoted and tied by law, habits, and customs. This sense of devotion and attachment controls not only all the princes hereabout, but also the earlier envoys to Petersburg who in spite of their warm reception, support, and rich rewards from us now have turned back to the other side. The khan is a shy young man completely in the hands of the ruling elders, who constantly point to their law."

On June 28, the anniversary of Catherine's accession to the throne, the soldiers with Shcherbinin planned to fire a salute. The general gave advance warning to the Crimean officials so they could inform the inhabitants and avoid alarming them. The authorities issued the following notification: "All residents hereby are notified that the infidels are going to celebrate a nasty holiday tomorrow with gunfire."

General Prince Shcherbinin had reported on May 12 that the Tatars everywhere were arming secretly and abandoning the seacoast for the mountains with all their belongings, refusing to sell horses to the Russians at any price. In intercepted letters the Tatar leaders implored Turkey to dispatch a fleet to aid them, writing: "We weep day and night while we long for help to come. Although our common people are gathered and armed, they cannot win by themselves. Indeed, were it not for their fear of us, they already would have accepted Russian sovereignty."

A certain friend of the Russian chargé d'affaires in Bakhchisarai, Peter Petrovich Veselitsky, told him: "Everyone here is saying that when General Shcherbinin arrives and we resist his overtures, suddenly he will realize the inability of his few soldiers to ravage our country. Yet much time will elapse before a large force can arrive, and meanwhile peace will have been made with the Porte. People here are aggrieved that circumstances were permitted to come to such a pass without resort to arms."

Eventually Shcherbinin was obliged to yield on the issue of the ceremonial audience. The khan did not accept the presents—pens and sabers—which Sahib-Girey recognized as signifying a pledge of subservience and obedience to the empress, nor did he agree to kiss the imperial patent. The audience took place on July 4, after which Shcherbinin had a conversation with the khan.

Introducing the matter of Russian protection of the Crimea's independence, Sahib-Girey pondered, "Why is it necessary to protect a free man?"

"Freedom without protection is not freedom, because it always is liable to extortion," countered Shcherbinin.

When the conversation touched upon the likelihood of stationing Russian garrisons and naval vessels in various Crimean towns, Shcherbinin suggested that the khan might find refuge there were the Turks to intrigue for his overthrow. He threatened the khan with the prospect that without Russian patronage he would not last three days on the throne. But an unmoved Sahib-Girey answered: "Let us assume that disagreements and disputes break out between the Crimean people and the garrisons stationed in their towns. Supposing the garrison troops are the cause of this dispute, yet place the blame on the Crimean people. Who will be the mediator, who will determine whether the insult came from the Russian garrison or the Crimean people? When there is no mediator between us, our ruin is as clear as the difference between night and day."

Throughout the negotiations regarding a treaty of alliance between Russia and the Crimea the Tatar plenipotentiaries stubbornly maintained that, "since we are free, it follows that we have the right to make the treaty or not make it." To postpone a final agreement the plenipotentiaries insisted that the fortresses Russia demanded were controlled by the khan; they could not comply with Russia's demands because it was really the khan's affair. And the khan said that without his elders he could do nothing.

But the khan and these stubborn elders were in the minority. Aside from them, there was a Russian party among the Crimean dignitaries. Deputies from the Nogay Tatars[36] agreed to all of the Russian demands, including the empress's request that Russia occupy the fortresses of Kerch and Yenikale in order to safeguard Tatar independence. Sahib-Girey signed the treaty, in which he swore that he and the Crimean people were abandoning the Ottoman Porte forever and would remain under the patronage of the most serene sovereign, the Great Catherine, and her heirs.

During these negotiations the khan's brother, Crown Prince Shagin-Girey, was living in Petersburg[37] and was able to acquire the favor of the empress, as is apparent from her letters to Frau Bielcke and Voltaire: "There is here now a crown prince-sultan, the brother of the independent Crimean khan. He is a young man 25 years old, remarkably intelligent and desirous of educating himself. This Crimean dauphin is a most amiable Tatar, handsome, wise, learned in ways non-Tatar. He writes verse; he wants to see and know everything. Everyone has fallen for him. He doesn't miss a single theater performance. On Sundays after dinner he goes to Smolny convent to see how the female students dance.[38] You will say that this is like allowing a wolf into the sheep fold. Have no fear; this is how things are managed. In the large hall there is a double balustrade; the girls dance within and the spectators gather at the balustrades. This is the only occasion when their relatives can see our young ladies, who are not allowed out of the convent."

In November Shagin-Girey was released to return to the Crimea, on which journey he had to pass through Moscow. Count Panin wrote to the commander-in-chief of Moscow, Prince Mikhail Nikitich Volkonsky,[39] who had received that position upon his return from Warsaw. "As to a personal meeting between your excellency and the eminent Tatar, be aware that he is well endowed with native acuity and good judgment. However, he is proud, haughty, arrogant, and glories in the antiquity of his family, which is descended from Genghis-Khan. Here he has refused to make the first visit to anyone; it even had to be spelled out to him formally that he should visit *me*. I tell your excellency this at great length for a reason: however natural and proper it is on your part to show him respect by your announcement and greeting, it is equally advisable and necessary, considering their ignorance and crudeness as Tatars and based on their servility and cowardice toward the Turks, for him to make the first visit to your excellency in view of the importance of your post, your rank, and your distinction. Then, should you reciprocate, do so without ceremony, not so much out of duty and reciprocity as out of your personal courtesy and good manners."

When Prince Nikolai Abramovich Putiatin, who accompanied Shagin-Girey, started to tell the crown prince he should make the first visit in Moscow to Prince Volkonsky, Shagin refused to agree. When Putiatin persisted, the crown prince requested to bypass Moscow and continue on the road by which he had come to Petersburg, complaining that his poor health would not permit him to inspect a city as large as Moscow from a carriage. The crown prince continued: "I am a man of the steppes, educated in the mountains among the herds, not possessing civilized manners. I am not of the proper quality to mingle with such eminent personages." But his demand not to sojourn in Moscow went unheeded. Putiatin upon arrival in the city advised Volkonsky that Shagin-Girey did not wish to make the first courtesy call, whereupon Volkonsky sent his adjutant to the crown prince to show him everything of interest in the city, beginning with the armory.

Shagin-Girey's stay in Russia was not easy on the imperial treasury. Not counting his maintenance of 100 rubles a day, immediately after his arrival he received 5000 rubles in addition to a rich fur coat, other clothing, a fur cap, and a silver table service, then another 10,000 rubles, and upon leaving 20,000 rubles and a saber studded with gold and precious stones. For his suite he received 10,000 rubles. To mark his visit to Tsarskoe Selo he was presented a ring and an expensive snuffbox. And finally, when he started complaining about debts he could not pay, he was passed another 12,000 rubles. Count Panin complained to Prince Vasily Mikhailovich Dolgoruky that Shagin-Girey lived most sumptuously in Petersburg without the least attempt to exercise restraint. Panin wrote, "Although he gave every evidence of deepest gratitude here, nevertheless it would not be excessive for your excellency to disclose to him delicately at the proper moment that out of personal respect for him, he has been awarded more than the Crimeans and their leadership deserve in view of recent events. It is advisable that upon his arrival in your town (Poltava) he pay the first visit to you." Shagin-Girey extended this polite gesture to the conqueror of the Crimea: he understood the importance of the commander of the Second Army for the Crimea's future.

Petersburg, then, was not satisfied with "recent events" in the Crimea. We have observed that Frederick II predicted these developments long before. He repeated his prophecy as the year 1772 began, convincing Godefroy van Swieten,[40] the Austrian ambassador to Berlin, that he should not fret over the clause about Tatar independence. "It is in this stipulation that all the difficulty lies," said Frederick, "for the Russian empress associates it in her mind with glory, and it will be extremely difficult to force her to relinquish glory. Everywhere triumphant, she now demands that her vanquished enemy liberate a people held in slavery. Seeing solely the good of humanity in this, she fails to understand why the execution of such a magnanimous intention might be delayed. Her inflamed imagination compels her to view the matter this way.

"But if we reason dispassionately we find that this supposed independence is a chimera, an empty word. Let us suppose that the Tatars are declared independent. Can Russia possibly hope to win their allegiance? It is inconceivable that these people would feel any gratitude whatsoever to Russia for liberating them from the Turkish yoke because the yoke does not exist. The Porte makes and breaks khans, but a khan has no power other than military command. His income consists of 300,000 to 450,000 rubles annually, which he receives from Constantinople. Each horde is a separate small republic with little concern for who names its commander in war and who pays him. I can tell you this with certainty because of exact and detailed information gathered by emissaries I maintained in the Crimea during the past war. Do you really believe that this Tatar independence is so dangerous?"

"These considerations," answered van Swieten, "are so obvious that they cannot remain hidden from anyone who examines the situation carefully, and it follows that they cannot remain hidden from the Russian court. Since Petersburg is adamant on this clause, I am forced to conclude that it is not at all a chimera, that Petersburg has very dangerous views, and that independence is merely a word cloaking a plan for outright dominion."

"But," objected the king, "should Russia later be inclined to subjugate the Tatars, the Porte always will have time to mount opposition."

"It will be too late, your majesty," answered van Swieten. "For a long while the Porte will be in no position to resist. Therefore a peace must be arranged that will restore and support equilibrium in the east and will not leave the Ottoman empire in an uncertain existence." Frederick repeated that peace negotiations must begin immediately inasmuch as nothing good might be expected from continued hostilities.[41]

AUSTRIA AGREES TO PARTITION POLAND

The negotiations with Turkey began in 1772 but were not destined to end that year. They resulted instead in an agreement to partition Poland. On February 1 Panin informed the Council that Vienna had consented to assist in opening peace negotiations between Russia and Turkey. Panin also communicated the report from Prince Dmitry Mikhailovich Golitsyn[42] that Vienna, in Kaunitz's words, wanted no division of Poland. Since Russia and Prussia had struck an agreement, however, Austria would join in. Austria would prefer to receive its share from Turkish rather than Polish territory. Vienna desired to conclude the matter with minimal delay and to confirm it through an alliance with Russia and Prussia. According to Golitsyn's report Kaunitz told him: "It seems to me that it has not escaped Count Panin's shrewd mind that, assuming the purpose of partition is the preservation of balance among the states, it might be possible to take shares elsewhere than Poland. If Polish territory does not prove suitable for an equal partition among the three states, a means can be found to take a bit of land from another state which will be compelled to agree whether it wants to or not in light of the concert among the three courts. I suggest that Russia ponder this possibility."

"You must certainly mean Turkey," observed Golitsyn.

"Of course!" replied Kaunitz. The Austrian chancellor thereupon began hinting that it would be most expedient to proceed discreetly with this new proposal, and thereby preserve the secrecy of the partition of Poland. He especially desired that it be kept from France and England, who might regard it as contrary to their interests and oppose it with all resources.

Meanwhile Kaunitz instructed van Swieten in Berlin to propose to Frederick II first that Prussia acquire Austria's share of Poland in exchange for Silesia. Should the king not consent, van Swieten was to demand for Austria what Emperor Joseph desired: Belgrade and part of Serbia and Bosnia. Were Frederick not to comply even with this, van Swieten then should demand Ansbach and Bayreuth. Finally, as a last resort, he might agree to Austria's equal share of Poland. As was to be expected, Frederick rejected the first proposition. "No, that is impossible," he told van Swieten. "I am demanding only Polish Prussia. Take your share where it best suits you, but not at my expense. The emperor himself promised me never to consider the return of Silesia, and Prince Kaunitz solemnly and formally repeated the same thing. I am neither able nor willing to agree to any partition of areas I now rule."

Then van Swieten broached the topic of rewarding Austria at Turkish expense, and the king quickly acceded. At least that is how van Swieten described the conversation in the report to his court.[43] But Frederick himself in a dispatch to his envoy in Petersburg, Count Victor Friedrich Solms, wrote that to van Swieten's first proposal he answered, "My gout is confined to my feet. To accept such proposals as this I would have to suffer from gout of the head. We are dealing with Poland, not my possessions."

Van Swieten responded: "The Carpathian mountains isolate Hungary from Poland. Because our potential acquisitions lie across the mountains, they are not very profitable for us."

To this the king replied: "The Alps separate you from Italy, yet you doggedly hold on to Milan and Mantua."

Van Swieten continued: "It would be much more advantageous for us to acquire Belgrade and Serbia from the Turks."

Frederick rejoined: "I am quite pleased to hear that the Austrians have yet to undergo the ceremony of circumcision of which they are accused.[44] I am pleased to learn that they wish to receive their share from their friends, the Turks."

On February 9 Panin read the Council his letter to Prince Golitsyn proposing that Golitsyn inform Vienna that its latest declaration had satisfied the empress. Panin asked Golitsyn to communicate to Vienna the plan devised by Petersburg and Berlin regarding Poland and to ascertain exactly what Vienna wished to receive, making assurances beforehand that Russia would agree to Austrian gains from Turkey as well as from Poland.

Actually, Petersburg was more than delighted by the latest news from Vienna. It now seemed certain that Austria, in agreement and alliance with Russia and Prussia, would assist in reaching an advantageous peace with Turkey. This appeared all the more certain now that Vienna desired Turkish territory as booty, something Russia had suggested long before but which then had been rejected.[45] Catherine fancied an early and brilliant finish to her war with Turkey and Poland and the conclusion of a triple alliance among Austria, Prussia, and Russia to guarantee the peace and provide an opportunity for Russia to strengthen its finances and undertake vital domestic reforms.

The convention with Prussia concerning Poland was signed on February 6,[46] and Catherine thanked Frederick, attributing to him the change in Vienna's policies. Prince Henry congratulated his brother on his success, predicting that if the triple alliance lasted, the three powers would control the destiny of the entire continent. Frederick was shrewder than his brother, forecasting an inevitable struggle between Austria and Prussia for influence in Petersburg.[47]

But Austria once more changed its plan. Maria Theresa's conscience had begun to torment her. She explained: "We are allies of the Porte and have accepted its subsidies. I would never stoop to steal from it. Therefore we must not consider acquiring Serbia and Bosnia, the only Turkish provinces that have any value for us. That leaves Moldavia and Wallachia, lands that are unhealthy, laid waste, open to attacks by Turks, Tatars, and Russians. They have no fortresses. In order to defend them, it would be necessary to expend millions of piasters and many lives." As Moldavia and Wallachia were not suitable for Austria, they were to be offered to Poland as compensation for the wealthy regions partitioned by the three powers. Maria Theresa's conscience did not forbid this, although she refused to approve a partition unless Poland received something in return.

The tough-minded Kaunitz pounced upon Maria Theresa's conscience from another direction. "Would the empress in truth deign to subject millions of her subjects to the horrible war which inevitably would ensue following the destruction of the balance of power?" asked the chancellor. To assuage the empress he renounced the claims to Bosnia and Serbia. Indeed, it would have been very unwise to annex those territories and offend the Turks. Kaunitz had never recommended acquiring them; they were the dream of Joseph II. Kaunitz all the while favored claiming land along the lower Danube as far as its mouth and awarding Moldavia and the remainder of Bessarabia to Poland. There was no injustice in this plan because Turkey had lost those areas already. Maria Theresa grudgingly consented, repeating nonetheless that she never intended to seize anything from Poland.

At this juncture Emperor Joseph offered a further alternative to Kaunitz's plan. "How," asked Joseph, "could we defend a frontier extending from the Adriatic to the Black Sea? By what right would Poland make demands on us if we wrest nothing from it? Is Austria obligated in any way to compensate Poland for the injustices it may suffer at the hands of Russia and Prussia? Moldavia and Wallachia are indispensable for us, but Bessarabia may be apportioned to any government except Russia. Our border should run from the Pruth to the Danube. Were we to return Bessarabia and what is left of Moldavia and Wallachia to the Turks, we would have to receive Orsova and Belgrade in exchange. It is essential that Russia pretend to want to keep everything for itself and then cede Moldavia and Wallachia to us. For Bessarabia the Turks will give us the two cities mentioned above."

Maria Theresa in despair insisted that this terrible wrangling must cease. She lay no claim to either Polish or Turkish territory. Kaunitz cautioned her that Russia and Prussia already had agreed to partition Poland. Hence Austria must follow one of two courses: either oppose the partition with its armed forces, or passively face the terrible peril of a significantly strengthened Russia and Prussia. Since he could not recommend either option, the sole remaining alternative was for Austria to issue its own demands. Maria Theresa granted at length that this was the only avenue left open.

Curiously, a dispatch sent to van Swieten in the wake of this consensus repudiated the proposal made through him that Austria receive territorial compensation from Turkey on grounds that the plan was van Swieten's personally and not the result of his government's instructions. As for its acquisitions in Poland, Vienna thought it best to define its share only after Russia had declared what it desired. Austrian historians do not explain this shift in Austria's policy,[48] but there is an explanation. Prince Golitsyn informed Petersburg that on February 10 (Old Style) he was called in by Kaunitz, who met him with a paper in hand—the February 5 (New Style) dispatch from van Swieten in Berlin. Kaunitz read it to Golitsyn and added that he had sent a courier to Berlin conveying his disapproval of van Swieten's suggestion to reward Austria at Turkey's expense. Golitsyn expressed amazement at this contradiction, for the Austrians had enunciated precisely the same proposal to him not long before. Asked for an explanation, Kaunitz replied: "There merely appears to be a contradiction. Our court is seriously disposed toward making certain acquisitions at the Porte's expense should it prove possible without insulting Turkey openly. It can be done if Russia, which by the right of conquest controls vast Turkish territories, retains some of them and afterward cedes others to a third power."

Apparently the young emperor and the old chancellor hoped to acquire land from both Poland and Turkey by striking an agreement with Prussia in Poland, where the shares of the three powers were supposed to be equal, and with Russia for Turkish territory. Russia would cooperate fully merely to gain a much needed peace by dint of Austrian mediation. Furthermore, the scheme was designed to estrange Russia from Prussia and bind it to Austria. Petersburg's warm regard for Prince Joseph Lobkowitz, Austria's minister to Russia, and its allusions to the restoration of their former alliance and trust confirmed these hopes. Emperor Joseph wrote his brother Leopold: "The king of Prussia regards our immediate ties with Russia quite enviously, and who knows, the Porte's imprudent behavior may well provide us with justification for interference in its affairs. Perhaps next year we will fit Belgrade and part of Bosnia into our pocket as we did the Polish province this year."[49]

But Frederick maintained a jealous and attentive vigil. He directed Solms to apprise Petersburg of the conversation with van Swieten on Silesia and Turkish territories. "Vienna's hesitancy to apportion Poland with us," wrote Frederick, "derives from its desire to win the hearts of the Poles, who are henceforward to concentrate their hatred on the Russians and us. As for the annexation of Belgrade and Serbia, I reminded van Swieten that two years ago the Russians proposed all sorts of gains for them at the Turks' expense, but that Austria rejected those proposals. In my opinion, Vienna is wholly undeserving of the efforts made on its behalf. Austria must be limited to a bit of Poland, in order to punish it for its earlier behavior."

This hint worked. When Frederick's missive was read to the Council in Petersburg during its February 11 session, the Council decreed that, "whereas Austria shrinks from receiving an equal share of Poland, but seeks to direct Polish indignation at the partition to Russia and the king of Prussia, Vienna must be limited to no more than an equal share of Poland." Thus Kaunitz's entreaty to Golitsyn fell on deaf ears, which caused Austria's strange behavior during the congresses at Focsani and Bucharest.

Rapprochement with Russia was vital for Austria if it were to persuade the Russians to forsake their ties with Prussia and restore the previous alliance (pre-1762).[50] But circumstances were not yet such that Russia had the necessary incentive. The foreign policy of Elizabeth's reign had been dictated by the unsettling, aggressive, and dangerous intentions of Prussia. When Austria was driven to the brink, Russia found it necessary to support Vienna as a counterweight to Prussia. Even France had to alter its centuries-old policy for this reason. But now Russian and Austrian interests adjoined in the Turkish question. Austria might successfully woo Russia were it to decide to act decisively and explain itself candidly. But Austria had no desire to do so, primarily because of the danger of Prussian influence on Russia. Vienna presented its case either in sharp, hostile terms or enigmatically.

Thus, less by the craft of the Prussian king than by deficiency in Vienna, it proved impossible to persuade Russia to abandon its Prussian ally for Austria. The Polish question could barely inspire the concept of a triple alliance among Russia, Prussia, and Austria, cemented together solely by their interests in Poland. Petersburg should have been much enamored of the idea of a tripartite alliance, for Russia, in light of Austria and Prussia's notorious rivalry, naturally would play the exalted role of peacemaker. Yet a triple alliance failed to materialize for the very reason that the ill-fated Northern alliance[51] had collapsed—the rivalry between Austria and Prussia. Their interests were totally at odds; no alliance could include both of them. This became abundantly apparent at the first try.

On June 6 Panin wrote Golitsyn in Vienna: "I am delighted that the courts in Vienna and Berlin are beginning to deal with each other much more openly than in the past. Events seem to point toward their realizing the benefits of a firm alliance among our three states to preserve and strengthen the general peace and tranquillity of Europe. What benefit will Europe, especially Germany, find in our system? Is it rationally conceivable that any power might arise to oppose it? Surely the reactions of governments outside the alliance will be based on the degree to which our system shifts the balance of power to one side or the other. When all is said and done, the peace and tranquillity of Europe by rights will rest in our hands.

"Because you can speak candidly with Prince Kaunitz, you might mention these considerations to him informally and dispassionately, as in essence reflecting my own thoughts. The truth of the matter is, I can think of several issues requiring deep consideration and raising serious difficulties, but quite frankly I do not think it entirely impossible to include them in the common bond of agreement. Among other problems that come to mind regarding Germany are the forthcoming inheritance settlements in the electorates of the Palatinate and Bavaria.[52] Is it impossible to open the door to a new order without resorting to force of arms? Can nothing be settled by negotiation? Should it be possible, might not the conflicting interests of Berlin and Vienna be reconciled in this case? When both sides display sincerity and good will, might advantageous means be found for the house of Vienna to cooperate with Berlin rather than Versailles? It would seem impossible for it not to ally with either one or the other in order to prevent jealousy and interference from both.

"As I am confident of Prince Kaunitz's honest intentions and goodness of heart, I do not doubt that he will consider such an arrangement in order to increase his own satisfaction and glory. As for me, both by personal inclination and the magnanimous sentiments of our empress I might consider it my special good fortune to participate in it. Should Prince Kaunitz think it proper to respond by permitting me to take the first step in that direction, I humbly beseech you [Golitsyn] to assure him that I will accept his view and proposal on the matter with sincere pleasure and cooperate so fully that Prince Kaunitz will not regret entrusting confidence in me."

Kaunitz replied forthrightly to Golitsyn's message. "In my opinion, all treaties of alliance and friendship are valid and beneficial only when the contracting powers are convinced wholly of each other's good and sincere intentions. Following this principle, for my part I want never to forsake an alliance with Russia, for I am certain that this union has great utility for both courts, and what is more, I can place full confidence in the integrity of the Russian court, on which I do not hesitate to rely on all occasions. But I reason differently as regards Berlin, whose secret and avaricious policy is all too familiar. I am absolutely persuaded that Berlin's current close ties with Russia forever will be designed not to allow the two imperial courts to effect a rapprochement. Incidentally, it seems useless to me to initiate new ventures just now; better to postpone other matters until the completion of the current Polish business."

Shortly thereafter Golitsyn learned that Emperor Joseph had told a confidant: " The more I ponder the Polish question, the more I realize that the two imperial courts devoted insufficient attention to their true political interests when they decided to partition Poland. Obviously Frederick will derive the greatest advantage from it, for it unites the two main parts of the kingdom of Prussia, increases its commercial capabilities, and adds territory valuable on its own account. All this gives him preponderance. Consequently I think that Austria and Russia would do better to ignore Poland and further their mutual interests through acquisitions from Turkey."

Conveying this information to Petersburg, Golitsyn wrote; "The empress-queen is showing a decided aversion to the Polish affair and is taking no part in it." Golitsyn's evaluation of the state of Maria Theresa's emotions was entirely correct, but the emperor's opinion noted above apparently was leaked to Golitsyn intentionally in order to remind the Russian court of the possibility and the need for new agreements and new ties concerning Turkish relations. That Joseph's view was identical to Kaunitz's, and that both dreamed from the beginning of winning significant acquisitions at Poland's expense before turning on Turkey, becomes manifestly clear in Joseph's letter to Leopold quoted above, proposing to seize Polish provinces in 1772 and to annex Belgrade and Bosnia the following year.

In order to realize the latter ambition, Austria somehow had to prolong the Russo-Turkish war and exhaust both powers, thereby compelling Russia to turn to Austria for support. To this end, when Golitsyn informed Kaunitz about the collapse of the Focsani congress, the chancellor failed to display "the proper sensitivity of spirit, but simply answered that he was surprised at how the Russian envoys had initiated the talks with a proposal that should have come at the end." Kaunitz had to speak in this manner in order to reveal how inconsequential were the Russian negotiations and to demonstrate the mistake the Russian court was making not to accept the aid and mediation of Austria by entrusting affairs to the inexperienced Orlov rather than to the most skilled diplomat, Thugut.

The Focsani congress broke down and the Bucharest talks began. Russia, fearful of a revolution in Sweden, yielded to the Turks. These events were extremely advantageous to Austria and fortified its hope that its aspirations in Turkey might be achieved. But first it was necessary to settle the matter of Poland as profitably as possible.

FINAL NEGOTIATIONS ON THE POLISH PARTITION

After Austria declared its desire to participate in the partition of Poland and Russia signed its own convention with Prussia concerning the partition, Frederick was well satisfied—pleased with Russia and even with Austria. "The signing of our agreement," he wrote to Solms on March 1 (New Style), "gave me endless satisfaction. I have always regarded this treaty as a new bond which should create an unbreakable friendship between the other two courts, and it would be hard for me to express to you how pleased I am by this turn of events so propitious for both courts.

Because Austria would subject itself to considerable risk by deceiving us, I am confident it is now acting in good conscience. France is another matter altogether. In consideration of France's current situation, Vienna may well deceive Paris without fear of punishment. One can at least count on this mutual guarantee of our acquisitions in Poland, pledged formally and ceremonially by Vienna. In time this might lead to an alliance among the three courts, against which I of course would never speak a hostile word; on the contrary, I would be very happy, for nothing else could consolidate peace in Europe for very long. The fact is, when three powerful courts such as ours are allies and friends, no other court would dare do anything to drive them apart. So you see there are many reasons for saying that I am at a loss for words to express my great joy that things have taken such an advantageous and pleasant turn."

On March 6 Frederick wrote: "I was pleased to hear that Count Panin began the negotiations with Austria on a friendly note. No doubt agreement soon will follow. Prince Kaunitz, fearing French or English interference, will hasten to conclude it as quickly as possible. You ask me how to set forth our claims upon Poland. I think that a short, simple manifesto would be best. I am sending you a draft to show Count Panin. He can make whatever minor alterations seem appropriate to him. I think that, having communicated it to the Poles, it would be inappropriate to transform the matter into a barrister's brief. The three courts should simply announce jointly that they have satisfied their own demands, which Poland, unconcerned with justice, would never have done. Now nothing forces us to hurry in establishing control over the partitioned area of Poland. Count Panin can rest assured that I will keep a tight rein on my impatience. Incidentally, I think we ought to finish this Polish business before the congress opens in Turkey. Speaking of the Turks, it will be simple to compel them to digest the partition of Poland by intimating that it is the reason for Russia's restoring Wallachia and Moldavia to them."

But Frederick's obvious satisfaction soon vanished. On April 21 (New Style) van Swieten revealed to him Vienna's claim in the partition—all of Galicia and Red Russia,[53] whose possession had allowed the Polish kings to designate themselves Russian sovereigns. "The devil take you, sirs! I see you have an excellent appetite," said Frederick, surveying the map. "Your share is as large as Russia's and mine put together. Truly, you have an excellent appetite!" Van Swieten explained in detail that equality of shares did not consist in size of land mass, but primarily in political significance; by this standard the Russian and Prussian shares were much more important than the Austrian. Polish Prussia was the ideal acquisition, for it rounded out Prussia's borders and eased internal communications. Austria merely would acquire land whereas Prussia would gain an entire kingdom. "True," the king replied, "the acquisition of Polish Prussia is profitable for me. But on the other hand, it consists solely of sand. It seems to me that consideration must be given to the fertility of the soil and the size of the population. Ultimately, it matters little whether your share is slightly larger or smaller than mine; I will not pick at nits. But if you will pardon my saying it again, you have an excellent appetite."[54]

But Frederick had prior knowledge of Austria's claim. On April 18 he had written Solms: "The share of the partition that Austria has granted itself is as large as Polish Prussia and the other Prussian and Russian acquisitions combined. What is more, it includes the salt mines belonging to the Polish king, which alone bring an income of a million thalers a year. For this reason make a special effort to focus Count Panin's attention on the greediness of these claims in order to prevent his becoming a marionette controlled by Prince Kaunitz's cunning. I explained to you the harm that would befall my own salt industry were Austria to receive the Polish mines. It appears from the Russian empress's last letter that she is anxious to conclude matters with Vienna. I have not the slightest inclination to impede this. I would want only to persuade Russia to reduce Austria's demands somewhat, at least to cut out those districts which it would harm me for them to control."

On April 22 Frederick sent Solms another missive. "The most delicate issue remaining is to define Austria's share in the partition of Poland. I am waiting impatiently for Russia's reaction to Vienna's claims. If Vienna receives everything it desires, there will be no balance among our acquisitions. The scales will tilt in Vienna's direction, the more so as Austria is already stronger than I at present. To restore the balance, we must expand our shares. But if Russia does not become too impatient, I trust everything may still be settled amicably in Petersburg."

Berlin's anxiety, as it happened, soon subsided, for Frederick discovered a means of reconciling Austria's demands with Prussia's advantage. According to the English ambassador in Berlin, Prince Henry, Frederick's brother, wrote to someone he trusted: "Austria's demands are excessive; we shall have to haggle with Vienna as we would with a tradesman and complete whatever transaction we can. If the Austrians will not reduce their demands, we shall increase ours. They are afraid of a rupture, but that will never occur. The participants can find profit only in cooperation."

In Petersburg the empress met with the Council on April 13 to hear Vienna's claims on Polish territory. The Council resolved to attempt to exclude the salt mines and the city of Lwow from Austria's share, the former for the reasons cited by the king of Prussia and also in order not to deprive the Polish king of his chief source of revenue, and the latter because Poland should not lose the city where the charters of the Polish nobility were compiled and preserved. On the basis of this decision Russia proposed that Vienna limit its share, estimating that Russia stood to receive a population of 550,600, Austria 816,000, and Prussia 378,750.

Solms notified his king that Panin had spoken already with Prince Lobkowitz about the impossibility of accepting the Austrian demands. Frederick, expressing the hope that Panin's reproach would initiate appropriate action, wrote Solms on May 17 that it was imperative to end the affair quickly, for France would pounce on every source of disagreement between Austria and Prussia. Indeed, according to information received in Berlin, France hoped to succeed in its intentions by inciting the Porte to continue the war, absolutely convinced that its entreaties and inducements would receive a warm welcome in Constantinople. The French ministry also planned to intimate to Joseph II that he preferably take tentative steps towards reconciling Russia and Turkey. He would profit more were the two states to exhaust each other, while he continued to accept Turkish subsidies. In the opinions of the French war and naval ministers, France should propose to the Porte that it expel the Russian fleet from the Mediterranean. Emboldened by this diversion, Turkey might then resume the war and recoup its losses. As a result of such daring actions by France, Vienna would return to its French alliance in order to escape the entanglement with Russia and Prussia it had entered into unwillingly.

"These plans were actually proposed," wrote Frederick, "but since France lacks the necessary means—the system, firmness, and money to execute them—they will probably be rejected." Count Belgurski, the Polish ambassador to France, upon learning that Austrian and fresh Russian troops had entered Poland, drove at once to Versailles to inform the Duke d'Aiguillon.[55] The latter listened with displeasure and impatience, as if he knew much more. When Belgurski asked whether France would abandon Poland to partition by its neighbors, the duke replied:

'How can we help?Your impotence is so overwhelming that our efforts would have no effect. This event is the natural consequence of your disunity and the nasty intrigues of my predecessor.'"

Frederick continued: "The king of Poland and his relatives are directing their wrath against me primarily. They would have preferred for Russia and Austria to seize three times as much as I. They are hoping that the Porte will refuse to make peace after learning about the project to partition Poland. Furthermore, they would like to engender dissension among us. Lastly, they hope that distant powers will oppose our acquisitions."[56]

The matter dragged on, irritating Frederick acutely. "I am enclosing a letter from the Russian empress," he wrote his brother Henry, "which reveals that she is already less satisfied with the Austrians than formerly. Prince Kaunitz is injecting all the spirit of backbiting he can into the negotiations. This infuriates me, for it delays the occupation of our share and leads to untold unpleasantness with the Poles and other powers, to whom I hardly know how to respond while such an unsettled situation continues. I have seen a large section of our claim. We are gaining most of all as regards trade. We are becoming masters of all products and all imports into Poland. Most importantly, as masters of the grain trade, we need never suffer famine."[57]

The aged Frederick's young imitator, Emperor Joseph, likewise burned with impatience and strenuously complained to his brother Leopold about Vienna's slow progress on the matter. He wrote that under no circumstances ought Austria yield to Russia's demands. Indeed, Austria must obtain part of the Cracow military district to strengthen communications with Silesia and Moravia. The salt mines were essential as practically the sole source of revenue in all Galicia. And Austria must acquire Lwow, alone suitable for becoming an administrative center. On June 17 Joseph informed his brother that General Richard d'Alton had occupied the salt mines and administered the oath of allegiance to its officials. On July 9 Joseph wrote Leopold that affairs in Poland continued to proceed agreeably; Austria had snatched Tyniec from under Russia's nose (soufflé).[58] The sturdy monastery of Tyniec, where Polish confederates[59] had gathered to make a stand, was besieged by the Russian Colonel Alexander Vasilievich Suvorov[60] when Austrians under the command of General d'Alton appeared. D'Alton repeatedly requested that Suvorov hand over Tyniec to his army, for the confederates would surrender willingly to them and needless slaughter would be avoided.

Suvorov steadfastly replied that the confederates must cast themselves on the mercy of the empress and surrender unconditionally. In addition, he had no authority to lift the siege of Tyniec without an order from the commander-in-chief, Alexander Ilich Bibikov.[61] Thereupon d'Alton shifted his camp closer to Suvorov's and many Austrian officers began to infiltrate into Tyniec without permission. When Suvorov warned d'Alton that any Austrians in Tyniec who fell into Russian hands would be treated as enemies, d'Alton moved his camp a bit farther from the monastery and promised Suvorov not to allow anyone else to enter Tyniec. Nevertheless, on the night of June 23 under his orders twenty infantrymen and ten unmounted hussar infantry stole in turn through the Russian sentry line and into Tyniec. A second unit was hailed by Russian sentinels, hid in a rye field, and was taken prisoner by a Russian picket.

On the morrow d'Alton informed Suvorov that there were no more confederates in Tyniec, only Austrian forces. Therefore he, Suvorov, was not to fire into the monastery but must lift the siege. Suvorov replied that he could not believe this, since no Austrian units had entered the monastery inasmuch as d'Alton had given his promise. As a matter of fact, Suvorov continued, several deserters had fled into Tyniec just the night before, but he assured General d'Alton that these deserters would be returned when the monastery fell. Meanwhile, the siege and shooting would continue as before.

At that juncture d'Alton demanded permission to convey food supplies into Tyniec for his men, or else he would surround Weliczkowski castle, the Russian headquarters, and forbid foodstuffs to pass inside. Suvorov repeated that as there were only insurgents in Tyniec, no Austrian forces could be there and he could allow no victuals to enter. Bibikov soon received a report of these events from Suvorov and began to fear the prospect of armed conflict. For this reason he ordered Lieutenant General Romanius[62] in Lublin to advance on Tyniec and try to ease the hostility between Suvorov and d'Alton. But if the latter were to persist in his hostile behavior, Romanius should inform Bibikov. The Austrian general in Warsaw, Count Rishkur, gave assurances that d'Alton would be replaced in consequence of his misdeeds. Bibikov simultaneously directed Suvorov to eschew drastic action. Apparently Rishkur then informed d'Alton that he could operate securely, as Suvorov's hands were tied by Bibikov's order. Before Romanius arrived, d'Alton broke through the Russian cordon and occupied Tyniec and then, when the general arrived, showed him every possible courtesy.

Meanwhile Frederick II advised Petersburg to accede to the Austrian demands so that Prussia might add Dantzig and Thorn to its share[63]. On July 10 Solms sent Panin a letter. "There are two methods of combatting Austria's refusal to accept a reasonable settlement. First, one might openly oppose Vienna's intentions. But this would have far-reaching consequences; it would preclude the pacification of Poland and increase the confusion. Russia and Prussia would fail to attract the Poles to their side against Austria, which would return to its old ties. A general war in Europe would result, and to what end? It would be hard to tell. Even if the war ended in our favor it would sow the seeds of another conflict because of the enmity planted among the states participating in it.

"The alternative consists in adjusting to the circumstances by meeting Austria's demands. But in that case it would be unjust for the king of Prussia not to be rewarded for his substantial friendship with Russia, evidenced by his retraction of claims to parts of Poland more valuable for Prussia than are the Cracow salt industry and Lwow for Austria. If the Russian court, to preserve Europe from a new war, prefers to concede the Austrian demands, I may flatter myself with the anticipation that it would not oppose the Prussian king's intention to supplement his share with Dantzig and Thorn. If not included, these territories, surrounded by Prussia's new possessions, would negate the chief advantage of the acquisitions from Poland, the rounding out of the kingdom's possessions. Only on condition of receiving these towns will Prussia consent without difficulty or disgust to the seizure of such extensive and strategic lands by its powerful and dangerous neighbor. This solution alone will afford a peaceful and timely settlement of the matter. I fear that if arguments continue about equality of shares, a disastrous collision between Berlin and Vienna may result."

Solms recommended to Prince Lobkowitz that Austria not oppose Prussia's designs on Dantzig and Thorn. Lobkowitz informed Panin and received his soothing assurances that Russia would never agree to Prussian annexation of the towns in question.[64] But for this pledge Austria likewise had to relent.

On July 12 Frederick wrote Solms that Austria was relinquishing claims to the districts of Lublin and Chelm, but would not renounce the salt mines and Lwow—this was Vienna's final offer. "Having considered Austria's conditions thoughtfully," wrote Frederick, "I have concluded that we must accept them or fail to achieve a satisfactory agreement. I am not telling Russia what to do; I am simply stating my opinion." In another dispatch, dated August 5, the king revealed the reasons compelling him to bow to Austria. "Russia's talks with the Porte have led nowhere. France and England are keeping a baleful eye on the partition of Poland. Perhaps they are both exerting every effort to entice Vienna from the Russian-Prussian system and persuade it to reach a hurried agreement with Turkey. Should their intrigues succeed, the peace conference will be ruined, matters will become much more confused and entangled than heretofore, and untangling them will encounter insurmountable difficulties."

The letter Frederick sent on July 12 (New Style) was read to the Council on July 16 (Old Style) along with Vienna's reply to Russia's objections concerning the salt mines and Lwow. Kaunitz wrote that his government would acquiesce in excluding the districts of Lublin and Chelm but could not yield on the salt mines and Lwow. To compensate for the loss of the salt mines, the aforementioned provinces might be returned to the king of Poland. The price of salt could be established with Poland while the treaty was being worked out and the nobility's charters might be transferred from Lwow to Lublin. The Council decided to accept this and sign a convention with Vienna for the partition.[65]

On July 31 Frederick wrote Solms: "Baron van Swieten just left me. He told me about a new draft of the manifesto dealing with the occupation of the Polish lands written by Prince Kaunitz himself and not differing essentially from Count Panin's draft. The Austrian minister thinks that since there is a difference in the positions of his court and Russia's there ought to be differences in the manifestos as well. I read the draft carefully and found nothing objectionable.

"In politics there is a general rule: if incontrovertible evidence is lacking, it is better to express oneself laconically and not to go into details. I know well that Russia has much license to act that way with Poland, but one cannot say the same about us with Austria. All things considered, it is best that we conform with Prince Kaunitz's ideas."

With the Polish question settled, Vienna decided to inform Frederick about its views on Turkey. On August 30 Frederick wrote Solms: "Several days ago I met with Count Dietrichstein in Neisse. I think he was sent there to test me. It is clear from his conversation that the emperor and Lascy are not satisfied by acquisitions from Poland. They want to drive the Turks out of Europe and seize all the Hungarian territory situated on the left bank of the Danube. They would be pleased, should the Focsani conference be broken off, to help Russia drive the Turks from Europe and, if they succeed, mind you, permit Russia to annex Moldavia and Wallachia. I think they ardently desire an alliance with Russia for this purpose but fear the French and Spanish would create diversions in Italy and Flanders. Therefore they are turning to me. To gain my support they will renounce their acquisitions in Poland, enabling me to incorporate the entire course of the Warta river and whatever I desire in the neighborhood of Silesia. I wanted to learn what they intend to do about Greece, but they have given it no thought as yet. I prefer that Count Orlov make peace with the Turks; but if that does not happen we shall see a new scene, and the matter of a treaty of alliance will be raised, whereby Vienna probably intends to make all arrangements with its new allies. I calmly agreed with Dietrichstein on the feasibility of Austria's plan so long as our two courts act in good faith. But we must apprise the Russian empress fully from the beginning. What pleased me most about this candid conversation was that Count Dietrichstein did not attempt to camouflage the poor relations between his court and Versailles." Frederick then directed Solms to inform Panin in detail about this latest development.

The Prussian ambassador in Vienna, Edelheim, soon notified his sovereign that Maria Theresa again was exhibiting indecision about Poland by expressing remorse over her role in the partition. Once, in a foul mood, she reproached her son the emperor severely, attributing the source of her difficulties to his conclaves with Frederick II. The emperor grew quite annoyed, and it was rumored that the daily arguments between mother and son were growing more frequent and bitter. Prince Kaunitz, who had played a principal role in the events leading to these scenes, sided with the emperor. Communicating this information to Solms, Frederick wrote on November 15: "Count Panin has nothing to fear. All he need do is allow Prince Kaunitz freedom of action. A shrewd minister, he knows the disposition and character of his sovereign and will manage to soothe her anxious conscience."

In a second dispatch, dated November 21, Frederick informed Solms that Maria Theresa continued to suffer pangs of remorse and had resorted to her religious advisors. Her confessor told her that as he knew nothing about the legal pretexts for her seizure of Polish territory he could not view the partition as a grave sin. Other churchmen affirmed that the laws governing states and rulers differed from those applicable to private persons; there were times when the empress might govern with an eye solely to her political interests. The latter opinion was ascribed to the Jesuits.

At the August 13 session of the Council Catherine initialed a rescript to Count Zakhar Chernyshev ordering the occupation of the territory taken from Poland to begin during the first week of September. Chernyshev, who had been the first to favor partition, was designated governor general of White Russia. On September 27 (New Style) the king of Prussia received the oath of loyalty from the inhabitants of Polish Prussia. The same day he wrote Solms: "Tell Count Panin he can reassure the empress in my name that now, on the day allegiance is sworn in Polish Prussia, I promise her that she has not bound an ungrateful man; I will let no occasion pass without displaying my gratitude to her and Russia not by lipservice but by action."

And what was occurring in Poland in 1772, while its fate was being decided conclusively by its three neighbors?

THE REACTION IN POLAND

Early in the year the primary interest and chief topic of conversation were as before the oppressions of the Prussian troops.[66] The French agent reported to his court: "At the very time that the king of Prussia grows all the more hated Russia apparently desires to soften its earlier treatment of the Poles. Bibikov's order for strict discipline among the soldiers is evidence of this. Conversation centers on the Prussian oppression directed against the clergy, which Benoit explains by the fact that the clergy is chiefly responsible for the trouble. By hampering the clergy, the king is helping Russia pacify Poland." Only on February 29 (New Style) did the agent write: "Frederick's actions reveal his desire to win permanent advantages: he aspires to take possession of Warmia province, for his generals have demanded the bishop's archive."

Gerard, France's man in Dantzig, knew more, informing his court on March 5 of the conclusion of an agreement to partition Poland, whereas his colleague in Warsaw wrote only on March 25: "Saldern[67] says that the affair will end poorly for Poland; the king of Prussia will certainly get Polish Prussia. From the other direction, the courts of Russia and Austria clearly are nearing rapprochement. It is possible that Vienna will consent to Prussian gains if they restore Silesia or leave under Austrian rule the Polish lands Vienna now controls. Russia likewise will attempt to reward itself at Poland's expense. Thus Poland apparently is on the verge of falling prey to its neighbors."

On May 16 the agent in Warsaw reported: "Although general opinion regards the partition of Poland as an accomplished fact, the Czartoryskis[68] maintain that this is nonsense."

At the beginning of the year the crown chancellor, Mlodziejowski, visited the Russian ambassador, Baron Caspar Saldern, with complaints about Prussian oppressions. "Would you think it proper," he asked, "for Poland's king to dispatch an envoy to her majesty notifying her of the oppressive behavior of the king of Prussia?"

Saldern made use of the occasion to express his thoughts. "I think the empress will receive no ambassador from Poland so long as disturbances continue here. She remembers very well everything that has gone on here for a number of years, noting not only the indifference to her on the part of the Polish throne but also the open opposition to her every good intention. How can you expect the empress to intercede for Poland with the king of Prussia when he is the only monarch acting in concert with her? What makes you think my sovereign would display churlishness to a friend by interceding for the Poles, who are neither cold nor hot, and who can be regarded as enemies of Russia? I am not talking about the confederates alone, but about all those who, while not openly involved in the present troubles, work underhandedly and crowd into Warsaw.

"I do not exclude even the court. Her imperial majesty will not forget the coldness, inattention, inconstancy, and improper behavior displayed by the king and his family in protecting the very group of people indignant at their own king,[69] who has been upheld by my sovereign. After my declaration I had several conversations with the king's uncles and the vice chancellors and told them of her imperial majesty's intentions to give satisfaction to Poland, revealing that the empress had agreed to revisions of the most substantive points of the previous treaty.[70] That is, she will provide clarifications regarding guarantees and will not oppose limitations on the rights of dissidents, so long as they consent to sacrifice a portion of their rights in exchange for removing the pretext for malicious people to practice brigandage under the guise of religion.[71] As far as domestic affairs are concerned, the empress has requested merely retention of the liberum veto for all nobles.[72] These conditions seemed to satisfy the king's uncles and vice chancellors. But did they really intend to take advantage of the good intentions of her imperial majesty and proceed to the business at hand?

"The Russian commander has said that we have but few troops in Poland to support our cause, that the republic faces a crisis, and that the situation cannot get worse. I fully understand what he meant; he intended to say that we have a war on our hands that might go unsuccessfully for he surely must know that we have 12,000 troops in Poland—enough men to support those who seriously desire to take advantage of our good disposition rather than increase the disorder by their own inactivity.

"Other than the empress no one supports both king and republic, but does this increase their trust in her? No, the king is turning the other way, deluded by the expectation of support from a neighbor which heretofore has not evidenced the slightest glimmer of friendship and favor. On the contrary, he gives succur to people who encroach on his authority and very life. Vienna sees and knows everything the king of Prussia is doing in Poland. Under different circumstances Austria might oppose him; now, however, it has seized Polish territory and may have something else in mind as well. Russia's empress is demanding prudent friendship with King Stanislaw and the republic, congruent with Poland's natural constitution. If the king and his friends prefer to remain passive and insist on being ambivalent, she can not be blamed for taking measures appropriate to her dignity and the interests of her empire.

"I predict that Poland must expect extreme disorder. This is not the first time that I have reminded you that last summer you lost the most propitious moment to calm Poland with your own forces and Russian support. I tried to make you understand that letting that favorable moment escape meant that Poland's calm no longer would be that of a free nation, but that its laws and peace now would emanate from the hands of your neighbors. When complaints started about the behavior of the Prussian king I warned Stanislaw and you that Frederick would cause you much more pain and that he more than anyone else was exploiting Poland's disorder."

Thus were pronounced the indictment and the verdict. This was Saldern's last official act, following which he asked even more persistently to be relieved. In a letter dated January 24 he had implored Catherine to recall him from Warsaw, or at least not leave him there beyond September, citing his poor health. Saldern wrote Panin: "I can no longer sleep, and my stomach refuses to digest anything." But he was left there until September. Panin ordained his silence in a letter of February 28: "Our current relationship with Vienna has altered totally the nature of the political coalitions, movements, and intrigues associated with your post. A plethora of matters suddenly have lost their significance—affairs which otherwise might deserve our attention, as for example (1) the thinly disguised offer of the Czartoryskis to mediate a rapprochement of the Russian and Austrian courts. This rapprochement already has taken place, and the Czartoryskis can be thanked for their service only by providing them the satisfaction of the unexpected by letting them learn of the agreement from its consequences. While awaiting a denouement they may conduct their own secret correspondence, to which they attach such importance. (2) By the same token we must remain silent in the face of Polish grievances against Prussia. Our agreement with the king of Prussia has been signed, after which it would be contradictory for us to call attention to the complaints against his troops; our interest requires that he oppress the Poles with ever greater intensity, thereby assisting us while terms are being settled with Poland."

At the end of May a Prussian officer in Marienburg notified a Polish official that the annexation of Polish Prussia to Prussia was no secret, that it followed from the treaty with Austria and Russia.[73] The Polish ministry therewith informed the foreign ministers of it in the following phrases: "Unfortunate Poland, devastated for five years by its own inhabitants and its neighbors, is to be relieved of its best provinces by powers with which it had no cause for a clash, who had no legal pretext for complaint. Indeed, Poland had cause to rest its hope and trust in one of them. However cruel and rapacious the behavior of Russia toward Poland, however unjust the undertaking of the king of Prussia, the behavior of Vienna, equally violent and unjust, is the more despicable for it was grounded in guile and duplicity."

Saldern maintained a deep official silence during his last days in Warsaw. Observing his fallen grandeur, the Poles turned their entire attention to Bibikov. Saldern could not help sending Panin a denunciation of the supreme military commander. "Bibikov's behavior," he wrote, "is totally at odds with the Russian system. The king and his brothers and uncles have taken advantage of his weak side: women control him—the wives of Marshal Lubomirski, Hetman Oginski, and others of the king's party. He does not appear likely to come to his senses. Chancellor Czartoryski, that old fox, summoned the daughter of Przezdziecki from Lithuania for this purpose.[74] Bibikov does everything these people put into his ear through their womenfolk. He does not get a single day off to regain his senses. They take him hunting, or for a ride in the country, or to a ball—in short, entertainment of every variety, accompanied by the basest flattery and servility by the Poles. Thus they are ensnaring him. He has passed several evenings at Madame Oginska's, despite General Ivan Ivanovich Weimarn's order to Russian officers to stay away because of her husband's and family's behavior and the gambling there. But Bibikov is permitted to do whatever he wants. He has lost touch to such a degree that he persecutes everyone whom the Czartoryskis and the king's brother despise. You can surmise the number of opportunities the military commander has to oppress whomever he wishes. I used every means I could to dissuade him from this and sometimes succeeded, especially when I did it in writing: he was afraid I was sending copies to the court. He abandons all discretion whenever his vanity is aroused. Indolence, which stands foremost in his manner of living, is bringing everything to a grinding halt. Oftentimes as many as sixty orders have lain on his desk unsigned for a week or longer."

But reports like these now hurt only Saldern himself. Everyone assumed he was sent to Poland because of his close friendship with the preeminent minister, Count Panin. He returned to Petersburg far less distinguished a man. He had had his reasons for not wanting the post in Warsaw. For one thing, he enjoyed the reputation of a most skillful negotiator. Unfortunately, as hopes rose that he would succeed in settling matters in Poland, the proportionate danger loomed that failure might destroy his reputation. Failure seemed increasingly possible to Saldern, especially in that negotiations already were being handled from Petersburg and by the king of Prussia. Several years earlier Frederick had collided with Saldern over the Northern system, after which the king of Prussia developed an extreme hatred for the Russo-Holstein minister, exacerbated by Saldern's opposition to Prussian influence in Copenhagen.[75] Saldern, it goes without saying, repaid Frederick with the same sentiment. When he was posted to Warsaw, the Prussian king commented about him to van Swieten: "This man is arrogant, obstinate, and proud, and thinks God knows what about himself."[76]

But if Frederick failed to appreciate Saldern's presence in Warsaw he must have been more chagrined to see him in Petersburg at a most critical juncture in the settlement of the Polish question. It is understandable how advantageous it had been for Frederick that no one very close to the leading Russian minister was hostile to Prussia, who advocated the necessity of rapprochement with Austria in order to contain Prussia. In fact, one cannot ignore the fact that after Saldern's departure for Warsaw Panin increasingly yielded to Prussian influence. It is common knowledge that Berlin skillfully used Saldern's absence.

The English envoy in Petersburg, Robert Gunning, reported to his court that the king of Prussia, long aware of Count Panin's overarching conceit, was nourishing this passion so adroitly that he had converted the leading minister to his devoted follower. Frederick often sent Panin gifts which, though not valuable, always were accompanied by a hand-written note filled with the most flattering sentiments. They achieved their goal, bending Panin to view every situation as though through the eyes of his Prussian majesty. Panin virtually worshipped Frederick II. This being the case, it is easy to understand the cooling of friendship between Panin and Saldern, who retained his former low regard for the king of Prussia and took advantage of every opportunity to express his feelings, which became well known to Panin through both open and privy channels.

As was noted earlier, Saldern related to Panin his conversation with Mlodziejowski in which he singled out Frederick II as the sovereign most profiting from Poland's troubles. On other occasions he expressed himself even more clearly and forthrightly. Gerard reported from Dantzig on May 6: "The tsaritsa feels she is placed in an awkward position and wants the other states to compensate for her impotence, she having frustrated the plans of the king of Prussia. This pattern of Catherine II's is re-enforced by the statement Saldern repeats from time to time that the king of Prussia deceived his sovereign, Catherine." Saldern took the liberty of telling the Dantzig city secretary, "The empress does not approve at all of the views of the king of Prussia, but the overwhelming need for peace compels her to shut her eyes and agree to execute his plan." What is more, Saldern charged the secretary to recommend to his master the unification of Dantzig with Thorn and Elbing either as an independent state or under the protection of the Polish crown.

Austria's ambassador in Warsaw, Baron Karl Emerich Rewiczki,[77] related to his court that Saldern resolutely was censuring the performance of Russia's leading minister. "Without the closest possible alliance between Russia and Austria," said Saldern to Rewiczki, "the king of Prussia will move both imperial courts into the background and himself receive the most important advantages." According to Rewiczki, Saldern wanted to reduce the great magnates of Poland to size and somehow equalize gentry property holdings, thereby reconciling the majority to the partition by liberating them from the oppression of their own countrymen. But Panin did not agree to it.

Chamberlain Baron Otto Magnus von Stackelberg[78] was named to succeed Saldern in Warsaw. The English envoy wrote his ministry concerning Stackelberg's appointment: "Inasmuch as nothing is accomplished without the counsel of the king of Prussia, the man named to succeed Mr. Saldern was selected with his approval, because his character is flexible and conforms to circumstances favoring his Prussian majesty. Therefore he is better suited for this post than his predecessor." We know only that Stackelberg set out with powerful prejudices against his immediate predecessor.

Stackelberg's instructions, signed on August 11, reveal the incentives that impelled Russia to favor a partition of Polish territory. "You certainly know that two other courts—Vienna and Berlin—have been observing Polish affairs and the Russo-Turkish war from different standpoints. Vienna had close ties with France whose policy, ever at odds with Russia's at all courts, strengthened and fortified the Polish rebellion with money, men, loud protests, and intrigues. Through substantial monetary bribes it induced the Porte to declare war on Russia. Under the influence of this kind of ally, Vienna has displayed friendliness toward the Polish confederates and offered them sanctuary. It has showed the Porte no less beneficence. The king of Prussia, on the other hand, loyally has fulfilled the conditions of his alliance with Russia. He has paid his subsidies, detained bands of confederates on his borders, and attentively monitored the behavior of the Austrian court, ever showing his preparedness to inform his ally of its actions. When Russia was doubly distracted by war with the Porte and the Polish insurrection, Vienna decided it had found a convenient occasion to reimburse itself with its own hands for its good will toward both the Porte and the confederates; without issuing a single claim of legality or pretense, it occupied Zips.[79]

"The less manifest attention Russia and Prussia paid to this development, the more the two of them discussed it at length in their councils and consulted on suitable measures. They recognized two alternatives. First, they could protest openly against Austria's behavior, opening negotiations to persuade Vienna to evacuate the occupied territory. In that case failure might mean the necessity to resort to arms and wage war on Austria. Second, they could act in concert with Vienna by issuing claims to certain areas of Poland. Since maintaining the balance of power among the three courts required them either to acquire nothing from Poland or else to receive equal shares, sound policy left them the choice of one of two alternatives.

"It was left to Catherine to determine which of them might provide the better means for restoring calm to Poland as quickly as possible while conforming with justice. She could not waver long. The first alternative, war with a power bordering on Poland, on such a vast expanse of land, would provide more fuel for Polish insurrections and thus delay the pacification of Poland interminably. The empress would subject her country to increased losses and considerable danger, and for whom? For the sake of a nation for which she already had sacrificed untold sums of money and numbers of men for many years! For a nation which was repaying her favor, beneficence and unselfishness with the most blatant ingratitude not only by waging open war against her but also by arousing a second, most dangerous enemy. The second option suggested the amicable cooperation of the three powers in pacifying Poland and deciding all questions which sooner or later otherwise might ignite a war between one or another of them and Poland. It presented the opportunity for reducing Poland's borders in order to bring its size into conformity with its constitution and the interests of its neighbors. Finally, and most importantly, the second alternative would preserve peace in that part of Europe. Having weighed all these considerations and made her decision, the empress busied herself with means for fulfilling it."

On September 7, Stackelberg and the Prussian minister, Benoit (the Austrian Baron Rewiczki had not arrived), handed the Polish ministry the proclamation of partition. After quick consultations the king and his closest advisors developed a strategy of delay, agreeing to nothing voluntarily. The three courts would be compelled to seize their shares by force. The Poles further decided to request aid from other European governments. They would play for time, bringing an entire labyrinth of cavilling and empty procedure to bear against the demands of the three powers. In speaking to certain people the king thundered against Russia; to others he implied that Catherine had agreed with him to form a confederation against partition. He even let this latter claim reach the ears of the Austrian ambassador in order to foment a dispute among the three powers. Stackelberg attempted to counter his assertions by hinting to the Poles that Russia was not acting as protector of the king; and since the Czartoryskis no longer held a monopoly on Russian relations with Poland the nation was not running the risk of being deceived.

At the end of October Stackelberg spoke with the king. Stanislaw Augustus was ready for him and gave full rein to his eloquence. "I have endured so much tribulation for the sake of my country," he said. "I have written my friendship and devotion to the empress with my blood. Seeing my realm plundered most dreadfully and myself driven to utter poverty, I can understand that those responsible can subject me to yet greater distress, but I no longer fear them. Beaten, near to dying from hunger, I have learned how to succumb."

Stackelberg coolly replied: "Your majesty's eloquence and power of imagination are equal to the best pages of Plutarch and ancient history, but this cannot serve as the subject of our conversation. Deign to return to the history of Poland and of Count Poniatowski." The ambassador next recapitulated the sequence of events resulting in the misfortune the king bemoaned. Bringing the story up to date, Stackelberg then wondered aloud what would happen to the king if 100,000 troops flooded into Poland, exacted tribute, forced the Diet[80] to approve whatsoever the neighboring powers desired and departed, leaving him as sacrifice to his enemies' spite? The king blanched. Seizing upon this Stackelberg began to demonstrate that Stanislaw's future depended on two conditions: the rapid convening of the Diet and renunciation of all intrigues which might embitter and mislead the Poles. The king promised his absolute compliance.

Stackelberg had not yet become accustomed to the fact that the unforeseen happened so often in Warsaw. Therefore he could not believe his ears when, two days later, the king invited him to a second audience and announced that he felt duty constrained him to send Frantiszek Branicki to Paris with a protest against the partition.[81] Stackelberg answered: "I can do nothing now but grieve for your majesty and inform my court of your behavior. Whatever can you expect from France against three powers who are able to shatter all Europe?"

"Nothing," answered the king, "but I did my duty."

On November 23 Stackelberg sent Stanislaw the following declaration: "There is a limit to the moderation which the justice and dignity of the three courts prescribe. Her majesty the empress hopes that the king does not want to subject Poland to the disasters inevitably following upon his majesty's sluggishness in summoning the Diet and proceeding to the negotiations which alone can save his fatherland." But at the same time that Stackelberg was taking measures to compel the king to alter his unfortunate conduct, Benoit repeatedly told him, "Leave the king alone; it will be all the better for us. We will take more."

Stanislaw Augustus felt duty-bound to protest the partition to France, admitting to Stackelberg that he anticipated no positive results for Poland therefrom. He spoke honestly, although he probably hoped that Western Europe would not remain indifferent to the audacious event in the East.

THE VIEW FROM FRANCE

The unfortunate reign of Louis XV was hastening to an end, squandering the remaining material and moral substance of the French government, which declared that a new war was impossible no matter for whom or for what. The only way left for France to demonstrate its power and prestige was adroit diplomatic intrigue. To be sure, France was famous for its school of diplomats, superior in cunning to the diplomats of other countries. This famous school dated from the age of Cardinal Richelieu. But this powerful, brilliant army represented by the corps of French envoys at foreign courts required a skilled commander in Versailles to direct its movements in a unified way toward the common goal. The director of France's foreign affairs, the Duke de Choiseul, had been such a masterful commander.

No sooner had Russia appeared on the European stage in the era of Peter the Great than French diplomats grasped its significance. When they proved unable to swing this new power into their orbit and when Russia thanks to mutual interests made an alliance with France's enemy Austria, they began a bitter diplomatic war against Russia in Turkey, Sweden, and Poland. The diplomatic revolution and the alliance with Austria, following the realization that Frederick II's Prussia was far more dangerous to France than the Habsburg monarchy, inclined France and Russia together in common operations in the Seven Years War. But Russia's shift in policy after Elizabeth's death rekindled the former enmity between France and

Russia, and the Duke de Choiseul, a true Frenchman possessing the
famous Gallic passion (*furia francese*), orchestrated the diplomatic
struggle against Petersburg's cabinet, for he realized that after the Seven
Years War Russia would be the strongest state in Europe. Moreover, he
sensed that the Russian sovereign, Catherine II, possessed the urge and
ability to increase her influence in Europe. Choiseul could not bear this,
for he wanted France under his leadership to retain its former primacy in
European affairs. He felt insulted by Russia's grandeur just as the representative of an ancient but declining family is offended by the success
of a young, capable, and wealthy parvenu. To counteract Russia he wanted to strengthen the bond of friendship with Austria through a dynastic
marriage of the heir to the French throne and Archduchess Marie Antoinette.[82] Russia, mirroring the moves of its opponent, aspired to take the
same step. As Choiseul built the southern Catholic alliance of France,
Spain, and Austria, so Russia envisaged a northern alliance. This northern
concert emerged stillborn because the interests of the three powers which
had to comprise its chief members—Russia, Prussia, and England—did
not coincide. But Choiseul was irritated by the consideration given to
Russia's initiative, by the open diplomatic struggle at every level, by Russia's emulation of French moves, and by Petersburg's persistent efforts
to countermine French policies.

The attempt to deflect Prussia from Russia turned out to be fruitless.
In Poland it proved impossible to prevent Russia from placing Poniatowski on the throne and issuing its notorious demands. Choiseul, however,
greeted the eruption of discontent in Poland. He welcomed the Confederation of Bar and began aiding the confederates with men and money,
for his primary goal was to continue the war and exhaust Russia. How
better to reach this goal than by rousing Turkey? Choiseul succeeded in
Turkey and meanwhile worked tirelessly in Sweden to augment the king's
power. In a word, Russia confronted Choiseul as its principal enemy on
every important political front. Catherine had every right to hate this
"coachman of Europe," as she termed Choiseul.

Frederick II had begun long since to console his ally concerning the
"coachman of Europe." The king of Prussia knew that Louis XV was
prepared to sacrifice his minister for any woman—not to say mistress (that
would be too blunt)—capable of pleasing him no matter how useful that
minister was for France. Considering Choiseul's fall to be well within the

realm of possibility, Frederick wrote Catherine early in 1769 that vigorous maneuvering against Choiseul had been initiated in Versailles; those
involved were attempting to oust him by means of the Countess Du Barry,
who had become the king's mistress. Along with Choiseul, wrote Frederick, would fall all his projects, for new ministers usually conduct affairs
differently from their predecessors.

Within two years the prediction came true. Late in 1770 Choiseul, un-
willing to grovel before Du Barry, was dismissed and exiled. The Duke
d'Aiguillon from Du Barry's party replaced him. Choiseul's dismissal
struck a decisive blow to French predominance in European affairs.
Although d'Aiguillon could hardly be termed incapable of recognizing
France's interests, he was concerned primarily about factions within
France and devoted the bulk of his attention to domestic affairs, court
intrigues, and factional struggles whose outcome would affect his career.
He was pleased when Choiseul's system collapsed and he could reproach
his hated predecessor for his mistaken plans or instructions. But
d'Aiguillon limited his reproaches to words. Notwithstanding his delight
at the failure of Choiseul's enterprises, he lacked the time, energy, and
ability to discard his predecessor's system instantaneously and create a
new one. Therefore d'Aiguillon did not interfere with the schemes of
Choiseul that seemed assured of success—for example, in Sweden.
Although he desired a rapprochement with Russia, it was difficult for him
to initiate anything. He would have been pleased to contradict Choiseul's
policies entirely, except that he was slow to begin and allowed affairs to
drag. He had no general plan of action and nothing was completely
clarified.

Early in 1772 the Russian chargé d'affaires Nikolai Konstantinovich
Khotinsky[83] held a conversation with the Duke d'Aiguillon about the
peace conditions Russia had offered Turkey. Khotinsky noted that Russia's bestowal of Moldavia and Wallachia ought to bring peace, whereupon d'Aiguillon looked at him askance and exclaimed: "But who will
get the Crimea?" Then, a little more quietly, he added: "You know the
Turks have no intention of yielding anything."

"In that case," queried Khotinsky, "how are we to be rewarded for our
military successes or compensated for the expenses they entailed?"

The duke answered coldly, lowering his voice: "I think the compensation should be monetary. Their preparations make it obvious that the

Porte is not shrinking from a fourth campaign. They know that your squadrons are in no condition to hold out much longer at sea, which is not surprising in light of the fact they they are forced to remain in service ten months of the year. As a result your ships have rotted and sailors are perishing. The Turks know that you are having difficulty raising enough recruits for the army because of the plague. Your garrisoned regiments have been depleted and money is in short supply. Even your ministers receive their salary in paper."

"Ever since the war started," retorted Khotinsky, "I have heard those arguments. The people who make them have waited a long time for us to become exhausted. True, the war is burdensome for us. But we have no state debt and the costs of maintaining an army are lower in Russia than elsewhere; thus we can bear the expenses of war longer than wealthier states than ours. As concerns the navy, Lieutenant Proshchin and Lizakevich, a translator, who are returning from the navy through France, have informed me that everything is fine in the squadrons."

"The recruitment levy is a severe burden for the gentry," shot back d'Aiguillon. "They now have to turn over every eighth man."

"You have received false information," said Khotinsky. "We are raising eighty thousand troops at present, so that the lot falls on hardly every hundredth man, for upwards of nine million people are enrolled in the soul tax lists."[84]

"We have detailed information," the duke persisted; "when one subtracts children, old people, and freemen not many remain who are suitable for service. Your sovereign's intention to maintain an army in the Crimea, another on the Danube, and a fleet in the Greek islands[85] is undeniably bold, but such plans ought to be masked, lest in the event of the war's continuation they do not achieve their anticipated success. As an illustration you might take our march into Bavaria. The first campaign was brilliant, but thereafter the army wasted away through disease and insufficient recruits."

Khotinsky defended the utility of paper money, and d'Aiguillon replied: "On the whole that is an easy method of supplying money, but it is injurious because it usually leads to abuses. We underwent untold disasters because of it, as you can see for yourself."[86]

In March another curious conversation took place. D'Aiguillon began: "The balance in Europe will be destroyed if you succeed in imposing peace with Turkey on the three conditions of free access to the Black Sea, a harbor there, and independence for the Tatars. With these footholds you soon will be in Constantinople, and then who will be able to oust you?"

Khotinsky replied "Whoever wishes to."

"Who might that be?"

"You first," Khotinsky smiled, "and then the Austrians and the English."

"By then it would be too late."

"Do you seriously think that?"

D'Aiguillon said that he was absolutely serious.

"Quite honestly," Khotinsky retorted, "our gains from this war are more glorious than useful. As concerns freedom of the sea, let me remind you of our success on the Baltic, which is open to us. As you know, foreigners carry our commerce; despite repeated attempts to encourage our people to engage in maritime trade, they do not. Hence it is obvious that we have no inclination to commerce. And the Crimean Tatars are already independent."

"What do you mean, independent?" asked d'Aiguillon. "You have selected their khan to be your lackey. At the appropriate moment you will set them against Hungary and the other Austrian lands which they will ravage before Austria can react and concentrate its troops, which are scattered about Italy and Flanders. Might one postulate that you have ten, twenty, or is it thirty ships in the Black Sea? And how many guns? You are so powerful, particularly when allied with the king of Prussia. You are presently his friend and he fulfills your requests, but in time you will have to learn how to deal with him. Your location provides security. Who will attempt to attack you over such a distance? Yes, you do well to insist on these three conditions. I would do the same in your shoes, although I doubt the Turks will yield."

On March 11 Khotinsky filed his initial report about the rumors in Paris that Russia, Prussia, and Austria were arranging a partition of Poland. On March 27 he visited d'Aiguillon, who repeated his forecast: "Should the Turks evacuate the Crimea, in two years it will be in your hands and in four years you will occupy Constantinople." The duke's exclamation at the end of the conversation had much greater significance: "Vienna has made a big mistake!"

In a conversation in April Khotinsky said, among other things: "You might quite properly show yourself of service to Turkey, us, and all humanity by persuading the Porte to be a bit more accommodating."

"What? Are you suggesting that we urge accommodation," answered d'Aiguillon, "when we were the ones who pushed the Turks into the war? Moreover, our political credit is not very great. It was foolish of us to allow your fleet into the Mediterranean."

On April 26 Khotinsky wrote Panin: "Paris is absolutely certain that some part of Poland soon will be partitioned among Russia, Austria, and Prussia. You can imagine the anger and reproach felt in France. Paris doubted that Vienna would ever consent to break up Poland, for it would strengthen us and the king of Prussia, an enterprising and dangerous sovereign."

"What will France and Spain and England say when we suddenly emerge closely allied with those whom we formerly wanted so desperately to restrain and whose conduct we termed unjustifiable?" wrote Maria Theresa, an opponent of the decision to pursue the partition of Poland.[87] Kaunitz, presumably, cared not a whit about England and Spain's reactions, but he thought long and hard about what France's response would have been had its foreign affairs remained in Choiseul's hands. He felt it less necessary to stand upon ceremony in dealing with d'Aiguillon. The notorious southern alliance—Austro-Franco-Spanish—had been created and sustained by Choiseul alone; without him it languished and grew untenable. Austria ceased to depend on France for aid and influence, or to fear it. Joseph and Kaunitz no longer cared what d'Aiguillon or Louis XV would say.

As early as June 1771 Count Charles-François de Broglie, the French ambassador in Warsaw, wrote Louis about the French general Dumouriez's[88] failure to restore order to Poland. "It would be simple to find a pretext for opposing partition were Vienna genuinely concerned about the good of Poland, but I suspect that it does not want to see that unhappy land prevail. Overcome, Warsaw will submit more readily to the laws Vienna wants to prescribe for it; and its ambitious neighbors want to place it in precisely this predicament. Only your majesty can help Poland. The new ministry (of d'Aiguillon) fails to grasp that the fate of this republic should interest France politically. The ambassador recently posted to Vienna (Prince Louis de Rohan) understands it even less. This lack of foresight will doom our interests and our system in this part of Europe."

But these hints elicited no action. Louis XV already knew, and in greater detail, about the plan for partitioning Poland. The French envoy in Berlin had reported in March 1771 that the Swedish envoy there had told him: "It's all done. The king of Prussia has managed everything and the peace (between Russia and Turkey) will be signed within four months. Poland will pay for everything."

Early in 1772 Louis XV wrote Count Broglie that the Duke d'Aiguillon had besought the Austrian ambassador, Count Mercy Argenteau, to discover whether Austria really wished "to receive its share of the Polish pie, as everyone seemed to think." At long last Mercy told d'Aiguillon about the partition of Poland, intimating that the threat of a united Russia and Prussia had compelled the Austrian emperor and empress to participate in the partition, which in any event could not have been prevented. Vienna admitted that the deed was indefensible but it felt obligated to take part precisely to minimize an injustice which could be stemmed in no other way. This explained why its sovereigns were to receive so small a share in comparison with the other powers. Vienna regarded the event exclusively with regret, for it was tilting the balances far from its favor. As for the silence Austria was maintaining regarding its relations with Russia and Prussia on this issue, France was observing a similar silence as well. Vienna was aware that the Duke d'Aiguillon had contacted Prussian envoys and had declared to one of them that whatever happened in Poland was of no concern to France. The king of Prussia had apprised Vienna of France's desire for rapprochement with him. Thus Vienna, realizing that it could not depend fully on France, was forced to take precautions against storms it could not confront alone.

This explanation greatly angered d'Aiguillon, who warned that a lack of trust on Vienna's part could lead to a cooling of relations with France. Were this estrangement to continue, it might result in the rupture of their alliance.[89] But these threats could not frighten Vienna. Mercy reported: "Intrigues are absorbing everyone's attention in Paris and distracting from foreign affairs, so that there is little to fear. What the Duke d'Aiguillon has told me about Poland heretofore has hampered me minimally. He conducts affairs listlessly and unsystematically and often resorts to petty falsehoods. This method never can by very formidable and merely bids one use some caution and attentiveness. I see clearly that the arrangements regarding Poland have not harmed the king personally."

Notwithstanding this, Maria Theresa wrote Mercy: "No matter how certain of the king's feelings I may be, I hesitate to write him myself on this matter. Tell him whatever you wish in my name."

In a subsequent conversation with Mercy, Louis XV exhibited deep regard for Maria Theresa but asked in sport whether Joseph was getting on well with his friend, the king of Prussia. At that point Louis's mistress interrupted, sensing that his jocularity was edging into anger. "I am sure," she said, "the emperor knows the king of Prussia well enough to know that he subjects the entire world to chicanery and cannot be trusted to keep his word."

Mercy replied in the same spirit and the king added: "I hope that these difficulties will end with a minimum of harm."[90]

This hope seemed to placate Louis. The Duke d'Aiguillon was left to pronounce a homily such as that delivered to Khotinsky regarding the partition. "To the king of Prussia will fall the choicest piece. His ascendancy does not particularly concern us, but you will regret it some day. This is where the policies of the Duke de Choiseul have led, whereas it would have been more natural for our two states, because of their geographical positions, to live in friendship for our mutual benefit."

In the summer the French chargé d'affaires, Sabatier, was recalled from Petersburg and replaced by François Michel Durand de Distroff, who was transferred from Vienna.[91] This appointment alarmed both Austria and Prussia, particularly the latter, for Durand was known for his deception; he was a diplomat of the old school. D'Aiguillon said to Khotinsky about the transfer: "I will disclose this one thing to you; I am attempting to take the first step toward rapprochement with your court. Should your government not reciprocate, I shall back away. You are well acquainted with my manner of thinking, and it seems to me that the spite and intrigues of a certain private individual (Choiseul) should be scorned by our great states."

In September d'Aiguillon told Khotinsky in response to news of the failure of the Focsani negotiations: "I am amazed that your allies, particularly the king of Prussia, were unable to persuade or compel the Turks to end the war. But I do not think your court is so obliging as to believe that they actually were pleading for reconciliation. I confess that in their place I too would want nothing more than to see my neighbors consumed by their own greed. Perhaps we might have been able to serve you better than your present allies, but you cast us aside." Khotinsky noted that Russia had France to thank for the Turkish war. "But as you know," said the duke, "we continue to seek after one thing—to live in amity with you."

"You ought to add," noted Khotinsky, "that this policy really began only when you replaced the Duke de Choiseul."

D'Aiguillon retorted, "My predecessor has been gone for a full two years."

"All the same," replied Khotinsky, "we had no reason to suppose that in replacing Choiseul the French court was also altering its views."

"We shall see what Durand does," said d'Aiguillon, ending the conversation.

Khotinsky received a directive from his court to describe the reaction of the French public to the Polish partition. He replied that French political figures believed the partition grew out of Frederick's lifelong desire to annex Polish Prussia. They were surprised only that Vienna conceded this. As for Russia, they said that since it had no need to acquire new lands, it did not favor the partition of Poland at all, but distracted by war could not resist the desires of the king of Prussia by itself.

On November 8 Khotinsky described his conversation with d'Aiguillon in response to news about Durand's warm reception in Petersburg. Khotinsky began with a reproach: "A year ago we might have been where we are now had you followed my suggestions then to post your own man in Russia."

D'Aiguillon replied: "You know that I did what I could. I am not ashamed that we took the first step. I told our allies in Spain about this, and they agreed that the most prudent must be the first to act."

"Honestly, we were unable to move first," said Khotinsky. "But since matters already have reached their desired end, why are men inimical to the restoration of harmony between Russia and France given the means to postpone such a benefit by contradictory words and deeds from Versailles?"

"What does this contradiction consist of?" asked d'Aiguillon.

"The armistice has been extended and the negotiations will be revived owing to repeated Turkish requests. Yet a Paris newspaper writes that the Turks consented to this at our entreaty. From such reportage, apparently, we can conclude that you continue to wish us ill."

"I did not see that in the newspaper," replied d'Aiguillon, "but I remember hearing it from Vienna. It was probably printed inadvertently with other news. To prove that this is being done without ill intent, if you wish I will tell the newspapers to send you proof sheets and you can mark out of them everything you do not like."

"Thank you all the same, but that will not be necessary. I am simply requesting that you instruct them henceforth either to say nothing or to mention more discreetly the things which concern my court." D'Aiguillon promised to give them these instructions.

The next day they had another conversation. D'Aiguillon said that the empress had received Durand warmly and that everyone at court had treated him with extreme courtesy. He was especially boastful about the graciousness of Count Panin, who told Durand: "You may report to your court that we have no obligations that might prohibit us from being allied with France." D'Aiguillon stated that they would have to see what might develop.

Khotinsky replied: "Now we must expect those who oppose the restoration of friendship between the two courts to do everything in their power to prevent it and to prolong the previous mistrust. Therefore it is best that we not make an open show of our increasing cordiality."

D'Aiguillon surmised that the Prussians were most apt to sow this discord. Khotinsky added that they likewise had to beware of England. Although presently friendly with France, one must remember that they were natural enemies.

D'Aiguillon then stated: "The Prussian minister, of course, will assail you in order to learn something, but I hope you will relate nothing of our conversation. The Austrian and Sardininian ambassadors have complained to me that he disturbs them constantly with requests for news."

Catherine wrote on the letter in which Khotinsky told of this conversation: "This dispatch clearly shows that M. d'Aiguillon has the soul of an intriguer and a desire to stir things up." Her comment came in the wake of a powerful new irritation with France caused by the revolution in Sweden.

UPHEAVAL IN SWEDISH POLITICS

On March 23, 1772 Count Ivan Andreevich Ostermann,[92] Russia's ambassador to Sweden, informed Panin that the Prussian envoy, Count Denhoff, had requested him to incline Russia's government to permit Gustavus III to visit Petersburg during his trip to Finland.[93] By way of response, Catherine instructed Panin: "In answer to Count Ostermann about the Swedish king's journey here, tell him that I will not oppose it should his majesty insist on coming. However, I doubt that a visit can be arranged this year because of the cordon and other measures instituted by General Ehrensvärd. The general, knowing the extent of the plague in Russia, undoubtedly will restrict the king from visiting us. Therefore let

Count Ostermann tell us as soon as possible the exact year and month the king selects so that we not needlessly expend money twice, for preparations for a summer visit are quite different from those for a winter visit. In fact, the Swedish king himself has yet to make clear to Count Ostermann his desire to make the visit; the only person to mention it is the Prussian envoy in the name of his own king. Ostermann should inform us more precisely, neither encouraging nor dissuading my dear friend from staying home or coming hunting. It seems to me, however, quite flippant for a sovereign with troubles and hunger at home to flit about abroad." The intention to visit Catherine was devised, apparently, simply to divert Russia's attention from the changes the Swedes had resolved to make in their constitution.

Earlier events proved that the principal endeavor of Ostermann and the Russian party was to ensure numerical equality for their faction in the Senate.[94] This could be done solely by removing people in the other party from the Senate, and the two sides apparently had reached an agreement. But when it was proposed to exclude Senator Carl Frederick Scheffer, who was strongly favored by the French party, "every pretext for sparing him was raised," as Ostermann put it. Field Marshal Count Frederick von Fersen suggested to one of the leaders of the Russian party that his faction be content to expel only two senators. Ostermann recommended by way of compromise that two senators request to be dismissed, that Scheffer refuse the post of vice president in the chancellery of foreign affairs, and that Senator Baron Düben be chosen unanimously as president of the chancellery, with the king's approval. The vice-presidency was to be given to a member of the Russian faction, Baron Ridderstolpe, and all the leaders of the French party were to pledge their word of honor never to attempt to alter the balance of power in the Senate. The king likewise was to give assurances that Vice Admiral Christopher Falkengreen might enter the Senate, although his admission would raise its membership beyond the total allowable number, and the French party was to promise not to interfere in the course of the Riksdag's activities. Fersen did not object to these requests. At the proper time, Ostermann was supposed to yield and permit the vice-presidency to be occupied by a less dangerous member of the French party.

The Riksdag dragged on and money kept flowing from Petersburg, although Ostermann was instructed to try to adjourn the Riksdag; Russia found it difficult under its constrained circumstances to send some 50,000 rubles at a time to Stockholm. Soon Ostermann's reports began containing news of much greater import than the difficulties caused by the opposition party in the Riksdag.

To his dispatch of July 11 Ostermann attached a document handed him in greatest secrecy by the English envoy, who had received it by special courier. According to the document there was a reliable report that King Gustavus had met secretly with the French ambassador, Vergennes,[95] on May 20, telling him that he could no longer endure the innumerable insults constantly inflicted on him by government officials.[96] His patience was exhausted and he felt constrained to rescue the independence of the crown, which the people of rank sought to limit permanently under a Russian yoke. He would rather die than undergo such dishonor. The king then unfolded his plan of liberation.

In the Finnish island fortress of Sveaborg there was a cache of arms designated for the undertaking. Sveaborg's garrison troops consisted of foreigners who feared that the greed of government officials would reduce their own salaries and therefore were dissatisfied and ripe for revolt. The plan was for them to appear suddenly outside Stockholm.[97] Turning the turmoil created by their appearance to his advantage, the king would gather the four estates and propose a just and reasonable constitution. Retaining civil liberties and other rights for the estates, the constitution would eliminate only their freedom to cause mischief and to alter the nation's interests. The king expected the estates to concur out of fear. Should the men from Sveaborg be delayed in the islands or fjords by unfavorable winds or be driven towards Norrköping,[98] the king would advance against them at the head of his guards as though to prevent their landing; in reality he would unite both forces and return to the capital to deliver the final blow.

When Vergennes observed that the enterprise seemed to stake everything on one card with little likelihood of success, the king replied that he had considered all angles. He recognized that the plan was fraught with danger, but whatever the outcome he feared failure and worse eventualities less than the disgrace that cloaked his reign. He feared that his meekness heretofore had been regarded as weakness. The Russian party was exploiting this with the greatest impudence. It was time to prove himself in the eyes of Europe, and whatever happened he had decided to test his fortune.

Vergennes gave in and agreed to provide money for the enterprise. This news was corroborated fully in Vergennes's report to his court—how practised the English were at ferreting accurate news! Ostermann wrote Panin: "You are aware of my constant vigilance with respect to all earlier coups, yet I am powerless against the suddenness of this one; I can only encourage precautions, which, of course, I will not neglect to do."

Against Ostermann's suspicion and precautionary tendencies the king again advanced his idea of visiting Russia. He asked Ostermann to meet him on July 22 in the so-called Intoxicated Garden,[99] and actually arrived after eight in the evening, by which time most of the promenaders had departed. Gustavus III, after the usual excuses for making the ambassador wait, opened the conversation by saying that the following day he planned to inform the Senate of his intention to use his Finnish trip to visit the Russian empress, whom he had long wished to see because of their kinship and his esteem for her brilliant qualities.

Ostermann assured Gustavus that his sovereign would be extremely pleased to entertain such a valued guest, dear neighbor, and close relative, adding that he gave these assurances at the order of her majesty, who already knew the king's intention. Ostermann expressed his own pleasure that the king would take this most opportune occasion to confirm the truth of his high hopes concerning Catherine's good will toward Sweden. If this benevolence had not been expressed appropriately, she was not to blame.

The king smiled: "My visit with the empress, no doubt, will distress many Hats and Caps, whose obsessive desire to govern rules out personal meetings between sovereigns." Ostermann asked whether the king would prefer to make the journey in 1772 or 1773. "That depends," answered Gustavus III, "on when you adjourn the Riksdag."

"If I had my way," replied Ostermann, "I would adjourn it now. But your majesty knows better than I the circumstances obstructing its adjournment."

"Swedish fanaticism I know well," said the king. "In expectation of your closing the Riksdag when everyone least expects it, I decided beforehand to solicit permission from the estates to travel. When I receive permission, I will write to her imperial majesty."

On this note the conversation ended. The following day the king really did inform the Senate of his trip, emphasizing that as the end of the Riksdag

was unpredictable, he would not plan to leave before May 1773. Ostermann was not deceived and wrote Panin that all this had been devised
purposely to divert attention from the king's actual intentions.

The king succeeded in carrying out his designs. News of the agreement
among Russia, Prussia, and Austria on the Polish partition forced Gustavus
into haste fueled by fear to protect Sweden from the same thing happening
with its restive Riksdag, and to prevent Russia, recently freed from concern about Poland and, apparently, Turkey, from attempting to consolidate
its influence in Sweden. Four years earlier, in 1768, young Gustavus had
written in his journal: "In Warsaw two councils were called and as a result
the king and Senate turned for protection to the Russian empress. That
is shameful! Ah, Stanislaw Augustus! You are not a king and not even
a citizen! Give up your life in order to save the independence of your
country, but do not accept an unworthy yoke in the empty hope of preserving a shadow of power that will vanish on Muscovy's orders!" Later
he wrote: "The news from Poland never changes—anarchy and bribery.
The same will be true of us unless we take strong measures."

This view found public expression as well. Early in 1772 people read
in a certain widely distributed Stockholm magazine: "Time will turn
attention to our *tomorrow*. The same fate threatens us as did Poland, but
we can still find a Gustavus Adolphus. What has caused Poland's misfortune? It stems from the failure to enforce firm laws, the constant re-
duction of royal authority, and the consequently inevitable interference
of neighboring powers in its domestic affairs."

To coincide with the Sveaborg uprising an insurrection was planned
in southwestern Sweden, in Christianstad. It was to start first, with the
ostensible support of the king's two brothers.[100] The estates, assembled
in Stockholm, grew alarmed, recognizing the movement's goal and the
king's hand in it. Against the royal troops the estates hoped to defend
themselves with troops loyal to the constitution; they also expected the
Upland regiment to march to their defense. But Gustavus III kept a jump
ahead of the estates and on August 19 (New Style) made an impassioned
speech to the officers and soldiers, who with few exceptions took his side.
Guards were posted at the doors of the Senate and the most visible and
dangerous leaders of the opposing party were seized. The members of the
Secret Committee fled. In several hours all Stockholm was firmly in the
king's control. Two days later Gustavus read a new constitution to the
Riksdag's warm applause.

On August 10 (Old Style) Ostermann reported that not only had the guards, the artillery, the townsmen, and the collegial departments sworn to obey the king's orders and accept his form of government, but also the assembly of estates, albeit under duress. "That is all I have been able to learn," wrote Ostermann, "for I am deprived of my friends, who are so frightened that not one dares to visit me. The Senate and the loyalist leaders who did not want to take the oath have been arrested, as have been the speaker of the townsmen's estate, the secretary of the peasants', and several notaries."

Next Ostermann related his conversation with the chief instigator of the coup, Count Carl Scheffer. At an assembly at court Scheffer complimented Ostermann's conduct during the coup. "The king," said Scheffer, "is quite pleased by your course of action and bids you believe that he will employ his increased authority not to destroy the harmony between Russia and Sweden, but to reaffirm it. In the event that Sweden's strength increases, he has no intention, open or covert, of obstructing the empress's enterprises and conquests."

Ostermann answered that he would certainly communicate these assurances to his court; he felt compelled to note, however, that undoubtedly there were courts which would not regard indifferently a close alliance between Russia and Sweden. As for conquests, Russia was sufficiently large to have no further need of expansion.

Scheffer caught Ostermann's reference to France and replied: "True, our king is aligned closely with France; but to please the latter he will never undertake anything against Russia. I am not playing games with you. France under the leadership of the Duke d'Aiguillon has altered the broad policy of the Duke de Choiseul, and has accepted the same peace-loving rules that our king intends to follow as well."

Ostermann laughingly answered: "If this is the truth, it is a shame that d'Aiguillon did not enter the ministry earlier, for we could have avoided war with Turkey." Scheffer nodded in agreement.

Forwarding this conversation to Petersburg, Ostermann noted that the participants in the coup had been careful to obtain the approval of the king of Prussia. Gustavus III personally assured each participant that neither Frederick nor Catherine would challenge the new form of government. Frederick II's sister, the widowed Swedish queen,[101] was indescribably overjoyed at the sight of the coup, said Ostermann, accepting credit for its origin. When it succeeded, she boasted proudly: "Now I recognize my blood in Gustavus."[102]

Without doubt the news of the Swedish revolution was the most unwelcome Catherine had yet received in foreign affairs. She regarded the coup as a French victory and feared that France would incite war between Sweden and Russia, threatening Petersburg and the exposed borders in Finland. Furthermore, war with Sweden would prolong the Turkish war and might lend sustenance to Polish opposition to the partition. In April 1771 Catherine had written Rumiantsev: "The king of Sweden learned of his father's death while in Paris. The French, from time immemorial our despised enemy, surely will attempt to provide several subsidies now in arrears. In Sweden the Hats may be scheming as well. Hence, relying on the mercy of the Almighty, we wait patiently for the Riksdag to adjourn. Should the Swedes choose war, I am prepared personally to defend to the death that part of our border which honor does not permit us to yield. But I suppose, correctly it would seem, that it will not come to this."

THE REACTION IN PETERSBURG AND BERLIN

But what happened next was what Russia feared most. Before he received Ostermann's dispatch, on August 16, Chernyshev read to the Council, with Catherine in attendance, reports from the commander of Vyborg containing testimony from an officer recently escaped from Sweden. He revealed that the towns were being forced to swear loyalty to the king alone, excluding the estates. Panin noted that Vyborg's governor had submitted similar reports. A letter had been sent to the governor on Catherine's instructions to welcome heartily any Swedish opponent of the coup who managed to escape. The Council discussed whether the king's coup would succeed and concluded it was still too early to tell. Regardless of the outcome, Sweden might suffer terribly. Were the coup to succeed, Prussia and Denmark were required by treaties to intervene together with Russia,[103] although Russia's war with Turkey would preclude its participation.

Expecting no real threat from Sweden for the remainder of 1772, the Council elected to remain in a defensive position and maintain an official silence regarding events in Sweden. It was thought advisable, nonetheless, to rattle the saber by positioning the troops in Russian Finland and the Petersburg light field command closer to the Swedish border and placing them under the command of an eminent general, and by arming a few ships and galleys. In addition the Council considered transferring several regiments from Poland to Finland. The empress confirmed all these measures. The Council named Major General Count Peter Fedorovich Apraksin to the new command and posted Chernyshev there likewise as a precaution. The Council considered joint action with other powers, but Catherine cautioned: "We should remember that as a rule combined actions are more harmful than useful; therefore let us not depend on others. Rather let us permit them to assist us on their own initiative. Thereby we will retain our ability to wage war alone."

At its session of August 23 the Council heard the dispatches from Ostermann, following which Panin read Gustavus III's letter to the empress conveyed by Chamberlain Taube. The king informed Catherine of the coup and assured her that he would strive for greater harmony between Sweden and Russia. Chernyshev, who had returned from Finland, used an updated map to demonstrate that Frederickshamn and Wilmanstrand fortresses were poorly situated and could not stem a Swedish invasion by themselves. He suggested strengthening them and erecting a new fortress between them. The Council decided that under current conditions, with the revolution an accomplished fact in Sweden and Russian forces tied down in faraway places, it was imperative for Russia's troops to remain in their garrisons in a defensive position. Count Panin confirmed that he had informed the Swedish and Prussian ministers that Russia's preparations were unavoidable because the coup in Sweden was not solely the king's doing; he had received assistance from a foreign power inimical to Russia (France). Panin charged Count Solms to seek Frederick's mandate of a similar show of force with his army.

But the king of Prussia preferred not to show force against his nephew. He had no reason to oppose the coup, for he did not regard the establishment of Russian influence in Sweden as beneficial for him. His worst fear was that his commitment to Russia would drag him into war. So he began to search for a peaceful solution. He wrote Gustavus III on September 6: "According to your majesty's letter you succeeded in refashioning the form of government in Sweden. Do you think that the matter will end with this domestic success? Do you not recall that Russia, Denmark, and likewise I guaranteed the former constitution? Remember what I told you when you were in Berlin. I fear that the consequences of this deed might prove worse for your majesty than the predicament you have escaped and that this revolution might have ushered in an epoch of extreme misfortune for Sweden. You are aware that I have obligations toward Russia. I assumed them prior to your show of independence. Honor and good conscience equally prevent me from violating them. It grieves me to think that you are forcing me into action against you—me, who loves you and wishes you every success compatible with my obligations. You are plunging a dagger into my heart, placing me in a difficult predicament with no apparent exit. I have written a similar message to the queen, your mother, telling her the truth. What is done, is done; the problem is to find the proper remedy. I will consider it the happiest day of my life when I discover a means to set these matters right."

Gustavus answered his uncle on September 22 with the statement that he hoped to find legitimation for his act in his people's love for him. He intended to emulate the conduct of his dear uncle when the entire continent had sworn to destroy him. "I hope," wrote Gustavus, "that you will acknowledge your blood in me."

Frederick replied on October 5 that he preferred not to see Gustavus in the position he faced during the Seven Years War. "In Sweden," wrote Frederick, "there are two parties inimical to each other. The king should proceed to their reconciliation and thereby strengthen the throne. But this can be done only in time of peace; therefore I am certain that your majesty will pay no heed to foolish urgings to quarrel with your neighbors."

Frederick was really in an awkward position. What if Russia demanded that he fulfill his obligations? He decided as a last resort to stall by means of negotiations until he could obtain some sort of arrangement, a concession from Gustavus III. Meanwhile the Russian, Prussian and Danish envoys must remind Gustavus that their sovereigns had guaranteed the Swedish constitution of 1720, and that therefore he should not make it necessary for them to fulfill their obligations. Frederick proposed this tactic to Russia in a dispatch to Count Solms on September 4. To Prince Henry the king wrote: "The Swedish queen informed me of the revolution's success. I congratulated her only on her son's escaping great danger and described all my anticipated difficulties if the king does not place limits on his authority. I see no other salvation for Sweden than compromise; the king must agree to accept Count Horn's plan.[104] I wrote along these lines to Russia. If compromise proves impossible, we will be thrust into war against our nephew; just the thought of such a war is abhorrent to me."

Henry displayed his sympathy for his nephew more openly, asking his brother to persuade Catherine not to become too alarmed by events in Sweden and convince her to concentrate on the Turkish war. Were she to hasten peace with the Porte in order to fight Sweden, she would lose substantial gains and subject herself to serious difficulties. Vienna again might cast its lot with France, which was obligated to support Sweden. "I agree," wrote Henry, "that it is difficult to find a middle ground between the interests of the empress and the Swedish king but, if merely to postpone action, I can hope for it."[105]

Prince Henry forwarded a letter to Catherine in which Gustavus justified his actions during the coup. Had he not anticipated it, he wrote, he might have been imprisoned or even killed. Catherine confided to Henry: "This might have been considered a family affair and we could have grieved or perhaps have become distraught. Unfortunately the Swedish revolution had other causes, as your royal highness knows quite well. The coup was instigated by French intrigue and money and not by some nebulous threat to the king or an altruistic desire to restore the nation's liberty. I am convinced that the coup was a machination of the power most unfriendly to my policies, and that the sovereign, my close blood relation, has been deceived by that power. I feel grief as his relative, but what am I supposed to feel as Russian empress, the guardian of my people's security?"

Catherine's irritation increased when she heard that the Swedish government was sowing rumors that Russia entertained hostile designs. She wrote Ostermann: "I think you are in a good position to show the Swedes in due time that they are in no position to challenge their neighbors. They certainly know that the surrounding states will react automatically and not be deluded by the empty compliments of their perfidious king. Significantly, they are giving the nation another object to divert attention from its proper condition."

In their concern for the Russian empress's anxieties the king of Prussia and his brother found comfort in the news of the failure of the Focsani negotiations as a development that would deflect Russia's attention from Sweden. On September 20 Frederick wrote Solms: "Having learned of the abrupt end of the Focsani congress, I can give no better advice to Russia than to mask its anger over the Swedish revolution. This should not be difficult; Sweden is in no condition at present to threaten Russia." When he heard that the Council had decided on August 23 to retain a defensive position toward Sweden, Frederick was ecstatic.

In consequence of this decision of the Council Panin wrote Ostermann: "The various pieces of our political concerns and arrangements are not yet clear enough to permit us at this time to define and temper specific policies for taking up arms and initiating operations against the arbitrary despotism installed by the Swedish king—or at least not those policies most practical, appropriate, and advantageous for the glory of her imperial majesty and the substantive benefit of the state. I can say this much, however, without fear of being wrong: our future actions will be undertaken jointly with allied and friendly courts. When time raises the curtain for open measures we will not appear on the stage alone, but insofar as possible with dependable allies. Until now we have maintained a discreet silence regarding the intentions and deeds of the Swedish king, content simply to prepare our defenses and militia gradually and secretly.

"It is true that we regard the destruction of the Swedish form of government an event of the gravest import with potential for dangerous consequences in the future. We also believe it easier now to incorporate, defend, and preserve something built through laws, oaths, the passage of time, and custom, and dedicated to the national good, than later, after these basic foundations are discredited altogether, to restore the discredited and undo the new system in its turn. Disregarding this principle for the present we must not aim to reimplement the former constitution without amendment, its articles and ramifications intact.[106] At the very least we must institute a new system of government guaranteeing essential freedoms for the Swedish nation and providing untrammeled security from neighboring powers. These principles and those of the former system of government must be affirmed as fundamental laws without their subjection to the king's arbitrariness and capriciousness. In all probability this middle road will achieve success, given enough time, for both the king and the nation will find they have gained something. The former will have preserved a fraction of what he stole, and the latter will regain what was most precious for its well-being and public safety under the previous constitution. Meanwhile, in order to preserve several alternatives for future action in favor of Sweden's freedom, you must attempt, without raising the slightest doubt or suspicion about yourself, and furthermore without publicity or affectation, not simply to preserve but to enhance the friendship and goodwill of representatives of the party favorable to us. You are to encourage these men, who should prove dependable under trying circumstances, by holding out hope of an imminent coup against the current subjugation of their homeland. This will commit them to gradual, skillful, and uncompromising preparation of their friends' spirits for a future struggle for the general good.

"Knowing the nature of Swedish mores, I agree with your observation that even many of the Hats frankly deplore the overthrow of the previous form of government and would be delighted to lend every effort to restore it. If you will, please keep an attentive eye on these men. Try to gain their confidence, and warm up to them should they warm to you. Among the most eminent Hats, I imagine that the present Senator Count Fersen is deeply interested in discussing the unlimited despotism the king has seized hold of. He knows the moods of the more distinguished of his colleagues; for this reason it may prove very useful in time to draw him to our side. It is more suitable for the Danish court to curry favor in Scania than for us, since it is closer to Denmark than Russia.[107] Nevertheless, keep in mind what is happening there; whatever action we take in Finland will be stronger and more lasting should there be simultaneous movement in Scania. If you find reliable, useful friends in Scania, do not let them go, but rather do all you can to keep their friendship secret as long as possible, since eventually they undoubtedly will yield to Denmark, which will use its power to make gains there for itself alone.

"Circumstances in Pomerania are totally different.[108] We are relying there on the swiftness of military operations on the part of our ally, the king of Prussia, who is, of course, utterly reliable. We are relying also on the impression the German empire will have of these developments and the political situation of its chief members, especially Austria. I have said all this to reach the following point: when our own policy becomes visible, and particularly when peace is concluded with the Porte and our armed forces and resources are freed completely of other concerns, I want you to inform me of your studied opinion about the possibilities of operations in Finland and Scania so that I can transmit your ideas to her imperial majesty. We want our measures to be coordinated with Denmark's in order to reinforce each other.

"Therefore we must have definite advance knowledge of the mood of the Swedish people, particularly the army and other military organizations. Indisputably, the king managed to persuade most of the military to support his coup and still has their loyalty. It may be debatable whether the army's enthusiasm will enable the soldiers to attempt to regain Sweden's former glory. Should it, this enthusiasm may well prove to be capable and successful, a threat to Sweden's enemies. However, the army's enthusiasm might be of the ambitious and smooth-tongued variety, concerned simply with gaining more rapid promotion and other rewards from the young autocratic sovereign."

Petersburg feared that the king of Sweden, whose courage had been demonstrated in the coup, might attack. It worried that France would incite Gustavus III to fight Russia in order to interfere subsequently in Poland and Turkey. France, however, satisfied with the success of the coup, wanted the new order in Sweden to be established peacefully, yet feared that Russia would attack a vulnerable Sweden and draw France into a declared war on the former's behalf. And Versailles's greatest fear was of war. The new French minister in Petersburg, Durand, found Russia's irritation with France difficult to salve while Russia held France responsible for the *unfortunate*—to use Panin's expression—Swedish revolution. Durand assured Panin that his court continued to seek, as always, happy harmony and fellowship with her imperial majesty. France helped initiate the turn of events in Sweden without the least intention of bringing harm to Russia. He added that France had advised Sweden earlier to rekindle an alliance with Russia and continued to urge it. At France's request, furthermore, England considered the change in Sweden to be a domestic disposition and was finding no need to interfere. Durand noted that his sovereign would be quite saddened were Russia to think he sought to give it cause for concern or fan the flame of war in Europe.

Panin replied that her imperial majesty was convinced of Louis XV's personal inclination to preserve peaceful relations. But France's policy throughout her reign had prevented him from observing his own wishes. For ten whole years the French court had opposed Russia in Poland, Sweden, and Turkey. France had helped precipitate Russia's war with Turkey, as Durand must have learned as a result of his constant involvement in diplomatic affairs. Panin contended that Russia had not behaved similarly and had made no treaties or agreements against France. Durand's sudden arrival had given Russia reason to think that he was sent to interfere with and nullify the three courts' agreement to break up Poland; Russia feared he would incite envy and lack of confidence among them or possibly generate some sort of alarm in Russia. If this assumption had any foundation, Durand might be certain beforehand that such intentions would fail. Russia could not escape being alarmed by Swedish events. No longer could it rely on the alliance with Sweden, for now Stockholm's policy was not formulated by the estates but solely by a young, enterprising monarch who had violated his oath. Therefore Russia stood ready to do whatever was necessary for its own protection.

In conclusion, Panin gilded the pill, enlarging upon his respect for Durand as a man grown old in diplomacy and esteemed for his skill in its practice. He expressed the hope that the French ambassador would fulfill his mission sincerely, providing his court with the truth, unlike his predecessors who malevolently filled their reports with lies. Durand, embarrassed by this unexpected declaration, replied that affairs in Poland were inconsequential in relation to his arrival in Russia. His court considered the partition as final and did not intend to interfere in an undertaking of the three great powers.

Panin had personal motives for being candid with Durand. Frederick had written Solms: "I will advise Count Panin repeatedly to take care with Durand. By all accounts I have received, the goal of his embassy is to reshuffle the cards and to overthrow Count Panin. It is for this purpose that Durand, a master of intrigue, was chosen."

THE DANISH REVOLUTION

In Denmark there also occurred a revolution of a special sort. The first letter Panin received in 1772 from Russia's ambassador in Copenhagen, Ivan Ivanovich Mestmakher, related that on January 5 (Old Style) the king and queen had attended a court masquerade together.[109] The king left around midnight and the queen with her favorite Struensee at three o'clock. At five the king was awakened by three unexpected visitors in his bedroom: the widowed queen, Juliane Marie, Crown Prince Frederick, and Count Rantzau. Juliane began to speak about the disastrous position of sovereign and state in the wake of the queen's shameful weakness and Count Johann Friedrich Struensee's unpardonable outrages. Juliane persuaded the king to arrest the queen, her favorite, and all their accomplices. Orders to this effect were drafted and signed. Count Rantzau went to arrest the queen, whom he found in bed. After some resistance and demands to see the king, Queen Matilda surrendered. Struensee and his accomplices likewise were arrested forthwith and incarcerated in the fortress. When the people learned about these developments a large crowd gathered on the square before the palace, raising joyful cheers. The shouting crowd accompanied the king as he and Prince Frederick wound through the streets in a ceremonial carriage. Women waved white handkerchiefs from the windows and in the evening all houses were illuminated.

When Mestmakher heard the news his first thought was to use the event to reassert the policy of Count Johann Hartwig Bernstorff, the former foreign minister.[110] He discussed the matter with the English envoy Keith; they went to visit Count Adolphus Sigfried Osten,[111] who received them singly, Keith first. Keith expressed his court's desire to see the policies of Count Bernstorff restored and summoned Osten's cooperation, stressing that it would please Russia as well. Osten heatedly replied: "I do not think foreign powers should dictate to the king whom he must appoint as ministers."

Following Keith's departure Mestmakher entered. He congratulated Osten on the happy occasion, adding that one further development would complete his happiness. Why had he, Osten, taken a back seat to Rantzau throughout the affair?

Osten answered that he could not talk long with Mestmakher, for he was hastening to leave the palace. He had learned of the development at eight o'clock in the morning, when he was summoned to the king. He had suggested to the king that out of esteem for the Russian empress he ought not name Count Rantzau to direct foreign affairs, but as a reward must post him to Holstein.[112] The king had agreed. Thereupon Mestmakher let Osten "feel" the excellent opportunity the coup presented to return to the policies of Count Bernstorff and demonstrate loyalty to her imperial majesty. Mestmakher suggested, furthermore, that Osten would not have to take this stand without recompense; he would become the head of the Department of Foreign Affairs and sit on the Royal Council, and the younger Bernstorff would assume the title of grand chancellor. Osten replied: "We have not had a grand chancellor for many years, and we certainly cannot start now." Moving toward the door of his study, he added: "We do not like foreigners here."[113] Mestmakher let him "feel" that Count Bernstorff's great services to Denmark were known throughout Europe. No one considered him a foreigner, especially now that his actions were exonerated by the arrest of the people who had driven him from office. The entrance of a third person interrupted the conversation.

"We have cause to think," Panin wrote to Mestmakher, "that the revolution that took place in Copenhagen was quite necessary to save Denmark from total depravity. It will prove beneficial for the future in restoring order to Denmark's affairs. I hope this crisis will help confirm the mutual interests of Russia and Denmark, should the latter abandon its former flightiness."

Panin felt that Osten was not at all inclined to be used by Count Bernstorff and suggested that Mestmakher secretly approach the queen mother. As the person chiefly responsible for the coup she now would enjoy a strong position and would wish nothing save the best for the elder Bernstorff because of the immense service he had rendered her in time past. As for the fate of those held under arrest, Panin wrote that it was neither necessary nor proper to treat them with severity, least of all by pronouncing a death sentence. By granting mercy the king might draw closer to the manner of thinking and magnanimous deeds of his natural ally and friend, Catherine.

Osten informed Mestmakher that the king had denied Count Rantzau a place on the Council solely out of regard for the empress; Rantzau had been sent to command the troops in Holstein. Also as a gesture to the empress, Count S. Germen was to be relieved of all duties and retired to Holstein. As Osten said nothing about Bernstorff, Mestmakher considered it indecorous to mention his name. Instead, he directed his efforts toward influencing the queen mother through several people loyal to Russia. One, Count Haxthausen, intimated to the queen mother that without Count Bernstorff's return the Holstein matter, with its promise of gain for Denmark, could not be concluded; consequently Denmark would lose both important acquisitions and in Bernstorff a distinguished servant. The queen conceded that she had long favored Bernstorff's reinstatement, but she feared it might prove impossible or entail enormous difficulty. She wondered whether Bernstorff's return would be in the people's best interest, for he had many enemies. Mestmakher attributed the queen's apprehensions about Bernstorff's popularity to Osten, who had raised the issue with the English envoy by asserting that the Danes did not like Bernstorff, blaming him for the accumulation of a large state debt.[114]

Bernstorff's death quickly ended these machinations for and against his participation in the new government. The Russians had placed great reliance on him, illustrated by Catherine's comments to Frau Bielcke: "I felt boundless grief at Bernstorff's death. I think that order and prosperity in Denmark are buried with him; although I have not said this before, I am convinced that no one there now is capable of firm action. I would not be surprised to see Queen Matilda reappear on the stage. I admit that it is difficult for me to believe every rumor about the plans of this queen and her Mr. Pill (Struensee—formerly a doctor)." Catherine's view of

Danish affairs was tempered by the memory of her own experience and her awareness of the childishness of the Danish king.

Meanwhile the commission investigating Struensee and his accomplices set to work. Mestmakher wrote his court that Struensee was unlikely to escape the death penalty. People were saying that if he were merely imprisoned the queen, who had been freed, would release her lover out of her sustained passion for him. The king would be too weak to prevent her. Bloody vengeance might then be expected from them and the people, who hated Struensee, would revolt.

Upon reading Mestmakher's letter Catherine wrote Panin: "If they fear the queen's vengeance now, they will fear it much more should she find her favorites dead; it would not be the same as finding them alive. In my opinion, if the Danes allow their weak king to break the fast and spill blood once, he will demand the head of almost everyone. Post this in the next mail to Mestmakher."

Unfortunately, Mestmakher's effort came to naught. Struensee and Count Brandt were executed. "The news from Denmark fills me with horror," Catherine wrote Bielcke. "How could they chop off the heads of those unfortunate men? They executed them because the sovereign does not know how to be a sovereign. If he were a different man, I wonder how things might have turned out? The prosecutors are doubling as judges, which makes my hair stand on end. The execution defies common sense because they were not alone in their guilt. It is terrible to do business with people who are mentally unbalanced. I know what the cost of this will be; I was in the same position myself.[115] Were the Danes to make a conscious effort to develop their young king's natural disposition to cruelty they could not do a better job. I feel an aversion for judicial murder with its most inhumane details. Only the most horrible revenge could have carried things so far. Now the Danes have to watch out for their own heads.

"Either I am very mistaken or there are hidden designs to deprive the king of his freedom. They took his wife away from him against his will, and God only knows what they yet will do or force him to do. I despise inhumanity and inhumane people. I realize that they justify the execution by claiming that they feared a popular uprising should mercy be shown, but this is a poor excuse. Had they wished to pander to the emotions and tastes of the masses they could have conducted many trials. As it was they chose the most unfortunate and contemptible role open to them."

Russia's desires were ignored on another front as well. Despite the king's promise Count Rantzau, a faithful champion of France, was not posted to Holstein, but received a seat on the Royal Council. Incidentally, he was not there long. He soon realized that the public interest and Denmark's obligations to Russia necessitated his departure from the government, and he retired on a sizeable pension.

The same fate awaited Osten the following autumn, although Russia regarded him quite differently than Rantzau. Osten had informed Mestmakher covertly that he sensed a pronounced coolness toward him at court following the arrival in Copenhagen of Prince Karl of Hesse. Osten had hoped to overcome this indisposition in time, but shortly thereafter was denied admittance to see Prince Frederick, with whom the Military Council met. Osten had expressed his displeasure and was placated. But the Military Council met again without inviting him, although other dignitaries were invited whose understanding of military affairs was less thorough than his. Thereupon he had sent the king a request to be retired but had received no answer. Mestmakher grew greatly alarmed at this news and began exploring how he might delay Osten's retirement, during which time he might correspond with his own court.

In the Royal Council Joachim Otto Schack-Rathlou was loyal to Russia.[116] Mestmakher informed him of his absolute surprise at the sudden disfavor of the minister for foreign affairs. The consequences of such major shifts were well known, especially now, at this critical period of foreign relations with respect to Sweden. How would other courts, especially Russia, regard this development? Could the empress and other European leaders, cognizant of the king's poor health and minimal participation in affairs, be expected to show confidence in the Danish government's resolution or stability when for no reason—or at least unknown reasons—the foreign minister suddenly was relieved of his office?

The intimation reached the right ears. Prince Frederick agreed to deny Osten's request for retirement, whereas Schack informed Mestmakher merely that it had been postponed. Schack did not consider Osten an effective minister: his incessant intrigues served to reduce his credit at court and with the public and his cowardice allowed the French and Spanish diplomats to influence him. At their instigation he currently was opposing mobilization in the Council, an action proposed in light of events in Sweden. Mestmakher asked who might be appointed to Osten's post.

Schack named two: Councillor to the Conference Schumacher and the former envoy to Sweden, Baron Juel.

Mestmakher's actions pleased his government immensely. Panin wrote him: "Nothing could have been more discreet than your behavior in the matter of Count Osten. True, his character has its shortcomings. Nonetheless there is no doubt of his attachment to our system; we dare not comply with his dismissal. Were it possible to choose a worthy successor more devoted to us, I would say that of all the Danes it would be Schack. Therefore I am instructing you to explain to him that should he agree to assume Osten's position I would offer no objection to the latter's removal. Otherwise I would prefer that Osten remain in office, particularly while circumstances continue to be critical in Denmark. His dismissal, without any apparent reason or fault or without minimal preparation of the public, could be read by Danes and every government in Europe solely as consequence of some dark intrigue. This would damage further the prominence and credit of the Danish court, fallen altogether too low already. To restore them, Denmark does not need sudden, inexplicable reversals of policy, but moderate and well conceived actions."

ENGLAND'S REACTION TO THE EVENTS OF 1772

Queen Matilda's prosecution for her relationship with Struensee, the annulment of her marriage, and her expulsion from Denmark could be expected to vex her brother King George III of England severely. But this family affair could not be allowed to precipitate a clash between England and Denmark. A fairly strong protest was expected from England against the Polish partition and the Swedish revolution. The English envoy in Russia, Lord Cathcart, eventually was recalled because he failed to negotiate a Russian alliance and because the Russians replaced Count Ivan Grigorevich Chernyshev with Aleksei Semenovich Musin-Pushkin.[117] The English ministry had grounds to suspect that Lord Cathcart lacked skills in conducting its affairs, for on one other notable occasion he had displayed a lack of shrewdness and the inability to obtain needed information.

As late as April 1772 he warned his court not to place any credence in rumors of a Polish partition. "As far as I know," reported Cathcart, "the king of Prussia has communicated nothing definite to either Russia or Austria and has received no questions from them concerning present circumstances. Neither of these courts has changed its tone. I have long been convinced and warned the Russian ministry that the king of Prussia has his own interests in view and indubitably will use all means to acquire Polish Prussia when the war is over."

In May 1772 King George instructed Cathcart's successor, Robert Gunning, to file a detailed report on the reactions of the empress and her ministers to a proposed alliance with England, which envisioned a general northern alliance and negotiations regarding a treaty with Sweden.[118] Should the Russians insist upon a subsidy, Gunning was to communicate the request to London without raising Russia's hopes. If in drafting a treaty of alliance the Russians represented the Turkish war as a *casus foederis*, he was to reject that article. Should the Russians desire England's mediation in concluding the Turkish war, he was to agree on the condition that England be chief mediator. Gunning was instructed to dispel the suspicions of Catherine and her ministers that England opposed Russian acquisitions on land or sea in the Black Sea area. England viewed only one possibility with disfavor—the free passage of Russian ships from the Black Sea into the Mediterranean.

On July 6 Gunning asked Panin categorically: What fate awaited Poland? After a long pause, Panin replied that nothing had yet been decided conclusively regarding that country, but he could assure Gunning that there was no danger of the general peace being violated there. When asked what sort of reparations Poland's neighbors would demand of it and whether Vienna and Berlin had reached prior agreement on them, Panin replied that to his knowledge there was no compact; desiring apparently to end the conversation, he denied there was the least danger that a new war would flare up. On July 10 Gunning reported that Russia intended to receive a share of a partition of Poland.

England did not protest the Polish partition despite French attempts toward a joint declaration. Upon receiving the announcement of the partition from the ambassadors of the three participating courts, the English minister for foreign affairs stated: "The king is willing to assume that the three courts are convinced of the justice of their claims, even though the motives that compelled them to act in such a manner remain unknown to his majesty." This answer settled the matter.

As for the Swedish revolution, at first the English ministry informed Gunning that his British majesty was concerned about it and was prepared to act in concert with the Russian empress to preserve the Swedish constitution. He was even prepared to pay subsidies, if only it was not too late. But under no circumstances should Gunning set a monetary sum or other definite measures. He was to promise nothing besides his king's burning desire to preserve the Swedish constitution and his readiness to undertake appropriate action toward this end.

Gunning later received a more candid intimation that the king had no greater interest in Swedish affairs than to use the Swedish question to form an alliance with Russia; he would do nothing about Sweden until the matter of an alliance was resolved. Gunning realized this decision would be a long time in coming. Whenever he spoke with Panin about improving relations between Britain and Russia the Russian minister answered very impolitely, Gunning thought. Panin told him that he stood ready to sign an extremely close alliance with England the moment he received assurances of the stability of the British ministry and the king's confidence in it. Gunning replied that he regretted very much how easily Panin, with all his perspicacity and honesty, was dealing in mercenary and false pronouncements. Gunning had to report to Whitehall that his words made a weak impression on Panin, demonstrating the extent to which Frederick II had succeeded in imposing on Panin his views on this subject. Nevertheless, despite Panin's aforementioned answer, Gunning wrote his ministry that he would bend every effort not to alienate Panin, for despite his shortcomings his character was far preferable to that of the Chernyshevs, even though Count Zakhar by application and speed could accomplish more in one hour than Panin in a year.

On September 14, less than six weeks after his hostile remark about the English ministry, Panin revealed to Gunning, in absolute confidence, Russia's intentions toward Sweden, as a demonstration of confidence in Gunning and the ministry. Throughout the winter Russia planned to feign indifference to the revolution, but by spring it would have sufficient troops in Finland to lend weight to its words, in which sense it had not yet spoken. By then twenty naval vessels would be equipped. Denmark would move fifteen thousand troops to the Swedish border and command a fleet of twelve ships. The king of Prussia would occupy Swedish Pomerania. Should the king of England support Denmark with subsidies or put a fleet on maneuvers, which might protect the Danes, Catherine would be pleased immeasurably. With everything in readiness, Panin would propose that the four courts issue a joint declaration to the Swedish king that they desired a restoration of the constitution of 1720. Panin thought the joint declaration alone might be adequate to achieve their goal. If not, it would be easy to compel assent. Panin then showed Gunning the correspondence between the Swedish king and his uncle the king of Prussia. Frederick's letter, Gunning noted, left no doubt in Panin's mind about the sincerity of his Prussian majesty.

Panin's candor did not arouse the impression in England that he had anticipated. Convinced that Russia simply followed the king of Prussia's initiatives, the English ministry saw a Prussian plan in Panin's proposal. In light of what is known about relations between Prussia and England, it stands to reason that England had no intention of assisting the plan. Thanks to the Prussian king Poland had just been partitioned, and now Frederick II desired Swedish Pomerania. England's minister of foreign affairs cautioned Gunning that Panin should think twice and seriously weigh all the consequences of the proposed plan before acting on it. Its consequences might be to return Austria to a close alliance with France. The latter and Spain could be expected to support Sweden. A general European war could follow, at the very moment Russia lay exhausted from its protracted war with Turkey. Panin's plan looked like a Prussian plan and Swedish Pomerania, apparently, represented a reward for the Prussian monarch's aid. According to ideas of national security fashionable today, this was a bagatelle. But the king of England would view it otherwise; while he sincerely desired to preserve Sweden's free constitution, he preferred not to do it at the cost of reducing Swedish territory. After the Russian court's inattention to England, the latter chose to avoid a war from which it could lose much and win nothing. Therefore Gunning as much as possible was to distract Panin from these questions.

THE SIGNIFICANCE OF THE POLISH PARTITION

In the end, the year 1772 did not justify all the hopes with which Russia had welcomed it. The Polish affair could be considered finished thanks to the consensus of the three courts. But Russia's most urgent desire— peace with Turkey—was not fulfilled. Furthermore, it appeared that the Swedish revolution might be ushering in a war more dangerous and difficult than had been the struggle with the Polish confederates.

Events in Poland and the closely related war with Turkey produced an unexpected consequence, the union of White Russia and Great and Little

Russia.[119] There is no evidence that a single Russian contemporary opposed this development on either political or moral grounds. To the extent that Catherine's contemporaries censured this event, they did so years later out of systematic hostility to Catherine's policies generally and Panin's activity in particular, and from animosity towards the Prussian alliance and its consequence. By that time these harsh judgments were influenced by opinions expressed in extreme Western Europe, difficult for a Russian to oppose. The Russian contemporaries of the annexation of White Russia stood very close to the historical course of events that necessarily led to this union. They were seized by the spirit of these events, they breathed the fresh legends about the derivation of this development, and thus were bound to endorse it heartily. They were participants and not idle judges. A mere century had passed since Little Russia, wrested from Poland and preferring subjugation to the sultan to oppression by Polish masters and Catholic priests, requested the Great Russian tsar to receive it in the name of their common faith.[120] The supplication was granted and a struggle began which apparently would end quickly with the decay of Poland and the complete gathering of Russian lands. Tsar Alexis received the title "Tsar of all Great and Little and *White* Russia."

But great events in history unfold slowly, as in nature everything great grows and develops slowly and only what is weak shoots up quickly and just as quickly fades away. Little Russia alone, and at that not in its entirety, was united during Alexis' reign, following a long and tortuous struggle. Yet the process had just begun and the great question continued to await its turn, despite numerous obstacles and delays, constantly reminding everyone of its presence. The Catholic Pole was unable to live in harmony with the Orthodox Russian and oppressed him in every way possible—and a great deal was possible. No wonder the Russian people rejoiced when it became clear that the time had come to decide the Russian question in Poland. Even those who had drifted away from the faith of their fathers, the Russian faith, welcomed the opportunity. They wanted the Russian cause to succeed; they awaited the victory of toleration over fanaticism. Sympathetic to Russia's complicated policy regarding the creedal or dissident question, they sympathized as well with its result, the union of White Russia. No one considered this union unjustified.

The Poles with sword in hand opposed the decision on the creedal question that Russia extracted, and Russia therefore had to go to war with them, although it was engaged at the time in another war, more dangerous and more difficult. The Polish government, incapable of open animus, showed its enmity covertly, insulting Russia more by its behavior than had the confederates who fought the Russian army. No agreement or settlement could be reached despite concessions which Russia unwisely ventured to make. The matter was fated to be decided by arms, and the Russians emerged victorious both in Poland and in Turkey, which had a close relationship. Everyone knows how war ends for victor and vanquished; White Russia was annexed by right of war, by right of victory. There could be no question on the Russian side of its justice or injustice.

Catherine could not help rejoicing over the acquisition of White Russia. She regarded this development as a purely Russian accomplishment which would assure her place in Russian history as one of the gatherers of the Russian lands. It was particularly momentous for her that it occurred before her son achieved his majority. But her happiness was tainted by a bad taste; her brilliant victory, the gathering of Russian land, was a partition.

Catherine felt embittered by the manner in which two neighboring powers, without engaging in war or losing a single subject on the Vistula, Dniester, or Danube, had seized equally large slices of Poland gratis. The king of Prussia's share was particularly remarkable for its advantageous location, for rounding out his borders, a condition sought by all sovereigns. Unquestionably Prussia had become both larger and stronger; it had gained the greater prestige. The French envoy mockingly pointed this out to Russia, and Russia had to bear the sneer without answering.

Aside from the political disadvantages, the inequality of shares, the strengthening of Prussia (which Russia had no reason to desire), and the disturbance to the balance of power (to avoid which the partition first was proposed!), there was a drawback of another sort. No one could raise moral objections to the acquisition of White Russia by right of war; however, this was only a third of the partition. Prussia and Austria had seized Polish lands with no justification, or to be more correct, by the right of force. Russia, acting in concert, participated just as fully and bore the same responsibility. Russia's indisputable right was besmirched by Austrian and Prussian lack of right and swallowed by it.

Frederick prattled on about Russia's right and his and Austria's lack of same, but his self-betrayal remained buried in the archives for years.

Meanwhile, people aware of this weak spot have tried with all kinds of untruths, and indeed are still trying, to strengthen it, to exculpate Frederick and ascribe the responsibility to Catherine. The Russian empress knew full well, they argue, that the Prussian king must be rewarded for his alliance, subsidies, and assistance in obtaining a favorable peace with Turkey. Since her sole means for rewarding him was with Polish lands, she had in mind the bishopric of Warmia, for which Poland might be compensated with territory won from Turkey. But Frederick insisted that Warmia was worthless and demanded Polish Prussia, persuading Russia and Austria to participate in a partition. Catherine's plan would have gained immediate peace with Turkey on Russian terms, assisted by its ally Prussia, which would have received its due reward. As the price of this assistance, however, Frederick rejected Catherine's plan and forced Russia to serve his interests and goals. Petersburg knew he had to check Austria, incapable of action without considering him and particularly incapable of action against him. Instead, Frederick merely used the spectre of Austria to bully Russia, contending that it was well nigh impossible for him to provide assistance for Russia in the war. Thus he not only demanded such an important share of Polish territory but also insisted that Russia return Moldavia and Wallachia to the Turks, a step that forced Russia to retract a promise made to their population.

It insulted Catherine's vanity to see herself as a tool for achieving someone else's goals, particularly the goals of a sovereign she considered her loyal ally. She was affronted that this loyal ally forced her to serve his interests and furthermore directly opposed her own interests on the question of Moldavia and Wallachia. She could not forget the way he treated her peace terms , softening only when they agreed to let him take what he wanted; but even here he tried to strike out one of the most essential peace conditions dealing with the Danubian principalities. Catherine could not forget that he ignored the negotiations with the Porte and advised indifference to the Swedish revolution. It insulted Catherine to realize that the luster of victory in an arduous war, of Larga, Kagul, Chesme, the winning of the Crimea, and the victories of Suvorov in Poland were tarnished by the ambivalence and even overt resistance of an ally concerned solely with his own interests and turning Russian victories and Russian blood to the advantage of rounding out his own realm. The French chargé d'affaires Durand informed his court that the Russian people blamed Count Panin in particular for strengthening Prussia. Grigory Orlov said publicly that the people who negotiated the partition deserved the death penalty. Panin himself conceded that circumstances had pulled him far from his own desires.[121]

Ironically, at the very moment the alliance between Russia and Prussia seemed to be strengthened conclusively by the convergence of their interests in Poland, it was substantively undermined, especially in Catherine's view. Frederick's assurances of gratitude and readiness to repay Russia for its assistance in acquiring such an advantageous share of the partition now must have seemed a mockery. Catherine was silent and had to remain silent for some time. Circumstances, the political *conjunctures*, forced her to retain the established arrangements for many more years and permitted no expression of her honest opinions to the Prussian king. But the necessity of long concealing her emotions did not weaken them, especially when they combined later with other incentives.

Readers many years removed from these events and capable of viewing them unemotionally might naturally pose the question: How could Catherine be angry with a sovereign who preferred his own interests to those of others? What was wrong with his aversion to strengthening his neighbors, in his opinion already strong and dangerous? One must assume that such behavior is to be expected and criticize it with extreme care, particularly when dealing with Frederick. It is easy to pass judgement years later; it was much more difficult for the participants to maintain their calm in the midst of action and the heat of passion it aroused. The old system had been changed. An alliance with Austria and France had been forfeited for one with Prussia. An attempt was made to justify the shift by pretending that under the old system Russia was fettered to Austria and served its interests. Under the new system, however, dependence on foreign interests was more pronounced. People often display anger toward others when they should be angry with themselves.

Frederick II apparently had strengthened his hand in Petersburg. Chernyshev had no stake in a Prussian alliance; these inclinations were developed under Panin's control. Panin, without a Saldern to restrain him, fell at length under Prussian influence. Grigory Orlov lost favor. "So Count Orlov has been formally disgraced," wrote Prince Henry to his brother. "He merely muddled affairs, and I am delighted with his removal because of my interest in your alliance with Russia."[122]

Frederick was unable to relax, fearing French intrigues or rapprochement between Austria and Russia, and waged a campaign in Petersburg against these dangers. Despite his shrewdness, he did not foresee the conjuncture of Russian and Austrian interests that sooner or later would lead to a Russo-Austrian alliance. We have seen how Frederick calmly accepted the condition of independence for the Crimea and attempted to win Austrian support. He foresaw correctly that Tatar independence would drag Russia into greater difficulty. But Frederick did not realize that it would deflect Russia's attention from the north and the northwest to the south and southwest; this naturally would weaken the significance and import of the Prussian alliance. Polish relations would become a secondary consideration and Turkish affairs assume primary importance.

To relieve the problem accompanying Crimean independence, by finally resolving the issue in its favor by annexing the Crimea, Russia had to turn its entire attention to Austria in order to forestall its opposition. It was essential for Russia to secure Austria's assistance, and to that end to enter an alliance with it. But an Austrian alliance rendered the Prussian alliance untenable. Thus the one of Catherine's terms for peace with Turkey that did not alarm Frederick in the least, since he saw in it only a source of difficulties for Russia, and which on the contrary, greatly alarmed Vienna by its results—this condition led Russia to break the Prussian and form an Austrian alliance. Catherine's personal relations could only contribute to the policy reversal, because for her the Prussian alliance ended in 1772.

II

WAR AND POST-PARTITION DIPLOMACY, 1773-1774

COLLAPSE OF THE BUCHAREST CONGRESS

We have observed that at the end of 1772 the Bucharest negotiations ground to a halt on the question of the towns in the Crimea demanded by Russia. At the start of 1773 Obreskov reported that the entire impasse involved two towns, Kerch and Yenikale, which the Turks refused to yield, threatening to quit the congress should Obreskov not seek further instructions from his court regarding the towns. Soon thereafter he reported a lessening of the Porte's desire to end the war, ascribing it to the intrigues of Russia's enemies in Constantinople.

Writing the Prussian envoy in Constantinople, Zegelin, Obreskov urged his cooperation in persuading the Turks to give up Kerch and Yenikale. Zegelin raised the matter with the reis-effendi [minister], responsible for foreign affairs, who replied: "The Porte has done everything possible to conclude the negotiations successfully. It consented to give up Azov and Taganrog, granted guarantees for Georgians, Moldavians, and cossacks, and acceded to commerce by Russian subjects on the Black Sea and in the Greek archipelago, although the maritime powers unanimously advised against it. The Porte conceded that for security from the Tatars Russia might strengthen itself however it wishes. But the prosperity of the Ottoman empire depends upon its refusal to yield Kerch and Yenikale. A Russian pledge never to build naval vessels there would provide no security, for Russia could stand in full preparedness on the Don and at the first dissention with us transport war materiel to Kerch and Yenikale. In three or four months a Russian fleet of twelve or fifteen ships might appear on the Black Sea and dictate policy to Constantinople. Our decision is final; should Russia yield on the issue of Kerch and Yenikale, peace will be achieved. But if it persists in its demands we will continue the ill-fated war, despite the chance that we may all perish. Should it be predestined for the Turkish empire to fall, we cannot escape it."

Obreskov likewise corresponded with the Austrian internuntius in Constantinople, Thugut, anticipating his assistance in ending the war. But the Prussian Zegelin wrote Obreskov that "Prince Kaunitz has protested to my sovereign that I intimated the following to the Porte: if it fails to achieve peace soon, in the spring the Austrians will join the Russians in depriving Turkey of its former possessions.This leads me to conclude that we can expect no support from Austria in accelerating the negotiations, because in fact the intimation ascribed to me would be the best way to bring the Turks to their senses. Even if Vienna fears that this would bring peace too soon and possibly interfere with its hidden designs, I do not see why it opposes such a hint which in no way will harm Austria, since Austria's minister is not directly involved."

Field Marshal Rumiantsev was likewise unhappy with Zegelin, sensing in his letters "the mouth of a wolf and the tail of a fox...." It appeared,

Rumiantsev wrote Obreskov, that "our enemies' friends are also our enemies, whereas our friends measure out good will and assistance to both sides solely in accordance with their own benefit and advantage. They recognized the articles constituting the chief stumbling block for the peace negotiations, more as a mental fixation than as representing real danger, but they have yet to offer us their good services or propose a strong, convincing argument to incline those who are across the table from us to an agreement."

Meanwhile Catherine wrote her reactions to Obreskov's reports for the January 3 session of the Council: "Russia is demanding free navigation on the Black Sea. All other Turkish protestations are moot and irrelevant, for large naval vessels cannot sail the Black Sea's shallow waters. Consequently the Russian naval vessels launched on the Don are in fact smaller than any Turkish merchant ship now seen on the Black Sea." Catherine added orally that it would be reprehensible for the empire and her own glory to put up with orders and instructions from the Turks after Russia's glorious military success. Thereupon the Council proposed to the empress that Obreskov must be provided new instructions in the event that the Turks became obstinate and would not conclude peace without limiting Russia's access to the Black Sea or denying it bases in the Crimea. In that case, reasoned the Council, it would be better to agree to limited access to the sea than to allow the Turks to reestablish themselves in the Crimea. Russia's merchant ships could always, if necessary, be converted into naval craft. Peace under these conditions would still be glorious and advantageous, whereas it would be truly deplorable were the war to resume, especially when affairs with Sweden were so tense. The empress replied that fear of the Swedes implied doubts about Russia's strength. She refused to alter her demand for full navigational rights until the Council furnished her more compelling reasons for compromising.

On January 26 Obreskov had written Panin that "a pronounced change has taken place in the Porte's inclination to achieve peace; not only does the immediate success of the negotiations seem in doubt, there is also danger that the congress itself soon will be ruptured." The Porte clearly did not intend to concede a single Black Sea port to Russia. Obreskov did all he could to hold the congress together. Knowing the boundless greed of the sultan, he proposed that Russia would abandon its demand for monetary reparations should the Porte accept the remaining conditions.

His offer was forwarded to Constantinople, and the answer was announced at the conference on March 9.

The Porte offered to pay twelve million rubles to redeem the territory occupied by Russia. In order to induce Russia to abandon its claims to Kerch and Yenikale and agree to limited navigational rights on the Black Sea, Turkey would pay another nine million. Obreskov made it clear that were the Porte to offer all the treasures of the world Russia would not abandon its demands.

Thereupon the Turkish plenipotentiary, Abdul-Rezak-effendi, announced that there was nothing more to be said and he was leaving. Obreskov told him to send a request telling how many wagons he needed. This embarrassed the Turk, who then said: "If we break off negotiations it will be hard to resume them later and keep the war from dragging on and on. It would be better to continue our talks than to drop them, but let us not do it face to face. I will cross the Danube and you can stay somewhere on this side, and we can continue the negotiations in writing." Obreskov agreed. The plenipotentiaries parted most cordially and embraced almost to the point of tears. "I can say with candor," wrote Obreskov, "that having spent nearly a lifetime in this nation, I have never found such a decent and virtuous man."

Obreskov moved to the small town of Roman. Zegelin wrote him from Constantinople that, contrary to his expectation, the collapse of the second congress had not brought severe disappointment to the capital. It was preferable to continue the war than to find peace on Russia's terms. The reis-effendi had asked him: "Could we really sell out the Tatar khan, as Russia demands? That runs contrary to our laws and our religion, for it is impossible for two Moslem sovereigns to reign in close proximity. Their khan must acknowledge the sultan as his superior or the sultan must be subjected to the khan. Equality is impossible. This is our constitution, which can be changed solely by the total collapse of our empire. To yield Kerch and Yenikale is tantamount to making them dependent on Russia, which would soon build an awesome fleet there and dictate policy to us."

Prior to the breakdown of the Bucharest talks Petersburg had instructed Obreskov to threaten nonrenewal of the armistice and thereby bring the Porte to agreement. But Rumiantsev demurred and wrote Obreskov: "To announce this, and to do so before it is necessary, would be tantamount to awakening them from their present lethargy and compelling them to take proper measures everywhere to be on guard. Incidentally, this not only would make it difficult for us to strike at any of their sensitive points but also allow them at times, because of the present weakness of our troops, to cause us to suffer losses, especially where we are undermanned. The more sudden and unannounced our acts, the more useful they will be. In my opinion, if it seems doubtful that we will conclude the desired peace it would be better to lull the enemy to sleep in his present military negligence and torpor than to compel him through fear to build his forces. If I am preparing action against you, need it be said, naturally you will take similar measures against me." Rumiantsev was annoyed at Count Aleksei Orlov,[1] who opposed the armistice and complained that his opinions were not being heeded, that he lacked the means to continue effective action, and that he was in an exposed position. Rumiantsev in his letters to Obreskov said regarding these complaints: "And what could he do in four months? Were three years too few for him to accomplish these great feats?"

THE RUSSIAN OFFENSIVE OF 1773

Rumiantsev was deeply angered that his army had been weakened the previous year by the loss of several regiments transferred in anticipation of war with Sweden. These regiments shortly were directed to return, but Rumiantsev wrote Obreskov: "When we raise our demands we fail simultaneously to seek the means plainly necessary to reinforce them— that is, to increase our forces against the enemy. Instead we weaken them within sight, so to speak, of our foes, who are watching. We can only hope that leaving behind the regiments taken from us last year, which cannot be ready for the first action because of their long march, will not elicit the same response from the enemy as did the departure of those regiments last year, from which the enemy drew encouragement. The armistice has not lasted long enough for us to stock sufficient supplies of war materiel. No conscripts and little of the necessary ammunition have been brought forward. Thus, if a campaign begins in March, we will hardly have the forces here to defend territory we now occupy against enemy attacks, much less mount significant operations of our own. Speaking as a friend, in fullest confidence, I confess that I have neither the health nor the mental strength for such difficult ups and downs, which I face alone, increasingly sapped by the necessary efforts to fulfill my tasks. Everyone else holds to the rule that if you want a hard peace you must be prepared for war, but we see things differently since the army here, as you see yourself, has so little of what it needs."

Field Marshal Peter Alexandrovich Rumiantsev

When Obreskov informed Rumiantsev that the negotiations might not lead to peace and therefore that he as commander in chief must be prepared to renew military action, Rumiantsev answered: "This will not be easy to do, since even conscripts have yet to arrive. While a part of the uniforms and clothing have come, we still need time to fit and clothe the soldiers. Getting all sorts of supplies here on time does not depend on me, but is arranged by others. Thus, we obviously cannot open a campaign at winter's end because we have too few men and inadequate supplies. Nevertheless I live by the Russian proverb, 'Though unhappy, I am ready,' that is, happy to do everything despite the various obstructions that are preventing preparations."

Returning to Orlov's antagonism toward the armistice, Rumiantsev wrote: "Our fleet has an open road, and is not tied to any particular island, whereas here every step must be won by force of arms. Consequently, the defense of vast territory acquired by occupation is quite different from sailing on the water without opposition. I cannot hide from you, solely because we are good friends, the thoughts toward which I am driven by my terrible loss of bodily strength. I have lived many years, remaining in the field out of love for my country and strong bent toward the military. Never having been fortunate enough to choose the occasion according to my own desires, I have borne what was laid on me and have done what was asked without complaint. Now attacks of illness so have sapped my strength that I can last barely a short time if there is a winter campaign. I do not kid myself about participating in further exploits. To conduct military operations one first of all needs physical vigor, but I have spent mine. Your political struggles, no matter how hot they get, have a way of quenching themselves. But our fights always flow with blood and are so violent that once overrun their weight rarely gives the fallen the chance to rise to his feet, and what is decided in one battle stands for entire centuries. Military battles and their methods are in the open for everyone to see; consequently, judgment and accusation are inescapable, and there is no room for self-justification. But your offices conceal from the penetration of others the ties and motives of your forces and their actions."

On February 28 Rumiantsev received an imperial command "To seize from the enemy by force of arms that which you have been unable to secure up to now by negotiations, by dispatching the army or part of it across the Danube and attacking the vizier's main army." Notifying Obreskov of his orders, Rumiantsev wrote: "I have you, my dearest friend, as God's witness, so to speak, of our situation here and therefore will not trouble you with further explanations, knowing that you are more astute than anyone else in seeing our strength and fitness for the task. We must overcome what previously were solid barriers, that is, break the enemy's power and occupy the towns covering the vizier's camp. At the same time we must scrutinize the task from every angle in order not to compromise in any way the security of places now under our protection, which leaves us able to advance on just one objective. Because of your friendship and partiality towards me you easily can imagine my difficulties here. I must add that the season is not appropriate for this type of campaign; the cold forces us to search every hut for the enemy; in combatting the severity of the weather you only wear yourself out and find yourself unprepared for action at a better time."

Rumiantsev expressed the same idea to the empress in a communication concerning the problems of crossing the Danube, sending her the opinions of generals Saltykov, Potemkin, and Weissmann about these difficulties.[2] Furthermore, the king of Prussia advised not to cross the Danube. None of this availed; Catherine insisted on the crossing.

In April the Russian army successfully moved to the offensive. Turkish efforts to cross to the left [northern] bank were unsuccessful. A Russian column under the command of Colonel Klichka crossed the Danube, defeated the Turks several times, and returned, as Weissmann had done in 1771. Turkish attempts against Zhurzha and Slobodzeia ended disastrously for them. In May Suvorov, who had been transferred from Poland to the army on the Danube,[3] practiced his brilliant talents here as well, seizing Turtukai [Tutrakan]. However, "a failure occurred apparently owing to the fortunes of war, which do not always favor one side." According to Rumiantsev, Colonel Prince Repnin suffered the defeat. Wounded, Repnin became a Turkish prisoner, along with two majors named Divov and several staff officers. "The territory acquired by the enemy in that battle changes our position not a whit," wrote Rumiantsev, "and the loss of so few men would mean nothing in itself. Except for Prince Repnin, the Turks still would not have taken a single notable prisoner in the entire war. Because of this, but even more because of the personal good will I feel for his family, it is deplorable that this happened.

Meanwhile we are proceeding to repay the enemy with interest. General Weissmann and his corps are already on the other side of the Danube, and I am pushing upstream along the bank of the river seeking further action."

Weissmann soon sent the field marshal tidings of victory. On May 27 at Karasu he fell on an enemy force, consisting of twelve thousand infantry and cavalry and inflicted a defeat. The Turks lost more than a thousand men killed; the Russians captured their entire camp and sixteen cannon. Rumiantsev thereupon decided to cross the Danube at Gurobaly or Bali-Bagas. But six thousand Turks with cannon stood there. The field marshal ordered Weissmann to advance toward their rear from Karasu and Potemkin to disembark and move directly toward their front. On June 7 both generals simultaneously approached the enemy's camp from different directions, while the field marshal with the main force appeared on the opposite bank of the Danube with ships fitted for a crossing. The Turks were struck dumb and at the first volleys broke and ran. The Russian cavalry galloped after them and killed more than three hundred men. The supply train fell to the victors. With the site selected for fording the river thus cleared, Rumiantsev the same day issued orders to ferry the troops across and himself crossed the Danube on the eleventh. After defeating the Turks once again on the Galitz river, the Russians set up camp outside Silistra.

Somewhat earlier, when Rumiantsev informed Petersburg of his intention to cross the Danube and the seizure of Turtukai, Count Grigory Orlov informed the Council that from the field marshal's present disposition he realized that Rumiantsev now intended to conduct the campaign as he, Orlov, had recommended to him a year before; namely, to ford the Danube between the Black Sea and Karasu and place the left flank of the army there. The vizier, on the other side of Karasu, would be unable to cut off the Russian troops because of the distance of the detour. On the contrary, he would face the danger of being cut off himself. Thus the army might be able to open a route beyond the mountains and, after alarming the enemy's capital, force him to make peace.

Having learned of Rumiantsev's crossing, Catherine on June 28, the anniversary of her accession of the throne, wrote him that since he had made that day happy for her, she was rewarding his son Mikhail with the rank of colonel, and she wished God's help in everything he did on the far side of the Danube.

To Voltaire Catherine wrote: "Your dear Mustafa must be thrashed thoroughly again after breaking off negotiations, two congresses and an armistice lasting nearly a year. This venerable gentleman in my opinion knows nothing about how to take advantage of circumstances. There is no doubt that you will see the end of this war. I hope that crossing the Danube will promote this doubly—by making you happy and by making the sultan more compliant."

RUMIANTSEV'S RETREAT

But Rumiantsev presented Catherine with the same bitter surprise in 1773 that Golitsyn had handed her in 1769. Despite several successful skirmishes with the Turks, the seizure of Silistra proved to be impossible owing to its strong garrison, which had been increased to thirty thousand men. When ordered to surrender, the commander answered that the Russians would not take a single stone or nail of Silistra. Numan Pasha left Shumla intending to attack the Russian army from the rear in coordination with an attack from Silistra on the other side. Weissmann advanced upon Numan Pasha and met him on June 22 at Kuchuk-Kainardji. The Turks were routed, losing around five thousand killed and twenty-five guns. But the Russians paid dearly for this victory; Weissmann was killed. Disregarding the fact that the Turks now were unable to assist beleaguered Silistra, Rumiantsev gathered his military council on June 24 and decided to return to the Danube's left bank. It was impossible to lead the terribly exhausted cavalry forward; there was no grass and they fed the horses reeds which, even so, were procured with difficulty and from a distance. The roads were nearly impassable and there was no one to fight, since they could not catch the Turks.

On June 30 the field marshal revealed his return across the Danube. "Foreseeing that my personal enemies will put me to a severe test," wrote Rumiantsev, "because the forces entrusted to me are considerably weakened I have ventured in clean conscience and in my obligation as a loyal subject to inform your imperial majesty of the difficulties encountered in the most recent crossing of the Danube. Envisioning it beforehand differed from the actuality only in that what seemed then to be very difficult turned out to be far more troublesome. The generals who accompanied me are witnesses to my utmost effort, sparing neither labor nor lives, to fulfill the supreme will of your imperial majesty. I had a small corps, although it was called an army, with thirteen thousand infantry, in action against the vizier's forces, which nevertheless were beaten and scattered. In a word, it was more than a test of what men can master or overcome. This difficult campaign quite exhausted my men. Our horses likewise were utterly spent, and I cannot hide from your majesty the difficulties now oppressing me as I go on the defensive. It is not easy for me to assume as firm a defense as before, since the positions are fallen down to the last stone.

"However, I can yet summon the courage to relate to you as an eager and loyal servant the situation across the Danube as I found it. If we plan to continue military actions there, we must not double but treble the army. An unassailable stance requires this many troops, for without them it is impossible to defend our position on account of the river's breadth behind us and the difficult fords, during which we could be cut asunder from all sides. In order to cover the fords we will have to post special corps so as not to tie the hands of those participating in the offensive, who will have to blaze a route through forest and mountains.

"My spirit long has been grieved that I have not been honored with a letter bearing signs of the monarch's benevolence, assuming that my loyal sentiments are reaching your imperial majesty's ears. It further distresses me that my intercession on behalf of numerous people serving under me has not benefited them. Without this, devotion declines among subordinates, whom I have no other way to encourage. Additionally, my numerous reports detailing insufficiencies and the necessity of reinforcements have obtained no results. I both sense and predict that I shall be found lacking if not in zeal, about which no one can lie, then in abilities, and I shall be made out to be a man who sees problems everywhere, and shall lose your confidence. I confess before your imperial majesty that, after serving not for the first time in a war lasting five consecutive years, I feel my physical and spiritual powers to be waning. Although it makes me happy to please your majesty's supreme will and the good of the fatherland, I fervently wish to see someone else in my place who will find better means than mine to satisfy both of these precious objects."

On July 15, in the empress's presence, Rumiantsev's official report was read to the Council, in which he related the details of his return to the left bank of the Danube. It made a strong impression. It was said that the field marshal's return would give cause for unpleasant rumors, would make the Turks haughty, and would delay the desired conclusion of peace. Dissatisfaction with Rumiantsev was expressed: his demands were too great, and the means did not exist to enlarge the First Army to the extent he wanted. Members of the Council wondered why he crossed the Danube without first considering all the complications. The battles he had fought in vain had put the army into disarray for at least two months. But the Council was not vexed. The situation could be helped only by satisfying, however partially, the field marshal's demands. Zakhar Chernyshev suggested that in light of the current state of affairs in Poland it might be possible to send the First Army several regiments from the corps stationed there. He added that in order to encourage the field marshal the Council must answer his report and inform him of this addition to his army. The Council acceded, likewise approving a second proposal from Chernyshev, to transfer Bibikov from Poland,[4] leaving Lieutenant General Romanius in command there. Catherine read the personal letter Rumiantsev had sent her, mentioned above, and having heeded his complaints granted that everything he proposed be carried out at once.

Rumiantsev's letter was written very adroitly. He related the most unfortunate events that had occurred and aroused powerful indignation against himself. But in order to allay this indignation he suggested in conclusion that should anyone else be capable of handling the campaign more expeditiously, he was prepared to offer him the reins of command. This was not a direct request to be relieved, but an open invitation to find someone as good as or better than he. It was impossible, need it be said, to find anyone better. It had been possible to relieve Golitsyn because Rumiantsev had been available, but there was no one else who could claim the victory at Kagul. Rumiantsev had no rival who might replace him on the Danube, so he could foresee easily that the indignation aroused in the Council would end with the decision to offer him encouragement, to enlarge his army, and to fulfill his demands about rewarding his subordinates.

But Rumiantsev found a skilled opponent in the war of letters. Catherine answered him candidly, with absolute dignity, condescendingly, graciously, continually expressing her complete confidence in his skill as a commander and her hope that he would conduct the war in the best way possible. Intimating that he erroneously presupposed he had enemies who sought to harm him with her, she indicated that he himself was responsible for the animosity in his army. Finally, she let him know that his allusion to retirement did not alarm her and that she stood ready to release him. But here she so skillfully removed any shadow of dissatisfaction or irritation that it was impossible to be offended and actually grant his request for retirement. "Loving the true good of the empire," wrote Catherine, "and thus desiring peace as much as anyone, I will tell you sincerely that the news of your retreat across the Danube did not make me as happy as your first crossing of the river, for which I congratulated you so sincerely in my earlier letter. For I think that your return to this side of the Danube will not serve to hasten peace. By the way, we shall pay no attention to the empty echoes of Europe, although our ears will ring with them for the next several months. They will, of course, die down of their own accord, after giving empty pleasure to those who hate us, but we will pay them no mind.

"Then there are your personal troubles, which you remind me are putting you to a severe test, at a time when the forces entrusted to you are reduced to extreme weakness, and because of which you paint me a vivid picture of the difficulties involved in crossing the Danube. After delving into those circumstances in as much detail as I could, let me tell you candidly, first, that I do not even know who these enemies are about whom you complain, and I have not heard about them except from you. Indeed, it was impossible for me to hear about them, since I close my ears to all private quarrels. I do not have people serving as 'ears'; I do not like tale bearers and gossip carriers who create discord with news which they often think up themselves. I have no patience with them. Such people usually do not have other qualities to gain esteem, only those base ones. I have become accustomed to blocking the ways to such intrigues and destroying them. Like you I have made it a habit never to judge people other than by their qualities and services, by the ranks which distinguish them from others, as well as for their deeds and their zeal. Thus I hope that you will judge my present and future disposition to you by the past, when you experienced well my benevolence to you and your many services to me and the state. I must admit along with you that your army is not great in number, but never shall I be able to forget the inscription minted on my obelisk, which honors your victory at Kagul, when with no more than seventeen thousand men you nevertheless gloriously defeated a multitude of the enemy.[5]

"I am very sorry that the arduous campaign you just undertook across the Danube and back exhausted these brave men so much and that the horses were utterly spent. But I hope that under your constant care, of which I am aware, both men and horses will be returned again to their former state of health. I can imagine that it will be difficult for you to restore your defensive position, destroyed to its foundation, since in one month you have had to assume three different positions, to wit: first, on this side of the Danube, then an offensive crossing of the Danube and beyond, and finally, your retreat across the river, having to reconstruct a defensive position all over again. All these, so to speak, crossings involve no small difficulty and anxiety. But having known your skill and tested your assiduous zeal, I do not doubt that you will know how to extricate yourself with honor from any difficulties in which you find yourself....

"As for your physical strength, through five consecutive years of war you have become so feeble that you fervently wish to see someone else like yourself in your place, who like you finds his happiness in pleasing my will and the good of the fatherland. This leaves me deeply sorrowful. Of course, to the extent that God upholds your strength of body and spirit the empire must expect nothing less than excellence from you in consequence of the glory you already have gained for it and for yourself. But having considered all this, if the usual human frailties do not allow you, to my sorrow and the sorrow of Russia, to find the strength to continue your skillful leadership, I will display the usual concern for you as I have before under similar circumstances."

In his answer, dated August 18, Rumiantsev admitted that he derived much comfort from the words and favors of the sovereign but did not want her statement regarding his enemies to remain without rejoinder: "I have them, unfortunately; otherwise why should I offer explanations about them before your imperial majesty, my monarch, for you are all-wise and capable of penetrating deeply into their activities and the reasons for their open opposition to me. They advance their own new contrivances of similarity, possibility, and accommodation in refutation of mine and give a different accounting of our troops on paper than exists in fact, thereby making me appear, while overcoming insuperable circumstances, as though either unprepared or inept. Every way they can they confuse the real athletes of war with others when it comes to receiving decorations. They honor not only those who because of old age are staying on the war's side lines, but also those who have withdrawn from service under various guises, who frequently under censure and out of favor with me found places on other staffs that were beneficial and advantageous, receiving double the salary due them under their previous post of service and rank. They (that is, Rumiantsev's enemies) have withdrawn from my charge units which were attached to me and by their continual presence were committed to my command. As a result, ambition has declined as a preferred mainstay of service, together with esteem for the commander; indignation and intrigues are sure to increase."

Rumiantsev concluded his letter as follows: "Because of the vast distances involved, I have no hope of borrowing reinforcements for the current campaign from regiments detached from the corps in Poland. Contrary to my true desires, but resulting from my extreme exhaustion (I have spent the last several days in bed), I trust that your imperial majesty's supreme mercy, liberally granted to all loyal and zealous servants, will grant me the liberty on the appropriate occasion to go someplace where there is at least a roof, to recover my last vital forces, for my health has been shattered by the humidity during this campaign and by the painful and harsh changes of weather."

In describing the actions of his enemies Rumiantsev pointed unmistakably at Chernyshev, who headed the War College. He also had reason to suspect Grigory Orlov, but Orlov at least had written him openly that the public was indignant with his manner of conducting the war.[6]

Rumiantsev had answered Orlov: "Receiving your excellency's most favorable letter, I perceived the depth of your indignation toward me and how unfortunate I am in the public's perception of me. Were this a parliament, in which the entire group comprised a court, and were cases decided now as they were in the tribunal of ancient Greece, the Areopagus, I might take issue with our public: who is (or should be) ungrateful to whom, I to the public or the public to me? I have spent my life in sweat and labor, not tasting the joy received for one's services. All laboring men have a measure and price for their deeds, but I alone seem fated to accomplish things time and again and receive only indignation for them. Let former deeds be forgotten and I will not remember them, but can my present situation really not touch the public, when our troops are triumphing over the Ottomans, while the naval forces stand idly by,[7] and everything requires unremitting labor? Public displeasure drove the best generals from Rome and Greece; their service was recognized only in

time of need, and then sometimes too late. My lot, apparently, is to receive
the same reward from my fatherland. I have been persecuted in the past
by general displeasure and must be prepared to endure this fate in my
old age, when the cause for my misfortune will be simply that I have
nothing to offer besides my service. I am sure, my dear count, that you
will not participate in the popular conclusions about me. I will erect your
kindness and friendship toward me as a wall against which the contrivances of those seeking evil for me will be dashed. Meanwhile we will
soon begin to drink the Danube's water."

Unfortunately they were to drink the Danube's water twice. Regardless
of the response from Petersburg, Rumiantsev was crushed with grief by
the impossibility of remaining on the far side of the Danube. "I can find
no solace for my aching spirit," he wrote Catherine, whose own frame
of mind was not enviable.

THE SECOND RUSSIAN CAMPAIGN

The English ambassador, Gunning, wrote his court that he had never
witnessed the empress in such distress. Her grief, in his opinion, stemmed
less from fear of a Turkish invasion across the Danube than from her
inability following uninterrupted successes to bear the slightest failure.

On August 10 Catherine spoke to the Council: "You request conscripts
from me for replenishing the army. This levy will be, as best I remember,
at least the sixth since 1767.[8] Altogether around 300,000 men have been
conscripted in the entire empire. I think, and you must agree, that the
defense of the realm requires this, but I sign the levy law each time with
heaviness of heart out of love for mankind, seeing that the levies have
yet to bring an end to the war despite our wreaking considerable damage
on the enemy and ourselves suffering terrible losses of men.

"Two questions naturally arise from this circumstance. First, have we
used the conscripts in such a way as to hasten the long desired peace?
Second, what do you intend to undertake for the glory of the empire with
this levy, which I will not raise at all except for the empire's benefit?
Without discussing our previous campaigns, now wreathed in laurels and
responsible for persuading the enemy to negotiate, in answer to the first
question I will address myself to the current state of affairs. It grieves
me to see that this campaign will come to an unfruitful end everywhere,
or has so ended already; all we can do now is look to the future without
a moment's waste. In order to resolve my second question, I repeat that

we must think hard, without hesitation, about our course of action in the ensuing campaign. You must decide whether you consider it is really best to deploy our land and naval forces exactly as they are now. Our current alignment is not bringing results nor do I consider it useful for winning our desired peace. In my opinion, our current strategy is more likely to bring us a second war on top of this one than to end the present conflict.

"From the levy you have proposed, I conclude that you are continuing to provision the army. I must remind you not to forget to bring the Azov squadron to full readiness for action. I particularly entreat and command you energetically to devise a plan that is unanimously acceptable. I exhort you to supply the various commanders of our forces with instructions to be prepared to move against the common enemy. Our efforts must be directed to a single object; that is, to achieve a felicitous peace, in which all the aforesaid will help us. Once again I enjoin you that all this not remain simply words written on paper."

After signing the decree for the levy, Catherine began speaking of the necessity of caring for the conscripts. Several Council members suggested that mortality among them resulted from the change in their way of life and the uncommon marches resulting from the empire's great expanse. The empress ordered the Senate and Count Chernyshev to investigate and take appropriate measures to stop the abuses taking place in levies and to bring the field army to full strength with garrison soldiers and the garrisons with recruits, in order to make life easier and provide better care for men not yet used to the army.

Following these orders, at the session of August 27 Chernyshev stated his opinion that the measures then being taken to increase the First Army to 116,000 men for the next campaign made it imperative to request from the field marshal his intended plan of action. Chernyshev argued that with the army's strength thus augmented it would be possible, posting the requisite number of troops on this side of the Danube, to cross to the other side and gain a foothold there. The Second Army, remaining in a defensive stance in the Crimea, could seize Kinburn with the navy's assistance. Should the First Army be in no condition to cross the Danube and remain in its current position, it would be necessary to detach a sizeable corps from it to help the Second Army conquer not only Kinburn but also Ochakov.[9] Meanwhile Russia must seek the desired peace through negotiations by setting aside several conditions, particularly the demands for Yenikale and Kerch, the acquisition of which would prove more harmful than useful (?).[10]

At this point Panin astounded everyone by suggesting the possibility of husbanding conscripts by dispatching garrison soldiers from regiments stationed in Petersburg to the army and replacing them with recruits. Chernyshev answered that in the Council's previous session the empress had given specific orders to do just that.

At the session of September 2 the procurator general[11] asked whether by making use of the treaty with England the Council might grant Count Aleksei Orlov the right to interrupt the supply of foodstuffs to Constantinople. Panin answered that Russia's earlier prohibition on transporting foodstuffs had aroused the dissatisfaction not only of France but also of the other commercial powers. Because Russia was in no position to oppose them, the prohibition could not be renewed at that time.

The members of the Council wanted peace so desperately that they agreed to restore all towns in the Crimea to the Tatars, including Kerch and Yenikale, and furthermore consented to limitations on Russia's rights of access to the Black Sea. Grigory Orlov alone opposed the majority, contending that no concessions would help, for the Turks would never agree to complete independence of the Tatars, even under the most extreme circumstances.

The king of Prussia suggested three avenues for gaining peace: (1) drive the Porte to agreement by force of arms, (2) invite the assistance of Austria, and (3) give up several conditions to which the Porte absolutely would not agree. Catherine evaluated these proposals: "To compel the Turks by force to sign a peace: to accomplish this Field Marshal Rumiantsev would have to command an effective army of eighty thousand men, besides which we would have to lay up stores for an entire year and place a navy on the Black Sea to occupy Varna.[12] The enterprise would require great expenditure and cost many lives. As for inviting Vienna's assistance in this important matter through a diversion from the direction of Belgrade, this would be the least advantageous for Russia because Vienna would seek to extract significant profit, which would conform not in the least with Russia's genuine interests or with the interests of other European states. Finally, to yield on the several conditions that are particularly harsh for the Porte is to sacrifice several gains in the cause of peace, and to reward oneself with Ochakov or Bendery for the concession. The first course is the most brilliant but also the most dangerous; the second is both the weakest and least politic; the third lies in the middle, between the other two. It is the most reliable way, and one can likewise consider it the most sensible."

In November a report reached Petersburg from the Prussian minister in Constantinople indicating that the Turks might offer Kinburn to Russia in exchange for retraction of the demands for Kerch and Yenikale.[13] As noted immediately above, the Council had consented earlier not to demand Kerch and Yenikale. Now it began to be said that the acquisition of Kinburn might prove useful for maintaining a Russian fleet permanently on the Black Sea, as well as for establishing trade there, not only with the Turks but also with Poland because of the accessibility of its water communications. To realize these goals it would be necessary to found a commercial city on the Dnieper below the rapids; Kinburn, separated from the mainland by a canal, would serve this city as Kronstadt served Petersburg.[14] For overland communications with Kinburn the Russians might receive from the Tatars the entire left bank of the Dnieper up to a width of five versts.

Count Panin, the "minister of foreign affairs" as people were beginning to call him, stated that it was hard for the Porte to surrender Yenikale and Kerch to Russia, but likewise difficult for Russia to keep them; therefore he called for the Prussian minister in Constantinople to be instructed to arrange the matter of agreement on this basis. But Orlov again objected. Kinburn was a small fortress lacking a harbor. It could not compensate for the return of Kerch and Yenikale and would serve no useful purpose. Commerce would be subjected to difficulties because of the rapids and shoals. If Russia felt obliged to return Yenikale and Kerch to the Tatars, it should try to receive in exchange Ochakov and all lands lying between the Dnieper and Dniester, along with Kinburn, and not allow the Tatars to settle in Bessarabia.

Others retorted that the Turks would not consent to this. During these disputes the Council admitted the error of its plan for Tatar independence, conceding that "for the total and complete separation of the Tatars from the Turks much more time and labor are required." Catherine herself retained the opinion that the Turks would not agree to cede Ochakov. Orlov proposed that the two sides agree to its destruction whereupon, after stipulating in the treaty that both sides remain free to build fortifications, the Russians might build a stronger fortress in Ochakov's stead. Should Russia acquire the districts between the Dnieper and the Dniester, a large number of Moldavians and Wallachians would move in quickly and settle there, and the territory soon would become a barrier between the Turks and the Tatars, preventing any overland communication between them.

Zakhar Chernyshev took exception to this view, arguing that this area would cost Russia dearly because fortifications must be built and garrisons maintained there. Orlov replied that there would be no need for fortifications. Someone noted that the Tatars would have a meager liberty if supreme authority in major matters were left to the sultan as caliph, or if Tatar judges were appointed by the mufti in Constantinople.[15] Thereupon Panin repeated his assertion that it was impossible to ratify Tatar independence overnight; this would require much more work. At last Catherine directed them to propose to the Turks, through the Prussian minister, that Kerch and Yenikale be left to the Tatars; in return for this concession Russia should receive Ochakov and Kinburn. The ambassador was to explain that the empress would never abandon the conditions of Tatar independence and Russia's right to sail on the Black Sea even if the war dragged on another ten years. Following Catherine's departure from the session, Panin raised another issue for decision: should peace with the Porte be concluded directly or through the mediation of Austria and France? The Council decided on a direct course, although that course heretofore had not resulted in the advantages that outside mediation might have brought.

No matter how Rumiantsev protested against the harsh impression produced by his retreat across the Danube, he fully realized that he could not let the year end with this impression. In October he dispatched two bodies of troops across the Danube under the command of lieutenant generals Baron Karl Karlovich Ungern-Sternberg and Prince Yury Vladimirovich Dolgoruky, who attacked the Turks near Karasu and completely destroyed them.[16] The entire camp with eleven guns, eighteen battle flags, three Turkish standards, and many military supplies fell to the victors. The Turks lost 1500 killed and 772 captured, including the three-tailed pasha Omer.[17] The town of Bazardjik, vacated by the enemy, was occupied by the Russians. Ungern and Dolgoruky were ordered to continue the advance without delay in order to "snatch" Varna and Shumla, as Rumiantsev expressed it.

At the same time Lieutenant General Potemkin besieged Silistra and Lieutenant General Fedor Ivanovich Glebov was maneuvered in his support.[18] Rumiantsev used these successes to evade making the plan for the next campaign for which Petersburg was asking. He wrote the empress: "I still feel the distress that gripped me on the retreat across the Danube, but your imperial majesty was pleased to find in my reports, in addition to the causes making this necessary, the result that followed upon the advice of all the generals. If any one of them had claimed to know a better course of action I, of course, would have followed it. I awaited the proper time and opportunity and exploited them more advantageously than sometimes the greatest plans can envision. We have captured many prisoners, among them some high ranking people. We took the enemy's entire artillery and the town of Bazardjik passed into our hands with scarcely any loss and without a single cannon shot, for the manner of attack and method of our operations produced such overwhelming success that the enemy fled of sheer necessity and from fear of the troops advancing on him, forfeiting his camp and forsaking the preparations he had made for winter.

"Plans, usually drawn up only at the beginning of a war or at the start of a campaign for the concerted administration of movements and supporting actions, and prepared by various hands far removed from the front, or outlined in general terms with allies, nevertheless undergo frequent changes. But when the commander closes with the enemy it remains to his skill to take further measures to suit the time, need and circumstances of the moment. For a long time I have used my troops to destroy the enemy; I have not reached them everywhere, just along a single river. Consequently, to whatever extent the enemy changes his daily position, to the same extent, especially now, we must plan our actions against him for the coming season. In my opinion, our operations will depend more on events and the initial judgment of them, for they open the way to significant operations if sound plans can be executed without hindrance or delay."

Arriving in Petersburg with this letter on November 14, Prince Vasily Dolgoruky[19] expressed his hope to the empress that within a week news would arrive of the success of Ungern and Prince Yuri Dolgoruky. But two weeks passed with no word, and on November 29 the news came that Ungern's attack on Varna had failed and that Prince Dolgoruky, after making a crossing toward Shumla, had turned back toward Karasu. The field marshal wrote nothing about what was happening at Silistra.

"What took place at Silistra?" Catherine wrote Rumiantsev. "You said not a word on this subject but left me in deep ignorance; my thoughts are gripped by uncontrollable excitement.[20] Yet, I am in no mood to place my trust in bombardment, which neither will compel the city to surrender nor damage it extensively. Although the consequences of the battle at

Karasu failed to sustain their initial promise, they nonetheless confirmed the soundness of our activity. For one thing, they affirmed our confidence in the bravery of our troops and revealed that in the field the enemy will not hold the upper hand under his present organization and disposition, at least in the sector where we attacked them. On the other hand, we learned that whatever action you might undertake beyond the Danube would advance our policies. There, of course, your every step either hastens or delays the nation's peace and the tranquility inseparable from its welfare. Thus I learned of the Karasu business with considerable pleasure. My sole regret is that it took place so late in the year that it cannot be as useful as if it had occurred some six months ago."

Having thereby implied to Rumiantsev that he had erred in retreating across the Danube and that he was responsible for prolonging the tiresome war, Catherine continued: "In order to prevent next year from passing so unprofitably and deficient provisions from hindering operations, I feel compelled to reaffirm in strong terms my instructions to fill the supply magazines on the Danube for the upcoming campaign in order to avoid delays in your operations on the opposite bank and to prevent the campaign from slipping past without our attaining peace through a concentrated use of arms. I anticipate receiving your opinion on these matters imminently, for your response has been sought repeatedly. Should you delay much longer, it is possible that your proposal will not arrive in time. Consequently, we might be behind schedule throughout the coming year, a situation neither useful, glorious, nor honorable. Regardless of the heartfelt enthusiasm and eagerness of the senior servants of the empire such as yourself, regardless of my labor or state of happiness, the world will judge you and me by our successes only. Our success justifies us in the public mind and censures us in turn, especially now when, after five years of successful warfare, the empire's subjects expect peace to result from your operations alone."

On December 30 Catherine made known her supreme will to the Council that it instruct Count Rumiantsev that after taking Varna and defeating the vizier at Shumla he not consider the Balkans as limits on his operations. The Council voted to prepare a rescript that, after expressing this determination, would leave the execution of operations beyond the Danube to Rumiantsev's good judgment.

ACTIVITY OF THE RUSSIAN NAVY

The break in the peace negotiations also called the Russian navy into action. Earlier, in September 1772, the newly arrived squadron from the Baltic Sea under the command of Captain Mikhail Timofeevich Koniaev burned sixteen Turkish ships near Patras.[21] Simultaneously Russian ships "dealt the enemy destruction and alarm" on the coasts of Egypt and Syria, where they supported the Egyptian pasha, Ali Bey, in revolt against the Porte. In 1773 Russian ships again appeared off the coast of Syria under the command of Captain Kozhukhov.[22] The Druses there were obliged to recognize Russian patronage and fight the Turks when the Russians did. The Russians besieged Beirut and forced it to surrender, thereupon presenting the fortress to the Druses, who by agreement paid them 250,000 piasters for it. This money was distributed throughout the squadron, after a tenth of it went to the commander-in-chief of the fleet. Among the ship captains in this expedition could be found Greeks and South Slavs from the coastal regions who, according to Admiral Grigory Andreevich Spiridov,[23] "served more courageously for their personal profit than if they had been fighting on salary alone." For reasons that remain unclear Orlov forbade neutral ships to enter the Dardanelles, ordering Spiridov to enforce this prohibition while the conditions of the armistice were being prepared.[24] But the Council decided to inform Orlov that this not only might deflect the Turks from concluding the armistice, so essential for Russia, but might turn all the powers against the undermanned Russian forces and thereby involve Russia in a new war with the French, "who hate us."

It displeased the empress that the navy, which lacked a landing force, was unable to contribute to the army's effort to force the Turks to peace. In the fall of 1773 Count Aleksei Grigorevich Orlov and Rear Admiral Samuel Karlovich Greig were in Petersburg.[25] Interesting discussions took place in the Council on the subject of their requests to strengthen the fleet. At the session of October 3 the empress asked the members what objective they would expect a new squadron in the Aegean Islands to achieve. The fleet already there was costly yet seemed incapable of harming the enemy. "If it can be utilized in any kind of operation," Catherine said, "and if land forces are needed, I will assume the responsibility for raising them." They replied that the squadron was to be sent at the request of Count Aleksei Orlov to replace ships that had rotted. They added that while the fleet might be unable to hurt the enemy, at least it would alleviate the army's predicament by drawing the enemy away from it.

Catherine said that Count Aleksei Orlov should be invited to attend future Council discussions of the navy, stressing that her love of order compelled her to take care that nothing in her empire be left without employ. Four days later, on October 7, Aleksei Orlov was present at a Council session. The empress asked him about the current state of affairs in the Aegean Islands and whether greater use might be made of the navy. Orlov answered that the timbers of five of his ships were completely rotted. During the current campaign, he said, he had intended to destroy Salonika and Smyrna to prevent the import of supplies to the enemy through those places, but illness forced him to leave the fleet. "I do not think," he said, "that an enemy fleet can appear in the Aegean. Ever since the Turks learned that our land forces are not numerous there, they have not feared them so much. They were defeated by a small force because they fear most of all the unknown. Having regained their confidence, they are now taking the necessary measures."

Thereupon Count Grigory Orlov spoke up.[26] "That is typical of the Turks, as of all ignoramuses; we must not give them time to think but try to make use of their confusion. And we must follow the same procedure in the peace negotiations in order to attain our desires more quickly."

Catherine said that in her opinion maximal benefit would be gained by an undertaking on the European coast alone because it was nearest the enemy's capital. Chernyshev and Aleksei Orlov objected that it would be impossible for a small force to gain a foothold on the European coast, for the enemy quickly could concentrate upwards of forty thousand men there. Thus the operation could have the single effect of alarming the Turks momentarily and strengthening their forces on that coast. Count Panin noted that ordering a new squadron to the Aegean might cause the enemy new concern, and he hoped that the Turks would renew negotiations during the winter. "It is my intention," the empress answered," that we not only rely on making peace but take strong measures to gain this in the upcoming campaign. A prolonged war will make people despondent, and for that reason no one wants peace more than I. Does the navy need more land forces, and if so, are twenty thousand enough?" Aleksei Orlov answered that with twenty thousand he could reach Constantinople itself.

"Might it be possible to take Gallipoli?" Catherine asked. "I might be able to add four or five thousand foreign troops to the navy." Chernyshev said that foreign troops would introduce too many problems, and Panin noted that hostile powers, upon learning of their use, might put up obstacles.

Count Aleksei Grigorevich Orlov

"Besides all the inconveniences of using foreign troops," said Aleksei Orlov, "every success will be ascribed to them. To avoid the opinion that we can do nothing without the English, I have always tried to use as many of my own officers as possible."[27]

The empress reminded him that Peter the Great had used foreign troops, that one must compare the inconveniences to the advantages. She left the Council after expressing in no uncertain terms her dissatisfaction with the course of the war. "The navy," she said, "is doing nothing, and the army little more; the enemy is taking advantage of our inaction, and we alone are to blame."

After Catherine's departure Aleksei Orlov proposed dispatching a new squadron under Greig before the ice closed Kronstadt and permitting it to strike any barbarians (Turks) it might meet. The Council concurred. Orlov further proposed that Russia not sign an armistice, for this would give the Turks time to take advantage of French advice. Concerning his own role, Orlov said that the empress apparently wanted him to continue to command the fleet. As a diligent son of the fatherland he would not shy away from the task, but he could not give full assurance that he would fulfill his assignment diligently because of his frequent illnesses. On October 21 Greig left Kronstadt with two ships of the line, two frigates, and six transport ships.

SHAGIN-GIREY'S OUSTER FROM THE CRIMEA

The state of affairs in the Crimean also must have aroused Catherine's dissatisfaction, for she had greater cause to say that Russia was wholly to blame for developments there. The previous chapter relates the story of Crown Prince Shagin-Girey's journey from Petersburg to the Crimea.[28] This Tatar dauphin captured the attention of Catherine and her court because of his talent, and with good cause. Transported from the steppes to the highest stratum of Petersburg society, he became captive to civilization, retaining only his Tatar cap and the memory of his descent from Genghis-Khan. But this memory did not live in him in vain. The marvels of civilization and the power which it had conferred upon former vassals of the Tatars aroused a dreadful ambition in Girey. He wished at all costs to use this fatal gift presented him by Russia. He desired to assert Crimean independence with Russian assistance and tear it away from senile Turkey forever. He wanted to become khan.

But this was not his only goal, for he had no desire to replace dependence on Turkey with dependence on Russia. He wanted to acquire the mighty tools of civilization, able to confer on him the power and ability to maintain independence. The insignificance of his Crimean possessions, need it be said, could have been seen as a major stumbling block, but Shagin-Girey knew that Genghis-Khan and Tamerlane also began with little and built extensive empires.[29] He dreamed of subduing the neighboring Caucasus and using its warlike population for conquest. He thought about the treasures lying untouched in the bosom of the fabled mountains, which would open to the voice of civilization and enrich the new Black Sea empire of the Gireys.

It was with these dreams that Shagin returned to Bakhchisarai. He repeatedly expressed his utter devotion to Russia to Prince Putiatin, who accompanied him to the Crimea, revealing incidentally that a faction existed in the Crimea that desired a return to Turkish rule. "With trust in God and in the intercession of the empress," said the crown prince, "I believe that I can manage those miscreants for now. I have entered a forest which long has stood neglected and without care. Should I not be able to straighten a tree bent with age, I will cut it down." Of his brother, the khan, he said: "Can a man attempting to ride an unbroken horse follow a path of his own choice when someone else is holding the reins?"

Shagin soon grew perplexed and justly irritated by Russia's concession in the negotiations with Turkey granting the sultan sovereignty over the Crimea in ecclesiastical affairs. By this agreement all judges in the Crimea were to be named by the mufti of Constantinople, and on Fridays public prayers were to be said for the sultan. "These developments," Shagin told Putiatin, "signify not only the Porte's supreme authority over the Crimea, but also the Crimea's former devotion to the Porte, for common religion alone does not oblige the Crimea to maintain close ties with Turkey. There are many Mohammedan governments which neither are subject to the Porte nor have the least connection with it." Bitter tears welled up in Shagin's eyes as he continued: "If this is how things will be, both my brother and I shall have to leave. Our predicament will be worse than that of a man threatened by a gigantic, poorly balanced boulder hanging overhead, which might fall on him at any minute. Under these terms our subjects, because of their inconstancy and herd instincts, will find means to make continual insurrection, not just alone but more so through the intrigues of the sultans (the Crimean Gireys), of whom there are not a few in Turkey."[30]

On March 13 Putiatin wrote Petersburg: "The general feeling of ill will towards us here is great, but the crown prince remains openheartedly loyal to us in spite of it. All the perfidious schemers of evil both hate and fear him and are devising ways to get rid of him."

As the crown prince told Putiatin, "I was well acquainted formerly with the debauchery of my countrymen, but now I find them ten times worse and more depraved than before. I cannot remain with people who are so ungrateful and so hostile to me and the Russians, because I promised her imperial majesty my eternal loyalty. Should the disorders continue and my powers not prove useful to Russia and myself, I will be forced to renounce my native land and seek asylum under the empress's patronage."

Upon the crown prince's return the khan had assembled a council of leading and influential men. In statements to the council Shagin-Girey extolled the liberality of the Russian sovereign and expressed his undying gratitude for it; he was eager for a Russian alliance as a prerequisite for lasting and continuous prosperity for the Crimea generally and for each inhabitant in particular. Shagin asked the council what made them inconstant, drove them to perfidy, deception, and oath-breaking. What did they really want? Did they desire freedom, which as the supreme happiness of human life could be obtained under the patronage of her imperial majesty?

"We are located between the two mightiest powers on earth," was the answer, "both of whom we fear in equal measure. Threatened by the one, we have agreed to all of its proposals, but simultaneously, fearing the other, we have feigned nostalgia for our former situation. We have been deceived and angered by Russia, which is taking advantage of almost every occasion to subject us to its brutality."

The crown prince contended that Russia had done nothing of the sort. If it wanted revenge for Crimean treachery it might transform their lands into wilderness and would do so if the Crimeans conducted themselves treacherously in their relations with Russia and behaved suspiciously toward the Porte, continuing their ruinous vacillation. "If you want to become free with Russia's help," said Shagin, "hand over to me forthwith the rebels against the general tranquility who have given cause for violating the oath." Shagin spoke heedlessly; he attempted to alter things too abruptly. A deep silence followed his demands. Irritated and unable to restrain himself, the crown prince let fly his last charge. "The oaths you have given," he said, "and the power entrusted to me upon leaving Russia make it incumbent upon you to obey me. Should you refuse to obey, I shall have to leave my fatherland."

They answered: "We will not hold you back. Many can be found to take your place, but meanwhile we are obligated to obey the khan, your and our sovereign, and him alone."

Afterward Shagin-Girey related to Prince Dolgoruky, the commander of the Second Army, his desire to make himself the autocratic khan of the Tatars, arguing that this act alone could assert the independence of the Crimea. Otherwise he could not even remain there. The Council in Petersburg, pondering Prince Dolgoruky's report on this turn of events, reasoned that the posture assumed by the crown prince was both understandable and justifiable, yet under the present circumstances no assistance could be given his intention to become khan. A revolution of this kind would violate Russia's agreements with the Tatars and lend the Turks cause once more to win them to their side. Russia could not expect a total estrangement of the Tatars from the Turks for many years. The Council instructed Count Panin to write to Shagin-Girey praising his zeal, explaining in general terms the impossibility of fulfilling his request while reassuring him of the patronage of the empress and promising in any event to grant him asylum in Russia.

Panin wrote Shagin-Girey on July 14: "Should affairs deteriorate to the extent that your security is in question and your further presence in your native land impolitic in bringing the Tatars to their senses, and your life be sheer misery, it remains for you to decide whether to accept asylum within the borders of her majesty's empire."

Shagin-Girey thus had no alternative to leaving the Crimea. He wrote Dolgoruky that "apparently God has driven him from his fatherland for his sins and has allowed him to wander in foreign lands and foreign courts." Shagin asked for residence in a place where no one would know him.

The empress answered Dolgoruky's report on October 4. "The crown prince, having perceived the danger under the present circumstances of his remaining in his fatherland and the preferability of becoming an exile in our empire, is unquestionably worthy of amnesty. He might serve furthermore as an example for the mighty in that he experienced our mercy when overtaken in this his extremity. Nevertheless, to preserve appearances we prefer that he remain near the frontiers for a while rather than appear immediately at our court, since in the latter event it might seem as though he were torn away and forever separated from his fatherland and his Tatars, and thereby please and encourage those who wish him ill. Likewise it would extinguish his memory among the peoples who so recently honored him sincerely and enthusiastically. Therefore, make him comprehend that their esteem for him requires that he not absent himself entirely or appear to despair of future participation in their government and affairs. Rather let him prepare to return and take action at the first likely moment." Shagin settled in Poltava, receiving for his maintenance a thousand rubles per month.

STANISLAW AND POLAND'S PROPOSED CONSTITUTION
News was discouraging from the Danube and the Crimea but not especially from Poland, although matters continued to drag along, preventing Russia from withdrawing the troops quartered there.

On January 18 Stanislaw Augustus wrote Catherine: "Amid the calamities that surround and threaten me, I dare to hope that I shall find in your imperial majesty an indulgent judge of my actions since the parcelling out of Poland—a judge the more merciful because your majesty possesses a natural spirit of justice and personal grandeur and, if I may add it, prior kindness toward me.[31] Undoubtedly you will appreciate everything I had to do to fulfill my duty, preserve the spotlessness of my reputation, and extinguish the rumors, unfortunately widespread, that I knew about and even participated in the agreement relieving Poland of part of its territory. This painful experience has taught me all too well that it is not enough just to be innocent in a case and that slander can be fatal for even sovereigns (especially in a situation resembling mine). You know this and thus I believe that in the depths of your heart you suffer too from the disasters befalling me. I believe that you are wondering how to ease them. Permit me to address you again as my benefactress and friend, and deign to hear my view of past and present.

"I have long since recognized the difficulties of a situation where it is impossible to combine one's desires with the demands of duty. For six years and more these difficulties have tormented me. Torn between gratitude, which urged me to follow your views, and opposition to these views because of my submission to the nation's will, I have spent the entire time devising ways to eliminate this paradox but have met invincible opposition from both sides. I refer your imperial majesty to my efforts in this direction and the many polite but insistent requests directed to you. I did all I could to preserve my people's tranquility, to encourage the beginnings of prudence and the nation's true interest!

"And what has been the result of these concerns? Among the people for whom I sacrificed everything I encountered an assassin's knife.[32] And you, the sovereign to whom I preferred nothing save my duties, deprived me of a portion of your mercies as though I were an ingrate. Thus my integrity was the cause of my misfortunes. Is there really no remedy against these disasters? Your majesty so eagerly makes of honor a virtue; you so jealously protect honor in supporting yourself, and you are so worthy of it. Can it be true that in my case alone honor means nothing to you? No, I let myself hope that I have endured a prolonged and difficult ordeal which must have an end and bring its reward. You are able to do everything for me and my fatherland. I entrust my personal interests absolutely to you. But I must make entreaty for this unfortunate remnant which still must bear the name of Poland. You have only to have the desire, and everything is possible for you. Your allies value your resolves the moment you express them. If they forced you to harm Poland, compel them in their turn to do it good. Gain this most valuable advantage compared to them, one with enough honor to please you.

"I have searched high and low for relief but have found it nowhere. Utterly helpless, I see the moment coming when my people and I will have to bow to fate. I sense this and do not intend to oppose it in vain. But before enduring the blows of fate, I implore you not to refuse me the consolation of telling me what you will do for us and how your sense of fairness will reward us. Should any hope of saving Poland be impossible, please deign to receive a request to lighten Poland's fate, however slightly, for I consider it essential under the circumstances."

"Your forthrightness requires me to repay you with like candor," replied Catherine. "My character knows no other language, and I have used this idiom every time I have spoken with you about your interests

King Stanislaw Augustus of Poland
(formerly Count Poniatowski)

and the interests of your people. Ever since circumstances changed and assumed their present form, I have been unable to consent to or favor any arrangement more or less peculiar to the situation of your realm without consulting my allies. I refer to your majesty's predicament and to that of the populace. When I alone intervened in your affairs, did I not do everything, did I not sacrifice everything in order to settle matters to the advantage of the Commonwealth? Driven to extremity by the intrigues and factions of your people, I had to enter into a compact with two other neighbors of Poland in order that our united strength might end its disturbances and disasters, which were beginning to reverberate in our own states.

"Despite the various difficulties the Poles brought to my affairs, my agreement with your neighbors did not lose sight of the welfare of Poland. This welfare consists for your majesty in the integrity of your crown, and for the nation in a lasting peace, in a free government more proper, tranquil, and secure for the nation and its neighbors. As concerns the details, my minister and the ministers of the two other courts have the same instructions. Because I have spoken so candidly with your majesty, I might forever reproach myself were I not to add that I will lose every hope of seeing you emerge in a strong position following this agreement if you now heed the fatal advice of those whose intrigues threw your realm into the abyss of disturbance and contention, into an anarchy that threatened its final destruction, from which it was redeemed solely by the intercession of the three neighboring powers."

The instructions to the ministers of the three courts referred to by Catherine were sent to Stackelberg on February 24. They read: "If you observe that the king of necessity seems disposed to follow the views of the three courts, you may make an agreement with him regarding the intentions of the Diet, after, of course, it is certain that no interests, intrigues, or foreign influence may interfere to the detriment of the three courts. The king is excluded inasmuch as in this purely national process it is reckoned useful to admit representatives from every faction so long as they sincerely desire to end the disturbances in their fatherland" (these lines were penned originally by Catherine herself).

"The ministers must have a known number of loyal men in the local diets who can be counted on to guide matters to the desired ends.[33] In selecting these men not only quantity but also quality must be kept in mind. Since force alone cannot induce the members of the local diets to approve the policy of the three courts, we will have to resort to bribery not only in naming deputies but also in giving them instructions. For this reason the three courts are establishing a cash fund with their ministers; the share of each court shall be a minimum of 150,000 to 200,000 thalers. This fund will be administered by the three ministers, and nothing will be spent without their unanimous consent. Agents sensitive to the strong and weak sides of each local diet will propose to the ministers which method must be employed primarily, or to which degree all means must be used. The ministers will decide accordingly on military force, admonition, or bribery. Since there is no possibility of accomplishing anything in a free Diet under the liberum veto, the ministers must form a confederated Diet (under the knot of confederation, as the Poles used to say).[34] The agents selected by the ministers must be men of the middle class bound neither to the court in Warsaw nor to the Saxon party,[35] and aware that the sole possibility of improving their lot consists in ending the calamities that have beset their fatherland.

"When the Diet opens the ministers will charge it to name a deputation to negotiate with them. During these negotiations the ministers will refuse to discuss the rights of their courts to the provinces designated for partition, or any limitation or diminution of the shares of each court. They must insist on a full and absolute cession from the Commonwealth. The ministers must demand all archives and documents relating to the lands being ceded. As concerns the constitution of the Commonwealth, representative government must be reestablished and affirmed in perpetuity. In the future Polish noblemen alone may be elected king; the king must have been born in Poland and be a landowner there. Foreign princes are forever excluded. Sons and grandsons of a previous king may not be elected immediately following the reign of their father or grandfather but may be chosen after at least two intervening reigns. The liberum veto at least remains immutable law.

"The ministers must keep in mind above all the preservation of the present king on the throne. All reforms must be inclined toward restoring equilibrium among the power of the king, the Senate, and the gentry *(ordre equestre)*. To ensure this, the king must not augment his power vis-a-vis the two other bodies in the government by means of his relatives. Thus, the king's relatives must not occupy any governmental posts. It is impossible to limit their rights absolutely, for rights belong to every nobleman; therefore it will be decreed that the uncles, brothers, fathers, and cousins of the king and queen may not be ministers, high military commanders, senators, military governors, or castellans, but may occupy lesser posts. The king's privy council will consist only of senators appointed by the Diet.

"Whereas the king's influence on the military and finance commissions has alarmed the people, these commissions must be abolished and the duties of supreme military commanders and treasury officials be restored to their former importance, if the majority wills it. But abuses which existed heretofore must be prevented from recurring: military commanders must not have the right of life and death over soldiers, and treasury officials must not be permitted to dispose of the state's monies arbitrarily. These powers must lie with councils under the military commanders and treasury officials, whose members will be named not by the king but by the military governorships every two years. The troops now under the king's command will be transferred to the supreme military commanders, and hereafter the Polish king will not have troops of his own nor will forces of the Commonwealth be under his command.

"Whereas the influence of the magnates, and especially the royal house, on the courts serves to oppress the people and violates the balance of power, the presiding judges and members of courts will be chosen by nomination and the military governors. Furthermore, the laws must be published, which might free the courts from dependency on the king and the magnates.

"Whereas the gentry, which constitutes the third branch of government, is relatively weaker than the two other branches, the king and the Senate, and meets but periodically in its diets whilst the two other powers are continuously active, it would seem well to make it possible for several delegates from the gentry to sit in the Senate between sessions of the Diet with the right to protest all decisions not coinciding with the constitution and privileges of their estate.

"Whereas the crown lands have declined as a result of the partition, several estates must be added to them to raise the king's annual income to at least 400,000 ducats. Distribution of the remaining estates shall follow the distribution to the king with the stipulation that no single house (*maison*) may be awarded more than two estates if together they yield more than eight thousand ducats yearly income, so that if one has a single estate bearing that much revenue, it may not receive another.[36]

"The Poles unanimously favor an increase in the size of their armed forces; this in fact is necessary in order to maintain tranquility and order. As matters now stand, the government has considerably fewer troops than several private individuals, who are able to laugh at the authorities with impunity. It would present no danger to neighboring powers if the armed forces of the Commonwealth were increased to six thousand men.

"Whereas the question of religious dissidents is one of the most basic to Poland's tranquility, the three ministers must contribute to an agreement between the dissidents and the Catholics. Both sides can make concessions. The dissidents can withdraw their demands to have seats in the Senate and ministerial posts, and the Catholics can refrain from punishing those who leave Catholicism for another confession. This is a barbarian law which cannot be endured any longer in an enlightened age. The remaining rights of dissidents must be upheld absolutely." (*"Especially the right to be a deputy in the diets,"* added Catherine.)

One of the articles in the instructions stated that the king was not permitted to buy lands in Poland and Lithuania. Catherine struck out the article with the statement: "I struck out this article because in an elective kingdom the king's estates pass again after his death to the gentry *(terres nobles).* The article merely would increase the Polish outcry needlessly. He who has nothing to live on cannot buy land."

POLAND'S REACTION TO THE PARTITION

Also at the end of 1772 Catherine wrote Panin on the matter of Stackelberg's reports about convening the Senate: "After reading this it occurred to me to use this occasion to release to this Senatus-concilium those senators we are holding in Kaluga.[37] At first glance this may seem an odd concession, but in fact it can generate several useful impressions. There is no reason to fear them because the three powers hold the whole nation in obeisance. The example made of these people will frighten those who are timid. Many will learn from this how little we value their intrigues and intriguers. Others will praise our action. For still others it will remove one more excuse to cry out against us, and there will be some whose attention will be attracted more to this voluntary act than to the partition itself. Among them will be the relatives and clients of the released senators. Now, I ask you to give me any reasons you can think of for opposing this idea. None come to my mind. If there are none, so be it. This cannot be at all pleasant for the Czartoryskis, since the detainees were the original incendiaries (*boute-feux*) of the Saxon party. As far as the other senators are concerned, this eliminates the opportunity to avoid the congress which must meet in order that the Diet achieve the character, or better yet, the composition we want." No objections occurred to Panin, and the men imprisoned at Kaluga were released.

The first to return from Kaluga to Warsaw was Cajetan Sołtyk, bishop of Cracow. As Stackelberg put it, Cicero could not have made more noise on returning to Rome from exile. All Warsaw began to stir. The papal nuncio, bishops, and everyone who was important went out to meet him. Crowds of common people surrounded his carriage with the cry "Vivat!" Sołtyk was dressed in shabby clothing, his bald head was uncovered, and he had a distressed appearance. He sat with downcast eyes, continually making the sign of the cross. The doors of his house immediately were thrown open to the poor; he himself went on foot to church and said mass.

Stackelberg met him at the house of the king's sister, where Sołtyk was visiting in the company of fifty Benedictine monks. Stackelberg told him that his piety might be more credible to the public had he remained quietly at home, resting from his journey. Sołtyk calmed down considerably after these words. He twice came to see Stackelberg, who likewise visited him once. All three meetings were devoted to "quenching the bishop's enthusiasm with the weapons of reason and the obvious." Success apparently remained on the side of the lion tamer. Sołtyk said repeatedly that he would not take a single step or utter a single public word without consulting Stackelberg. He asked the envoy's permission to address the empress and received it. His letter was couched in the most respectful terms.Sołtyk thanked her for her kindness, asked forgiveness for the past, and entrusted himself to the supreme protection of the Russian sovereign.

On February 19, 1773 the Polish government answered the declaration of the three courts concerning the partition of Poland, saying that the excessive demands of the three courts, reinforced by expressions of accusation and reproof, had insulted the sensibilities of king and Senate; the three courts had not observed the proper respect due the king and the Commonwealth, whereas the prudent behavior of the king deserved otherwise.

Despite this accusatory tone, the king recognized the serious threat to Poland implied by a denial of the demands of the three courts. On advice from the Senate he carried out their wishes, calling a meeting of the Diet for April 19. Also on the Senate's advice he solemnly petitioned the three courts to withdraw their troops from the Commonwealth's territory before the local diets convened, in order that they and thereafter the Diet might proceed freely and the national will be expressed without pressure or danger. The ministers of the three courts decided not to force an issue over the tone of the Polish response. From the start they had followed the practice of permitting the Poles to make emotional declamations so long as they remained without consequence. Thus the Poles had the comfort of using harsh words yet affairs proceeded generally as the three courts desired.

The local diets had to open in March 22 but people loyal to Russia who had been dispatched into the provinces revealed to Stackelberg that they could not guarantee that a single deputy among their friends would come over without the promise of financial support, for they were in dreadful penury. The instructions to the ambassadors of the three powers distracted Stackelberg's attention unwillingly from the local diets to the Diet. He wrote Panin that he was convinced it was impossible to institute the change demanded in the law on apostasy. "The blind fanaticism of the Poles, for which they will sacrifice everything, poses a lesser difficulty on this point than that of Vienna, in particular the empress-queen's sensitivity to the religious question. At the pope's behest she has instructed Baron Rewiczki to protect religion, especially on this point; Rewiczki has informed me that he has received these instructions and is conducting a separate correspondence with Maria Theresa on that topic. However unjust the law may be in itself, I beseech you not to insist on a change, for this point is potentially the most hazardous to our compact with Vienna. Furthermore, the introduction of dissidents into a legislative assembly— a matter quite problematical aside from this difficulty—happens to be impossible. Finally, the form of government advocated by the three powers, with its limitations on royal control, will arouse the opposition of the entire royal party. Only by placing the king between fear and hope was I able to lead him into compliance and influence the Senate. As soon as Stanislaw Augustus discovers his fate he will begin to raise heaven and earth to avoid becoming a puppet king. If we have all the friends of the court against us from one side, and provoke and arouse the remainder of the nation with the religious question, so dear and sacred for the Poles, you can guess what will happen. Similar opposition would develop to our gift of estates to the king should we attempt to seize them during the lifetimes of their present owners."

In reply Panin said that if the abolition of the law prohibiting religious conversion were to meet with serious difficulties, it could be amended or even left unchanged. With regard to the king's new estates, Panin suggested following the nation's desire. Panin also sent a supplement to the instructions, on which Stackelberg and his colleagues had to agree: the king could be given the right to have a guard of two battalions of foreign troops, for which a specific sum was to be designated; otherwise, when the allied troops quit Poland, his life might be endangered because many Poles hated him for his alleged role in the partition.

For the present, Panin first of all demanded that Stackelberg reach agreement with his Austrian and Prussian colleagues. "Take care not to raise the suspicion that we aspire to supremacy, for the matter can be completed solely if the three courts retain their complete equality. Do not tie your hands with obligations which block our path to greater influence. Do not overburden Poland independently of the other two courts. Do not alienate the Poles by actions which might be attributed to us alone. This is all we can do at present. Rather than appear overly concerned for the future, it might be useful to don the mask of ambivalence. Let them think what they will—that this is your personal style of diplomacy or that it is the policy of your court. In any event, you must believe that this will make our cause victorious."

As the Diet drew nearer Stackelberg complained primarily about Sołtyk, who once more sought to defy the designs of the three courts. When Stackelberg seriously reprimanded his behavior in a letter, Sołtyk answered: "Immediately upon my arrival in Warsaw, in my first conversations with you and with the ministers of the other two courts, I let it be known forthrightly that I will not approve of your intentions against Poland. I have reiterated several times to you in private that a Pole who approves of the partition of his country sins against the covenants of God which forbid anything of this kind, and whoever supports this deed is its accomplice. I told you that everyone is obligated by natural law to defend the right of his fatherland if he does not want to be a monster. And I said that if we senators supported partition we would be breaking our oaths. Who gave us the right to make our brothers slaves and thereby acquired the same power over us? I have told you repeatedly that I will do everything for you if your demands do not run contrary to my conscience and honor. You assured me that with your knowledge of my character and manner of thinking you would not venture to tempt me. Go to Colonel Bakhmetev and the other officers who guarded me in prison: did I not tell them that I prefer to spend the remainder of my days in a dungeon, even in Kamchatka, on bread and water, than to receive freedom at the cost of the welfare of my fatherland and my conscience? I repeated the same thing to you as well, and even added that I would sooner lose my life than sign a verdict fatal to my fatherland. Not desiring to confirm the partition, I cannot favor a Diet; not wanting a Diet, I cannot favor the local diets: therefore I am exerting every effort to break them up.

"I am telling you the whole truth, yet you reproach me by asserting that I have not kept my word. You are reproaching me for devious conduct, specifically by your allegation that I proposed my brothers and cousins and other relatives to you as future deputies. What you call deception I would call a political ploy or cleverness permitted under such circumstances—ultimately, a *restriction mentale*. You must remember that from my youth I studied under the Jesuits."

Stackelberg answered him: "I did not study under the Jesuits and I abhor Machiavellianism. I have never used religion and morality as pretexts for masking the interests of my passions. Fanaticism, personal interest, and intrigues are the cause of Poland's misfortune, not neighboring powers. Common sense, true patriotism and prudence must bring this misfortune to an end. When you find the essence of these virtues in your heart I beseech you to inform me, and I will receive you with open arms. I am not going to answer you concerning the intentions of the courts; they are none of your business."

"Sołtyk is mad," Stackelberg wrote Panin on April 1, "mad enough to be locked up. I wrote him a letter designed to end all relations between us. I preferred not to receive letters from him but gave instructions to keep him under observation. Truly this man has done something evil. It is remarkable that the Diet is gathering. Without Sołtyk's insinuations it might not have been as boisterous as it is going to be. The Poles were regarding the partition as an inevitable misfortune, but now they are talking about the collapse of the Bucharest negotiations and the conditions under which the treaty must be written. At last, in another week, the curtain will rise and a great drama will begin to play itself out. I can assure you that it will bring difficulties we are not anticipating. Arousing fears and making threats leave little impression. And this while foreign troops are swallowing up the entire incomes of private individuals."

THE DIET MEETS

The Diet opened under the "knot of confederation." Hardly had the royal and the Lithuanian marshals of the confederation entered into the assembly hall and the first deputy from Cracow opened the session with the declaration of confederation than a huge Lithuanian named Tadeusz Rejtan stood up and cried out for the entire castle to hear, "I do not allow it!" This cry was repeated for three days, and the Diet collapsed. When the royal marshal of the confederation, Count Adam Poninski, rose to strike the floor with his cane to restore order, as was customary, Rejtan seized another cane and stood up in the marshal's stead crying, "I am the marshal and I can be just as good a marshal as one chosen in the dark and in secret!"[38]

Benoit and particularly the commander of the Prussian troops, General Lentulus, proposed to Stackelberg that Rejtan be seized. Stackelberg replied that since his Prussian majesty was an equal participant in affairs he, Stackelberg, was agreeable for the Prussian hussars to seize Rejtan. But Stackelberg had decided not to use force. The ambassadors of the three allied courts had nothing to fear from the cries of madmen. He would take it on himself to force the king to accept the treaty in his palace, without entering the embassy building. To fulfill this promise, Stackelberg summoned both chancellors and asked them to notify the king that if he did not proceed to the treaty within twenty-four hours an order would be issued to mobilize the troops.

The king demurred and invited Stackelberg to a discussion on April 11. At their meeting he repeated his previous words and laid before the Russian the inconveniences and delays that his entry into the Senate chamber would create if Rejtan and his colleagues were there, as in all likelihood they would be. The king consented to convene the Senate in his palace and order the chancellor to repeat Stackelberg's threat, and to summon the marshals of the confederation.

"It is all done," Stackelberg wrote to Petersburg. "The marshals made their speeches, the king proceeded to the treaty, and the senators signed individually. The chambers will meet jointly on the 13th; Rejtan and his followers are frightened and begging for mercy. All is calm."

But it was much more difficult to pass the new constitution. The king dared tell Stackelberg that under no circumstances could he permit a diminution of his rights. We have seen that the Diet had to reach agreement with the ambassadors through representatives of the Senators and deputies. It was still possible for the ministers of the three courts to name delegates from the Diet from among those loyal to them, but the king named the senators. The senators then sent the king a list of the people they favored, which included all the ministers, among whom were his relatives. Stanislaw rejected this list with incomprehensible obstinacy. The three courts began to think again about mobilizing troops. But Stackelberg wrote Panin, "I beg to petition that, if the Poles yield on every point, the troops must evacuate the Commonwealth. I must fling poor Poland at the feet of our most august sovereign and beg for her mercy on it. All of Great Poland has been reduced from a rich and populous province into virtual wilderness because of the occupation of Prussian troops, since Poland must supply them with forage and a contribution of forty thousand thalers a month. Meanwhile the deputies in the Diet are doing their utmost on our behalf. It is not surprising that they are becoming estranged from us out of despair."

In consequence of the king's political speech the Diet composed a note to the ministers of the three courts. "The allied courts have communicated to the Polish ministry a rationale supporting their claims to certain Polish lands. The Polish ministry has countered with a summary of Polish rights to these lands, rights based on visible proofs. But since the Commonwealth finds that its response has not received due attention, and that the three courts continue to insist on their demands, Poland finds it necessary to propose to the three courts that all four parties agree to accept the friendly mediation of neutral powers, who will establish the proper rights and claims based on treaties. This will guarantee that the three neighboring courts not be plaintiffs and judges in their own case."

Stackelberg answered: "The three courts have presented to the Polish ministry a statement of their rights based on irrefutable proofs, whose rectitude is the more incontestable because of the lack of objection from the Polish side. As one who has signed the document, I cannot give another answer apart from upholding the several declarations of the three neighboring powers, particularly that of January 22 (February 2), in which they outlined in sufficient detail Poland's designated alternative: final approval of the matter by June 7 or an increase in the three powers' demands.

In spite of such decisive and immutable language, this signatory watches sadly and compassionately as the Diet wastes time in trifles, cavils, and disputes over semantics. Meanwhile the day of judgment is approaching and the culprits responsible for these delays display no fear. They must answer for the insidious argument that the powers must not be plaintiffs and judges in their own case. Who is to blame for their finally being forced to render justice? What is to blame is that spirit of ambition which, borrowing all voices and assuming all forms, has aroused sedition, fanned the flames of internecine war, and produced a bloody struggle between Russia and the Porte which has continued for four years. To this argument I would add the following: if the Diet within one week does not name representatives to negotiate with the ministers of the three courts, no one will answer for the consequences."

INTERFERENCE FROM THE KING

"We have performed a very intricate task," Stackelberg wrote Panin. "We assembled the Diet, created a confederation, and persuaded the entire nation to approve a treaty with the powers. Yet the king is mounting every imaginable hindrance and delay!"

On April 26 the three ambassadors were sent to Stanislaw Augustus to entreat him not to create obstacles for them, but Stackelberg expended his eloquence in vain. The refrain of the king's every answer was the same: "I cannot oppose the partition, but I will never allow a delegation from the Diet to decide my rights and our form of government."

Stackelberg explained that the negotiations on the partition of Poland and talks concerning its domestic structure were inseparable. He said that the peace of Europe depended on it and that by resisting the king could bring disaster to Poland. The appointed day was approaching and the ambassadors would issue orders to mobilize the troops. At this point the king expatiated upon the illegality and impossibility of reducing his rights and upon the bad government structure that would result at the hands of the three courts, who had no understanding of Polish laws, and by the action of a few Poles who were hostile to him, the king. The ministers assured him that nothing had been decided yet about his rights and that the chaos in Poland rendered the abuse of its government sufficiently clear to the three courts; the argument concerning his enemies was irrelevant, for he might be able to name the entire Senate. Everything was in vain.

Suddenly he stood up and said that the following Monday he would speak for the last time in the Senate.

Hardly had the ministers of the three courts left the palace than the flowery phrases of the king began to resound through the city. In Stackelberg's words, Stanislaw spent the day showering everyone with tears, pathetic posturing, and garlands of rhetoric.

On April 27 the three ambassadors let fly the rumor among the Poles that they were drafting orders mobilizing the troops, which was, moreover, absolutely true. But news came from the palace that the king was girding for a protest against the entire situation, intending if necessary to abdicate his throne. This news forced the ambassadors to resort to a strong measure, but what specifically were they to do? Benoit and Lentulus produced letters from the king of Prussia authorizing extreme measures in the event of the least resistance. But Stackelberg reasoned that the personal resistance of the king ought not subject the entire people to ruin, especially since his resistance had nothing to do with the partition. They decided ultimately to spark rumors throughout the city that orders had been given to mobilize troops and send the Russian, Austrian, and Prussian quartermasters to arrange billets in the homes of prominent personages. This measure evoked the desired fear in the Poles, and the appearance of a Prussian squadron half a mile from the city completed the impression.

At 8:00 a.m. on May 1 Stackelberg assembled all deputies of the Diet at his residence and in the presence of his Austrian and Turkish [sic] colleagues tried to explain how reckless they would be to subject themselves to military measures at a time when even the king was consenting to the partition; his opposition was only on domestic questions, at a time when none of those issues had been decided—nor would they be settled without the advice of the Diet. At that moment two squadrons each of Prussians and Austrians passed through the streets. The three ministers had brought them into the city under conditions laid down by Stackelberg, that they leave Warsaw as soon as their purpose was accomplished; namely, when the Poles were frightened. All Warsaw was struck with horror at the sight of these troops. The king alone, encouraged by his small council consisting of his mistress and two foreigners, a Swiss and a Frenchman, challenged the three powers to war, intimating to the deputies that the latter sought to introduce an aristocratic government composed of twelve tyrants. Appearing before the Diet, the king proposed approval by majority voice vote of his bill naming the representatives to negotiate with the ambassadors. A different bill had been drafted by the ambassadors. The king's differed from theirs by not empowering the representatives to make final decisions but requiring them to submit matters to the Diet, which of course would lead to delays.

Thereupon the marshal of the confederation, Poninski, approached the throne and reminded the king that he, the marshal, alone had the right to call for a majority voice vote; the king and his faction did not have this right. The bishop of Kujawy, Antony Kazimierz Ostrowski, rose and in strong language showed the king what he was exposing the nation to.[39] Many senators expressed similar opinions. The younger Prince Sulkowski, the palatine of Gniezno, whom Stackelberg termed a subterranean creature, directed his courageous oratory against the king and strongly impressed the gathering by saying that his majesty, safe on the throne, risked nothing himself, but was subjecting to danger the life, honor, and property of his countrymen. The motion was made to send deputies to the ministers of the three courts with the request to extend the deadline two days. The king objected even to this motion. Then they went to a voice vote; the majority sided against the king. The ministers of the three courts granted the Diet's request, extending the deadline to May 3, and charged the deputation to transmit to the Diet a protest against the king's bill as having been written without due esteem for the three courts.

The allied ministers spent May 2 confirming their majority in the Chamber of Deputies; by general agreement they spent twenty-four thousand rubles for this purpose. At the same time they intimated to the king's relatives that the first consequences of carrying out his threats naturally would fall on them if they were unable to find the means to dissuade his majesty from his obstinacy, both fatal and useless. Furthermore, the ministers composed a declaration designed to remove the Diet's least inclination to accept the king's bill. The magnates presented this declaration to the king and urged him to yield and not subject them to certain death by his obstinacy. Stanislaw answered that he would reveal his decision to the Senate. But when he made his appearance he began as before to encourage his party by words and gestures to call for passage of his bill, for which he proposed a written ballot. Despite his efforts, the majority voted for the bill proposed by the ambassadors of the three courts.

When he described all these troubles to Panin, Stackelberg complained about his colleagues, particularly the Austrian Baron Rewiczki. According to Stackelberg, Rewiczki was totally unequipped for his task; he was weak, easily influenced, and lazy. His secret was known to two Italians, who used the condition into which the envoy fell after dinner for nefarious purposes. Benoit was an intelligent man who generally acted in concert with Stackelberg, but he had no influence whatever over the Poles.

The king from his perspective described his own troubles and his unhappy situation to his mother surrogate, Mme. Geoffrin.[40] "I swear on my honor that I neither gave nor promised anything to anyone in the Diet who remained loyal to me to the end. One hundred thousand foreigners are cruelly devastating Poland and particularly oppressing those who do not please them. The three ministers lavished large sums on the Diet. The foreigners saw that there are honorable and courageous men in the country for almost half the Diet resisted their gold and their might. But alas, what does all this accomplish when there is no money and no army! The day after the vote on this wretched matter I was told: 'Had you received a majority you might no longer be king and the rest of Poland might have been divided among us.' The king of Prussia bears this in mind constantly.

"Now, despite the fact that the three courts have taken whatever they desired, their troops are still stationed in Poland, eating free at Poland's expense. The Russian minister promises that this will end soon. The Austrian also expresses this hope. The Prussian does not do even this. His sovereign, so it seems, is busy concocting ways to force his allies to consent to his taking even more territory from us. The emperor, it appears, considers himself obligated to do us as much evil as the king of Prussia, and the Russian empress is so occupied by the Turks that she can do nothing to prevent the king of Prussia from harming us. Since May 14th I have been totally dependent on the mercy of the three courts. I am starving; they are arming themselves against everything that is dearest to me. Nonetheless, I must maintain outward calm and play with some sort of dignity the worst of roles, think it could be worse, and attempt to avert the worst from the realm, to save a few kernels which might vegetate until more suitable weather."

NEGOTIATIONS WITH THE DELEGATION OF THE DIET

On May 8 the representatives were named to negotiate with the ministers of the three courts. The king appointed all the senators who were present and the marshals designated sixty men of the gentry, for a total of one hundred men. When everything seemed settled, an obstacle emerged at the outset of the negotiations. This time the Poles were not the problem; on the contrary, they now were hastening the matter.

Rewiczki had received no instructions from his court, and the most monstrous rumors were circulating about the cause of this delay. Finally his papers arrived, and negotiations began on May 22. A day later Stackelberg complained again about Rewiczki: "He is a good man and my friend. In the past he has followed my lead absolutely. But now he is supporting the king's party and also from all appearances inclining his government in that direction. I do not suspect that he has been bribed, for I consider him an honest man. But it seems to me that the king has promised to follow the ideas of the empress-queen regarding religion, and that Rewiczki has become involved in the plan by means of the papal nuncio. They are resolved that dissidents will never participate in legislation." Stackelberg supposed that Rewiczki was supporting the king's faction out of personal conviction and inclining his court to this view, but in fact Rewiczki was acting on Vienna's instructions, which ordered him to attempt to strengthen the king's power and possibly limit the liberum veto so that Poland might play the role of a buffer state (*puissance intermédiaire*) between Russia, Prussia, and Austria.

Stackelberg soon was driven to complain about both his colleagues. Rewiczki announced that the boundaries of Prussia's share as presented by Benoit were clearly out of line with the convention of the three courts; therefore he could not guarantee that his court would continue to support the initial plan. On Rewiczki's map the river Podorze—a name no one recognized—seemed to be the boundary, and the Austrians assumed that what really was meant was the river Sbrucz.[41] Rewiczki maintained that he could not continue the negotiations because of the Prussian map and because he had not yet received from Vienna the originals of his commission as plenipotentiary, only copies, and a draftsman had not arrived with an accurate map. Stackelberg rushed to Benoit; could he not persuade his king to use the general terms of the convention in the treaty on partition; clarifications could be made on the spot through commissioners whereas the king's explication was holding up the entire procedure.

Benoit answered that Frederick's decision was immutable and would permit no changes to be made to the map that Benoit had been sent. Furthermore, if the Austrians took the Sbrucz as their border the king of Prussia would be dissatisfied with his present share. So the affair dragged on and the Poles, agreeable to everything, lost their patience in the face of utter ruin. The Prussians forced them to deliver enough foodstuffs and forage for thirty thousand men when they had only five thousand. Stackelberg wrote to Prince Vladimir Sergeevich Dolgoruky[42] in Berlin, asking him to propose to the Prussian ministry that Russian [sic] forces pay for everything, and that in the future the three courts arrange to purchase their supplies and forage as long as the Poles conformed to their wishes. Dolgoruky answered that Frederick would comply with the desires of the two imperial courts on this account and that Benoit would receive orders to that effect.

After Rewiczki received instructions from his court to pay for everything all that remained was for the three courts to agree to act identically. But Benoit constantly avoided this, although in Stackelberg's words at first he was offended by the barbarity of the Prussian officers in Poland. Stackelberg was convinced that if arrangements were not made for Austria and Prussia to pay for everything they consumed in Poland no power on earth could force them to leave the country. Such was the spirit of economy reigning in Vienna and Berlin.

In that regard Panin sent a directive to Stackelberg. "Whenever the Prussian minister proposes to use force and it seems to you that other means remain open, keep his urges under control and agree with him only as a last resort. Tell him everything the Prussian soldiers do that seems excessive and flagrant, but speak as friend with friend, minister with minister, without giving the appearance that your court is meddling. Show him that the short-term expense of feeding his troops in a foreign land is nothing compared to the necessity of extricating Europe from the crisis it is in. But you can set yourself against Rewiczki's indifference toward domestic affairs more directly. If he drags his feet because of the religious question, you may remind him that from the time negotiations began with his court everything wanted for the dissidents was communicated to it. Thereafter not only was nothing more demanded, but you even chose not to demand abolition of the criminal law against apostasy or a mixed court, which obviously can exist no longer in its previous form because of the union of Mogilev with Russia's possessions. It can be changed somewhat by the consent of both sides. Since Catholicism retains a glitter and perfection in Poland which it does not have in Germany, nothing will constrain Vienna, from the standpoint of either conscience or advantage."

As to the provisioning of troops, the three ministers agreed at length that all would purchase beginning on July 1. But until then the Prussian and Austrian generals insisted that arrears be paid without fail. During the levying of arrears the Austrian general so exceeded the Prussian in his demands that the Poles called the Russians angels, the Prussians copies of humans, and the Austrians devils.

Not until mid-July, upon urgings from Petersburg, did Berlin and Vienna agree to insert their own terms of the convention into their treaties with Poland regarding the partition, saying nothing about which rivers and streams would, in Stackelberg's words, perhaps carry them directly to Warsaw, for when Vienna insisted upon a particular boundary river Berlin said the Austrians were going too far and it would go farther too.

When negotiations finally opened in August between the Diet's representatives, the so-called delegation, and Stackelberg, the delegation handed him a brief written note (remarque). "Some time ago your excellency received a reply from the king to the empress's claims regarding Poland. The Petersburg convention among the three powers, presumably deciding our fate without our participation, does not allow the necessary attention to be paid our reply. The sole cause of this conduct is the weakness of the king and the Commonwealth, which forces us to bow before the fate prepared for us. Nevertheless this delegation cannot imagine that neighboring and allied states have paid no attention to the rights of the king and the Commonwealth, based on the most sacred laws, both divine and human. Poland particularly had hopes for the empress of all the Russias, who like her predecessors has taken a special interest in the prosperity of Poland and affirmed that she would never seize, nor allow anyone else to seize, territory belonging to the Commonwealth. Although now she is acting altogether differently, we continue to believe that she will receive our petitions, particularly since the Commonwealth has entertained not the slightest intention of violating the ancient friendship and alliance with Russia."

Stackelberg answered: "Poland had a right to base its hopes on her imperial majesty. These hopes have been justified by the most sincere and unselfish concern the empress has shown Poland since she mounted the throne. But what was the consequence of her friendship, so durable and bought with such great sacrifices? With regret I turn the delegation's attention to the terrible picture of the disorders and devastations of its fatherland. What might have become of Poland? Would it have been sacrificed to greed, private interest, and ambition papered over with the apparition of liberty, which Poles assumed was endangered by the guarantee brought by Russia for the preservation of that very liberty? What might have become of Poland had Russia, feeling justifiable revenge, deserted it in its convulsions, which might have led inevitably to death?

"In spite of an excessively bloody war with the Turks which Poland instigated, Russia has not ceased to prevent the total dismemberment of the Commonwealth, to struggle for years against the ingratitude and combined efforts of those who deliberately stirred up the country in order to dominate and oppress it. Half of Poland has been warring on the empress, and the government has approved through its inactivity. The voices of well-intentioned citizens have been powerless, as have the statements of Russia's ambassadors. During a terrible clash of interests among powers people are not won over by the metaphysics of a multitude of proofs, which inevitably serve to embellish secret arrangements. They judge by deeds not words. The events I refer to speak for themselves and there is nothing I can offer in rejoinder, as though the Commonwealth had no intention of violating its former friendship and alliance with Russia. It is enough that the empress sincerely desires their renewal. But the incontestable rights to the lands in question, rights presented in my government's declaration, will brook no opposition. I am not talking at this point about Russia's right to increase its just demands or require compensation for the awful war Poland instigated against Russia."

While this answer was being read to the delegation Ostrowski, the bishop of Kujawy, hotly announced that the reading must stop. It was necessary first to inquire of the Russian ambassador which people he blamed for the ruin of Poland. "Every true citizen should be acquitted in the eyes of the fatherland," said Ostrowski. "Woe to those who were the tools of its distress. It is our responsibility to bend every effort to uncover their names. If I am guilty, punish me first for the crime shameful for him who had to commit it and even more shameful for the nation if it forgets to avenge itself therefor. If I am guilty, let me be the first to be thrown into the Vistula."

Ostrowski's vehemence quickly spread to the entire assembly, and everyone began to lay claim to his love for the fatherland, his jealousy for freedom, and his true gratitude to the Russian court for the concern and protection which it had shown Poland at all times. Extravagant criticisms were expressed concerning those who stood in the way of Russia's good intentions, and loud glorification of Great Catherine was heard.

Prince Anton Sulkowski, deputy from Lomza, supported by Prince Marcin Lubomirski, delegate from Sandomierz, and then by the entire gentry, proposed a note to Baron Stackelberg in the name of the entire assembly asking him to name those who were guilty. The assembly approved, the note was presented, and Stackelberg answered: "The greater part of the members of your eminent delegation must have been struck by the obvious equity of the policies of the empress, my sovereign. I fully sympathize with the ardor with which the delegation wants to uncover the perpetrators of the evils referred to. But I, just as the other two ministers, have instructions not be become involved in any other business until the main task is resolved for which the Diet was convened. As soon as the three treaties are signed I will not oppose an investigation of the behavior of those who broke the sacred bonds uniting Russia with Poland and who rejected the empress's every proposal for reconciliation."

The unrest kindled by Ostrowski's speech severely frightened the elder Czartoryski, the Lithuanian chancellor.[43] He paled when the bishop cried "If I am guilty, let me be thrown into the Vistula." It was clear to Czartoryski that he would undergo this bathing first. The "family" had to endure the humiliation, hearing out the reproaches and threats in silence. Voices were heard to mutter that if people with evil designs on the life of the king had their heads and hands chopped off, it was unjust to spare the murderers of the country.

Stackelberg boasted to Panin that his answer to the delegation's note struck fear into Russia's enemies without interrupting the negotiations. The next day he had an appointment with the king, whom he found in great confusion. Stackelberg told him that he must use the circumstances to begin to be king, not just the nephew of one. The king, however, ended the conversation with a plea to save his relatives. Stackelberg answered that this was not necessarily in his power, but he would try at least not to compromise him, the king, if he was willing to safeguard the proceedings from further intrigue.

THE DISSIDENTS
There still remained the complex question of the dissidents. The dissidents handed Stackelberg a petition for the empress. "Since the current Diet is supposed to decide and confirm henceforward and forever the fate of the dissidents in Poland, we venture to implore the powerful protection of your imperial majesty. Our opponents, driven by fanaticism and politics, now are striving harder than ever to deal us a mortal blow and deprive the non-Roman Catholic gentry, who are closely aligned with your majesty's interests, of all rights and advantages of inheritance, which alone give the gentry its character and serve as the sole means for their survival in the Commonwealth. The certitude of your imperial majesty's protection and the solemn guaranty which you vouchsafed to grant the treaty of 1768 provided us with the resolution and the capability to endure the impoverishment and persecution which have descended on us during the disturbances. We sacrificed our every possession, and many of us our lives, without making the slightest move that might have aroused suspicion of ingratitude toward our most august benefactress.

"In light of the foregoing, it would never occur to us to suggest that the empress, whose generosity, charity, and wisdom are the source of wonder for all Europe, might desire to abandon this part of the Polish gentry, which holds no other means for fighting for the justice of its cause save the lofty protection of your imperial majesty. But now there are those who wish to strip this portion of the gentry, hated solely because it hastened to the shelter of your imperial majesty, of its right to participate in legislation forever. This is the only right that can guarantee us freedom of worship and all other advantages accruing to a well-born citizen."

Conveying this entreaty to Panin, Stackelberg wrote: "I do not see the slightest ray of hope for attaining the right for dissidents to become deputies in the Diet, and I dare say in advance that this point will prove impossible to win. Besides the fanaticism of the nation, the participation in this matter of the Viennese court, whose view of the issue is well known, promises nothing of comfort for the dissidents. The papal nuncio, although a friend of humanity and peace, will not keep quiet. His position, his character, and the nature of his ambassadorship force him to speak; it is enough for him to give the word and the whole country once more will be engulfed in flames."

Then the delegation complained to Stackelberg that agents of the bishop of Perejaslaw were persecuting Uniats, hiding behind the presence of Russian troops on Polish territory; they were taking away Uniat churches, and so forth.[44]

Panin, from whom Stackelberg had sought instructions, wrote him: "According to the constitution of 1768, the churches taken from the dissidents had to be returned to them. If some have been returned, their number is few in comparison with those still in the hands of the Catholics and Uniats. Under the present circumstances it is best for us and the delegation to quench this issue, which can only raise fanaticism anew among people who already have caused so much trouble. We cannot agree to abolishing what was done to implement a treaty concluded with us; we cannot agree for the people we protected so diligently to be sacrificed to their former persecutors. Field Marshal Rumianstev writes that all complaints about the Greeks (that is, the Russian Orthodox) are exaggerated. If we believe every complaint of our people as easily, we will present reports that are just as important and numerous. What has been done to return churches to the Orthodox must remain in effect, and to preserve order and tranquility a joint commission must be appointed.

"As concerns the dissidents generally, it is too bad that you are losing hope of retaining their right to participate in the Diet, especially because there is no place to retreat to on this point. The empress's instructions, which I will repeat for you, are precise: use the assistance of your colleagues; bend every effort to combat the nation's resistance, and do not allow any difficulty to hold you up. You may make a single concession, namely to a limitation of the number of dissidents elected to the Diet and to silence about the necessity of choosing them. It will turn out that their right will not be real, or will be little realized, but at least it will be preserved. If even this is impossible to obtain, explain that you simply do not want to hear about the matter of the dissidents, and that you have been forbidden to participate in anything that concerns them. The exclusion of the dissidents from lawmaking, proclaimed at a Diet under the auspices of the three courts, would be a blow more fatal for them than all the former constitutions which gradually stripped them of their rights. Her imperial majesty, having abandoned out of love for peace her demands for places for them in the Senate and ministry, will not betray justice and her glory by signing their destruction and totally abandoning them."

THE RIGHTS OF THE KING

Panin required Stackelberg to solicit the help of his fellow ambassadors on the matter of the dissidents. Stackelberg wrote him that as soon as negotiations were completed about the lands to be ceded and the ministers moved to domestic questions, the concert among the three allied courts would be broken. Benoit continued to support Stackelberg, but Baron Rewiczki suddenly changed his language and ignored the arrangements the three courts had introduced to pacify Poland. He announced pointblank that the diminution of royal power shocked his court. It is easy to understand how much this encouraged the king and his party. The king abjured the right to name persons directly to senatorial and ministerial posts, consenting to choose from among three candidates for each position recommended by the Permanent Council.[45] For this concession he demanded the right to appoint all officers of the general staff and guards and the commandant of the guards regiments; in short, he demanded the right to head the armed forces.

Stackelberg could hardly believe that Stanislaw Augustus was unaware of the degree he was strengthening the determination to decrease his power by revealing his views on government so clearly in his demands and especially by disclosing the plan to imitate the king of Sweden at the first convenient opportunity. Members of "our party," as Stackelberg termed them, asked him to found a new guards regiment for the king but not to leave the old one under his command, with which he might undertake a revolution at some future time. Stackelberg succeeded in persuading his colleagues to propose the following terms to the king: were he not to insist on appointing officers to the posts on the general staff, but promote them in order of seniority, and were he to renounce command of the guards of the Commonwealth, a personal guard would be organized for his complete disposal, its cost underwritten by the Commonwealth. Should the king renounce his right to make appointments to judicial and revenue posts, he would be permitted to appoint bishops, senators, ministers of the realm, and foreign ambassadors from among three candidates proposed by the Permanent Council. The Permanent Council would choose the candidates by secret ballot, and the members of the Permanent Council themselves were to be chosen in the same manner by the Diet. Finally, the king must refrain from distributing estates.

After negotiations with the king these terms were stated as follows: he retained the right to appoint to all church and civil posts except bishops, governors, castellans, ministers, and military and finance commissioners. He was to choose these appointees from three candidates per post, selected earlier by the Permanent Council by secret ballot. In the military the king would appoint officers in the Polish militia and in the four infantry militia units bearing his name. In the remainder of the military, officers were to be appointed by seniority. The king lost the right to distribute crown lands, the profits from which were to be employed in financing the realm. The Diet was to appoint members of the Permanent Council by secret ballot. But now, in the first instance, the king had to have the consent of the ministers of the three allied courts before naming senators, ministers, and members of the gentry who had to serve on the Permanent Council. The four guards regiments were placed under the control of the state, as they had been under Augustus III, with the sole distinction that whereas in the past the chief military commanders held complete authority they now shared it with the military commission. Both the chief military commanders and the commission were subordinated to the Permanent Council. The king would receive an annual sum for maintaining a two thousand-man military command, which he might deploy as he wished.

These terms were worked out jointly by the king and Stackelberg. Stanislaw Augustus had asked that the Austrian and Prussian ministers not participate, to which they willingly agreed in order to avoid such unpleasant work. When it was finished the king sent Stackelberg a letter: "You were an instrument in the awful ceremony in which I was innocently sacrificed. You saw the bitterness of my suffering. Undoubtedly you felt compassion and must want to bring me medication and relief. But this cannot be if the empress does not renew her friendship for me. I implore your assistance. I have been miserable for so long that she must at last be touched. This final blow pierced my heart, because it violates my dignity and because she was the one who directed it—she, before whom my heart is in no wise guilty. But in the end, even had she thought me guilty, I have atoned for this pernicious assumption, I think, dearly enough."

Frederick the Great
King of Prussia

After seeing the king's letter Catherine penned the following note to Panin. "As concerns the king and his brother, I ask you to think of something we can do for them. First of all, I will willingly restore, and persuade the two other courts to restore, whatever the king had before the partition. It seems to me that Count Chernyshev had instructions to work out an account for this; I will prod him."

FREDERICK'S VIEW OF RUSSIAN OPTIONS

Events in Warsaw, it stands to reason, were bound to generate shifts in relations among the powers participating in the partition. What was happening on the Danube continued to be intertwined thoroughly with developments in Poland. Russia continued to demand assistance from its allies in gaining the earliest possible peace with the Porte.

On February 9 (New Style) Frederick II wrote Solms: "The news about the peace talks in Bucharest disturbs me greatly. I am afraid that the congress has dissolved already. The obstinacy of the Ottoman plenipotentiary must be ascribed to French intrigues. In the meantime I will fulfill as best I can the instructions of Count Panin. Although I am not in immediate correspondence with the emperor, Panin can rest assured that I will communicate to his majesty the admonition to give Thugut specific instructions to work with greater ardor at the Porte for the cause of peace. My only fear–and not without cause–is that this remedy will come too late, after the collapse of the congress. If this happens, remember the project offered by Vienna that I revealed to you when I was in Silesia last year.[46] Vienna seriously seeks to acquire Turkish lands next to Hungary and for this purpose to enter into alliance with Russia against the Turks. If negotiations break off, you can be sure that Vienna will make every effort to carry out this project, which is close to the emperor's heart. Meanwhile the failure of the congress will echo loudly in our negotiations in Poland, creating much greater difficulties than if peace were at hand. I know of no other means for overcoming these difficulties than to have forced the Poles to accept all our demands."

Frederick intended that this letter be shown to the Russian government. But his tone was different when speaking with van Swieten for communication to Vienna. The conversation took place February 20 (New Style). "The news from Constantinople," began the king, "does not hold out hope for peace. The Turks absolutely refuse to yield two fortresses in the Crimea (Kerch and Yenikale), maintaining that the surrender of these fortresses will threaten the security of Constantinople. They prefer to continue the war, even though it might lead to the destruction of their capital and the dissolution of the empire, because disaster is inevitable in any event in another thirty years. On the other hand, the Russians declared that without cession of those two fortresses in the Crimea the peninsula is not worth talking about. I am expecting to hear at any time that the Bucharest congress has broken down. The Turks themselves expect it and are preparing for it, assembling as many troops as they can. This development displeases me greatly, because I see no way to help in the matter."

Van Swieten replied: "Can it not be hoped that Petersburg, which must want a shortened war, will reduce its demands in light of the Porte's decision to risk everything rather than be subjugated to Russia?"

The king demurred. "No, the Russians are enraptured by their good fortune. Truly, it is as difficult to handle good fortune as it is bad. Enraptured by successes, they placed the most onerous conditions on the Porte. They realize now that the most opportune time has passed but they do not want to retreat, considering that to be degrading. They will be obliged to continue the war because they have requested too much. There will be at least two more campaigns which, in my opinion, result in no particular advantage for them. They have occupied everything on the near side of the Danube and can do nothing more there. It would be exceedingly dangerous to take troops across the river since it would be overly difficult to sustain the required communications. They would have to use the greater part of their army for that purpose, and the remainder, the element which would cross the Danube, would be incapable of operating effectively because of its small size. Raids alone, even if they reached to Adrianople and farther, would not decide anything.

"By the way, in spite of the good harmony which now exists between your court and Petersburg, I am not sure you would look with favor upon a Russian advance beyond the Danube. At the very least they would have to inform you of it beforehand. Another project has been communicated to me from Petersburg which I strongly advised against. It was to devastate Moldavia and Wallachia, to burn everything, after evacuating the inhabitants, in order to reduce those provinces to a veritable wilderness, and withdraw their troops to the Polish border beyond the Dniester, leaving twenty or thirty thousand in Tataria. This plan is totally inhumane and absolutely disgusting. At the same time it might prove dangerous since the Turks, in spite of the devastation, have the capability of approaching close to Poland, where they might raise a great revolt; we must hold them farther off for the success of our plans. I see one way to facilitate the matter: that is, for Russia to request your assistance against the Turks in exchange for your annexation of Bosnia and Serbia. In this case the war would not drag on and you would not be left without profit."

Van Swieten promised to transmit this proposal to his court and wrote Kaunitz that it undoubtedly shielded the most expansive designs by the king of Prussia, namely the farthest possible extension of his territory. Van Swieten offered the conjecture that Frederick desired to interfere in Russia's war with Sweden and acquire Swedish Pomerania. To keep Austria from disturbing his plans he hoped to occupy it in Turkey, where it might also make acquisitions.

But the Austrian envoy did not recognize another point of view: more than anything else, Frederick wanted to acquire Dantzig and Thorn. To gain the consent of Russia and Austria, he was pointing them toward acquisitions in Turkey conditioned on their prior concession of the entire Vistula to him. Earlier he had preferred that Austria not acquire lands from Turkey because above all he wanted concerted action by the three powers in Poland. Now that this combined move was completed to his satisfaction he thought about one thing only: how to acquire Dantzig and Thorn, without which the Polish initiative would seem to him incomplete.

To prevent Austria from becoming afraid of France should it begin to expand at Turkey's expense, Frederick told van Swieten: "The French may rage, but they have no strength; for this reason they have exchanged their lion's skin for that of a fox. They are doing all they can to drive us apart. You may not be aware that they proposed to Petersburg that France mediate peace with the Turks in exchange for Russia's consent to free France's hands to maneuver in Constantinople. But their proposal failed; I take credit for that. So there is nothing to fear from them. They are in no condition to wage war. It is true that they have hopes for Spanish subsidies, but this source cannot provide enough. A war waged on someone else's pocketbook, on alms, can be neither energetic nor protracted. Besides, I know for a fact that the king hates the very word war. And the minister who suggests it to him undoubtedly will lose his post. As you know, in France, as in several other countries, ministers love their positions more than they love the state."

But Vienna refused to consider joint policy with Russia against Turkey. It hesitated to look for acquisitions with weapons in hand since it was uncertain which acquisitions the king of Prussia wanted to make gratis. Frederick II had excellent students in Vienna who, following in the footsteps of the master, likewise intended to acquire something from Turkey, gratis. After receiving a negative answer to his proposal, Frederick tried another tack. "Still," he said to van Swieten, "one must expect the breakup of the Bucharest conference any day now, and if the war continues one must decide what to do. Russia is saying that should there be no peace, it no longer will hold to the proposed terms, especially on the return of Moldavia and Wallachia."

"You know, my lord," answered van Swieten, "what we would have been obliged to do had Russia intended to keep Moldavia and Wallachia, and therefore you can conclude what we will be forced to do if those circumstances are repeated."

Frederick understood by this that Austria did not wish to assume an open stance against Turkey out of fear of France. "What is there to fear from the French?" he asked van Swieten.

"We fear," he answered, "the inevitable loss of our possessions on the Rhine, in Italy, and in the Netherlands, which we would not be able to defend."

"Do you not suppose I would be your ally in this general war?" asked Frederick.

"Your majesty will have enough to keep yourself busy with your own possessions," replied van Swieten.

"But why do you believe in the possibility of this general alliance against us?" persisted the king.

"We do not have to suppose this possibility," answered van Swieten, "thanks to the general unrest and envy produced throughout Europe by our treaties of partition and alliance. Fear has given birth to suspicion and increased anxiety. If they see that our alliance is limited to the partition of Poland, which no longer can be prevented, the uneasiness will be cut short and suspicions and fears will dissipate. Thenceforward it will be possible to hope for the preservation of the general peace. But should they see in our alliance with Russia against the Turks the existence of precisely those dangerous consequences which they fear, there is no doubt that all Europe will unite against the three courts and the broad intentions which they justly suspect the three powers have."

"This danger will pass," answered the king, "if we ally ourselves even closer. This is why I would like a tripartite alliance to be signed. Then we will be the masters of peace and war and possess the true means for realizing the plan of the Abbé Saint-Pierre" (for lasting peace).[47]

That Frederick desired war with no one, least of all Sweden, is apparent from a letter he wrote to Solms on April 24. "If I expressed suspicions to you about Durand's intrigues and his improper relations at the Russian court, I did so on the basis of my letters from Paris. The French boast that he is performing essential services for his court. Rumors are widespread in Versailles about dissatisfaction between Russia's empress and the grand duke, a decision to remove Panin, and a coming revolution in Russia. As concerns your news that Durand informed his court about the fortifications of Kronstadt and the poor condition of the Russian navy, France may well use this news to fan the fires of youth in my nephew, the Swedish king. It might use these tales to convince Gustavus III that present circumstances are most propitious for a break with Russia. Since I would be very distressed if my relatives caused new difficulties for my ally, I have tried to devise some means of forestalling this eventuality; here is what occurred to me.

"Having assumed that a break with Sweden is inevitable and that Sweden actually will attack Russia, the latter can calculate that I will fulfill to the letter my obligations as an ally. But is there perhaps a way to avert the storm? The only reasonable means that France could use to force Sweden's king to make the break is the suggestion that Russia unquestionably is scheming some sort of blow to restore the previous form of government in Sweden; it would be much more advantageous to him to anticipate this and attack Russia during the Turkish war without waiting for peace when Russia, its hands free, could turn its full force against him. This argument seems to me very natural and liable to make an impression on Gustavus. In order to compel France to remain silent and forestall the consequences of its inevitable suggestions, I have no choice but to explain everything to the Swedish king amicably, either directly or indirectly."

Russia informed Frederick that if the Bucharest congress collapsed its troops would cross the Danube. Frederick commented on this, writing to Solms on May 1: "I will not hide from you my impression that transporting the entire army of Field Marshal Rumiantsev across the Danube would be particularly dangerous and difficult. The Russian army would be subjected to a thousand hazards there, not to mention the difficulties of obtaining food and ammunition. When you realize how wide the river is, you perceive the difficulty the army will face should it experience the least setback and be forced to retreat along the river. A siege of Ochakov, it seems to me, might have been more natural and less dangerous. This year's campaign will require much more prudence and care than the previous ones."

When he received confirmation of the collapse of the Bucharest congress, Frederick wrote: "It is really sad that the Bucharest negotiations again have come to naught. I have grounds for assuming that had Vienna beem more resolute in its counsel to the Porte the talks surely would have been more successful. As far as I can conclude from reports, Vienna still retains too much of its former awe of France; it lacked the courage to make stronger representations in Constantinople." But Frederick contradicted himself. Only one thing was true: either Austria did not want to insist on peace because of its relations with France, or by other calculations it desired to use the continuation of the war for its own ends. So in a dispatch on May 25 Frederick returned to the latter explanation: "Kaunitz wanted to raise every conceivable obstruction in order to force Russia to need Vienna's assistance and then sell this assistance at the highest price."

In August Count Ivan Chernyshev had a long talk with Frederick II in Potsdam. Frederick discussed his relationships with the various powers. He had nothing kind to say about the English. He reproached them for concluding the recent peace with France secretly without resolving the question of French occupation of Prussian lands, thereby forcing him to reconquer them militarily.[48] But far more insulting had been the English proposals to Kaunitz of an alliance and aid to wrest Silesia from Prussia and to cool Peter III's admiration for Frederick. "At present," said the king, "I have no need of an alliance with England. I am satisfied with the Russian alliance and have need of no one else. Russia is in a different situation; it may well have reasons for agreeing or making an alliance with England. In that case, by way of Russia I would be in some sort of liaison with England. At my second meeting with the emperor Kaunitz was also present. He has the same opinion of the English as I: he considers them to be less than loyal allies, and as an example he cited their behavior toward the Austrians after the peace of Aix-la-Chapelle."[49]

Next Frederick began to speak about his friendly relations with Empress Catherine and Russia. As though ashamed of his attempt to expand his borders at Poland's expense, he said through his teeth: "It is generally accepted that when they give you a river it means the upper reaches; the empress decided not to award it to me, and I agreed." He then continued with a smile. "The Austrians declared that they always intended to follow to the letter the stipulations of the convention about the partition. But afterwards it became clear that boundaries could not be described on paper exactly as they appear on site, which is why they want to start with that. I know their greed. They want to seize more, which is why I am sending someone to watch them. If they do take a bit more, naturally I too will redefine my borders as the geography permits."

Chernyshev interjected: "If her imperial majesty decides that the three powers must be held to the agreement expressed in the convention, it will not be to keep from giving Prussia more but to show the world the firmness of the three powers' intentions. For this reason it is not possible to expand your borders under the pretext that the other fellow has seized too much, else the Polish question reach the point that it can never be settled amicably."

Frederick preferred not to continue this conversation. He stated that the issue in Poland was simply to win consent to acquire the territory in question; it did not involve entanglements in explosive domestic questions. Shifting the conversation to the issue of war and peace with the Turks, he stated: "Peace is absolutely necessary. The campaign must be considered over, and not particularly successful. Should the desired peace not be achieved this year, you must spare no expense and use every means to force it on the Turks in the next campaign.

"It is impossible to foresee all the complications that can follow in Europe. As for the Swedes, I am certain that they will attempt nothing, especially this year. Even if they undertook something, the 25,000 Russian soldiers stationed in Finland and near Petersburg naturally will be sufficient, particularly if the Swedes simultaneously must to do business with the Danes. I have thought quite a bit about what the Swedes might be able to do to you. They have no more than 45,000 soldiers, and of these must leave some at home and in garrisons. Let us say that five thousand are enough for this. Another ten thousand will have to be set against Norway. Then there will remain against you only twenty thousand [sic]. Be assured that should you fail completely against the Turks, France will try to incite the Swedes against you. More than anyone else, France's creature Count Scheffer is encouraging and abetting the king's hatred for you. Scheffer planted the idea in the king from his youth that he can achieve fame in the world only by unlimited attachment to the French system and close alliance with France. I saw them both here. My nephew, the king, is no fool, but everything bad and French has so captivated him that he is as flighty as a young Frenchman.

"It is preferable for you to become reconciled with the Turks without outside assistance. But should this prove impossible, you must go running to the Austrians. They desire desperately to interfere in this war, but they want you to ask them repeatedly. Their appetite is unquenchable; they want to repossess Belgrade and the other losses from the last war. I know the Austrian court well and will describe it to you briefly. The emperor is a young man. He is impatient to become famous, but he is honest and firm. His mother is a player of farces like no other on earth. Kaunitz is not only a double-and triple-dealer, but even a quadruple-dealer.

"I have often thought as to how you might deal the most grievous blow to the Turks, but unfortunately I do not know the terrain and therefore cannot speak without erring. Nevertheless it seems to me that it would avail you, leaving the largest part of the army north of the Danube near Zhurzhev or higher, to proceed with the rest of the army along the right bank of the river directly toward Varna. Provisions might be brought along the river and by sea. This movement would force the enemy either to leave the mountains, to come out of the crevices and give battle, or to run to the defense of Adrianople. It is a great pity that Silistra has not been taken: then you would stand with a foot firmly planted beyond the Danube." Chernyshev noted that Silistra could be taken only by assault, which would involve considerable bloodshed. "You use too little artillery," said the king. "You need a hundred cannon and thirty to forty mortars since the Turkish defenses consist of firm, high walls. But you might have taken Ochakov on the present campaign." Chernyshev noted that it was difficult to transport artillery there.

On October 5 Frederick wrote about the dangers of crossing the Danube a second time. "If the Turks were to cross the Danube first and Count Rumiantsev defeat them, he might be able to pursue them across the river; the pursuit of a defeated and therefore dispirited army always goes successfully. But should the Turks remain in their camp the field marshal will find himself playing for high stakes. Having crossed the Danube to attack them, he will be risking everything to gain everything. I am not going to say that such a brave blow cannot succeed. Military fortune, which to this time has smiled on the Russians, might smile on them again, but the destiny of war is fickle and its former affections do not vouch for the future. Failures are as possible as successes. And I cannot hide from you that in Russia's place I would not begin to second-guess fate so much."

AUSTRIAN PERSPECTIVES

In Petersburg Solms gave Panin the dispatch from Goltz, the Prussian envoy in Paris, dated November 4. The dispatch said that the French were concluding, from letters from Petersburg, that Panin did not enjoy the full grace of his sovereign, having to divide it with Prince Orlov and Count Chernyshev, who were quite close to each other. The letters added that these magnates did not seem to be such enemies of France as Count Panin, that the French and Spanish ministers often were seen with them, and were giving their courts hopes concerning the positive inclinations of Orlov and Chernyshev toward France. The Duke d'Aiguillon, speaking with Goltz about some awards Panin had received, asked him several times: "Do you think that he really will retain the management of foreign affairs and that the favors shown him do not presage a hasty removal from affairs?"

Goltz was informed that Durand had been instructed to inquire in Petersburg whether Russia would agree to negotiate peace with the Porte using France as an intermediary. If so, France would try to obtain from the Turks concession of the two Crimean harbors on the Black Sea.

Petersburg immediately informed Vienna about the French proposals, thinking that this would induce Austria to promote Russia's conclusion of peace with the Porte. On February 12 the Austrian ambassador to Russia, Prince Lobkowitz, was handed a paper entitled "Contents of the Conversation of Count Panin with Prince Lobkowitz." The paper included the following: "France's effort to create entanglements in Europe's political affairs with the single goal of preventing the agreement of the three courts concerning Poland, or as a last resort, to prevent the execution of this agreement, is well known to Vienna. Here in Petersburg Durand does not cease pressing the advantages Russia would reap from a close alliance with his court. Under such an alliance Russia would conduct its affairs from an unresolved position; Durand is suggesting directly and openly an alliance among Russia, France, and Sweden. This suggestion obviously is offered to cool Russia, to weaken its activity in fulfilling the designated agreement. Although the French have no real hope of dissuading Russia, they nonetheless like to point out the great advantages it might receive from new relationships. There is not a court where France has not been intriguing against the partition of Poland. Even the British ministry is seduced to such an extent that it supports in Constantinople all French intrigues against peace because of the Black Sea trade. It is well known that the Russian court has abandoned Moldavia and Wallachia out of respect for Vienna; no other considerations could have persuaded it to make this sacrifice. Taking this into account, it would have been an act consonant with justice and Austria's love of peace for it to instruct its ambassador in Constantinople to open the Porte's eyes to the double intrigues of France, which is working to benefit Sweden simultaneously in Petersburg and in Constantinople, and to announce to the Porte that if it allowed itself to be persuaded by someone else's views to continue the military disasters Austria not only would abandon it to its military fate but would take Russia's side in the event of a Swedish diversion in order to uphold the European balance, as previously it had taken the side of the Porte."

Kaunitz attempted to convince Prince Golitsyn that he had ordered the Austrian envoy to support Russian interests in Constantinople with candor and energy. He added that Austria anticipated receiving some sort of favor from Russia. "We would have been very grateful," he continued, "had Russia not given cause for a break with Sweden, if it had limited itself to removing features displeasing to it in Sweden's new form of government through peaceful negotiations." Kaunitz asked Golitsyn to write about this more frequently to Count Panin.

Golitsyn answered that obviously Russia hardly would begin a new war thoughtlessly, but the fact was that France by its intrigues had encouraged the Swedish king to enter into whatsoever agreement it could. How could Russia view without alarm the existence in Sweden of a form of government contrary to its guaranty and its interests?

Kaunitz seemed somewhat discomfited by these words and said: "What has Russia to fear if the Swedish king is gifted with talent and courage? No matter how talented or courageous he is, he will never be able to compare with you in status: Russia infinitely surpasses him thanks to its resources. Besides, it has Denmark at its disposal, it has the king of Prussia as an ally, and solid friendship with Austria."

Golitsyn thereupon noted that the policies of governments are not guided by the present but by future dilemmas and distant dangers. He maintained that Sweden's transformation from aristocratic government to unlimited monarchy clearly would create a concentration of power that would give Sweden great abilities. It would be far more dangerous for Russia should the unlimited power of the Swedish king become a tool in France's hands for constantly interfering in Russia's affairs.

Kaunitz did not answer this directly, merely enlarging upon how desirable it is to avoid a war which might have far-reaching consequences. He made further assurances of the Austrian envoy's sincerity and zeal in support of Russia's interests in Constantinople. Indeed, he was prepared to instruct Thugut to incline the Porte to a reconciliation, but Emperor Joseph was of another opinion, convinced that Austria would not render service to the Porte thereby. If Austria simply did nothing to prevent peace, Russia would have no right to complain. France likewise would be friendlier were Austria not to exert itself too eagerly for peace, for France feared that a Russia freed from the Turkish war would turn on Sweden. Finally, the longer Russia remained at war and matters remained undecided, and as long as the king of Prussia paid annual subsidies, Russia and Prussia would remain pliant on the Polish question. Kaunitz was obliged to insist on winning peace in his dispatches to Thugut, which he could show Golitsyn, but in secret dispatches he informed him that these admonitions for peace were not being taken seriously in Vienna. It was implied that such strong insistence on peace from Austria could be beneficial only to the Porte, for its rejection of Russia's demands would produce the strongest impression in Petersburg, which would conclude that Austria's most convincing arguments had availed nothing.

When Golitsyn informed Kaunitz of the collapse of the Bucharest congress, the Austrian chancellor said calmly: "From this truly regrettable event one can see what necessity and importance the Turks place on the two Crimean fortresses, Kerch and Yenikale, which the Russians have demanded."

"In my opinion," retorted Golitsyn, "such obstinacy by the Turks merely can add to the unremitting intrigues of those ill-disposed toward Russia. The Turks will acquire no advantage by their obstinacy. I am absolutely amazed that the Porte, disregarding the new proposals given it by Count Thugut, broke off the congress. It is obvious from this how little it values Vienna's proposals." Kaunitz was silent for a moment and then began to lead the conversation to another subject.

After receiving detailed information from Panin about the breakdown of the congress Golitsyn once more visited Kaunitz to communicate it to him. After hearing an exposition of the matter, Kaunitz assumed a serious expression that indicated neither approval nor disapproval. Then Golitsyn began to speak: "Keep in mind, Prince, that at least my exposition of the matter represents a sincere explanation from one friendly court to another; nothing is contrived or hidden. We would be very happy if our conduct of the negotiations with the Porte were to seem to your court to have been as correct and consistent as it really was."

"In due time," answered Kaunitz, "but in order to judge your policy dispassionately, I must imagine myself in the Turks' place. According to you, you are demanding little. But according to them it is too much."

In October Emperor Joseph II asked Golitsyn about the crossing of the Danube by Russian troops: "Do you not think that a crossing of the Danube is somewhat risky?"

"Sire," answered Golitsyn, "there is no doubt that the attempt is courageous and full of risks. But since the enemy did not come to us, we have to go to him. Incidentally, if our troops were unable to accomplish every aim of the crossing, at least they held a decisive superiority over the enemy."

"True," said Joseph, "the troops quitted themselves well, and I am impressed by the lasting glory won by your arms. Would only that it had brought peace more quickly."

"Sire," answered Golitsyn, "that does not depend on us."

"You are right," replied Joseph, "the Turks are obstinate to the point of impossibility; what have we not done to persuade them—but their one answer is that it is impossible to accept the Russian conditions! Your insistence on Kerch and Yenikale is one of the principal stumbling blocks. They think that with these two fortresses and the fleets you will have there you will control the Black Sea and besiege Constantinople."

Golitsyn disagreed. "All these dangers are groundless; both Kerch and Yenikale are unsuited for naval fleets. Regardless of that, the Porte would have nothing to fear in peacetime when our ships have the right to sail on the Black Sea. In the event of war we would bring into action the dockyards at Taganrog, Azov and Voronezh since the Kafa Straits, in the hands of our allies the Tatars, always will be open to us. The Porte does not want to give these two places to us for the sole reason that they will serve us as guaranty of the independence of the Tatars."

Joseph smiled. "They say that Tatar independence, on which Russia is insisting so much, is not at all to the taste of the Tatars themselves, and that you are forcing it on them."

"That is possible," replied Golitsyn. "A people long bent to the yoke and tied to the Turks by common faith and morals might seem to lack the desire for instant freedom. We might not have started opening their eyes to benefits they do not understand had it not been in our direct interest to do so. Liberating this rapacious people from the guardianship of the Porte and making it responsible for its own actions provides security from their raids for our borders. Your lands will profit from this too."

"How is that?" Joseph asked.

"For one thing, we evacuated many Tatar hordes from Bessarabia to the Kuban.[50] If war breaks out between Austria and the Porte the latter no longer will have at its disposal the mobs of brigands who previously devastated whole areas in the twinkling of an eye."

Joseph exclaimed, "Well done! These considerations seem to me to be basic. However, should the Turks persist in their stubbornness, can you achieve peace soon?"

Golitsyn hinted: "Our peace with the Porte will be concluded very quickly if Vienna uses the very best exhortations on our behalf."

Again Joseph smiled. "I understand; you have in mind cannons."

"Exactly, Sire. Surely the very closeness of such a lengthy war is uncomfortable for a neighboring power. Then, thanks to the untiring concern of those who envy us,[51] the Turks unwittingly are becoming more disciplined; they are learning how to wage war with Europe. With this advantage added to their natural abilities and methods, they are becoming considerably more dangerous than they were heretofore."

Joseph said, "I disagree with that. Not even considering the main string (Mohammedanism?), the spirited and effervescent character of this savage people in accord with their form of government can never tolerate the discipline in which we hold our soldiers."

Golitsyn added: "I hope to God that your majesty's assumption never proves incorrect, but considering all the circumstances, care in this regard is not inappropriate." At this point the emperor suddenly shifted the conversation.

THE VIEW FROM FRANCE

Berlin, Vienna, and Petersburg spoke constantly of France's intrigues. What was the topic of conversation in France? In March Khotinsky wrote Panin: "The French government considers the agreement of the three courts—the Russian, Prussian and Austrian—as a strange alliance for all, and it is not clear which they suspect most. For this reason I am afraid France has employed every contrivance to frighten the English, who might fall into such a trap and begin, if not to cooperate with France's efforts, at least to push for peace, and France will not fail somehow to distort and stir things up."

France feared most of all a Russian attack on Sweden, which would compel France to offer Sweden subsidies at a moment when there was no money. In vain Khotinsky assured d'Aiguillon that Russia had no intention of attacking Sweden. The duke answered: "Nonetheless, it is the same as if you told me that you would remain at Versailles, while I could see with my own eyes from the window that the horses remained harnessed to your carriage. Why will you not offer the Swedes a guaranty by signing a treaty with them?"

In August news arrived that Major General Prince Ivan Sergeevich Bariatinsky had been appointed minister to France.[52] This news silenced the rumors about war, and stocks went up at the Paris exchange. D'Aiguillon told Khotinsky that Durand was showering praise on Bariatinsky.

"This appointment might even ease your agitation about Sweden," noted Khotinsky.

"You know," answered d'Aiguillon, "the king's manner of thinking and my intentions. You know that we desire above all that this appointment lead to the closest possible harmony." Khotinsky reminded him that France was arming, whereupon the duke said, "We do not want people to consider us absolutely powerless."

In August instructions were issued to the new minister, Prince Bariatinsky. They are noteworthy as an explanation and justification of Russian policy during Panin's administration of foreign affairs. They were written by Panin himself.

"The direction of mutual affairs is apportioned by the chief powers according to the ability of each to seize its share. Until the reign of Great Catherine Russia, despite its successes in the Seven Years War, played a secondary role (?), following everywhere the lead of its allies (?). At the time of her majesty's accession to the throne there were two parties in Europe: in the first were France and Austria, backed by Spain and a significant number of imperial princes. Opposing them were England and the king of Prussia. The king of Portugal and several imperial princes were allied with England, and Emperor Peter III suddenly switched from an enemy to the most intimate ally of Prussia. Consequently, even here, revising the continent's political system, Russia nonetheless remained in its significance a power dependent upon outside interests. At the conclusion of peace England managed to force advantageous terms on the Bourbons, holding on to many and significant conquests, and the Prussian king emerged without loss. As little influence as Russia was able to exert on the peace talks which laid the foundation for the future configuration of Europe,[53] owing to the sudden break in its policy instituted by Peter III, it had even more difficulty acquiring influence later. Her imperial majesty's wisdom and firmness quickly overcame this difficulty, and the world suddenly realized in amazement that our court had begun to play a role in the management of general affairs equal to that of the major powers, and in the north, the leading role. England, whose interests are identical to ours, and more significantly whose insular position required an ambivalent policy towards the continent in peacetime, viewed this political development with extreme pleasure because it had found in Russia a new opponent of France, easing its own burden.

"Austria and Prussia were so exhausted from warfare that at first they gave little thought to advancing their influence beyond the boundaries of the German empire. Later, seeing that Russia began to act independently and according to its own policy, because of their mutual envy they began to compete in seeking friends and allies, but with one difference: Vienna from its former habit of conforming Russia to Austria's own views (?) attempted here also to make us dependent on its policy. The king of Prussia, however, allowed her imperial majesty primacy in general relations between them, desiring only to gain her friendship and as her ally to safeguard the unity and security of his lands for the future, knowing from experience that Vienna burned with envy of him and of course would use the first convenient occasion to retake Silesia.

"It was not hard for the empress to decide which side was more advantageous and useful for the glory and merit of the empire, particularly because Vienna was allied closely with France, whose influence reached everywhere and especially in the north obstructed the strengthening of Russian influence. Russia's preference for the Prussian ally cannot have been to Vienna's taste, which is why it began to promote French intrigues against us everywhere while preserving a certain moderation and complete outward decorum. But France was offended by our war with Turkey, sensing that Russian influence was being strengthened through the loss of its own. The prime minister, the Duke de Choiseul, feeling his personal honor at stake, began to lay hold of every allowable and not a few disallowed methods.

"The general system France erected against us consists in placing the strongest obstacles in our path, now that our influence and significance are at least equal to those of France, in an effort to reduce Russia to its former inability to act independently and remain obedient to foreign interests. The French ministers at every court now are following this plan, although the Duke d'Aiguillon is obliged to mouth the platitude that since his ministry commenced France has observed every outward propriety. In Petersburg Durand offers assurances that his king is amicably disposed toward the empress and wishes to be of service to her. Two means to his ends are the renewal of the defensive alliance between Russia and Sweden and French mediation in arranging peace with the Porte. Yet all this is being done from the former intention of depriving our policy of independence. France realized that its successes in the struggle with us failed to meet expectations and therefore decided to reorient its policy and put its big guns here in Petersburg. The plan was to use the Swedish revolution and the breakdown of negotiations with the Turks in the hope that the multiplication of our worries would induce us to seize upon France's flattering proposals joyfully and without reflection. It is a subtle idea, designed as it is to demonstrate how incapable we are of handling our own affairs. But France's subtlety could not stand against the wisdom of her imperial majesty, who shrewdly rejected the French proposals."[54]

Bariatinsky received instructions to follow Catherine's lead should the French repeat similar proposals to him. Concerning French mediation, Panin in deepest secrecy informed the English envoy Gunning of the following. The famous writer Diderot, sojourning in Petersburg in 1773, had handed the empress a paper containing the conditions of peace with Turkey which France would be obliged to obtain for Russia were its mediation accepted.[55] Diderot explained that he had received the paper from Durand and could not refuse to transmit it to the empress; otherwise upon his return to France he would be imprisoned in the Bastille.

Catherine told him that in consideration of such personal danger she forgave the impropriety of his gesture and told him to inform Durand of the use she had made of his paper, and with these words she threw it into the fire.

Besides this, Durand called on Panin three times with proposals of mediation and alliance with France on terms that would be advantageous for Russia. Each time he received the answer that Russia did not consider the present moment suitable for increasing its obligations and that it was satisfied with its current arrangements. Nevertheless, Catherine was very sympathetic toward the amicable intentions of his most Christian majesty and more than anything sought an occasion to convince the king that she held him in esteem and valued his friendship.

Panin assured Gunning that while he was directing foreign affairs Russia would never accept French mediation. But Gunning, filing his report to his ministry, noted that despite Panin's enmity for France, had Orlov been in Petersburg there might have been sufficient grounds for fearing success by the proponents of a French alliance.

THE CRISIS SUBSIDES IN SWEDEN

Meanwhile Sweden anticipated a Russian attack and to assure its safety followed France's suggestions to the letter. "Those who side with us," wrote Ostermann, "claim that they failed to resist the revolution solely because of uncertainty whether Russia would come to their defense. They believed that the yoke placed upon them by the king would be removed as suddenly as it was put on. There is not a single Swede who doubted that this moment will come. Until it does, any movement, as you wisely and shrewdly will understand, not only would be in vain but might prove to be a most harmful enterprise. Consequently, in my opinion, any payments to prepare minds would be excessive, except for limited secret assistance to extremely needy people already on our side, for which enough remains from the last money I received. I must be the more careful since even without this our rivals have accused me of preparing a conspiracy; now they have begun to say outright that following the conclusion of our war we intend to attack Sweden together with Prussia and Denmark.

"Knowing the intention for the future of her imperial majesty, as decency allows, I will not cease strengthening secretly the dissatisfaction here, meting out insinuation and sincerity in accordance with the confidence shown to me. I have compiled a list of people whose dissatisfaction is certain. But since they are marked by the king as Russian proteges and are estranged from the government, one hardly can expect anything from them other than veiled assistance, as their every step is followed. We have not yet succeeded in drawing the royal brother, Prince Frederick, from the king and bringing him to our principles, and none of the great lords will reveal his feelings. Should an uprising or mutiny flare in the regiments it will come from the lower officers, not the high-ranking men of the bureaucracy. It is hazardous to count on the firmness and modesty of Prince Frederick. Two days before the king issued the royal decree assuming command of the regiments in Ostrogothland, as news arrived of an uprising in Christianstad, the prince publicly made assurances at table that he would stand up to lead the people in defense of liberty. When he received the decree, however, he declared, shrugging his shoulders: 'The king is my brother; I cannot stop him. Whether I wish to or not I must defend him.' Duke Charles also schemed against the king, but without result.[56] The feeling of kinship in the royal family is very strong. They argue often and quickly, but soon become reconciled again."

News of Russia's arming in Finland forced Gustavus III to form a military council at the beginning of March from senators counts Lieven, Scheffer, and Fersen and Baron Falkengreen.[57] The king proposed sending several regiments and the Estland artillery of four hundred men and sixteen cannon to Finland.[58] All senators except Scheffer proposed as a first step gathering of reliable information as to whether the empress actually intended to attack Sweden. They considered it useful, before arming any troops, to assure the empress in the king's name that he had no intention of disturbing her. Sweden likely would receive similar assurances from Catherine since military preparation is the quickest way to cool relations between states. The king consented not to dispatch the regiments and artillery to Finland, but on the other hand concurred with Scheffer that it was not necessary to send assurances to Petersburg which might produce an answer unpleasant for Sweden.

Every means was employed to assure that there would be no Swedish military movements. Scheffer called on the English minister Sir John Goodricke and spoke about the rumor widespread in Europe that the Swedish king had signed a treaty with the Porte which obligated him to create a diversion against Russia in exchange for a large subsidy. Scheffer swore that the rumor had been concocted by Sweden's enemies. Not only was there no treaty, on the contrary, the Swedish minister at the Porte, Zelzang, had been instructed to place no obstacles in the way of peace between Russia and Turkey. "Scheffer's assurance," Ostermann wrote Panin, "might have had a certain resemblance to the truth had he not so shamelessly made clear to Zelzang his instructions."

Ostermann was convinced that Turkish money was arriving in Stockholm however it might be concealed by treaty or French cloak. After these events Scheffer requested an appointment with Ostermann and began the conversation by invoking the king's name: "You are well acquainted with his majesty's repeated assurances of his most sincere desire and steadfast intention to preserve good harmony with the empress. The king, who retains this burning desire, instructed me to confirm it to you once more, adding that heretofore he has sought similar assurances in vain from the empress, notwithstanding the news about Russian preparations in Finland. Now he has received confirmation that eighteen thousand men have been moved in and seventy-five galleys and an entire squadron outfitted.[59] He is unable to conceal how much this news would have disyurbed him were he not relying fully on the friendship of her majesty, based on kinship. Meanwhile he has taken several precautionary measures but instructed me to repeat the assurance that they were undertaken solely for defense, and in no way for offense. As soon as he learns from your lips that her majesty intends no operations against him, he will cease preparations for war forthwith."

"Scheffer's conduct," wrote Ostermann, "stems from the fact that he and his gang have sniffed out the people's distaste for war. Now he is attempting to extricate himself from this labyrinth on behalf of the national peace, which is why he is so concerned about our reply; in the event of a favorable answer he could suppress all movements and in the opposite case continue them intensively, even to the extent of assembling an extraordinary diet."

Petersburg prepared the following answer for Ostermann to give Scheffer in reference to their previous conference: "From the moment the king ascended the throne her imperial majesty has assured him constantly of her sincere friendship as a close relative, of the interest she takes in his prosperity, and of the trust she places in his desire to establish complete harmony between the two powers. Animated by these feelings, the empress received the king's latest assurances with fresh confidence and renewed pleasure. Her imperial majesty despises secret ways. Throughout her reign she has conducted her affairs in the sight of all Europe and can do no less when dealing with a sovereign who is likewise a close relative. By this immutable law of her own policy she instructs you (Ostermann) to offer assurances that in everything done and being done in her realm there is not the least intention to attack Sweden. It was not she who took the first step to alter the existing state of affairs in the north. Her war with Turkey was drawing to an end when Sweden received a new form of government. This change and the military maneuvers immediately thereafter and continuing uninterruptly have lent courage to Russia's enemy and the peace negotiations have stumbled on obstacles originally not there.

"Naturally the empress has had to pay attention to events in Sweden where intensified preparations have been made for war. In Russia, on the other hand, troops normally stationed on the northern borders recently were transferred to the south because of the unexpected declaration of war by the Turks. So it was with the naval forces. Every military command was weakened thereby. The northern borders were stripped of troops owing to the momentary need. But there was no desire to leave the borders wholly bare, nor should they have remained that way in consideration of the changes that have taken place in Sweden. The empress affirms that her every concern in past and present is for the natural defense of her realm and that of her ally, the king of Denmark. Should the Swedish sovereign offer solemn assurances that he has no desire to attack Russia or disturb it in any way, and should these assurances extend to Denmark as well, the empress will assure the king that she holds not the slightest intention of attacking him and wishes to preserve the peace and amity between their realms. As for the proposal for a closer union between Russia and Sweden communicated by the Swedish envoy at the Russian court, Baron Ribbing, this is a matter for more settled times when there is little possibility of misinterpretation."

When Ostermann read this response to Scheffer the latter said that he could hardly have expected firmer assurances; although he might have made several observations about the Swedish maneuvers mentioned in the response, he considered it more proper to refrain.

In November the king himself told Ostermann in private that his sole desire was to convince the empress of the sincerity of his friendship. To remove any cause for doubt he was announcing his intention to visit Finland early in June of the following year. He would not make the trip in 1772 solely to avoid various rumors about its aims, but now he was disclosing privately his desire to visit the empress on that journey. For this reason he asked whether Ostermann had received an answer to his previous question on this matter.

Ostermann replied that the sovereign naturally would recall how he, the ambassador, had assured him in the name of the empress of the pleasure with which she would receive such a dear guest and blood relation.[60]

"True," Gustavus said, "but whereas certain events have taken place here since then, it isn't appropriate simply to repeat the previous assurances. Therefore it would please me greatly were you to communicate her imperial majesty's response to my ministry. I am eager to visit such an illustrious monarch, renowned worldwide, and to convince her personally of my high esteem and peace-loving feelings, which is why I wish to receive an invitation from her majesty."

Catherine told Ostermann to answer that she continued to nourish the sincere desire to become acquainted personally with the king, her neighbor and close relation. Panin on this occasion wrote Ostermann: "His majesty's arrival naturally would be more agreeable after peace has been signed with the Turks than during our present difficulties. However, now that he has made known for the second time his desire to visit the sovereign, he leaves us no decent way to hinder his intentions."

DENMARK DRAWS CLOSER TO RUSSIA

We have noticed that in her relations with Sweden the empress not in the least drew away from her ally the Danish king. On New Year's Day, 1773 the new Russian minister in Copenhagen, Ivan Matveevich Simolin,[61] in the most vivid colors (but in less than brilliant French) described the relationship of Russia and Denmark. "With my knowledge of affairs I can assure your excellency," he wrote Panin, "of the sincerity and inviolability of feelings of the entire royal family and the ministry concerning the empress, her policies, and her interests. They have decided never to part ways with her for the integrity and welfare of Denmark are inseparable from the interests of the Russian empire. It remains to our court to incline Denmark and its armed forces into accord with our views and interests. The members of the royal family regard France as a beast (les personnes royales regardent la France comme la bête), and I never miss an opportunity to strengthen this view among the ministers. Your excellency observes how suitable is the present for establishing and confirming Russian influence in the north and excluding French influence. Denmark awaits merely an indication of her imperial majesty's pleasure and wishes to conform fully with it and demonstrate that its devotion to her has no bounds."

But shadows soon crept across this brilliant scene. On February 16 Simolin wrote that the minister of foreign affairs, Count Adolphus Sigfried Osten, was wavering, offering resistance to Denmark's arming, which the Danish court accepted as much for the security of its own borders as for fulfillment of its obligations to Russia as an ally in the event the Swedish ruler made a demonstration or diversion against Russia in order to persuade the Porte to continue the war. When the Council discussed the matter of appointing officers for the squadron being fitted for the next spring, Osten did not limit himself to open opposition but also chose covert ways to reach his goal. He went so far as to hint to important personages of the royal house that it was still uncertain whether the Holstein affair would be settled. This suggestion conclusively damaged Osten in the eyes of the queen and Prince Frederick, who were loathe to deal with him on official matters. It was dangerous to permit such a man to confer with foreign ministers and read diplomatic correspondence. It was hard to imagine that his conversations with the French envoy, which continued for hours, involved nothing more than the weather, as he claimed.

For some time Simolin had detected a certain embarrassment in Osten's conversations with him, especially his desire to avoid talking with him or to cut short a conversation when the French and Swedish envoys might be watching. The members of the royal house felt the need for his removal, but who should replace him? They sought advice from Count Panin in Petersburg, but before they received an answer the suspicion against Osten intensified. The Prussian envoy, Baron Arnim, told Osten that he had written Frederick about the rumor going the rounds in Copenhagen, to the effect that the king of Prussia would not look kindly on Denmark's arming. Arnim received the answer that Danish armaments caused Frederick not the least uneasiness and that under the present circumstances he could only approve Copenhagen's precautionary measures. Prince Frederick and others who were privy to Frederick II's reply thought that Osten would announce it without fail in the Council, but the minister of foreign affairs remained silent despite the significance of the message. Furthermore, a report reached Copenhagen from the Danish envoy in Vienna about the comment of the French ambassador there, Prince Louis de Rohan. "France and Sweden," said Rohan, "remain calm concerning the disposition of Copenhagen's court because a change of ministries soon will take place in Denmark advantageous for the policies of both these states."

It was revealed at last that Osten had kept a spy at court, Chamberlain Triberg, who simultaneously had a suspicious relationship with the French envoy, the Marquis Blosset.[63] It was then decided to dismiss Osten without awaiting an answer from Petersburg and to place Privy Councillor Schack temporarily in charge of foreign affairs.[64] When Simolin was informed, he answered that it was entirely attributable to the wisdom and insight of Prince Frederick, particularly because Schack long had enjoyed the confidence of the Russian court. Then, informing his court of the retirement of Osten, Simolin wrote that it was necessary to end the Holstein business, since in doing so Russia was winning the entire kingdom, whose strengths and resources would be forever at its disposal. A second reason for resolving the Holstein dispute quickly was that France was leaking rumors that Grand Duke Paul Petrovich would never approve a treaty depriving him of his patrimonial possessions.

Soon the queen and Prince Frederick expressed their regrets to Simolin that Schack was refusing the department of foreign affairs, when he was the only man capable of occupying the office. Simolin suggested that they delay the royal appointment of another official, for perhaps Schack would become comfortable in that post. Unfortunately, the year before, Schack, to alleviate Osten's worries, had told him that he would never accept his position. In the end, it was possible to find a loophole, namely to leave Schack permanently *ad interim*, not appointing him minister of foreign affairs. The queen and prince promised not to hurry things. It was obvious that Simolin desperately wanted the Holstein dispute to be ended during his tenure and with his assistance. He twice wrote Panin that the matter of Holstein alone could lead Schack to abandon the foreign office. Should he see an opportunity to resolve it, and thereby win everyone's gratitude, he might yield to the urgent solicitations of the court and his friends.

No amount of exhorting could sway Schack. Count Andreas Peter Bernstorff, a nephew of the late minister of the same name,[65] was appointed minister of foreign affairs. His best recommendation was that he was trained to be hostile to France and well disposed toward Russia; he was a friend of Schack, who remained the soul of the Royal Council. At his first meeting with Simolin the new minister declared his unyielding adherence to the Russian alliance, saying that he was reared on the principles of this policy and his sole ambition consisted in making indissoluble the bonds uniting Denmark with Russia. On May 31 Schack brought

Simolin the happy news that the treaty giving Holstein to Oldenburg and Delmenhorst had been signed in Petersburg.

Simolin later informed Panin that the Swedish minister in Copenhagen had proposed a close alliance between Sweden and Denmark to the widowed queen. The queen responded that this would be possible if Sweden could incline Petersburg to the alliance; otherwise Denmark could not accept such proposals. The Swede replied that this was quite impossible because Russia was so remote. "Nevertheless," answered the queen, "Russia is a neighbor of Sweden and by its position, power and influence is capable of participating in all the affairs of Europe, especially of Northern Europe." With this the conversation ended.

Osten's behavior, although resulting in his overthrow, caused concern in Petersburg. It demonstrated that France had not abandoned hope of restoring Denmark to its side. To lose the alliance of Denmark at a time of strained relations with Sweden was difficult for Russia. Therefore Russia sought an agreement with England, the former subsidies to be paid not to Sweden but to Denmark. Petersburg considered this proposal all the more imperative when news came of France's efforts to draw nearer to England.

RUSSIAN-ENGLISH RELATIONS

From London Musin-Pushkin wrote that for some time open objections had been expressed there to Russia's ambitious designs, to England's timidity, to its inclination toward a close alliance with France, and to the sound policy pursued by Prussia. On March 20 Musin-Pushkin asked Lord Suffolk in jest when Britain's treaty of alliance with France would be signed.[66] The minister, responding in kind, said that the matter had been settled but then, assuming a serious expression, raised Musin-Pushkin's hopes with the strongest assurances that England could not conceivably forget its geographical position. It could never prefer a French alliance to the Russian, for Russia came closest to sharing its most palpable interests. In order to mold a sound policy, however, England must have full knowledge of Catherine's slightest intentions regarding both Turkish and Swedish affairs. England's current harmony with France existed solely because there was at present no reason for dissatisfaction between them. But the current situation could not possibly negate the grounds for competition and distrust which always would remain as insurmountable obstructions to an alliance. Suffolk added that he was saying all this not in his name alone but was speaking for the king and the ministry.

On the basis of news from Paris and his own observations Musin-Pushkin reasoned that negotiations of some sort were under way between France and England. He discussed this with Suffolk, who neither confirmed nor directly denied the Russian minister's doubts. "It shouldn't seem remarkable that under the present critical and somewhat indefinite situation France should make some type of proposal to the English court, but I am not yet able to tell you about it. You must be prudent and patiently wait to draw your conclusions. Count Panin's silence with respect to our minister Gunning serves as proof for me that you do not intend as yet to initiate a new war; Sweden will never offer the least cause for war, especially while France is incapable of providing substantive, untrammeled help and Denmark stands mobilized and prepared to attack Sweden at a moment's notice."

Meanwhile, in March Panin in a conversation with Gunning reminded him of an alliance necessary primarily for protecting Denmark from French encroachments. Should England choose to obligate itself to Denmark, its alliance with Russia necessarily would follow. Gunning answered bluntly that it was impossible to approach his court with this proposal since it merely cited Denmark in place of Sweden; the English government had announced once and for all that it would not pay subsidies to another government. Panin asked whether London's thinking ought not be influenced by the great transformation in Europe since subsidies had been requested for Sweden; shouldn't they recognize that whereas in Sweden English subsidies won but a single faction, now they would gain the entire Danish navy. In Panin's opinion a general war was not far off if measures were not taken immediately to avert it. First of all it was necessary to draw Denmark away from Sweden, which alone would be merely a weak ally for France. When an alliance was concluded between Russia and England both states would have nothing more to fear from French intrigues. Gunning "out of respect for Panin" reported these statements to his ministry, which replied again solely "from personal respect for Panin" (incidentally, not at all respectfully, but drily and sharply) that the Russian proposal hindered English policy and decisions already repeatedly announced and thus was quite unacceptable. To adopt it would mean yielding primacy to those who with the conclusion of an alliance between Russia and England otherwise would have to follow them.

In May the empress decided to talk personally with Gunning about an alliance on the same basis, that England first conclude a subsidy treaty

with Denmark. Perhaps the suspicion that Panin, to please England's enemy the king of Prussia, did not handle the matter with the requisite care
forced Catherine to take this step, not entirely in conformity with her notions about the dignity of the Russian sovereign. "Let us see now, is it
really impossible for us to end our tedious negotiations concerning an
alliance?" she asked Gunning. He answered that the matter was complex.
"How can it be done?" continued Catherine. "Denmark needs assistance,
and your interest no less than mine requires you to offer it. No northern
system worthy of the name can be built without Denmark; this is an
excellent occasion on which to reveal our alliance."

Gunning replied that the English ministry steadfastly stood by its
decision not to allow any obligation benefitting Denmark as a condition
of an alliance with Russia, that this alliance was viewed as the basis of
a great system. It was necessary first to lay the foundation, and to erect
further construction upon it later.

"I do not see," objected Catherine, "why we cannot combine these two
matters either by means of a secret and separate article or in two different
treaties."

The envoy answered that something similar had been suggested in the
past concerning a Swedish subsidy, but had been rejected in England.

Catherine persisted: "In that case why make a treaty? Will it contain
no conditions whatever? What then will it consist of?

"Like all defensive treaties it will define mutual aid," answered
Gunning.

"In what way will it be reciprocal?" asked Catherine. "Owing to the
complexity of your commercial and political interests, you are infinitely
more liable than I to quarrels and ruptures with various powers. I have
only one enemy, the Turks, yet you refuse to include them in the event
of an alliance."

"In my opinion," answered Gunning, "Russia has as many enemies
as Great Britain. Although our enemies are powerful, we do not expect
to become a burden to our allies in the event of an attack because of our
favorable location."

To this Catherine responded, "What good might come out of such a
general treaty? Of what use will it be to me?"

Gunning answered her questions with a question of his own: did the
empress suppose that a treaty of alliance between England and Russia
would make no impression on the majority of European cabinets or

preserve peace in the Baltic Sea? And was not the latter circumstance important for the possessions of her majesty?

Catherine ended the conversation by saying, "I find that affairs are conducted differently in London than here. Neither Russia nor England, however, will be able to remain long in such a situation."

But England decided that it was better to remain as it was, that a subsidy for Denmark could not serve as the basis of an alliance treaty with Russia. Furthermore, Gunning was instructed not to allow the Russians to include in the treaty a guarantee of the usurpations in Poland. And as before a Turkish assault on Russia was not to comprise an event of alliance.

THE MILITARY SITUATION IN THE BALKANS

It was clear that security in the north depended exclusively on the march of events in the south. More specifically, it depended on Rumiantsev's successes in 1774.

As remarked earlier, in the last days of 1773 Catherine had instructions sent to Rumiantsev that upon capturing Varna and defeating the vizier he not halt at the Balkan mountains but proceed onward to win peace. Peace was essential, for in the east it was imperative to extinguish Pugachev's fire.[67]

When in January 1774 Stackelberg transmitted to Petersburg a letter from Constantinople discussing the anticipated death of the sultan, Catherine wrote Panin, "I consider this latest news, which I heard through Stackelberg from Tsargrad, to be so important that it seems to me it should be communicated without delay to Count Rumiantsev with the instruction that he try as much as possible to seize the moment. In my judgment, this occasion can be used not by a feint but by actual attack on Silistra and Varna. Victories there—God grant them—will serve as their own peace proposal to the vizier. I am instructing you to prepare a rescript authorizing Count Rumiantsev to make a peace treaty without a moment's waste. Such a moment when lost does not return."

Stackelberg's news turned out to be accurate; Sultan Mustafa died and his brother Abdul-Hamid took his place.[68] The following directive was sent to Rumiantsev from Petersburg: "Since previous experience has shown that such an important change likely will lead to some unrest in the seraglio and a degree of disorder in the Porte's general political and military measures, prudent perception demands that we prepare ourselves as quickly as possible to make maximum use of the enemy's bumbling following his change of government. In our abundant desire to serve the empire's true benefit, that is, to attain most quickly the long desired and highly valued peace, we are authorizing you to assemble as rapidly as possible, and of course without any publicity, a body of troops to cross the Danube at your first order and strike Silistra and Varna, together or separately, should blunder and disorder begin to appear among the enemy's troops owing to the change of government. It is our will that if you capture both towns, or even one of them, you utilize the enemy's terror to propose to the vizier a renewal of the peace negotiations on condition that they are brief and that the obstacles separating you both as supreme military commanders be removed."

The news arrived that the new sultan had given full authority to Grand Vizier Mussin-Zade.[69] Simultaneously assurances were received from Vienna and Berlin that Zegelin and Thugut were of one mind, having forsaken all mutual envy, and would attempt to urge peace on the vizier since his reputed love of peace surely would be linked to his desire to remain in Constantinople to prevent seraglio intrigues. Catherine wrote Panin: "The postscript from Prince Kaunitz, which Prince Lobkowitz read you, seemingly was composed to eradicate our doubts about Vienna's duplicity. It has occurred to me now to make use of the accession of the new sultan; the hazards of pride and other personal circumstances and feelings which persisted in our discussions with the last ruler do not affect him. For this reason I think you should ask Prince Kaunitz to announce once more our preparedness to hasten the peace whenever they want to discuss it. He should tell them that a rescript and plenary powers are now being sent to the field marshal."

With such impatience to achieve peace as soon as possible, it stands to reason its conditions had to be softened to the utmost degree. In the Council's session on March 10, with the empress in attendance, Count Panin proposed dropping the demands for Kerch and Yenikale to please the Tatars, and limiting Russia's demands to Kinburn and free access to the Black Sea for merchant ships only, which in need might be converted into naval ships. All members of the Council concurred except Count Grigory Orlov. Catherine deferred resolution of the questions. At the following session on March 13 they decided not to transmit these conditions to the Turks immediately but to reveal them one at a time in view of Turkish stubbornness and "pressing state needs for the soonest possible return of peace and tranquility to the fatherland."

Petersburg placed much hope in Vienna's promise to instruct Thugut to inform the Porte that, in light of its obstinacy in accepting the Russian conditions, Vienna was forced to abandon the terms it had wrung from Russia regarding Moldavia and Wallachia, whose fate now would depend wholly on the course of the war. "God grant," wrote the empress to Rumiantsev, "that your arms, festooned with laurels, be covered equally with garlands of peace. When negotiations with God's help reach the point of actual discussions with the grand vizier a path will open naturally which, contoured to his ideas and desires, must be followed to begin the bargaining. We think that it is shortest of all to continue from the point where the Bucharest congress stopped, accepting in advance all articles either actually signed there or at least held in essence by the verbal consent of the Turkish envoy. The entire difficulty of peacemaking consisted in two points: ceding Kerch and Yenikale with their surrounding areas to Russia, and freedom of navigation for all vessels on the Black Sea.

"Having recognized well enough that Turkish opposition on these two points is insuperable, the Porte considering them vital to its very existence, we have decided, in order to restore precious tranquility to the fatherland, to withdraw to a limited right of navigation on the Black Sea and to leave Kerch and Yenikale to the Tatars if the Porte agrees, having recognized their freedom and independence, to grant them full possession of all fortresses in the Crimea, in Taman and in the Kuban and all territory from the river Bug to the Dniester, and if Turkey yields us the city of Ochakov and Kinburn castle with their environs and the steppes as far as the Bug. If you must, you may demand merely the destruction of Ochakov, and as a last resort leave Ochakov with the Turks and take only Kinburn and its surroundings up to the Bug. You may stipulate only commercial sailing on the Black Sea."

The vizier, staying in Shumla, sent an official across the Danube with a letter to the pashas who were Russian prisoners. Rumiantsev returned the Turk to Shumla with letters of reply from the pashas, and with him Rumiantsev's own officer. The latter recrossed the Danube to the Russian side accompanied by the same Turkish official, who this time brought letters to the field marshal from the vizier and the reis-effendi inviting him to renew the peace negotiations. The two commanders-in-chief began to correspond about the peace conditions, which quickly showed that the Turks were aware of Russia's difficult position making it agree to anything. The vizier yielded Azov alone. He did not want even to hear about ceding Ochakov or Kinburn. He agreed on navigation for Russian commercial ships on the Black Sea and Sea of Marmora, but the construction and sizes of the ships were to be defined precisely (so that they could not be converted into naval vessels). About the Crimea he spoke in the vaguest terms, not at all in line with Russia's demands. The Tatars were to exercise their freedom in accord with the prescriptions of Islamic law, but this meant nothing specific.

Panin on this occasion wrote Rumiantsev a long letter: "Since the Bucharest congress I have noted that the Porte, in speaking of freedom for the Tatars, insensitively is inclined in all references to incorporate in the word *freedom* the word *independence*. Our duty to be on guard keeps us from letting it use this cunning trick of its barbarian politics. Therefore, your excellency, I ask most diligently that in your remarks during the negotiations you link together the words *freedom* and *independence*, and during the composition and signing of the peace treaty that you make sure they are placed side by side and that the Tatars are not subordinated to anyone's political and civil domain besides God's alone."

Petersburg grew alarmed at the slowness of the negotiations. It grew suspicious that the vizier purposely intended to drag them out to exhaust our patience and bargain for better conditions for the Porte or use the occasion for a test of military fortune, besides waiting for a favorable change in circumstances. In this state of alarm Panin wrote Rumiantsev that "peace is absolutely essential for our land; we therefore covet it and must strive for it." He requested that Rumiantsev explain to the vizier that he and all of the Porte's ministers were mistaken if they believed the calumnies of those who begrudged peace, as though the resources of the Russian government were totally exhausted and it was in no condition to continue the war with its earlier successes. But even were its resources exhausted Rumiantsev held an asset which no power nor change of European circumstances in the Porte's favor might take away from him. This consisted in converting the war from offensive to defensive, but first razing all occupied Turkish fortresses to their foundations and totally evacuating the towns and settlements, sending all inhabitants and their belongings to Russia where there were still many uninhabited places suitable for settling. Resettlement of the population of Bessarabia, Moldavia, and Wallachia would be adequate compensation to Russia for all expenses incurred, and for the Porte it would be a decisive blow from which it could not recover.

WAR BRINGS PEACE

We know that Rumiantsev had no sympathy with these Assyrian-Babylonian methods. For the victor of Larga and Kagul there was a more appropriate way to compel the Turks to peace. This method was a strong offensive stopping not even at the Balkans. In April Lieutenant General Michael Fedotovich Kamensky's corps crossed the Danube and in May stood near Karasu.[70] Suvorov's corps, which had crossed the Danube near Girsovo, was in close support of it. Kamensky and Suvorov decided not to move toward Varna and Silistra but toward Shumla, where the vizier was camped. After defeating a five-thousand-man Turkish force, Kamensky occupied Bazardjik on June 2, and on the same day Rumiantsev crossed the Danube near Gurobaly with the main army and likewise moved to the attack toward Shumla. The vizier sent a force of some forty thousand men toward Bazardjik, in the direction of Kamensky, but it was crushed near Kozludja on June 9; the hero of the day was Suvorov. After this victory Kamensky preferred to halt but Rumiantsev, knowing how Petersburg was thirsting for peace and awaiting it solely through the offensive into Bulgaria, demanded that Kamensky immediately advance on Shumla. By June 17 Kamensky was a mere five versts from this fortress, and Brigadier Ivan Alexandrovich Zaborovsky had crossed into the Balkans and hit the Turks there. The vizier sent a proposal for truce; Rumiantsev chose to reply that he would hear nothing of it. The vizier then suggested reopening the congress but Rumiantsev did not agree to that either. Thereupon the vizier sent two plenipotentiaries to Rumiantsev's main camp. Learning this, Rumiantsev proceeded with two infantry regiments and five squadrons of cavalry to the village of Kuchuk-Kainardji under the pretense of joining Kamensky's corps outside Shumla.

The Turkish envoys arrived in Kuchuk-Kainardji on July 4 and requested an immediate opening of negotiations. But the more they pleaded the more strongly Rumiantsev resisted, maintaining that he was bound for Shumla and could not stop. This forced the Turks into compliance when the field marshal at last agreed to begin negotiations. He designated Prince Nikolai Vasilevich Repnin[71] to represent Russia because a flood on the left bank of the Danube prevented Obreskov from arriving promptly. On July 10 the peace treaty was concluded and signed on the following conditions:

(1) The Tatars were to be free and independent of everyone save God himself in their civil and political affairs. In religious matters Islamic law was to apply to them without, however, threatening in the least their freedom and independence. All land and fortresses in the Crimea, the Kuban, and the island of Taman were to be handed to the Tatars except Kerch and Yenikale, which were to be retained by Russia.

(2) Russia also was to acquire Kinburn castle with its surrounding area and all the steppe between the Bug and Dnieper rivers, but the Porte was to retain Ochakov, Moldavia, Wallachia, and the Aegean islands on conditions beneficial for their inhabitants.

(3) Commerce and navigation for commercial ships were allowed on all waters, as well as navigation from the Black into the White (Marmora) seas and return, and in this regard Russian subjects were to enjoy the same privileges granted to the subjects of France and England.

(4) The porte was obligated to recompense Russia 4.5 million rubles for its war expenses.[72]

Prince Repnin himself carried to Petersburg the news about the negotiations he had conducted and their results.

A rescript sent to Rumiantsev upon receipt of the tidings of peace expressed the utter joy surrounding the event. The rejoicing was particularly great because Petersburg had lost hope of an advantageous peace. "This peace is erected as a creation of your hands; through it you have declared to us concomitantly your most notable service to us and the fatherland," Catherine wrote Rumiantscv. "We proclaim your service in the full extent of labor and heroism in which you had to be armed throughout the long war to ward off the might and arrogance of an enemy who until now has been accustomed in his fortunate wars to levying harsh laws on others. The measure of our good will to you and your service has been confirmed and we of course shall never let it escape our attention that Russia is indebted to you for a glorious and advantageous peace which no one expected, or could even prudently suspect, given the notorious obstinacy of the Ottoman Porte. Envy itself cannot argue with this truth, since on one hand the Turks, deprived of the Crimea and the Tatar hordes, also have been deprived for the foreseeable future of a significant number of troops, who were all the more useful because their maintenance cost the Porte nothing. And our acquisition of three harbors on the Black Sea grants us the means to harm the Porte in its most sensitive places if it again attempts a war with us in consequence of outside intrigues."

A rescript had been written for the commander of the Second Army ordering him temporarily to evacuate the Crimea, posting garrisons in Kerch and Yenikale, when news suddenly came from Dolgoruky that Seraskir Pasha Ali Bey had landed troops in the Crimea. Khan Sahib-Girey not only offered him no resistance but also handed over the Russian resident, Veselitsky.[73] A second rescript then was sent: "Since you have not yet informed us in detail we do not know how the Crimean khan was able to unite with the Turkish commanders and summon the courage to yield our resident to them while you and the army under your command were encamped right in the middle of the Crimea; consequentially, other than telling you to stay close to the khan and insisting on maintaining every possible contact with him and communicating with the resident, we can offer nothing more than generalities in this current instruction." These generalities rested on the fact that it was now unthinkable to evacuate Russian troops from the Crimea; troops could be withdrawn only when the last Turk had departed the peninsula or as they left. The rescript also said: "You and other reliable sources have warned us for some time about the present khan's bad qualities and incapacity for governing, but the situation we are in at this time with respect to the Crimea and other Tatar peoples gives us no proper grounds for deposing him that would be accepted as valid according to the right of birth and voluntary election by the entire community, especially at a time when the Tatars are being weaned away from Turkish rule. Therefore we must defend him if the Turks intend to depose him. On the other hand, if we are to give neither the Turks nor the Tatars the least cause for enmity, we must hold to the highest scruples in order not to be thought the instigators."

Dolgoruky sent word that he was withdrawing his troops from the Crimea and submitting his request to retire to Moscow because of his poor health, yielding his command to the senior lieutenant general. All this was granted him.

Meanwhile bad news began to come from Rumiantsev as well. For the final settlement of peace arrangements he had sent Colonel Khristofor Ivanovich Peterson to Constantinople, but Peterson informed him that arrangements were not being made.[74] The Ottoman council of state, the Divan, was demanding changes in several conditions of the peace treaty. The Prussian envoy at the Porte, Zegelin, also wrote Rumiantsev about this. But the field marshal's regard for the news from the latter is apparent from his curious letter to Peterson (October 24): "Zegelin praises the reis-effendi and represents him as a zealous defender of peace. But we have reason to know that he does not favor peace. Zegelin wants to frighten us with the Turks' readiness for war, but in a previous letter he himself described the Porte as so terribly exhausted it could not raise its head. Therefore take care with him and find out whether the trouble is coming from him or from some other source. It easily may be that the Prussian minister, excluded from participation in negotiating the peace, now wants to make himself indispensable. Should the reis-effendi or anyone else stall for time or refuse to accept the peace treaty word for word, make them understand that their behavior will halt the evacuation of Moldavia and the fortresses remaining in our hands, where our army remains at full strength. The reis-effendi asked you on what basis Austrian troops occupied the better part of Moldavia.[75] I am transmitting the following information to you to be held in strictest confidence: we must intimate our true views candidly on this matter to the Porte. Find the safest way to convince the Porte that Austrian occupation of Turkish territory is, as far as we are concerned, an entirely unauthorized action; we do not have and never will have the slightest part in it. Make this statement orally, not in writing, to the grand vizier himself or a trusted aide of his. I repeat that this must be done in utmost secrecy since our court's position in this matter is very delicate. We must not be compromised either in Vienna or at the Porte. I authorize you to promise 100,000, 200,000 or even 300,000 rubles to whoever can destroy the intrigues of the people ill-disposed towards us, oversee the treaty's ratification, and send it to Petersburg without any changes."

Rumiantsev directed all these efforts in Focsani, lying in bed, where he was chained by an agonizing illness. In August the empress, apprised of Rumiantsev's dreadful illness, decided to return Repnin to assist in concluding the peace; were the field marshal to recover, Repnin was to go to Constantinople as ambassador; in the other eventuality he was to take command of the army. On September 14 Repnin arrived in Focsani and the next day wrote Potemkin in Petersburg: "I found the field marshal still extremely weak and unable to get out of bed, although he is now out of danger. He looks pitiful as does everyone else here. The whole town has been turned into a hospital. Igelstrom was quite ill, but is already up and about. Zavadovsky is on his back, Asch, Velda, Prince Andrei Nikolaich also[76]—in short, practically everyone is sick with high and low-grade fevers. Of all the field marshal's staff, only his huntsman is healthy. All others are either in bed or barely dragging themselves about. The field marshal directed me to express how absolutely grateful he is for the part you played during his illness and for all your signs of friendship to him. He lacks the strength to write but will as soon as he is able. Considering that in three or four weeks the field marshal will have regained his desired strength, I do not see the necessity of my staying here with him. You know, my friend, that he needs no assistants. Do me the kindness of asking not only for instructions but also for gracious advice on this from the empress. I fear that the Turks, should they learn that our ambassador came galloping by post, might think that we have extreme need for haste, and therefore might give rein to their pride; but it is impossible to conceal this information since it is widespread in Petersburg and many people are writing here from there. Lay all this before her majesty, and if I am so fortunate that our thoughts coincide, entreat imperial permission for me to come to you once the field marshal regains his health. Please, my friend, do not delay me by your answer, although the embassies, of course, cannot be set up before next spring." The Council decided that it could permit Repnin to return to Petersburg.

UNRESOLVED PROBLEMS IN THE CRIMEA

Rumiantsev had not yet recovered from his illness when a new responsibility was laid on him—command of the Second Army, which had remained without a commander following the departure of Dolgoruky and settlement of the Tatar question. Rumiantsev wrote the empress on this score: "As concerns the qualities and disposition of the Tatar people, there is little reason to expect them to remain at peace and make proper use of their freedom and independence in the near future. I am basing my opinion on the fact that Shcherbinin, Veselitsky and Prince Dolgoruky, who had dealings with them, wrote unanimously and repeatedly that the Tatars were filled with utter disgust for all benefits associated with her majesty and would never abandon their desire for submission to the Porte as before. They are now seeking this formally, as the vizier reminded me in his letter; and Prince Dolgoruky wrote that they have sent delegates for this purpose to the Porte."

Actually, Turkish troops left the Crimea, the navy sailed from its shores back to Constantinople, and the resident Veselitsky was freed. But the Tatars had no desire to accept the independence given them. It was difficult for the sick field marshal to lead two armies, especially under such circumstances. "I am giving quarter neither to my health nor to my very life," he wrote Catherine, "against the advice of doctors, who think that worry associated with the administration of policy is the chief hindrance to my recovery. I am sacrificing my last energies daily to fulfill my duty. But weakened as I am by this prolonged illness, I can hardly administer even this army, and I fear that in such condition I might let something slip even here." Rumiantsev asked either that Prince Dolgoruky be renamed commander of the Second Army or that someone familiar with the area be appointed.

Meanwhile the grand vizier addressed a letter directly to Rumiantsev expressing the desire to change the terms of peace, namely concerning the Tatars and the Danube principalities for which privileges had been stipulated at Kuchuk-Kainardji. Rumiantsev replied: "I do not wish to disguise the utter amazement that laid hold of me when I saw the contents of your letter. A matter so solemn as the peace concluded between the All-Russian empire and the Ottoman Porte, authorized by their sovereigns, will tolerate neither delays nor detours in its implementation. I must tell you, albeit without accusing you, that not one point in the treaty can be violated without violating its every article, and its cornerstone is sincerity and scrupulousness. A change in the sacred treaties following their signing would be scandalous for the dignity and glory of the imperial courts. Although what is said frees me of further explanations, I want to make note of the following out of friendship for you: the Tatar peoples, as free and independent, are not being forced into anything repugnant to Islamic law. Their complaints and requests—even if they really have come from them—do not accord the right to this or that power to enquire into them. The Tatars now are an independent people dependent on no one, and with regard to this Russia and the Porte have mutual obligations which must be observed regardless of Tatar desires. You yourself say in your letter that the war continued for several years because of disagreement on the conditions decided at Kainardji; is it really possible to demand some change in them again and thereby fan the coals of former disagreements?" In a report dated November 5 Peterson congratulated Rumiantsev; the firmness of his answer had produced the desired result: the Porte decided to ratify the treaty with no changes.

But a mistake permitted at the beginning is found to be permanent at the end. The mistake made at the beginning of the Crimean negotiations by the proposal of Tatar independence was reinforced when the Turks received religious jurisdiction. Immediately upon signing the peace of Kuchuk-Kainardji Panin wrote Veselitsky concerning its conditions as relating to the Tatars: "Although the Porte recognizes the Tatars as free and independent in political and civil matters, there remains nevertheless the proviso that in ecclesiastical matters, because they share the same religion as the Turks and consider the sultan their supreme caliph, they are conformed to principles specified by Islamic law but without limiting in any way their political and civil liberty. From earlier observations at the Focsani and Bucharest congresses of the spiritual obligations of the Tatars to the Turkish sovereign, they would seem to consist of the following. Each new Crimean khan elevated to this rank by voluntary election informs the Ottoman throne through a charter sent with an authorized courier which requests the confirmation or blessing of his dignity. Second, the Crimean judges, because justice and Islamic punishment are closely related in Islamic law, are invested by the cadilesker of Constantinople; there is a formal act of blessing although not necessarily at first occasion, but timeless once done, which the Tatar authorities require of their present and future judges.

"Third, in the Crimea and other Tatar places the sultan's name is raised in prayer every Friday in the mosques. Undoubtedly the Porte will continue to try immediately to bring these three points into full practice. Opposed to this persists the danger that the Tatars, in their ignorance, superstition, and unbounded loyalty to the Turks, might not make progress in civilization and will remain as it were imprudent, going further than can be reconciled with their present independent status. So let the Tatars sound the name of the sultan in their mosques. But the moment you learn of the khan's intent and preparations for informing the Porte of his status and entreating its approval of his rank, and about formal investiture of

Tatar judges, you may request that the first letters sent to the Porte about the freedom they have acquired be communicated to you. Should you find these letters in any way out of character with the present situation of the Tatars, you are to try to correct them through explanations to the khan and the Crimean officials in order that the khan appear before the sultan not as a slave but as a lord, acting strictly according to religious convictions."

Thus the Tatars were placed between two fires: between the sultan, whom they must consider their spiritual leader and object of their prayers, and Russia, which at the first opportunity would demand enmity with the sultan, forcing the Tatars also to declare themselves against him. It is understandable that the Tatars, especially their clergy, with all their might would seek to escape this difficult situation, namely by returning to yesteryear. Others, like Shagin-Girey, who wanted a completely new order of things, full independence of the Porte, were extremely dissatisfied by ecclesiastical dependence on the sultan, which in their view had no religious basis.

Shagin-Girey appeared on the field again at the time of the Nogay rebellions.[77] Early in 1774 Prince Dolgoruky advised Petersburg of the debauchery of the Nogays, who were tempted by gifts the khan distributed to them after the Porte sent him to Sudjuk-Kale. The Edichkul horde revolted and seized the Russian district commander and his troops. At first the Council determined to counteract Turkish money with Russian money, granting Shcherbinin permission to use 35,000 rubles for this. But it was impossible to help with money alone. Lieutenant Colonel Bukhvostov gained much greater success by defeating the rebellious Nogays several times and driving the crown prince sent by the Turks from the Edisan horde. Shagin-Girey was sent to undertake the final pacification of the Nogays.

Panin wrote him a letter on February 26: "The reception of the news at her imperial majesty's court that your excellency intends to go to the Nogay peoples to take charge of them produced great satisfaction. Undoubtedly you will strive while at the Nogay hordes, more so because of the better resources given you there, to administer your fatherland and the Tatar people as a benefactor and mentor. Your nature and perfect virtues are worthy of this. The Tatar peoples, delivered through her imperial majesty's magnanimous deed, in accordance with her singular love for humanity, from abusive slavery and bondage, are maintained in an independent status through your watch and care. Yet, amazingly and quite regretfully, their lack of scruples makes them scarcely conscious of the advantageousness and superiority of their present lot when compared to their previous contemptuous, hard, and poverty-stricken fate. Now they shall be brought all in all to wisdom and lasting order through your excellency, so that the glory of your name shall ring among their descendents as an example and for imitation. To accomplish your goal you will be aided not only with money but also with troops; above all, the twelve thousand rubles allotted annually for your living expenses in the Crimea will be delivered to you as long as you mean well. Should you because of personal danger be unable to remain among the Nogays, you may as before accept exile in the empire and expect all proper esteem."

Simultaneously, Prince Dolgoruky received a rescript: "Furnishing Shagin-Girey, the Crimean crown prince sultan now living under our protection in Poltava, with primary authority over the Nogay hordes is obviously one of the best and safest ways during a protracted war for holding these flighty people in a situation advantageous to our empire. The more worthy our effort is for going beyond mere appearances, the more important and necessary it is. And the crown prince will find in it, because of his condition and circumstances, a most suitable recompense for his loyalty to us. Let him be sent as quickly as possible to the Nogays and receive aid in troops and money in order to frighten those who oppose him by one method, and support those who wish him well by another. And provide a special escort to accompany him and observe his behavior. Up to thirty thousand rubles are allotted for helping the crown prince. It is our desire that his attempt to win authority over the Nogay hordes not have the least appearance of coercion, but observe all proper freedoms. His selection should appear voluntary. You must try to make the crown prince understand how necessary and advantageous it is for him to forswear harsh measures by employing our arms; rather he should seek agreement through indulgence and persistent explanation. Colonel Brink can fill the post of escort."

Shagin-Girey was sent to the Kuban and the Peace of Kuchuk-Kainardji made. Yet the Crimeans displayed a persistent desire to remain under Turkish suzerainty. The crown prince wanted to make use of this to attain his own goals; he disclosed to Shcherbinin that it was possible to induce the Nogays to protest the behavior of the Crimeans and elevate him,

Shagin-Girey, to the khanate were he given 100,000 rubles and some troops as a guard. When Shcherbinin's report was read to the Council on October 27, it "pronounced the crown prince's proposal quite useful for consolidating the Tatar region which we have conquered, and considered it possible to implement it among the Tatars alone, without inciting a quarrel with the Porte. Because of the money, all Tatars in the Kuban, even Djan-Mambet-bey, could be employed and undoubtedly would be stronger than the Crimeans. The Porte, not seeing any clear Russian participation and therefore hesitant to disturb the peace, would not have the nerve to support the Crimeans. The crown prince would be indebted to us for raising him to the khanate and would remain absolutely loyal. In this way the Tatars would grow estranged from the Turks imperceptibly, and finally might be made wholly independent of them."

But this time Shagin-Girey proved unable to accomplish this purpose. Rumiantsev, after receiving good news from Peterson in Constantinople, did not want to disturb the consolidation of peace through new movements from the Kuban. He told Shcherbinin not to allow Shagin-Girey's plan to proceed further. Petersburg concurred fully with the field marshal's opinion, and on December 15 the Council approved a rescript to Shcherbinin instructing him to delay the crown prince's plan temporarily, holding the Tatars in readiness, not permitting them to return to their old settlements.[78]

ORDER RESTORED IN POLAND

Despite the fact that developments among the Tatars did not presage a long future for the peace of Kuchuk-Kainardji, the obvious advantages won by Russia at the moment it was experiencing significant domestic difficulties must have made a strong impression on the neighboring courts. Until now they had felt quite free and easy because of their roles in the Polish question.

On January 23 Stackelberg wrote Panin from Warsaw that "From the king to the last deputy no one will dare speak out in favor of the Orthodox non-Uniats and dissidents, even if convinced in the depths of his heart that their cause is just. Fanaticism, instead of waning, has grown stronger! Fear does not gain the results now as it did previously because of Vienna's policy of hypocrisy. I invited the Prussian and Austrian ambassadors over and suggested that we discuss the dissident question, which soon will be placed before the Diet. I will not speak about Benoit. His opinions,

completely in accord with the justice of the matter, remain the same as
they were; his future activity will accord with his sovereign's interests.
Both of us tried to persuade Rewiczki, but in vain. He stuck to his guns,
arguing that especially considering the present situation, given the marked
decrease in the number of dissidents owing to the partition, it is improper
to award them a place in the Diet equal to the Catholics. In general his
court implied in Petersburg, and particularly in Berlin–which admitted
its validity–that Austria as a Catholic state could not intercede for the
dissidents. It is easy to imagine what impression such behavior by Vienna
has produced among the Poles. When I arrived in Poland I found the people
full of prejudices against Russia and blinded by their ingratitude. The
partition has strengthened these feelings."

On March 3 Stackelberg wrote: "Benoit promised me to act together
in the struggle against the increase in prejudice brought about by cooperation between the papal nuncio and Baron Rewiczki. The former
rattles on about anathema and the latter promises money and aid in the
name of his court, although he tells me he is neutral."

But the allies brought cooperation to a halt on more than the dissident
question. We noted that Austria had seized Polish lands along the Sbrucz
river.[79] Tidings now came that the Prussians had changed the boundary
line demarcated in the treaty and were seizing Polish territories. The Polish
delegation complained. The ambassadors began to threaten the Poles, but
received in answer: "Our admission of weakness forced us, through ceding
a better part of Poland, to cling to the hope of ruling the remainder
peacefully. But in light of the fact that even the remnant is not safe from
daily seizures there is nothing more for us to fear; we sooner would agree
to be drawn and quartered than to roast on a slow fire."

Stackelberg complained that this development was destroying the hope
of completing all formalities before May 6, the date of the opening of
the Diet. But the dispute was resolved when the delegation decided
unanimously to send some prominent people to Petersburg and Vienna
to request mediation. They decided to send the supreme commander,
Hetman Branicki, to Petersburg.[80] They also decided to send an envoy
to Berlin to ask Frederick II to stop violating the frontier.

Meanwhile the dissident question hung like a storm cloud over the
scene. Stackelberg wrote Panin on March 24 that "My position will be
difficult between Catholic fanaticism on one side and the sometimes petty
obstinacy of the dissidents on the other. These gentlemen, who provoked

justifiable insults, are demanding full equality without understanding the situation or taking into account the need to limit themselves to what is essential, since their number is insignificant in comparison with the number of Catholics. Each day I assure them that at least a certain number of them will be allowed immediately to participate in the diets, but this does not pacify them. They want full rights, including the right to be members of the Permanent Council. They will receive all this with time, but this is impossible to arrange now owing to Vienna's resistance and the new government's difficulties. We would need grenadiers to introduce the draft for the Permanent Council into the delegation if we explained that the dissidents were to be included. The future will be less frightening for them if under the new form of government the king and the most intelligent elements of the population can weaken the influence of the bishops and Rome generally."

Baron Rewiczki suggested to the members of the deputation that they stand firm concerning the matter of the dissidents and he would answer for the consequences. Stackelberg feared that the negotiations would founder on the point of allowing dissidents into the Diet . He wrote Panin that for this venture to be accepted, the empress must announce that she promised her intercession with the king of Prussia on the issue of Poland's boundaries—if the dissident question was decided according to instructions given her minister in Warsaw. If the king of Prussia under these conditions were to honor the agreement concerning borders, the dissident question, this cause of unrest in Poland, would be resolved forever.

The Diet assembled and again postponed its sessions, until August 1, in order to give the delegation time to settle the issues. The question of the borders would consume the most time. Frederick II was seizing territory on the grounds that Austria had grasped more than its share. Austria would not consider returning the strip involved, and moreover Rewiczki assured Stackelberg that if the king of Prussia retained what he had seized, Vienna would not be limited to what it had already taken. Stackelberg had not foreseen this end to things. At the same time Commander Branicki upset him by sending news from Petersburg that aroused all Poland.

Stackelberg asked Panin to appease Branicki. "This man," he wrote, "can be of service, but it is necessary to put limits on his imagination else he subvert everything. You must note that he wishes to be the autocratic pilot of the ship. Perhaps he has mentioned the king several times but this was done merely to observe decency. He holds Stanislaw Augustus in submission through a feeling which, passing for friendship, is more like fear. In his effort to become the sole leader of his party he is emulating everyone before him who was our tool. As soon as our patronage made them strong and rich, gratitude was blotted from their hearts and replaced by hatred when the Russian ambassadors, having noted that they were playing a secondary role, tried to elevate Russia once more to its rightful place in Polish affairs. Your excellency knows the difficulty the Russian ambassadors had, owing to Poland's anarchy and the power of the magnates, in restraining the present king and the ranking men from putting the empress's patronage to evil use. The king hoped to create an autocracy and the magnates were intent on oppressing their compatriots. Circumstances have changed but not their views. If nothing interferes, the king will do the same as he has always done, Poland will perish, and Branicki will follow the footsteps of the Czartoryskis with the difference that he is perhaps more honest but also more temperamental. Russia, the king (if only he wants to) and all honorable men will discover the means to combat wickedness in the National Council,[81] if only equilibrium, once established, is preserved. You so often impressed upon me Poland's importance for Russia, especially when, after the peace, a steadfast system arises toward the whole of Europe and we will have to protect this bulwark of empire ourselves, so useful in both war and peace and much more difficult to administer now that two other powers have come so close to it.

"Permit me to conclude my dispatch with some necessary reflections. The mainspring of fear, so powerful in dealing with the Poles, has been undermined almost completely for us because the majority of the important magnates of the kingdom are divided as subjects among the three powers. When our embassy intimates to them from here that their conduct might not please Russia, they turn to the patronage of the other courts, primarily of Vienna. If the mainspring of fear has been weakened, common sense requires that a mainspring of hope and good deeds be substituted. In this regard we must force Branicki to limit the king from energetically persecuting everyone loyal to Russia. You directed these poor souls to me in order that they receive their rewards here, since enormous military expenditures prevent the empress from rewarding them herself. But when I petition the king on their behalf he not only refuses but also disparages them in the delegation, declaring publicly that such is the fate of people who turn to a foreign power. It is easy to imagine the impression this arouses daily, and how in this way the king asserts his own policy of destroying our influence in Poland, whereas under the Saxon kings Russia became fully ensconced in Poland because of the regard its sovereigns had for our recommendations. If you do not make use of Branicki's sojourn in Petersburg to restore our former position, the king will be able to render Russia as insignificant in Poland as the most distant courts. There is one other area in which we must use Branicki, namely the negotiations the Polish king is conducting with every court of Europe regarding his personal interests and rule now that the king of Sweden has turned his head."

But even as Stackelberg was asking Panin to convince Branicki to act in accord with Russia's views it turned out that Branicki, in concert with the king, had gone to Petersburg to subvert the resolutions about the Permanent Council. Consequently, the royalist party in the delegation reopened the question of the council, opposing it vociverously. The king's supporters were brazen enough to maintain that there had been no agreement on the council between the king and the ministers of the three courts. This greatly irritated Stackelberg, Benoit and Rewiczki. "Only in Poland can such things be done!" Stackelberg wrote Panin. The ambassadors pointed to the written agreement with the king. The king instructed his supporters to declare that he had signed nothing. Thereupon Stackelberg displayed the note the king wrote him the day after the agreement.[82] In it Stanislaw Augustus explained that by agreeing to formation of the council he was making a sacrifice out of esteem for the empress.

In order to confuse the issue in the delegation the king's supporters began to insist that since three official ranks had to participate in the council the dissidents necessarily had to be excluded. The entire delegation began to insist on this. Stackelberg told them that they must not mix topics. They could talk about the dissidents later. The session was adjourned until the next day but in the meantime the king, who was hardly in a position to disavow his agreement with the ambassadors, declared that he had been coerced into it by threats. The question of the Permanent Council came up at the delegation's next session and the cry was renewed that dissidents be excluded from it. Stackelberg again insisted that they must not combine topics. Even Rewiczki took his side, but simultaneously left the impression in his speech that Russia had gone too far in the treaty of 1768 and that on instructions of his court he would participate most actively in upholding the essential rights of the prevailing religion in Poland. He even added that he would attempt to exclude dissidents from the Permanent Council. The book by Father Konarski helped settle the question of the Permanent Council by supporting a plan similar to the Russian one, only less favorable for the king.[83] Furthermore, the author introduced letters from Prince Czartoryski, the Lithuanian chancellor and the Lithuanian table attendant–the present king–which admitted that the plan was a saving compromise. The question of the Permanent Council thus was settled, but the disputes about boundaries and the dissidents carried over into 1775.

FREDERICK II INTERVENES

The border issue led to a strengthening of relations among Berlin, Vienna, and Petersburg. Russia's old friend, the king of Prussia, played the most prominent part in Russia's troubles during the first half of the year [1774]. He was quite distressed by the cossack rebellion in Russia,[84] but in his sorrow found comfort in the opportunity to insist that Russia hasten to make peace with the Porte by yielding in the Crimea and on the question of navigation on the Black Sea. He found further comfort in the opportunity to acquire a few more pieces of land from Poland. On January 4 the king wrote Solms: "Since I am Russia's friend, you must not doubt that I was deeply grieved by news of the cossack uprising. This spark must be extinguished before it produces a fire. This forces me to yearn more than ever for Russia to conclude peace with the Turks. Tell Count Panin that if the Turks are prepared to make the desired proposals, it is foolish to be concerned with details. I think that peace is more important for Russia right now than all the conquests it might make. Van Swieten has returned from Vienna complaining that the Russians are interfering with Austria regarding the borders of Galicia. Vienna, in his words, has resolved firmly not to renounce its possessions. Should Petersburg yield to the Austrians but make difficulties for me, that suggests that Russia favors those who envy it rather than its most loyal ally. It seems to me best for Petersburg to yield both of us these bits of territory, quite useful for us both and essentially trifles. And here, finally, is the news from France: Durand writes about his successes. At the Russian court, he says, the interests of the realm take back seat to personal passions. He wanted to stir ambitions with the reproach that Russia accepts direction from the king of Prussia. In Russia there is, in his words, an uprising, complications in raising soldiers and bad management of the war. These problems supposedly must lead to difficulties which will force Russia to appeal to France."

The following month Frederick wrote: "I approve the wise measures of Count Panin calculated not to arouse the enmity of Austria, especially under the present circumstances. But I do not promise Russia greater advantages because of its favors. Favors will never gain Russia the true friendship of Vienna. I am correct in assuming Vienna feels the same envy toward Russian trade in Turkey as France and England. Exploiting envy, France wishes ardently to promote strife among the three courts in order to mediate peace between Russia and Turkey. Be that as it may, if Russia really desires immediate peace with the Porte, it is entirely capable of winning it without outside mediation. The cost is merely easing the conditions regarding trade and the Tatars."

In March the king's advice that peace could be concluded faster through relaxation of terms grew even stronger. Frederick wrote that softer terms in no way would damage Russia's military glory, for its military fortunes had not changed. Crossing the Danube was always extraordinarily difficult. It was necessary to make peace before the vicissitudes of military fortune were tempted. The benefits of independence or subjection of the Tatars scarcely equalled the risk to which Russia was subject should fortune not smile on the Danube or in the Crimea. The king groaned at the very thought of it. Failures in Turkey would produce embarrassments in Poland more dangerous than ever. And it was inconceivable that the king of Sweden would not exploit the opportunity to reacquire the part of Finland now held by Russia. If the Porte proposed tolerable conditions, it would be best for Russia to make peace. On the vicissitude of military fortune Frederick spoke from his own experience.

In April Frederick grew deeply concerned about Austria's intention to seek Poland's outright assent to enhancing its share of the partition. In his view the matter must be settled among the three courts, which alone must be concerned about mutual equilibrium. Under no circumstances was this a concern of Poland. Frederick directed Solms to convey to Panin that were Austria to achieve an expansion of its share, he would add to his own and hoped in that case to receive aid from the court which was interested no less than he in upholding the balance between Austria and Prussia.

Petersburg knew well that preservation of this balance could lead very far, and therefore from the very first accorded poor reception to Austria's proposed extension of its border from the Seret (or the Podorze, as it was called in the treaty) to the Sbrucz. Panin in conversation with Lobkowitz stated bluntly that if the Austrians did not limit their claims there were no grounds for demanding that the king of Prussia not make further seizures. When Lobkowitz tried to explain that in this case Austria had a greater right than Prussia, Panin reminded him that, on the contrary, it was possible from the wording of the treaty to construe a Prussian claim to the entire Netze river whereas the Austrian reference to insufficiency of information, according to which an unnamed river appeared on the map, had no weight and gave no right to expand its borders to localities no one had in mind when the treaty was signed. Panin ended the conversation with the words that Austria must agree first with Prussia and then turn to Russia.

Austria began to see eye to eye with Prussia. Frederick II was displeased with Petersburg and told van Swieten that "This is clear chicanery from the Russian side. I find your declarations to be valid. I am not participating in the difficulties others are causing you. I am not at all envious of your share. Chicanery is being practiced on me, as on you, over trifles." When van Swieten told him that, considering Petersburg's point of view, Austria and Prussia must agree not to increase their shares but rather define their borders more advantageously and reduce their occupied territories somewhat, Frederick replied: "We must hold on to everything we now rule. We must uphold our rights." Frederick also explained why he expressed himself so decisively and paid no attention to Russia's dissatisfaction: Russia was in such dire straits that it was in no position to interfere in this dispute. The Pugachev uprising had taken 15,000 troops from Rumiantsev; the people were dreadfully tired of war, and the conscript levies were difficult to meet.

But Austria was concerned about more than Russia's opposition. From Warsaw Rewiczki wrote about new seizures by Frederick II. People were saying that he had moved his border from the Netze to the Warta.[85] Consequently, were the principle of balance in shares to be upheld, that is, were Austria to compete with the Prussian monarch in taking more, where would it all end? Austria had no desire whatsoever to see the final destruction of Poland. Rather, it wished to win the greatest influence there, to become Poland's patron, and therefore it declared to the Prussian ruler that it was essential to discuss boundaries with the Poles in the delegation. It is easy to imagine Frederick's irritation. In a dispatch to Solms he styled Kaunitz a horrible man, the proudest and at the same time the greatest swindler among mortals.

This break between Prussia and Austria led both powers separately to make their case in Petersburg. But Catherine did not want to change her outlook. She requested that the borders be established according to the treaty, exactly as Russia was doing regarding White Russia. Inasmuch as Frederick had announced that he would not yield an inch of the land he had acquired if Austria would not modify its claims, Panin again took it upon himself to persuade Lobkowitz to concede, once more expressing the view that had Austria not done so, the king of Prussia would not have thought of making additional acquisitions. When his admonitions failed, Catherine decided on direct entreaties to Frederick, Joseph, and Maria Theresa, admonishing them to be satisfied with the lands stipulated in the convention.

No sooner had Frederick learned of Catherine's decision to write him and the Austrian rulers than he quickly sent for van Swieten. "If you want to cede anything," he told him, "I beg you to tell me and I will issue instructions so that we will remain united. Branicki has upset everyone in Petersburg. Do you not see that it is in the interest of the Polish monarch to play for time in the hope that discord may appear among the three courts? All this is his doing. He forced Branicki to cry to Petersburg, blew the matter out of proportion, and requested the justice and patronage of the empress, who was hoodwinked. But it is only necessary for us to stand together. The storm will disperse.

"Do you want to know my opinion? We will be in no hurry to answer the letters of the Russian empress; emotion there is abating. I know the Russians: their first impressions are very strong but dissipate with time. The Polish ruler chose Branicki purposefully, knowing he would be heard in Petersburg and the empress would receive him, for he was loyal to her and Stanislaw Poniatowski when the latter was in Petersburg during Empress Elizabeth's reign.[86] Branicki knows how to utilize these old relationships and assured the empress that her glory requires her to protect the Poles, who are driven to despair. Consequently the letters were written. But this was not all; it was only a prelude. Branicki's plan was as follows: if after receiving letters from the Russian empress you did not renounce the areas you have occupied, Russia and Prussia were to have admonished you, and if even then you did not yield, the Poles would call forth the Commonwealth's collapse and attack you. We were to stand by peacefully. This beautiful plan was communicated to me in minute detail. I did not wish to answer it seriously and began to laugh. I let the empress feel that we would be assuming the role of Polish Don Quixotes and that I am not at all disposed toward this role.

"But it was essential to move quickly on the border question and not delay, either not answering the Russian demands for concessions or saying that we are prepared to yield if the others yield."

However reluctantly, Berlin and Vienna were forced to decide to require Polish recognition of the claims of both courts, and should the Poles not concur, to turn to Russia so that the three courts might resolve the dispute jointly. The Poles declared that the Austrian and Prussian claims could not be examined in Warsaw; it was absolutely necessary to send special commissions to the areas of the claims. Again reluctantly, Berlin and Vienna had to agree to this as well. It was to the Poles' advantage to delay in dispatching the commissioners. A year passed and Frederick angrily wrote to Solms: "I confess that I might have wanted to find a way to convince Count Panin of the necessity of making a stronger declaration to the Poles. So far these republicans have introduced thousands of difficulties in defining our boundaries, and Austria finds their commissioners just as inflexible as I. One must assume that this commission will not have the least success. The dispute will be passed on to the delegation and we will have even more troubles. Russia will draw the same lot on the matter of the dissidents, which I doubt very much will reach its goal without shrieks and clamor. The Poles in their foolishness think that Vienna and I will do everything possible to force Russia to withdraw its troops from Poland. The Austrian minister answered this request in general terms, but Benoit answered perfectly that since matters were far from being settled, it is impossible to think that calm has returned to Poland, even though the restoration of calm is the sole reason for the presence there of foreign troops. Consequently, the real issue is not about the departure of Russian troops, but about preventing Prussian and Austrian troops from reentering Poland because of the sluggishness and ill will in the negotiations."

"The Poles," Frederick continued, "are not as accommodating as they are perhaps thought in Petersburg. And the Diet will never end without Russian scolding. Almost two years have passed since the delegation was assembled, and what has been done? The issue of the Permanent Council barely has passed. Questions about the authority of the supreme commander, the army, election of the king, revenues, and dissidents re-main open and no one is even thinking about their resolution. If the dele-gation were to venture to take up disputes like these several years would drag on before we would finish them. Truly, neither I nor Russia nor Vienna can ever rely on the Poles. This nation is empty-headed and ava-ricious. Higher reasoning never makes any impression on them. Fear and money are the sole mainsprings of this heavy mass."

So it was necessary to appeal to Russia, to plead that it scold the Poles, but it was impossible to scold Russia after the peace of Kuchuk-Kainardji. Frederick had tried to suggest in Petersburg that the peace was unstable and that Prussia once more had obtained significance for Russia in Turkish affairs, but the attempt did not succeed. At the beginning of October Frederick forwarded to Petersburg Zegelin's dispatch from Constantinople, which revealed that the Porte intended to beseech the Prussian monarch to employ his good services to soften the terms of the peace of Kuchuk-Kainardji. Catherine wrote Panin: "You may answer in truth that not a single stroke of the present treaty can be changed without a new war. It would be better for the Porte to review what has happened in its neighborhood than to avert us slanderously from the sincere agreement with it which I intend to preserve inviolate." The last sentence referred to the Austrian occupation of Moldavian territory, about which Rumi-antsev had been corresponding with Peterson.[87]

SOME OBSERVATIONS

We noted earlier that in addition to Polish lands Joseph II's favorite idea was to take something from Turkey. At the beginning of 1774 Vienna was in a blissful frame of mind. Russia, occupied in the east with Puga-chev, must make a most unprofitable peace with the Porte, which could only be to Austria's liking. But suddenly there was a terrible disappoint-ment: Russia now was signing the most advantageous peace it could have desired! The indignation against the Turks was frightful. "The Turks," Kaunitz said, "completely deserved the misfortune which befell them, in part for their weak and stupid conduct of the war and in part for lack of confidence in the powers, especially Austria, which wanted to assist them in their predicament. Why did they not employ the mediation of Austria, England, and Holland? Each of these powers might have gained the most advantageous terms for them, and we all would have been satisfied. But this nation is predestined to perish, and a small but well-trained force is capable, when it decides to do so, of driving the Turks from Europe."[88]

If it was easy to drive the Turks from Europe, it was even easier to relieve them of some land. The Turks were in no condition to sustain a new war now. Russia was not prepared to fight on Turkey's behalf. The king of Prussia, having adopted the "Political Catechism,"[89] could not be angry when on the basis of this document states permitted themselves small acquisitions without bothering each other with notifications. The king of Prussia might take for himself anything, any place, and should he take too much Austria on grounds of equity would add to its share. Austria had merely to choose a more convenient area, and chose Bukovina, the part of Moldavia lying toward Transylvania, very profitable now in relation to Austria's new Polish possessions. Bukovina was occupied by Austrian troops. Turkey did not raise a finger. Petersburg decided to await the response of the Prussian monarch, and in general was very pleased by the conduct of the Austrians, as is apparent from Catherine's letter to Prince Repnin. "My desires often come true. Now the emperors (caesars) are quarreling with the Turks. I am prepared to bet that the former will be overcome but I, with my hands on my hips like the letter Phi (Φ), will stand watching them and on lips everywhere around me will be the words 'good officiating.'[90]

There remained France, the eternal advocate of the Turks, but France no longer reached as far as Bukovina. On January 9 [1774] a new envoy arrived in Paris, Prince Ivan Sergeevich Bariatinsky, and in April King Louis XV died, in consequence of which the Duke d'Aiguillon retired and was replaced by Count Vergennes, recalled from Stockholm. Bariatinsky wrote that the new king, Louis XVI, discussing the policies of Duke Choiseul, said that France had wasted much money in subsidies and pensions to no effect. "What is it to me," asked the king, "if Russia wars on the Turks and confederations are made in Poland, and why give subsidies to Sweden and Denmark? I will stop all these useless expenses." The tidings of the peace of Kuchuk-Kainardji produced a terrible impression, especially in the ministry. "It is incredible," wrote Bariatinsky, "to what degree envy is rising here at our successes. The Poles in France are in a profound state of grief. The Austrian ambassador rarely shows me candor; if he speaks, it is in general expressions with double meaning."

Given the situation in France Sweden was unable to count on more aid from there. In May Ostermann departed Stockholm for Petersburg, leaving the conduct of affairs to the resident, Alexander Stakhievich Stakhiev.[91] In July at a court ball the king approached Stakhiev and said that he could not possibly visit the empress that summer, but certainly would do so during the coming year, discussing it with no one in advance. Thereby he let Stakhiev know that for this year others had interfered with his desires. The king expounded on the need of a meeting with the empress. "In a personal meeting," he said, "I can do more in a quarter hour to advance the mutual prosperity of both courts than through ministerial correspondence over an entire year, especially in destroying misunderstandings and suspicions aroused by men of ill will and perhaps by certain of one's own people. I burn with desire to see the empress and in this meeting once and for all to close the way to unkind suggestions. I am well aware of the calumnies and instigations heaped on me in Petersburg on the occasion of the recent revolution here, which were related to me. I let them in one ear and out the other. And as concerns the revolution, I decided on it only after the estates intended to drive the senators from their chairs. In all fairness to you and Count Ostermann, you both made every effort to restrain the unlimited obduracy at that time in the three lower estates, but it was impossible to restrain it any other way than as I did."

On the subject of the peace of Kuchuk-Kainardji Stakhiev wrote: "The more glorious and profitable this peace is for our court, the less pleasant it is for Sweden and its followers, and more so because France embraced it with the hope of including in the treaty a guaranty of Sweden's form of government; that also was a reason why the king postponed his trip to Petersburg: the French ambassador Vergennes threatened that if the king went to Petersburg there would be no guaranty."

One final anecdote reveals how Catherine understood Russia's relationship to the European powers after the peace of Kuchuk-Kainardji. Immediately upon receiving news of the peace, an assembly was held at the court in Oranienbaum at which all foreign ministers were present.[92] The empress, sitting at cards and inviting the Danish and English ministers to play with her, said loudly, so that all could hear: "Today is a very happy day for me and I want to see only merry faces around me."

III

DOMESTIC AFFAIRS, 1769-1774

ACTIVITIES OF THE SENATE

With the establishment of the Council the Governing Senate in reality yielded primary importance to it.[1] The empress attended the Council's sessions very frequently, but no longer was present at meetings of the Senate, expressing her will by letter or through the procurator general.[2] Thus, on the subject of the punishment of Lieutenant Dubasov, who had murdered a steward of Countess Razumovskaya, a handwritten resolution was drafted: "In commutation of his ten-year stay in prison he is to be freed, and the Senate is to examine why such an important case remained so long without a verdict. In the future our Senate is to ensure with vigilant eye that cases demanding justice do not remain so long without verdict." Just under two years later the Senate received a personal decree from the empress: "It is so essential for the civil service and public order that directives sent from one office of civil administration to another be acted upon promptly and accurately; all this notwithstanding, her imperial majesty has noticed in numerous cases that this is observed so poorly and carelessly in some government offices that lawsuits and legal statutes of the greatest import either are not acted upon or not executed with the speed and precision which the service and their importance demand. Therefore her imperial majesty ordains that the Senate reiterate this most strictly in all government offices and likewise maintain supervision of all subordinate offices unremittingly in order that this indeed be done everywhere. Should such negligence appear any place, deal with it without the slightest indulgence and to the fullest extent of the laws. Come to decisions on fundamentally important issues without delay or hesitation, for no legal statute will provide the expected benefit if carelessly drawn and not executed at the prescribed time."

Notwithstanding this injunction to the Senate to watch "with vigilant eye," in 1774 we observe the resolution of a case first brought in 1765.

In the latter year two Little Russians, Zolotarenko and Cherny, testified that they set fire to the cossack village of Lugansk during its fair at the order of the bazaar foreman, Volosheninov.[3] Later Zolotarenko and Cherny testified in military court, following three applications of torture and fire, that they neither set fire to the fair nor had been instructed to do so by Volosheninov. Volosheninov confessed to nothing. The College of Justice acquitted Volosheninov, Zolotarenko and Cherny of burning down the fair. However, since Zolotarenko was obviously a charlatan, he was sentenced to be beaten with the knout and banished to Orenburg. On reviewing the case, the Senate did not uphold the knouting of Zolotarenko because he had endured excessive torture; it merely sent him to perpetual exile in Taganrog. Zolotarenko and Cherny maintained that they testified against Volosheninov because they could not endure the beatings and torture administered by the merchants who seized them at the fair.

As far as the interminable delays in resolving legal cases were concerned, Catherine issued a remarkable decision in 1769 in the case of the merchant Popov. In March a Moscow merchant held under arrest, Mikhail Popov, was brought to the Moscow Secret Chancellery from the Treasury College.[4] He was detained in consequence of his denunciation of crown agent Khlebnikov for making extra money on the sale of spirits. Popov was sent to the Secret Chancellery because, while under arrest, he stood up from his seat in a passion and said, "There is no justice in the sovereign." Catherine issued the resolution: "Erase Popov's careless words and return him to the Treasury College with instructions to complete his case forthwith so that he can see that there is justice."

The views of the Catherinian Senate with regard to the two following events indicate the peculiarities of the time. In 1771 the Ufa military governor, Borisov, reported to the Orenburg governor, and the latter to the Senate, that in the town of Ufa near the cathedral the sound of an invisible bell was heard repeatedly from overhead.[5] The Senate ruled that there must be a simple and natural cause for the ringing. The Orenburg governor was to select a reliable man and send him to discover the cause of the sound. A year later the Orenburg governor reported that he had sent one Garezin, an architectural ensign, to discover the source of the sound. Upon his return he reported that he had heard the sound repeatedly by day and night, only softly. Noting that in calm weather there was a noise in the church cupola that sounded like a swarm of bees, Garezin in the presence of the local archpriest ordered the cupola broken open. Tearing open the cupola caused a similar echo to resound. The cause of the phenomenon turned out to be the vibration of the wires supporting the iron cross atop the church. When the cross was removed nothing could be heard either in the church or in the cupola. The Senate ruled that the Orenburg governor be apprised that the Governing Senate concluded from his previous report that this echo could not have been a supernatural act, as the military governor empty-headedly and superstitiously had written the governor, but issued from a simple and natural cause. The Senate told him to find it for no other reason than to lead the local people out of their error. Therefore the Senate recommended that in the future when confronted with such events officials be more observant in their reasoning.

In this instance the matter was resolved by the decrees of the secular authorities. But in 1769 the Synod[6] informed the Senate that the bishop of Ustiug had filed a report that sorcerers and magicians had appeared among peasants of both sexes in the Pechora district near the town of Yarensk.[7] They not only turned others from Orthodoxy but also infected many with various diseases by means of worms. The Senate directed that whereas their sorcery and trickery consisted in plotting against other people's health, which in fact was harmed, the men who committed this crime were to be drafted into the army, although they might keep their wives, and the unmarried women and girls were to be sent to settle in Siberia. But before this decision reached Yarensk the sorcerers were sent to the Senate as having confessed that they had renounced their faith and had met with the devil, who had brought them the worms with which they had harmed people. The peasants testified to the Senate that they had been seized by the district police because of the raging at them of women possessed by the devil. They said that in the Yarensk military governor's chancellery they had been beaten unmercifully several times during the inquest; as a result of these beatings they had been driven to confess to things they had not done. The Senate ordered the governor of Archangel to dismiss the Yarensk military governor and his subordinate from their duties and to free the alleged sorcerers. Furthermore, he was to inform the chancelleries of all governments, provinces and towns of the case and communicate the order to the Synod. In 1772 the Synod informed the Senate that instructions had been sent to archbishops and other church notables forbidding them to initiate inquests concerning sorcery and magic since these matters were considered to be under the jurisdiction of the civil courts.

We have mentioned Catherine's testimony that she could not find a map of Russia in the Senate. In the fall of 1774, probably owing to the Pugachev uprising, the procurator general stated that the Senate had no reliable information about the distances between adjacent villages and towns, or to the government and provincial capitals lying nearest them. Nor did it know for certain through which landmarks, geographical features or habitations the roads passed to those towns, or what rivers the roads crossed, or whether there were bridges across them or fords. The Senate issued an order that all government, province, and district chancelleries be instructed to submit this information.

THE SENATE AND PROVINCIAL ADMINISTRATION

As regards the life of secondary institutions during the period under discussion, the following event is noteworthy. The president of the Main Magistracy, Count Tolstoy, and Procurator Sushkov were dismissed from office for the improper balloting of the members of the Moscow magistracy.[8]

At the level of regional administration the governor of Novgorod, Jakob Sievers,[9] continued to be distinguished by his vigorous activity. In 1769 he sent the Senate statistics on the number of births, marriages, and deaths for the year 1768 in his government. The Senate decided, having received the information, to send him a resolution to the effect that his fulfillment of his duty was so praiseworthy and energetic that it wished all the lord governors to furnish the Governing Senate with similar information. What was more, the information sent by the Novgorod governor clearly demonstrated that reporting his praiseworthy conduct through the procurator general could serve as a means for obtaining similar information from each governor about his own government.

But the Senate was obliged to forward quite a different message to the governor general of Livonia, Count George Browne.[10] He reported that on the basis of a 1766 manifesto he deemed it necessary to elect mayors and marshals for two-year terms. The marshal of the Livonian land assembly observed that the two-year term to which he was elected nearly had ended and therefore requested convocation of the assembly to elect a new marshal. The land assembly was convened in the proper manner, but only one person showed up for the election and four others sent written ballots. "From this," wrote Count Browne, "I conclude that the Livonian land assembly does not want to elect any more marshals or constitute a special body."

The Senate issued instructions to the governor general that, acknowledging the refusal of the Livonian assembly to elect a marshal to be quite reprehensible, the Senate charged him to make the land assembly listen to reason and convince it, in the most stern way, to proceed immediately to the election of a new marshal. Anyone not obeying should be treated according to the fullest severity of the laws.

Somewhat earlier, on a proposal by the procurator general the Senate ordered the staffs of the chancelleries of Riga, Reval, and Vyborg governments to learn the Russian language thoroughly;[11] those who knew Russian should occupy higher posts than those who did not because the welfare of the realm and their own well-being required it. Proposals forwarded to the Senate nominating candidates for posts had to specify who did and who did not know Russian.

During this era a new region, White Russia,[12] was added to the empire. During the related administrative structuring the newly acquired lands were divided into two halves. Part of the large Novgorod government was joined to one of them. Two new governments were set up, Pskov and Mogilev. Pskov government was divided into five provinces, of which two were Great Russian, Pskov and Velikolutsk, and three came from Poland—Dvinsk, Polotsk, and Vitebsk. Mogilev government was divided into three provinces, Mogilev, Orshansk, and Rogachev. The capital of Pskov government was Opochka and the capital of Mogilev, the city of Mogilev. Two major generals were named as governors, Krechetnikov in Pskov and Kakhovsky in Mogilev.[13] Count Zakhar Chernyshev was named governor general over both governments.

The empress, after notifying the Senate on September 10 of the union of certain Polish lands with Russia, instructed it to present an opinion as to where these newly formed governments were to direct judicial appeals. In its report the Senate stressed the necessity of making the inhabitants of the newly added lands equal at the outset with long-time

Russian subjects as far as possible. This would prevent them from claiming special laws or perpetual privileges and consequently the administrative difficulties that Livonia, Estonia and Finland continued to cause. Therefore the Senate considered it appropriate to subordinate legal appeals in these governments to the College of Justice, cases concerning hereditary estates and landed property to the College of Hereditary Estates,[14] and other matters to the relevant administrations. Since personal litigation in the governments was subject to local law and conducted in the local language, the Senate raised the question of creating separate departments for each of these governments in the colleges of Justice and Hereditary Estates for handling such litigation, and employing Polish translators in each college.

The selection of government personnel in the newly acquired regions was not everywhere successful, as is apparent form the report of the Mstislav procurator, Babaev, who recorded the numerous disorders and disputes in Mstislav province which sometimes went as far as murder. Not one such case at the provincial chancellery had been decided, for which reason the inhabitants brought complaints about the *voevoda*,[15] the district military governor, to the civil governor. Because of the *voevoda*'s absences from the chancellery for lengthy periods, discipline had diminished not only among the inhabitants but among the chancellery employees and the staff command as well. Frustration prevailed on every side. Incessant quarrels and scuffles occurred among the inhabitants; the poorest nobles, widows, and orphans were being ruined and could not find justice. The *voevoda*, Collegiate Assessor Lebedev, was said to be chronically ill. He rarely visited the chancellery and conducted some business at home, but nothing was known about this in the chancellery. His assistant, Rode, left the chancellery first thing every day for Lebedev's house and returned just before the end of the working day. A gentrywoman named Partsevskaya neither accepted orders from the provincial chancellery nor instructed her peasants to obey them. Her people inflicted great insults and torment on the detachments sent to discipline her and shot soldier Kvasov.

MEASURES TO RAISE REVENUE

During the difficult six-year war with Turkey the Senate was obliged to turn special attention to the tasks laid out by its founder [Peter the Great]: economy in expenditures, increase of revenues, and conscripting for the military—in short, "to collect as much money as possible since money is the artery of war." Immediately upon declaration of war by the Turks an assignat bank was founded.[16] The dark side of this institution was not slow in appearing. In June 1771 N.I. Panin received a note from the empress disclosing considerable alarm; her alarm shows itself because the message was entrusted to the man responsible for foreign affairs and the education of the heir to the throne, neither of which was related to this concern. "Please join the procurator general and Count Shuvalov (Andrei Petrovich, the director of the assignat bank) to investigate the details of today's discovery at the Bank of State Assignats that twenty-five-ruble notes have been altered into seventy-five, and inform me of your findings. Take whatever measures are necessary to ensure as quickly as possible that the bank's credit is not damaged by falsified assignats." The following day Catherine sent a second note: "Count Shuvalov wrote me that the thieves were found and confessed. He does not say whether prepared plates were found on them, but merely states obscurely that they embezzled up to five thousand rubles or spoiled ninety numbers in this way."

In 1772 occurred the affair of the two Pushkin brothers. One of them went abroad and returned with a press and type for making counterfeit assignats, but was seized at the border.[17]

At the time of the bank's establishment a million rubles worth of assignats were put into circulation, but at the beginning of 1774 an imperial edict authorized the Senate to circulate up to twenty million rubles in assignats, with the stipulation that when that sum was distributed from the banks new assignats were to be printed solely to replace old worn-out assignats returned by banks. The Senate instructed all government offices doing business with banks to exercise utmost care in fulfilling their obligations and not request assignats before they held the cash to pay for them in full. On no account were they to rely on the fact that cash would be available shortly.

The old Bank for the Gentry reported abuses to the Senate that it was incapable of combatting.[18] Although the bank had been very strict and taken every appropriate precaution to avoid forgery in mortgaged property, violators were not declining but from time to time were increasing. Therefore the bank petitioned that it investigate families desiring to borrow, particularly the number of male souls they owned and where the souls lived. The bank wanted the Treasury College to forward a list of landowners, which the bank would alphabetize, so that prior to making a loan it could determine whether a mortgaged estate was truly under lien, whether the property had been sold, and whether there was collateral. Initially the Senate decided to instruct the Treasury College to compile a list and send it to the bank, but several weeks later it changed its decision, informing the bank that the desired information was quite difficult to assemble. Inasmuch as directives had been issued to prescribe the precautions the bank had to observe when making loans, it was to act on the basis of the applicable decrees.

In October 1769 a decree was published for general information. "The present war with the Turks, which has increased expenditures over those of peacetime, requires that state revenues be increased proportionally. Although present circumstances require levying an extraordinary tax on the people in the furtherance of our common defense and security, nevertheless her imperial majesty, feeling maternal concern for her people, seeks to avoid burdening her faithful subjects more than is necessary even under these circumstances by raising state income in a less burdensome way than through increased taxes. This revenue may be found in the crown's profits from the sale of alcoholic beverages throughout the land." Spirits were to be sold at three rubles a pail, and a tax of three rubles per ten gallons added to French liqueurs.

In 1769 the empress charged two men renowned for their business acumen, Volkov and Teplov,[19] to determine how much tax the merchants and townsmen must pay during the war. The plan was obliged to adhere to certain fixed principles: (1) the overall burden be assessed equally throughout the empire insofar as possible; (2) the condition of industry and trade in towns, rather than population, be considered; (3) in calculating merchants, townsmen, and others, identify everyone who, although not subject to tax assessment, operated factories and industrial works and practised other lines of business typical of townsmen; and (4) because the tax was to be temporary, it be based on the short term.

Volkov and Teplov found that in 1769 there were 230 textile and 256 non-textile manufactures. The former worked 12,771 looms and in the latter the total capital turnover was 921,534 rubles annually. There were 111 iron foundries with a total yearly capital turnover of 1,192,540 rubles. There were 48 copper smelteries, with a capital turnover of 780,175 rubles. The number of merchants and handicraft guild members totalled 228,209.

Volkov and Teplov explained that they had followed the rule that if needs dictated new taxes they should be temporary and similar to existing taxes since this was the practice the world over. They found that a doubling of the annual tax on manufacturies and plants would not be burdensome. In this way 287,646 rubles could be raised. On the same grounds merchants would be treated equitably were the present tax rate of forty altyns increased to a ruble and a half per soul. State peasants should pay more tax as well, namely two rubles for quitrent and 70 copecks for soul tax. It was true that the poor townsmen in the small towns did not enjoy the advantages of the state peasants. But it was equally true that the sole cause of their poverty was laziness and negligence, and that prosperous townsmen paid for many of the poor whereas the peasant for the most part paid his own tax. In the entire townsman classification, according to the last census, there were 228,209 souls; consequently the temporary tax would bring in 342,313 rubles. By their reckoning the treasury each year during the war would receive new revenue of 629,959 rubles. On the basis of this report a decree announcing the new tax was issued on October 30 of the same year.

But if taxes must be increased, first of all it was necessary to collect old taxes and avoid appearances harmful to the treasury. At the beginning of 1769 the Senate admitted that although the collection of the soul tax and arrears was assigned primarily to the governors, nothing had been achieved despite persistent efforts by the General War Commissariat, the War College and numerous missives from the Senate.[20] Not only had arrears not been collected, new ones were accumulating from negligence alone, to the extent that the General War Commissariat in 1768 considered total arrears to be 644,000 rubles. In addition, the General War Commissariat did not receive reports on time; on the contrary, it was being paid in obstinacy and disobedience, as the conduct of the secretary and staff of the chancellery of the Moscow government demonstrates. Detained in the chancellery by the General War Commissariat, they drove off the sentry posted at the door and escaped. The Senate ordered the governors to pledge once again to finish collecting the arrears.

Needless to say, it was much easier to collect money due the state from one or several well-known personages. It turned out that the former governor of Kazan, Kvashnin-Samarin, had purchased spirits from Senator Count Ivan Larionovich Vorontsov for the state at an exorbitant price at a time when there was no pressing need to buy, resulting in a loss to the treasury of 31,511 rubles.[21] To restore this loss, the tax farmer, Shemiakin, was ordered to return 9,675 rubles, and he and another tax farmer, Belavin, were to give back another 5,084 rubles; the remaining 16,740 rubles was demanded from Kvashnin-Samarin. The Senate issued a directive to recover the money from Vorontsov and Kvashnin-Samarin.

There were complaints about contraband, and Count Münnich gave the empress a plan for stopping it.[22] Merchants in the customs house would receive labels from customs officials enumerating the names, quantity of goods, and the stamps affixed to the boxes or bales so that no merchant while on the road, before arriving at his approved destination, would dare to unseal, extract, or sell goods under fear of confiscation of all his wares. When merchants arrived with their wares at their appointed towns sentries must bring them directly to the highest local government office where the goods would be examined and, if something not listed on the label was found, it would be confiscated. If everything appeared in order, the merchants were free to sell their goods. This decree would be read in all border towns and villages at the churches, in order that the townsmen of different estates, and particularly the peasants, be encouraged to apprehend smugglers. Since most merchants with contraband hoped to acquire huge profits in the largest towns, particularly in Moscow, it would be necessary to establish there an office under the Main Chancellery for Customs Duties,[23] with one reliable man paid a good salary and having a sufficient number of subordinates. He must monitor all merchants arriving in Moscow and, when he found anything amiss, inform the chancellery to place under surveillance the houses and shops of the merchants he suspected of dealing in contraband.

The empress asked the Senate to review this plan. The Senate noted that when internal duties were eliminated and excise taxation was transferred to the ports and border customs houses it was calculated that excise duties amounted to less than a million rubles whereas they were actually more than a million, sometimes a million and a half rubles.[24] Therefore the Senate found no immediate need to change arrangements which had produced much profit for the treasury and great benefit to the merchants by allowing free and uninterrupted circulation. The use of labels to license the goods of those not under suspicion would be extremely unjust and burdensome for the merchants. It would be impossible for merchants to avoid harassment and the same ruin which prevailed under the internal customs duties. The peasantry, thanks to constant reminders in church, would be encouraged to pillage goods freely in the name of preserving public revenues. The Senate did not maintain that there was no neglect of customs taxes at the borders. This had been found before, and now open larceny by the director and other administrators had been discovered in the Boevsk border customs house.

The Senate suggested these reasons to account for smuggling: (1) there were too many customs houses, which allowed a merchant to choose one where he thought he might find a way to lessen duties; (2) the staffs of customs houses were not of the highest moral caliber; (3) the customs service ranked quite low in comparison with other institutions, and its employees were not paid well enough to serve solely from ambition and zeal for the fatherland. Therefore the Senate proposed providing labels for merchants at the borders and in ports for the sole purpose of allowing merchants to prove their case should they be accused of smuggling. It also proposed to limit the number of customs houses, assign to them officials who were deserving and honest, and pay them good salaries.

In 1769 state revenue reached 16,996,902 rubles, with 983,856 in arrears. Four years later income totalled 23,611,300 rubles, including 2,835,823 collected from arrears. There remained 4,544,017 rubles in arrears from previous years, and from 1773, 4,103,102 rubles.

In 1774, upon the conclusion of the Turkish war, the procurator general informed the Senate that the empress charged it with examining state revenues to determine whether some taxes were burdensome and should be lifted. The Senate recommended: (1) lifting all taxes imposed expressly for the Turkish war, such as the "contributions" from Livonia, the supplementary soul tax on merchants, and those on manufactures and plants; (2) elimination of several specified taxes (on boat and landing guards, dye works, eating houses, gems, benches in bath-houses, smithies, inns, barber shops, and others); and (3) halving passport fees for merchants and peasants.[25] This decision decreased tax income by 807,683 rubles.

Besides money the war demanded a larger number of conscripts. A decree was issued hastily to conscript unemployed sons of priests and churchmen living at home with their fathers and families.[26] This measure evoked many complaints about its impropriety, following which one bishop (Tambov) was deprived of his diocese. Oddities like the following came to light. In Moscow during the investigation of the sons of priests and ecclesiastics of the eight endowed churches in the Kremlin under the jurisdiction of the artisan and armory office, it turned out that there were many supernumerary church employees neither placed in that vocation by the bishop nor possessing anything in writing from a spiritual eparchy. They were church servitors on the basis of documents given them by the artisan and armory office and signed by its staff. The Senate ordered all supernumerary clerks and sextons to military service and instructed the artisan and armory office henceforth not to appoint servitors to the aforementioned churches but merely to recommend worthy persons to the bishop.

THE SENATE AND ECCLESIASTICAL RELATIONS

In other questions related to church administration the Senate found itself in a predicament regarding the Old Believers.[27] On one hand, the government professed toleration and practised moderation. Civil rights were returned to Old Believers. For example, they were permitted to take oaths and to testify in legal matters. The government did not wish to employ cumpulsion, but other methods were lacking. Distributing the pamphlet "Admonitions to Schismatics" to churches and monasteries scarcely could replace the vivid oral admonitions or the common-sense and impassioned preaching of the Orthodox clergy. Meanwhile the schismatics sensed the relaxation and began to act more boldly. The Synod informed the Senate that in 1765 schismatics had moved a church from the foreign settlement of Vetka to a spot near the Old Believer settlements of Klimova and Mitkovka. Services were conducted in this church according to the old liturgy. Another small church had been built recently near the settlement of Zlynka on the Iputa river, in the woods, on a plot of land on Maliiny Island, and services conducted there. But what is more, an inquiry by the Synod discovered that chapels built by the Old Believers still existed: one not far from Saratov, on the far side of the Volga, on the Irgyz river, which had bronze bells; a second in the fortress of St. Elizabeth in the outlying settlement; a third in Tsarevosanchursk command, in the crown district of Ustinsk, in Larionov clearing. In these chapels Old Believers publicly gathered in large numbers for prayers and even enticed Orthodox Christians from God's churches. The Senate resolved to report to the empress that it concurred with the Holy Synod to demolish the aforementioned churches and chapels in order that Orthodox believers not become confused or corrupted by them.

But some sects appeared which did not build churches and chapels. When the castration heresy[28] appeared in the middle of 1772 Catherine issued Colonel Volkov a curious order: "Rumor has it that in Orel district there has appeared a new variant of a certain heresy and that several peasants of various landowners have been summoned to the Orel ecclesiastical administration and found to be heretical. In such cases nothing is more necessary, on one hand, than to extinguish such irrational folly at the very outset and, on the other hand, to safeguard many people from arrest and incarceration in some local judicial institution, and from entanglements and oppressions that sometimes happen to innocent people. In consideration of this we have decided to send you to the town of Orel, where you must inquire of the local military governor and the ecclesiastical administration whether and where this exists there. If you find that a proper investigation has begun, assume control of it and all people implicated thus far.

"Fully informed about everything, you must conduct a general investigation together with the local military governor and his assistant to identify above all the instigator and proselytizer of this destructive heresy. If these people have not been found, issue orders to apprehend them immediately. You are to arraign those involved into three classes: (1) the instigator or instigators and those who mutilated others; (2) converts who proselytized others; (3) simpletons who, having been persuaded, blindly obeyed the folly of their mentors. As for those who have not been apprehended, when you learn their names and whereabouts, do not arrest them unless absolutely necessary. Let their leaders know discreetly that they are under close surveillance in order that they be restrained from any outrages.

"On completing examination of the first group act as you would with agitators against the public peace; that is, flog them with the knout in the dwellings where they preached their sermons and converted others and then send them to Nerchinsk for life.[29] The second group you are to beat with staves and send to Riga for work on the fortifications, and the third you are to send to their former dwelling places. We find it necessary to add here that during the inquest you attempt to discover the truth without torture and with greatest compassion. If you find that innocent people have been arrested, let them return unharmed to their dwellings as soon as possible. The sooner and without further publicity this affair is investigated and settled the more useful, for the less importance the government places on it, the less place such lunacy will find in empty heads and, consequently, the faster its attractions will disappear in the popular mind. We find it no less necessary to add that you must treat this matter as a common civil one, and not at all otherwise, and in meting out guilt be sure that the punishments employed are for civil crimes."

Notwithstanding this declaration that the castration sect represented a civil and not an ecclesiastical matter, the church was embroiled when the wives of twelve castrated peasants returning to their landlord requested permission to enter second marriages.[30] The Synod ruled that these women were wholly blameless and had the right to repudiate their spouses, who had scorned their marriage vows and thus destroyed the benediction of the church given them in matrimony. Having allowed the wives of the castrati to enter into a second marriage, the Synod barred the castrated peasants from Communion for seven years, except at death, and their confession was to be heard twice a year.

In 1769 several Old Believer preachers were banished to the fortresses of Azov and Taganrog and placed in military service. The War College was ordered to keep them under the strictest observation in order that they not communicate among themselves and not propagate their enchantments. But the instruction was not executed. The governor of Voronezh reported to the Senate that one of the exiled men, the soldier Stepan Kuznetsov, often left his unit for his former home in Voronezh, where he spread the Old Belief. Particularly ardent among his followers were women, among whom two peasants, Varvara Efimova and the daughter of Sergeant Ovchinnikov, the maiden Akulina, solemnly preached to the people on the town square about the necessity of crossing oneself with two fingers. Four psalms were found on the schismatics, which they sang at their meetings; indeed, Akulina Ovchinnikova and her mother Mavra testified that God had taught them these psalms. The Senate issued strictest orders that people banished to the fortress for deviation from piety under no circumstances must be allowed to return to their former homes. But it appended an instruction that a summary of all cases dealing with schismatics then being submitted to the Senate be sent to the Holy Synod for its attention. The Senate recommended to the spiritual leadership that in any inquest in an ecclesiastical court, extreme circumspection and care be taken in forcing people to come before the consistory, in order to avoid any oppression of those innocent of superstition so that "nothing be produced that resembles an inquisition."

As noted earlier, the Synod called attention to the fact that schismatics had built a chapel with bells on the Irgyz river. It also learned that schismatic hermitages had been formed on both Irgyz rivers to provide refuge for fugitives. The Senate instructed the governor of Kazan, Brandt,[31] to send a detachment there to inspect all the hermitages and at the same time to prevent the Old Believers from one hermitage from concealing themselves in another. By this mens forty-four fugitives of various ranks, both men and women, were found in them.

Ticklish relations of the same type continued with respect to Mohammedans. The Synod complained that in Kazan, despite earlier edicts, mosques had been built near Orthodox churches and that the former governor, Kvashnin-Samarin, with whose permission this was done, declared he had received permission in an oral ruling from the empress. Catherine dictated the following answer to the Senate's report: "As the Most High God tolerates all faiths, tongues, and creeds on earth the empress, coincident with the principles of His Holy Will does the same, desiring only that amity and harmony reign forever among her subjects. Incidentally, her majesty is pleased to instruct the Senate to announce that former Governor Kvashnin-Samarin granted permission to build stone mosques in accordance with the Great Nakaz, articles 494, 495, and 496."[32]

Two months later the Synod informed the Senate that Mohammedans arriving in the Barabinsk steppe were converting idol worshippers recently baptized into Christianity. Although the governor of Siberia had forbidden travel there to Tatars and natives of Bukhara, various enticements nonetheless were originating from them. The Mohammedans consequently requested the Senate to permit them to build mosques there. The Synod pointed out that the consequence of this would be that newly baptized Christians would be tempted and would cease going to church, especially to confession and the Eucharist. The Senate instructed the governor of Tobolsk not absolutely to forbid Mohammedans from entering the newly baptized areas, since they were allowed to enter for commerce, but that he observe stringently that they not lead the newly baptized astray. As concerned punishment by the knout of those abandoning Christianity, he must refrain from that entirely and instead seek to save them through the ministrations of the clergy, employing only admonition and affection, rather than punishment. As concerned the affirmation that it was permissible to build mosques, even mosques of stone, the governor must convince them that any such allegation was unfounded."

CRIMES AND PUNISHMENT

It has been observed that Catherine's basic desire to use suasion in the struggle against immorality rather than harshness inclined her to the church for assistance, as in the Zhukov affair.[33] During the years under review here she continued to follow this policy, primarily in affairs involving murder of peasants by their landlords. Concerning the gentry-woman Morina, who killed one of her female serfs, Catherine wrote: "Place her for six weeks on bread and water and send her to a convent for a year to work." By Catherine's decision the Belozersk gentry, the Savins, were imprisoned for half a year for killing a peasant and required to perform the penance of the church. The widow of Captain Kashintsev, for having a child with her serf and for the intolerable physical punishment of her maidservant, for which reason she hanged herself, was sentenced to six weeks in a convent at penance. The wife of a chess master named Gordeev was sentenced to prison for a month and church penance for torturing a servant girl, who shortly died. The Senate sought her pledge to refrain thenceforward from such treatment but the empress amended the Senate's decision, restoring her to her husband with the stipulation that he be responsible for preventing her from being so severe in the future.

The Senate reported on the punishment of the wife of Major General Ettinger for striking a peasant, from which he died. The empress wrote on the report: "The widow Ettinger admits that she whipped her man for deeds belonging under municipal jurisdiction rather than to hers inasmuch as flight, robbery, and such do not belong to household discipline. Communicate this to the Senate's Second Department[34] in order that the jurisdiction of the laws be preserved from exceptional intrusions." The Senate answered: "In order that other serfowners not interfere in matters of civil justice, since there is no exact precedent about this, information must be gathered by the commission for compiling a draft of a new law code[35] so as to devise a suitable law for such cases." But Catherine wrote on this, "The commission also is to issue regulations dealing with those who use cruelty against people."

Based on information about the poor treatment of serfs by the widow of Major General Khrapovitsky the Senate received an imperial edict to appoint a guardian for her. The guardian would receive the necessary information about her income, take charge of the widow's house and determine her people's moderate standard of living and dress, and set aside the remainder of her income for her maintenance. In the event of crimes her serfs would be punished by the guardian, who thus could elicit the respect and obedience they owed her.

Besides these instances of ill treatment of peasants, tortures and murders, the problems of serf relationships, a major interest of the landowners, carried them into crimes of another type. Furthermore, serfs seemed to be convenient, obedient tools of crime. The Senate sentenced the wife of an ensign, Fedosia Chegodareva, to punishment by the knout and exile to a colony in Siberia for causing the flight of a female serf of the wife of Lieutenant Tormasov and for other disorderly acts. Catherine wrote on the report: "Instead of corporal punishment, keep her on bread and water two weeks and then, depriving her of gentry status, dispatch her to Siberia." The gentrywoman Ingeldeeva was sentenced to the same punishment by verdict of the empress because she sold a runaway after changing his name. The Senate sentenced retired Second Lieutenant Karpov to death because he and his men visited the leader of the single homestead holders,[36] Kutepov, wounded him with a rifle and beat him with clubs, from which Kutepov died the next day. Catherine changed his sentence thus: "Deprive him of gentry status and his ranks and, having stood him under the gallows, brand his forehead with the word 'Brigand,' and send him to perpetual hard labor." The Senate sentenced retired sergeant Prince Ivan Meshchersky to the knout and exile in Nerchinsk for forging a travel permit and for stealing the belongings of several people. Catherine changed it: "Having deprived him of gentry status, send him to Siberia." The empress decreed the same punishment for a nobleman named Shushchov and a young woman named Chertanova for sheltering thieves and stolen possessions in their houses.

Catherine decided upon forfeiture of noble status and ranks, branding under a gallows with the letter "M" (murderer), and perpetual labor in the Nerchinsk silver mines for retired Captain Otiaev because he allowed his serfs to beat his wife to death. Retired Lieutenant Leskov killed a runaway peasant; his wife and sister-in-law Rodicheva knew about it and did not report it. The empress read her decision: "Having deprived him of his ranks and gentry status, brand Leskov with the letter 'M' under a gallows and send him to the Nerchinsk silver mines for hard labor. Free his wife; lock Rodicheva in a prison for repentance." Upon Catherine's verdict the wife of Ensign Vasiliev was put on bread and water for two weeks and sent to Siberia for theft and conspiracy in aiding the escape of someone else's young female serf. Ensign Ilin was deprived of gentry status and rank and sent to Siberia for harboring robbers in his house and for receiving stolen goods from them. The wife of Captain Mourinov was put on bread and water for four weeks, deprived of gentry status, and sent to Siberia for conspiring with her serfs to smother her first husband, Lieutenant Epanchin, with a pillow while he slept, which they then did. Ensign Simbirsky was deprived of his rank and sent into exile for beating a sexton who died two days later. Colonel Rachinsky lost gentry status and ranks and was sent to Siberia for murder. The wife of retired Ensign Avdulov was put on bread and water for four weeks, deprived of her husband's and father's surnames, branded with the letter "M" and sent to Siberia for killing her husband. Her daughter, an accomplice before the fact, was put on bread and water for two weeks and sent to Siberia. Identical to the punishment of Avdulova for murdering her husband was the punishment of Second Lieutenant Simonov's wife. Sergeant of the Guards Varakheev was deprived of gentry status and sent to Siberia for declaring another's estate as security with the bank and for inciting someone else's serf to thievery. So were Guards Corporal Yurev for falsely selling someone else's serf, Lieutenant Tiapkin for selling fugitives, and Ensign Stokhanov for selling someone else's serf as a conscript under false pretences.

Concerning the wife of Ensign Skripitsyn, who sold a fugitive serf belonging to someone else, the empress wrote: "Put her on bread and water for two weeks, and if her husband does not want to take her back, send her to Siberia, depriving her of her gentry status." The landowner Kultashev lost his gentry status, was branded and sent to perpetual penal labor for murdering his two brothers. His wife, who was responsible for starting the argument that resulted in murder, was sent to a convent for labor. Their son, Second Lieutenant Prokhor Kultashev, who tried to dissuade his father and mother from the evil deed, but who had been forced into involuntary obedience, was deprived of his rank and registered in the soldiery for long service. Retired Captain Turbin was deprived of his gentry status, ranks, and family name, taken to the scaffold, laid on the executioner's block, branded, and sent to perpetual labor for the murder of a young serf girl belonging to him. Retired quartermaster Neledinsky was sent to a monastery for penance because he flogged his mother with lashes and beat his sister with a cane.

This long, doleful list is explained by the premature edict of Peter III which allowed the gentry to retire from service whenever they chose to.[37] In state service a man with bad inclinations was kept in check by service discipline. He could not surrender himself to laziness; he was restrained by the company surrounding him, necessarily expanding his intellectual horizons, increasing the variety of his higher interests, and developing his personality. Now he was allowed while still young to break away from service discipline and live on his estate in the village. No longer the subordinate who trembled before the angry glance of a senior officer, he became a lord with full powers over a voiceless population in bondage to him. The more he had chafed at his low rank while in service, the more unbridled he now became. The slave became a lord. The absolute idleness and ignorance, the inability to occupy himself with anything intellectually or morally developing, the absence of community which otherwise might have developed—these conditions produced a moral downfall. The women, by their passionate nature, by the ease of their rising and falling, were even closer to temptation than the men. One must add that poverty, in the absence of moral restraints, impelled them powerfully to such crimes as luring away serfs, selling runaways, and offering them shelter.

The marshal of the Pronsk gentry reported to the Senate that at the assembly of the gentry for casting lots to see who would enter service,[38] more than two hundred sons of gentry showed up declaring their eager desire to enter service, but could not because various ones possessed neither the proper clothing nor boots. The Senate instructed the Moscow governor, for preservation of the gentry's liberty, to accept these half-educated young men's applications to enter service. The governor of Novgorod, Sievers, requested instructions about what to do with young gentry offspring whose impoverished fathers were unable to educate them. The Senate's reply was to place them in garrison schools at public expense.

But in introducing this doleful list we cannot help but note that gentry crimes involving peasants could not be concealed and were punished. Regarding crimes of peasants against gentry, there is the following curious resolution by the Senate in 1769. When extracts of governors' reports were read about acts of disobedience, mortal beatings, theft and robbery that peasants and serfs had committed against landowners, the Senate ordered them deposited in the archives because the governors had issued appropriate orders for the prevention of such evil deeds. We shall note the most important cases.

In 1769 in Simbirsk province the peasants of Ishevka village were punished for disobedience to their gentry landlady, Krotkova. In the same year the governor of Voronezh submitted reports about the disobedience to their owners, the Naryshkins, on the part of Little Russians settled in the villages of Krasovka, Elan, Rudna and Krasnoiarovka; he noted that the first two settlements had been restored to obedience by a military detachment. In 1771 Catherine confirmed Peter the Great's decree about not selling peasants without land. In a personal edict she absolutely prohibited thenceforth the sale of serfs without land in cases of both confiscation and auction; all town commanders were to observe this strictly. Peasants assigned to industrial enterprises[39] were to be given money for the days they spent on the way there.

PROBLEMS WITH FACTORY PEASANTS

The Senate began to pay particular attention to assigned peasants, as is seen in the following decisions relating to the Voznesensk copper-smelting complex. The Senate distributed decrees to the governors of Kazan and Orenburg instructing them to consult and designate which settlements of state peasants in their governments would be best to assign to the Voznesensk copper works. The governors were to report the distance of settlements from the mines, the distance of settlements from each other, and the number of souls in each. Thereupon the governors must report whether it was more beneficial to move the peasants to the copper works or simply to assign them.[40] The College of Mines was instructed to inform the Senate whether the Voznesensk mines had sufficient land for planting and hay and other needs to support the one thousand or so souls who might move there. The college was also to recommend the most appropriate and useful method for moving the peasants, how to assist them, and on what basis.

Although no uprisings involving industrial peasants occurred in the eastern parts of the empire, a powerful uprising broke out in the west at the Petrovsk blast furnaces near Olonets.[41] The primary cause of the uprising was that the peasants had been compelled, above and beyond their usual work, to quarry marble for the building of St. Isaac's cathedral.

This labor soon was lifted from them, but other tasks were intensified. The peasants were forced to deliver a thousand piles of charcoal, despite the fact that the furnaces consumed only a third of that amount. The management wanted to build four new furnaces, ignoring the fact that there was insufficient iron to keep them in production for even a year. At that juncture appeared the adventurer Ivan Nazarov Elagin[42], a man notorious for his bankruptcies, who told the peasants that if they petitioned the empress, proposing to pay three rubles per soul, they would be freed from work. The peasants believed him and filed the petition, refusing to work while awaiting its answer. This was in the summer of 1770.

The Senate dispatched an investigative commission to the villages involved. It proclaimed the Senate's edict to the peasants in each village, admonishing them to fulfill their assigned tasks immediately and unquestioningly. The commission likewise did everything possible to ensure that the peasants obeyed the edict, but for various reasons the peasants asked to be excused and did not want to work. The men most responsible for their recalcitrance were the registrar Nazimov and the peasant Kalistratov. The commission concluded its report with the recommendation that severe measures be implemented.

The Senate was displeased by this report, and found that the commission had not gotten to the heart of the matter discussed in its instructions; it had not investigated whether the peasants were in a proper condition to work or whether there were enough peasants to carry out the work. Furthermore, the commission gave no appearance of having carried out its task earnestly. Therefore the Senate ruled that whereas the blast furnaces and the peasants were situated in Novgorod government, Governor Sievers, as manager of the government, must visit the scene, take charge of the commission and, having discovered the cause of the peasant's disobedience, do whatever was necessary to restore the refractory peasants to proper behavior. The Senate trusted in his renowned discretion and care to take the proper measures. After quelling the peasants, Sievers was to examine their complaints of excessive industrial labor; if in fact it was impossible for the peasants to fulfil their industrial labor, he must devise new regulations covering everything pertaining to the peasants' welfare.

Sievers did not go to the scene of the inquest. In a letter sent later to the empress he said that he had been slandered to her as not having wanted to attend the inquest, whereas in truth he had asked to go there. Just before leaving he had received an instruction from the empress to go to the Polish border. Nevertheless, he reviewed the case and made recommendations about calming the situation, but his opinion was rejected rudely. Sievers ended his letter with the words: "I decided to be silent and would have remained silent had I not heard the peasants' mute complaints, the reasons for which must be important if they are heard from so far away." In Sievers's opinion, forwarded to the Senate, the chief cause of disobedience among the peasants consisted in the extraordinarily burdensome and disorganized assignments of workers and the delivery of materials at the busiest time for the peasants who, prevented thereby from earning a livelihood through agriculture, had yielded to despair. This situation was worsened because they were not informed of the new rate of payment for factory work. Another cause of these unfortunate people's despair was the disorganized administration of the Petrozavodsk chancellery. A third cause was that the commission sent there consisted of three men of various ranks who spent their time in correspondence and did not work together as well as might have been hoped had a single important personage been sent instead.

The Senate, after receiving this opinion, reported to the empress: "Although Sievers discusses the chief causes of the disharmony and disobedience, he was not there himself; therefore the Senate is unable to confirm his opinion but prefers to dispatch an officer with general's rank to take charge of the commission. The Senate has selected Major General Lykoshin for this task." The empress confirmed the report.

The order to dispatch Lykoshin was the last one made in 1770. Early in 1771 the procurator general received an imperial edict stating that her majesty deigned to find in the petitions from state peasants under the administration of the chancellery of the Petrovsk furnaces that those peasants again were being expected to cut stone for building St. Isaac's cathedral. This exaction from those peasants corresponded not at all to her intentions, especially since she had rejected specifically the proposal of State Councillor Kozhin[43] to use forced labor, preferring rather to quarry the marble with hired labor. But a week later the Senate heard the report of the investigative commission at the Petrovsk blast furnaces, which said that the peasants had been released from their obligation to quarry marble at the beginning of 1770 and therefore pointlessly belabored the empress with their petition. This fact, it will be remembered, was confirmed by Sievers's letter.

Lykoshin filed his first report in March. He suggested that the cause of all the disarray, of the neglected arrears, and of some of the lack of respect was that the selection of village elders, though done by general election, had been transformed into mere formality. In reality, elders were chosen by the foremost and richest local peasants, largely from men beholden to them, who therefore did their will. Illiterate, these village elders were so poor that nothing could be exacted from them to cover deficits. The rich peasants, who controlled the elders, did whatsoever they wished. As evidence Lykoshin presented a statement given him by Shuisk village indicating the degree of influence and strength of the peasant Korotiaev in that settlement. Several days later Lykoshin reported that his every effort to pacify the rebellious peasants had been unsuccessful and that depositions had been taken from them. From these depositions it was apparent that State Councillor Elagin had accepted a petition from the peasants, leaving them with the anticipation that he would place it directly into the hands of the empress and satisfy their request to pay three rubles per soul in lieu of the labor assigned to them. In general, the tone of Elagin's conversation had given good cause for peasant unrest and disobedience. Besides this, he concealed the petitioners who had come to Petersburg in his apartment, apart from the petition presented to the Senate. Lykoshin likewise requested the removal of Colonel Winter, who as the senior member of the commission was aware of Elagin's conduct but had not restrained him. The Senate carried out Lykoshin's requests.

Because his admonitions to the peasants went unheeded Lykoshin sent a detachment under the command of Captain Lamsdorff to pacify them. Arriving in the village of Kizhi the detachment found a mob of about five thousand people armed with rifles, boar spears, and other weapons. The mob greeted the detachment with invective and threats of annihilation. It demanded that the expected imperial edict be placed directly in their hands. Lamsdorff, realizing that his detachment was outmanned, was obliged to retreat. The peasants followed the retreating soldiers for about eight versts, crying: "You are lucky you did not start shooting!" When it learned of this incident the Senate gave orders to send Lieutenant-Captain Rzhevsky to the rebels with the original copy of the manifesto, if they would not trust one that had been printed. But Rzhevsky must not hand over the manifesto to the peasants; he must hold onto it. He must read the printed manifesto wheresoever the majority of the rebellious people would assemble, paying no attention to the size of the crowd and their arms. Where there were churches he was to compel the priests or deacons to read it, and where there were no churches the elders were to read the manifesto in the local government houses. Should a great crowd gather, the edict was to be read in the village squares, admonishing each and all that their crime resulted from the teaching of deceitful people living among them. As soon as everyone obeyed the law their complaints would be looked into. If they did otherwise, they would receive no mercy.

Lykoshin thereafter informed the Senate that every satisfaction was being shown the peasants' complaints. When they realized this, the peasants gave the commission a declaration on June 15, representing the views of 8,990 men, in which they admitted their offense and confessed they had been fooled by the false assurances of their brethren. Since now their situation had improved, they pledged full obedience. Lykoshin wrote that since Rzhevsky's arrival another 3,105 souls had complied with the law and set to work without complaint. Colonel Prince Urusov had been sent to bring the remaining peasants into obedience.

The Senate responded to this report with instructions to try insofar as possible to bring the remaining peasants under control without being harsh and severe, and to bend over backwards in examining and satisfying peasant complaints quickly, thus eradicating their dissatisfaction. But the Senate's policy was not followed. The commission reported that Prince Urusov, arriving in Kizhi district with a detachment, was unable to impose the necessary order without violence, no matter how he tried. He was forced to fire cannon and killed several peasants before the remainder offered to submit and return to work.

Sievers did not stop interceding for serfs. He wrote the empress: "The permission given the gentry to banish whomever they wish among their serfs to Siberia for settlement without a magistrate asking, 'what for?'—this liberty produces moving scenes every day. A peasant who cannot be conscripted because of his short stature or some other deficiency must be exiled as credit for future levies the landlord fears in the coming year. Many gentry even sell the receipts they get in exchange for sending their serfs to Siberia. I confess that not a day passes without my heart steeling itself further against such privilege. Siberia is gaining comparatively little if one considers the distance and the loss of people along the way."

The Senate adopted another measure for settling Siberia. It inquired of the College of Church Landed Property[44] how many villages and hamlets there were under its jurisdiction in Moscow province whose inhabitants did not have enough land and how many could be settled in other places. The college offered to give a full answer as soon as it had gathered the information, adding that only in Moscow district did there appear to be a significant shortage of land. The Senate then issued instructions to the College of Church Landed Property to calculate as soon as possible how many peasant families lacking land could be resettled in Siberia, to enable the Senate to report to the empress the comparative advantages of settling such peasants in the areas of Siberia where they were needed, as opposed to the minimal benefit derived from transporting serfs and peasants to the colonies, should that practice be resumed.

Whereas industrial peasants were provoked and complained of the unbearable burden of their labor, paradoxically peasants who had fled their various obligations found refuge in industrial enterprises. The chancellery of the Serpeisk military governor reported that the iron mines of the Demidovs[45] openly were receiving and offering work to fugitives and giving them fraudulent passports besides.

URBAN UNREST

Towns also suffered disorders. Novgorod's governor, Sievers, relayed to the Senate the insults, outrages, beatings, and murders inflicted upon various landowners by the inhabitants of Tikhvin. The Senate directed an inquest be organized, adding that this report and earlier cases suggested that such disorders, scuffles and murders occurred because the alarum was rung unnecessarily and without the permission of the authorities, when such ringing was permitted solely in case of fire or attacks by enemies and brigands, and that therefore proclamations must be published stating that except for the above henceforth no one was to dare ring the alarum when private quarrels and fights began.

Lieutenant Colonel Riazanov, sent with a detachment to deliver contracted timber to Saratov for colonists,[46] complained that along the way, in Syzran, the town inhabitants beat him and stole and burned his papers. Meanwhile the Syzran merchants, farming soldiers, and the town deputy reported that Riazanov and his detachment grievously offended the citizens by assaulting women and young girls.

The governor of Smolensk reported that in Viazma the merchants and magistracy officials were quarrelling vociferously and scuffling with the military garrison stationed there. In addition, a tax farmer named Baryshnikov complained about the police constable Zuev, selected for that post by the merchants as authorized by the magistracy.[47] Zuev disregarded a contract signed with Baryshnikov and ignored the merchants' frequent brawls in defense of the illicit trade in spirits. To halt this practice the governor proposed several times that the Viazma magistracy hand over police administration to the military governor's assistant, who would be answerable to the civil governor , but the magistracy refused to listen and used indecorous expressions and reproach in its statements referring to the civil governor.

Meanwhile the Viazma magistracy in complaints about the governor requested that it retain the power over police administration vested in it by the Magistracy Regulations.[48] The Senate ruled that the Viazma magistracy's disobedience to the governor was patently obvious and its brazen references to his person and authority were reproachful and unseemly. It therefore sent an injunction to the Main Magistracy to dismiss the Viazma magistrates and replace them with others elected from the local merchants. The Main Magistracy must assign a special deputy to investigate the dismissed officials. The governor must name further investigators. The insolence of the Viazma magistracy consisted in writing the governor three times about the illegal sale of spirits and the ruin caused two merchants by Baryshnikov, as well as in other insults and nonpayment of the assessed tax rate. The governor fully exonerated Baryshnikov and transferred police administration to the Viazma military district governor's assistant Bogdanov, a good friend of Baryshnikov. The magistracy opposed his decision and appealed to the Main Magistracy and the Senate itself.

But the governor of Belgorod, Fliverk, was not at all as pleased with the Senate as a result of his clash with the Kursk magistracy.[49] Fliverk complained that the Kursk magistracy had not permitted the single homestead holders in Kursk to register as merchants or in craft guilds although they had built tanneries and were engaged in shoemaking and other crafts. The governor asked that the Kursk magistrates be disciplined and that the Main Magistracy be instructed that there was no prohibition against registering single homestead holders in guilds. The Senate ruled that the circumstances portrayed by both sides revealed no compelling reason for punishing the Kursk magistracy; quite the contrary, the Senate found its action justified. The homestead holders were to return to their former status and be excluded from the guilds; since these matters by definition belonged exclusively to the magistracy, the governor must not interfere in them in the future.

From Kargopol came news of dreadful disorders among the merchants because of the salt tax and other issues relating to neglect and embezzlement of public property. The merchants beat a secretary named Piatnitsky unmercifully, and when the governor investigated, one of the informers, the copyist Popov, was found in the river with a stone tied to his neck. The peasants, who supported the military governor, his assistant, and his secretary, besought the civil governor not to believe the merchants' ridiculous petitions; the merchants were testifying unjustly that the military governor, his assistant, and his secretary had oppressed the peasants. The chancellery of the Rylsk military governor reported that certain merchants there, the Vykhodtsevs, had assembled many men and would not allow his detachment to dump the spirits illegally distilled there, and in general repeatedly insulted and deceived the tax farmers, yet the Rylsk magistracy, favoring them, would not request the personnel necessary for an investigation.

The continual complaints about expropriators exposed the weakness of the town corporations and their inability to govern themselves. Some merchants from Gzhatsk, the Sanburovs, Gurev, and Emelianov, complained about members of the town court, saying that they controlled lands that really belonged to the merchants. They did not pay the ten-percent tax due the treasury from the warehouses and shops they administered, and the places they allotted for building houses were unsuitable. They hindered trade. Furthermore, they consigned two leading merchants to resettlement in Siberia out of spite, as credit against future conscript levies.

The Tambov merchants Ivan Kuzmin the Younger, Vasily Rastorguev, Matvey Borodin, and Grigory Beliaev reported that the burgomaster of the Tambov magistracy, Tolmachev, had attested that the Tambov merchants Borodin, Rastorguev and Beliaev had raised more capital in their commercial and contracting ventures than they in fact had; now Rastorguev had left to manage the concession on tavern collections. The Senate's verdict: thirty-five Tambov merchants testified that the attestations had been signed by Tolmachev without the consent of all the merchants solely because Borodin and Rastorguev, without consulting other merchants, in visiting homes and shops gathered signatures in favor of electing Tolmachev as burgomaster, which the merchants did not want. Consequently, concluded the Senate, it is uncertain whether the attestations were correct. Furthermore, according to current records of tavern collections by the aforementioned merchants, there were arrears of about 9,000 rubles. Since it was debatable whether they should be granted the concession on tavern collections, the Main Magistracy must investigate forthwith whether the attestations granted them conformed to the regulations of the Treasury College.

From the very beginning of the war with Turkey domestic protection weakened and a rise in brigandage was to be expected. The chancellery of the Likhvin military governor described the beating of seven merchants by a band of thirty brigands. Following this the Senate heard news that robberies involving huge sums were occurring on the Volga, Kama, and White rivers; the iron transports of the Demidovs and Tverdyshev were plundered and their escorts variously assaulted. The Senate ordered the governors of Kazan and Nizhny Novgorod to prevent these crimes and catch the brigands, but this was not easy. In the colonies around Saratov bands of brigands appeared. They killed two men and set fire to several settlements and their grain and cattle, threatening to return. On the Kama there were estimated to be fourteen bands of robbers numbering from seven to fifteen men each. Robberies began to occur in Shatsk and Kasimov districts and the Temnikov Forest. That was in 1769. In 1770 the governor of Kazan reported that in the spring large bands of brigands appeared on the Viatka, Kama, Volga, and Sura rivers, killing and ravaging the inhabitants. A detachment sent to search for them caught thirty-eight brigands. In the fall the robbers descended on Frolishchev Hermitage (in Vladimir diocese), pillaged everything, and beat the superior terribly to find his money. Then news was received about brigandage in the Settlement Ukraine[50] and Voronezh governments, and Ufa and Galich provinces. Robbery appeared next in Balakhna in Tambov district. The bandits' strength and daring reached such heights that they attacked Kaigorod, ravaged and burned the inhabitants' homes, and stole the money from the salt tax.

THE ONSET OF PLAGUE[51]

The lack of troops to maintain order became all too obvious in Moscow during the troubles caused there too by the Turkish war. The Russian troops invading Moldavia met an enemy much more dangerous than the Turks—the plague. By the end of summer 1770 it had crossed the Russian frontier, spreading quickly throughout Little Russia, and appeared at the edges of Great Russia, in Sevsk and Briansk.[52] Moscow government was encircled from the south by pickets and the usual quarantine measures were taken. Instructions were given to surround Moscow with a palisade or cheval-de-frise, but this was not done. At year's end (December 17) the plague appeared in a remote section of Moscow, Lefortovo, in the small military hospital located in the Vvedensky Hills.[53] The chief doctor at the hospital, Shafonsky, informed the Medical Office of the dangerous disease.[54] He also informed the chief of gendarmes, Bakhmetev, who reported to the commander-in-chief in the capital, Count Peter Semenovich Saltykov[55] that, according to the doctor, fourteen people in the hospital had died from the dread illness since December 17 while two survived. On December 22 Saltykov wrote the empress: "The director of the hospital, Major General Famintsyn, came just this morning and gave a meaningless report except to say that this is nothing dangerous. May it please your imperial majesty to see from the reports of the chief of gendarmes and the Medical Office that the infection broke out in November. Famintsyn knew all about it; why then did he conceal it? The chief of gendarmes is a very prompt and conscientious man. I wish that all local administrators were as punctual and helpful to me under such needful circumstances."

On the same day, December 22, a council of medical specialists convened, consisting of Erasmus, Shkiadan, Kuhlemann, Mertens, von Asch, Veniaminov, Zybelin, and Yagolsky. They unanimously diagnosed the illness as the pest plague.[56] Doctor Mertens informed Saltykov and advised him to cordon off the hospital, which was done. On December 25 Saltykov wrote the empress: "Not relying on my own judgment, I called in Doctor Mertens and requested his advice, which endorsed everything already done. He requested moreover that entry into Moscow be absolutely denied to everyone, which is impossible to institute. In such a large city so many besides landlords eat imported food, and like the landowners, get food from their villages. Goods destined for the ports are transported through Moscow. Everything—meat, fish, and so forth—everything goes through this city. People come and go to local towns—even the Ukraine—from every direction. It is impossible to forbid entry. Passage from the Ukraine is, it would seem, essential: besides couriers the army requires many items and it is mandatory that the necessary troops and supplies be sent to our regiments at the front."

Then came 1771. Unsettling news began to issue from Moscow. On January 4 Saltykov wrote: "The sickness is now abating; cold weather is helping a good deal. Nothing has been said about it for several days at the Vvedensky Hills. Officers of the guard have been instructed to examine carefully arrivals from possibly infected areas, but there is no one travelling who does not have sufficient documentation—identity card or passport. As for the police pickets surrounding Moscow, since it is now winter the ditches are drifted with snow and can be crossed anywhere. It is impossible to establish a cavalry patrol, for every last regiment is greatly under strength."

On January 15 the commander-in-chief reported: "In the hospital in the Vvedensky Hills, where the pestilence first made its appearance, it seems to have run its course. The hospital is unable to determine for certain whether the disease was there or not, for no one has visited besides two military medics who are now quarantined. The doctor at the central hospital (Shafonsky) asked the Medical Office to investigate, but not one doctor has gone; they are making diagnoses without observation. Now I have summoned the local physician (Rinder) and sent him there. He went, but merely talked with the hospital doctor across a fire. The doctor reproached him for the fact that despite many requests nobody had come to investigate."

The frosts curtailed the disease. But when February came it began to thaw and with the warmth the pestilence could return. Saltykov proposed measures to prevent this. On February 7 he wrote Catherine: "Spring is approaching. May I suggest that you order all the sick (that is, at the hospital) transported from Moscow to various monasteries about fifteen to twenty versts away, placing a few in each monastery and providing physicians. No real burden will be placed on the monasteries, for the number of sick will be small and they will be in the open air. Moscow has enough uncleanliness without adding hospitals. The hospital here is located in a wholly unsuitable place, above the Yauza, where its sewage flows through the city. It would not be bad to decrease the number of vagrants in the city as spring approaches. The city is so heavily populated, and its buildings are small and crowded together."

The empress did not agree to move the sick into outlying monasteries, and Saltykov informed her on February 28 that the sentries had been removed from the hospital and sick people were entering it. There were two barracks at the small hospital in the Vvedensky Hills where the infectious sickness had appeared; they and the adjacent barracks, which were so dilapidated they were barely standing, were burned together with all their contents upon the advice of the chief of the commissary of the army, Glebov, and Chief of Gendarmes Bakhmetev.

Even as fire destroyed the dilapidated structures of the small hospital in the Vvedensky Hills the pestilence was stealing its victims in the very center of Moscow. On March 13 Saltykov reported: "On the tenth of this March I received a report from Doctor Yagolsky about the appearance of an infectious disease at the Big Woolen Court,[57] which is near Stone bridge on the bank of the Moscow river, from which 123 persons have died since January and 21 remain ill." Saltykov dispatched five physicians, who upon visual examination concluded that the illness was putrescent, infectious, contagious, and quite resembled the plague. Moscow had housed two departments of the Senate since 1763, the fifth and the sixth, which were supposed to take measures in cases of the greatest importance. The commander-in-chief assembled the senators, who decided that although an edict of her imperial majesty forbade it, utmost need dictated that the sick people in the Woolen Court be moved to the St. Nicholas on the Ugresha monastery.[58] (Moscow's Archbishop Ambrose concurred in this.)

Second, they agreed to move the healthy from the Woolen Court to a rented house in a field on Meshchansky street, assigning a physician to it and posting a cordon around it. Third, they decided to cordon off the abandoned Woolen Court. Before these measures could be taken about two thousand factory hands from the Woolen Court fled and began living all over the city, in consequence of which several corpses were picked up in the streets. Doctor Orraeus and Staff-doctor Grave,[59] who had observed the plague in the south in the army, informed Saltykov that the same marks were on the sick people in Moscow as they had observed on people afflicted with plague at Khotin. Saltykov notified the senators of the Moscow departments about this, and they decided to isolate in three monasteries the people already in quarantine houses, the factory workers who had fled the Big Woolen Court and the owners of houses where the workers had taken refuge. The sick were to be separated from the healthy, and those actually infected with plague put in Ugreshsk monastery. The senators further resolved to dress in appropriate clothing the medics and servants transporting the dangerously sick in order to protect them from danger. To prevent factory workers from wandering around town during Holy Week and from coming into contact with the workers who had fled the Woolen Court, factory owners were ordered to keep their workers in their factories all week. Until the workers from the Big Woolen Court who had hidden could be rounded up and no longer disturb the peace, public baths were closed throughout the city. It also was forbidden to bury the dead inside the city.

THE GOVERNMENT COMBATS THE PLAGUE

After receiving this news the empress instructed the Council to propose the following measures to halt the further spread of the plague insofar as possible: (1) quarantine everyone leaving Moscow about thirty versts from the capital on both main and secondary roads; (2) seal off Moscow as much as possible and not admit anyone without Count Saltykov's permission; (3) halt food transports seven versts from Moscow in designated places where the inhabitants could purchase what they needed on appointed days and hours; (4) the Moscow police were to build big fires at these market places between buyers and sellers and construct barriers and were also to prevent city residents from touching nonresidents and otherwise mixing. Money was to be dipped in vinegar;[60] (5) the archbishop of Moscow was to arrange reading of prayers concerning the infectious disease according to a form conveyed by the Synod. These prayers were to be read in all churches of his diocese, to calm the people's fear. This was to be done in the dioceses of Vladimir, Pereiaslavl, Tver, and Krutitsa as well. Quarantines were to be established for Petersburg on the Tikhvin, Staraia Rusa, Novgorod, and Smolensk highways at one hundred versts and set for seven days; if the illness did not appear by that time travellers and goods were to be allowed to pass. Their belongings had to be fumigated and paper and anything else deemed necessary dipped in vinegar. Immediately upon the roads drying all military detachments were to be sent to a camp neither too close nor too far from the city, each regiment or detachment separately; the locations were to be selected in advance and permission received. The naval command was advised to do the same. The guards regiments were considered to be included under the military command too.

The Council, discussing these measures, determined to propose to the empress the advisability of appointing a special official in Petersburg with extraordinary authority to take necessary measures promptly. This official also would have charge of sanitary pickets, of which three were recommended: at Chudovo, Bronnitsy, and Tver and Ladoga. As concerned Moscow, the Council decided to forward her majesty's points to Field Marshal Saltykov with the injunction that "this instruction offers methods for use as local perceptions dictate, insofar as the spread of the illness requires that they be implemented."

Doctor Orraeus and Moscow's governor, Yushkov,[61] were invited to the same session of the Council on March 28. The former declared that his duty and profession compelled him to admit that the illness was infectious; he had examined the sick personally. But Yushkov reported that the Moscow medical authorities disagreed among themselves on this subject.

The empress concurred with the Council's opinion and the task of establishing a quarantine was assigned to Lieutenant General Count Bruce.[62] The Council had determined earlier, on March 21, that Count Saltykov's age made it imperative to entrust the protection of Moscow against the pestilence to someone else, but had hesitated because this would be prejudicial to the commander-in-chief. The empress unhesitatingly handed command of measures against the plague in Moscow to Lieutenant General and Senator Peter Dmitrievich Yeropkin.[63]

Saltykov concurred on the necessity of local measures to cleanse Moscow both of the infected and of conditions conducive to spreading the infection. But he continued to oppose cordoning off the capital as impractical because of the shortage of troops and as extremely oppressive and therefore possibly productive of disorder. "There seems to be no need," he wrote the empress on April 4, "to establish a quarantine for everyone leaving the city; furthermore, it would be awkward. Likewise it is quite dangerous to prohibit entry into Moscow. Almost the entire city eats purchased bread. Should importation cease, there will be hunger. All work will stop. No one will go seven versts outside the city to make purchases but will pillage instead, and there is enough theft already. There is no way to seal off Moscow. There is no city wall; the White wall has been torn down.[64] There are no soldiers, so who will encircle it? It is better for people to leave for the surrounding villages for fresh air; the city will be less crowded."

Saltykov did not like Yeropkin's appointment, as was evident from his letter of April 21: "According to the will of your majesty all authority is handed to Lieutenant General and Senator Yeropkin. Every precaution has been taken from the first; it seems that there is nothing further to do since he need only watch over what has been established, for which all authority is transferred to him from me; I wish only to be kept informed."

Meanwhile the course of the disease in Moscow proceeded. On April 7 Saltykov reported that apart from the Ugreshsk and Simonov monasteries no one had died or become ill. On April 18 he wrote that 943 factory workers of both sexes had been removed from Moscow to the Simonov, Danilov, and Pokrovsk monasteries.[65] On May 25 the first department of the Senate in Petersburg received a communication from the Moscow departments to the effect that inasmuch as a majority of the workers who had fled the Woolen Court during the quarantine had been captured and only a few remained at large he had authorized the reopening of the baths for the enjoyment of the public. On May 30 Saltykov received the comforting news that the quarantined monasteries reported no new dead or afflicted; there were only nine sick persons at Ugreshsk. Therefore the empress published an edict to release the factory workers detained in quarantine in the Pokrovsk and Danilov monasteries and allow them to live anywhere in the city in private lodgings. This was done.

But beginning June 20 the plague reappeared in the Simonov monastery. Ten factory workers died and six became ill. Thereafter the illness began to increase in strength. Yeropkin worked tirelessly, doing everything he could. He instituted what would appear to be rigid supervision, in that anyone taken ill had to be brought immediately to the hospital, or to a so-called quarantine. The belongings of people suffering from plague were destroyed summarily. But neither Yeropkin nor anyone else could reeducate the people and quickly inspire in them support of the commonweal or ability to assist government decrees, without which the decrees would not be effective. On the other hand, neither Yeropkin nor anyone else could create people overnight to discharge the decrees or supervise their fulfillment—effective, honest people incapable of wrongdoing.

The inhabitants of Moscow feared the plague less than the hospitals or the so-called quarantines and therefore hid the sick, not informing the officers placed over each part of town by Yeropkin about them. Others, leaving the sick alone in their houses with no assistance or care, fled and carried the illness and terror everywhere. Some clandestinely carried the dead from their houses and cast them on the street in order to keep their infected belongings and avoid inspection by officials appointed for that purpose. The latter developed their own form of mischief, as is apparent from a manifesto issued by the empress: "It is our will that during the inspection of houses, both as to removal into quarantine and everything at the site, everyone and everything be treated by commanders and deputies with all possible humanity and solicitude, and that everyone receive full and proper treatment according to his physical condition. We forbid each and all to practice any oppression, suppression, crudeness, and discourtesy whatsoever. We especially reiterate that we most strictly forbid commanders and their subordinates to accept bribes, to force anyone, no matter who, to pay money or to extort under any pretext whatsoever during inspections or the removal into quarantine...It is rumored that at present there are many such irregularities in Moscow."

On August 2 Saltykov wrote that the plague had reared its head in Yeropkin's own house and the general therefore was shunning his duty. Yeropkin wrote Bruce that he could not handle his task successfully with the small number of men available to him. The Council decided to send Yeropkin a rescript urging him to remain at his post, notwithstanding the plague's appearance at his house. It also decided to appoint Senator Sobakin[66] to assist Yeropkin and in addition sent twelve guards officers from Petersburg to discharge his orders. Moscow's medical council[67] proposed selling spirits in taverns from the windows, denying entrance to buyers, and moving the settlement of economic peasants adjacent to the Earthen rampart. It also proposed selecting special police agents from among the best gentlemen in the city to inspect houses daily. It suggested further to use convicts to bury those who died of plague and carry the stricken to the hospital. In Petersburg the Council approved all these measures except the last, consenting to employ convicts solely for digging graves. At the same time it forbade export of any goods whatsoever from Moscow. Infected houses were ordered fumigated, primarily with sulphur. Couriers going to Petersburg were instructed to skirt Moscow.

We saw that in the spring the decision to cordon off Moscow was left up to Saltykov, depending on whether he thought the spread of the illness required it; at that time he thought a cordon useless and impossible. However, as the virulence of the plague increased the empress, in consideration of the danger threatening other regions and Petersburg, deemed it essential to order the commandant of Moscow to establish a cordon. On August 25, attending the Council, she declared that, "although it is hoped that what has infested Moscow is not actually the plague, I consider it essential to employ every means to destroy the illness raging there in order not to be responsible for neglecting anything."

Saltykov still opposed a cordon. "To institute quarantines," he wrote on August 30, "does not appear necessary at this time. It is too late. Almost everyone has left Moscow. Even the lowest people are fleeing; only a few sutlers and bakers are left. Everyone fears the quarantines. There are no food reserves. Nobody is coming to town and hunger is a real possibility. Winter is coming, but firewood is not being delivered. The people have lost heart and courage. Quarantines are most burdensome for the local populace and already there have been several threats against the pickets."

Moscow's senators[68] shared the field marshal's view and informed Catherine that it was impossible to cordon off Moscow because the city's situation, the condition of its houses, and the morale and habits of its residents all impeded it.

On September 5 Catherine brought to the Council the report she had just received from Saltykov in Moscow and the report of the Moscow departments of the Senate about the impossibility of cordoning off the city. She also brought a letter from Yeropkin to Bruce stating that in Moscow in two days 207 people had died of the dangerous disease and 615 from other illnesses. The Council instructed the Moscow Senate and the city's authorities that (1) quarantine houses were essential and it was imperative not only to maintain existing ones but to establish new ones, and inform the public about them, so that all inhabitants would notify their district police officers immediately when someone became sick so that they could be diagnosed and the stricken person quarantined if the illness was dangerous or suspicious; those who would go voluntarily were to be taken to a quarantine house or else stay at home isolated from everyone for sixteen days. Those infected with the illness were to be taken immediately to a quarantine house. When someone died of the dread disease only his room was to be fumigated, not the whole house, especially when the building was sectioned into apartments. (2) Quarantine pickets were needed around Moscow to safeguard the remainder of the empire and were to be placed on all roads from Moscow in the first settlements beyond the Treasury College rampart.[69] (3) Under no circumstances were people bringing cartloads of produce from other areas to be allowed into Moscow; they were to be shunted to sites beyond the Treasury College rampart where they were to remain sequestered from the city's inhabitants by a palisade. Commerce was to be conducted under police supervision. (4) The owners of eateries, bakers, kvas sellers—in a word, all traders in victuals—must not be considered idle and superfluous by other people in town; they must not be evicted freely from the city, especially in such an impoverished condition. At the least those who remained must be assembled and divided into groups, and elders appointed to look after and be responsible for them. (5) Although one could not say for sure whether there would be a shortage of foodstuffs in Moscow, since supplies usually were laid by from winter to winter—and it was even harder to judge now that most inhabitants had scattered—in case of need supplies could be obtained in nearby towns and villages and delivery sites selected where the city inhabitants might receive foodstuffs at normal prices.

Catherine personally drafted an answer to the Moscow Senate refuting its opinion that it was impossible to cordon off Moscow. "The first duty we have before God and the people He has entrusted to us," she said, "is to care for the welfare and health of our loyal subjects. We seek to sustain them despite the present difficult circumstances, not despondently but overflowing with memory of our debt to and love for the realm, with a spirit grieving over current circumstances in Moscow and unable to find peace and solace in empty regrets and sighs, but comforted solely by courageously seeking and instituting the measures and ministrations which only humane concern arouses for overcoming the human sacrifice suffered in the capital and preventing its further spread throughout the empire. These were the sources of the instructions which our Senate found inappropriate.

"We know from experience that the city's great size undoubtedly is a major obstacle to executing our instructions with dispatch, but we also believe that the potential harm to the city from doing nothing is far greater than the difficulty of obeying orders. The nature of the buildings, customs, and timeless habits increase the difficulties because the task at hand requires extreme care if we are to restore first the welfare and tranquility of the inhabitants and, second, make our measures permanent. But the vice or weakness best left unnamed must be reduced to a minimum in order not to destroy good and useful measures which must overcome obstacles rather than be frightened by them. Every effort must be made to ensure that personnel in charge of the measures are perfectly honest and without guile, and energetically pursue whatever they are assigned.

The officers will observe this closely, and not only they but everyone employed by the government, for all are bound by oath and honor above all to demonstrate solicitude and lend a helping hand whenever that can extirpate an evil harmful to society and one's own person. We must not weaken now and lower our burdened arms for the sake of our own repose, but adopt every idea to assist the measures created for the common security from the plague."

FURTHER MEASURES AND POPULAR REACTION

Meanwhile in Moscow on September 1 Yeropkin suggested to the senators that to eradicate the pestilence at the earliest possible moment, it might be appropriate to instruct Moscow's merchants to establish quarantine houses and infirmaries at their own expense for merchants who fell ill. They summoned the president of the Moscow magistracy and ten of the leading merchants of the first-rank and, sharing the proposal with them, urged them to agree to it. In addition, the senators decided to use the police to persuade other inhabitants of the suburbs to establish quarantines and infirmaries at their own expense. Yeropkin next stated that because so many of the criminals sentenced to transport were dying of the pestilence there were not enough available to remove corpses from the city and bury them. Since work at factories was at a standstill it would be advisable for the Senate to assign factory workers to this task. Twenty men could be raised from each district of Moscow at a wage of six copecks a day. The Senate adopted his suggestion. Besides Yeropkin, only three senators were in attendance—Sobakin, Count Ivan Vorontsov, and Rozhnov. But then on September 1 Sobakin, named as Yeropkin's assistant, announced that the dangerous disease had stricken people in his house, for which reason he no longer could head the commission entrusted to him or attend the Senate.

On the following day, September 2, the Senate consisted of three men— Prince Kozlovsky, Rozhnov and Yeropkin. The latter communicated sad news: during examination of the critically ill and deceased by Doctor Shafonsky and Guards Captain Volotsky in Lefortovo settlement, five men—the hospital's commissar, Lieutenant Kaftyrev; an employee in the office of the College of Hereditary Estates, Prytkov; Corporal Rakov of the Office for Building Houses and Gardens, and the retired hostlers Petrov and Piatnitsky—assembled a large crowd and brazenly and insolently refused to allow Shafonsky and Volotsky to conduct their examination, shouting that Shafonsky and other doctors were giving powders with arsenic to the sick and healthy in the hospital and thereby infecting the settlement's inhabitants. The Senate ordered Kaftyrev placed on bread and water for two weeks and sentenced the others to be lashed. Chief of Gendarmes Bakhmetev reported that while the stalls on Red Square trading in old clothing were being sealed one of the vendors, a soldier of the Synodal office, threw a rock from the crowd that fractured the head of a soldier. Although the rag sellers were seized, they were freed by the mixed crowd because of the small size of the police detachment. The Senate sentenced the soldier of the Synod office to be lashed.

The city's merchants complied with Yeropkin's proposal to build a house of quarantine. Old Believers then approached Yeropkin requesting permission to buy or build a quarantine house opposite Transfiguration village[70] on the Earthen rampart and maintain it at their expense, on condition of exemption from examination by doctors and orders from officers. Two of the petitioners, Pimen Alekseev and Ivan Prokhorov, were received in the Senate, where they were told that they might build a hospital at that location but could not be exempted from physical examinations and officers' orders. The petitioners agreed. On that day, September 7, four senators were present: Rozhnov, Pokhvisnev, Prince Kozlovsky, and Yeropkin. On September 12 only three were present— Rozhnov, Yeropkin, and Field Marshal Saltykov himself. The next day, September 13, Saltykov visited the Senate and again found only two others, Rozhnov and Yeropkin.

The old man lost his nerve and on the fourteenth sent the empress a desperate report. "The illness is multiplying so much and intensifying so much from day to day that nothing can be done to halt it other than every man for himself. As many as 835 people have died in a single day in Moscow, not counting those who are buried secretly in fear of the quarantines, and an additional sixty or more corpses are found each day in the streets. A multitude of the common folk have fled Moscow, especially bread and pastry bakers, sutlers, kvas brewers, and all who supply foodstuffs, and other artisans. Only with difficulty can one buy anything to eat. No one is working. There are no grain supplies. All nobles have left for their villages. Lieutenant General Peter Dmitrievich Yeropkin is laboring tirelessly to bring this evil to an end, but all his efforts are in vain. One of his house servants has become infected, which he requested me to report to your majesty and beseech merciful release from his command. Some of the people in my chancellery also have become infected, besides which people in the houses all around me are dying. I have locked my gates and sit alone, fearing the same misfortune for myself. I helped Lieutenant General Yeropkin every way I could, but there is no longer any way to help. The entire military garrison has been dispatched here and there, and government offices have stopped working; office workers everywhere are becoming infected. I grow so bold as to ask permission to absent myself during these evil days until the approaching cold weather quiets things down. Lieutenant General Yeropkin's commission is now superfluous and does more harm than good; all the district inspectors, sending messengers and travelling themselves, merely spread the disease. Factory owners now are building their own quarantines and observing their people. The merchants also are agreeing to take care of their own sick. The Old Believers are removing theirs into tents."

Without waiting for an answer to his request, Saltykov on September 14 went just outside Moscow for two days. Of course, it is impossible to justify this action. It is explained by the difficult situation of a leader feeling helpless and lonely. Everyone was leaving, the old man might have thought, they were deserting their responsibilities and leaving him alone, but what could he do by himself? How could he help? Yeropkin was making the necessary arrangements. He would stay behind, and Saltykov could breathe the clean air for two days. Surely his two-day absence would not have been noticed had there not been a riot in Moscow on September 15, the second day of the field marshal's absence.

The riot was accompanied by a terrible, loathsome, unprecedented occurrence—the murder of the archbishop.

MURDER OF THE ARCHBISHOP

In 1767 Moscow's metropolitan, Timothy, died.[71] He belonged to that group of people who are called good, and with this word escape a more exact definition of their character. Under the good metropolitan the abuse of the great powers residing in the bishop's advisory board or consistory gave opportunity for illicit activities and bribes. Timothy's successor was Amvrosy (Ambrose) Zertis-Kamensky,[72] a man with a different character. The energetic Ambrose, knowing well the disorder in Moscow because his prior appointment as archbishop of Krutitsa caused him to live in the city, determined to root out irregularities and enforce regulations and edicts—a difficult enterprise because one of the main sources of the disorder was the extreme poverty of the white or parish clergy.[73] Their obligatory marriage in early youth resulted in large families. To provide for their welfare and an appropriate education for their children would have been difficult even for a state wealthier than Russia. Poverty was the cause of their quest for the wherewithal to live and their loss of dignity; it was the source of the greediness so long and so easily criticized and laughed so hard at in literary works with no attempt to understand it.

Ambrose introduced order into the bishop's council[74] by prescribing for violation of orders "a fine with chains, restraint in irons, and deductions from salary without indulgence." Everyone who did not accept the new order was sent away quickly. Ambrose forbade marriage by young ecclesiastics until they had finished the course in theology or been examined by the bishop. He forbade ecclesiastics to change houses or move from church to church. He solicited from the Synod renewal of the edict of Peter the Great that permitted the clergy to have homes provided by the churches and thereby not to have to spend money to buy houses. Ambrose was notorious for his persecution of the so-called crossroads priests in Moscow.[75] He observed that "there is a large number of idle priests and other parish clergy in Moscow who, to extreme temptation, stand at Spassky crossing offering to perform church services for hire and create a major scandal by bargaining among themselves. In competing to offer the lowest price, instead of displaying the dignity befitting a priest, they hold filthy-tongued and heated arguments, sometimes even resorting to fisticuffs. And after the services, not having their own homes and land, they spend the rest of their time either in public taverns and private chophouses or, having drunk themselves into a stupor, disgracefully wander through the streets." Old men have related the story of the normal practice for these crossroads priests: they stood with white bread in their hands and when someone hired them to perform the liturgy but paid only a small amount they cried: "Do not bargain, else I will eat it now!" (that is, the loaf, and with it the ability to say mass).

It is easy to understand why an archbishop like Ambrose was unable to win the favor of the lower strata of Moscow's inhabitants, among whom were some who cared nothing about the practices he was persecuting. Others, however, accumulated complaints about the strict archbishop that were heard with sympathy by the first group because of their close proximity.[76] Ambrose must have known that these people did not like him; he even must have known the names of some of them. Their dislike naturally evoked his low regard for them.

Under these circumstances it was reported to Ambrose that on the square near the St. Barbara gates[77] a shameful scene was enacted against which the Ecclesiastical Statute[78] fulminated and the age of enlightenment cried out. On the wall near the St. Barbara gates for years there was an icon of the Bogoliubovo Mother of God. Suddenly, beginning in early September, continual prayers and vespers began to be said before it. A certain factory worker said that he saw this Madonna in a dream, and she had told him, "Because no one has prayed at her image or placed candles there for thirty years, Christ wanted to send a rain of stones on Moscow, but she begged him to substitute a three-month pestilence for the rain of stones." One might also cite the curious words of the nephew of the archbishop, Nikolai Bantysh-Kamensky,[79] which display strong dislike of the white clergy: "Idleness, avarice, and damnable superstition stimulated invention. At the beginning of September the priest of the church of All Saints at Kulishky devised a miracle with the help of a factory worker. (There follows the story of the factory worker's dream.) The vile goats (it is a sin to call them priests!), leaving their parishes and church ceremonies, assembled at the gates with pulpits, creating a marketplace not a pilgrimage." We note here only that there is no proof that a clergyman and not a factory worker thought up the miracle; the accusation remains unsubstantiated.

Bantysh-Kamensky described faithfully the archbishop's initial impression upon hearing news of the events near St. Barbara gates: all of it—the superstition, the false vision—was forbidden by the Ecclesiastical Statute and edicts and must be stopped. "He (Ambrose) considered it his duty, set out in the Statute and the monarch's edicts, to silence this disgrace. His first intention was to send the priests away and remove the icon (since there was no passageway through the gates for persons or vehicles because a stairway had been added) to the church of Sts. Cyrus and John[80] recently erected near the St. Barbara gates by her majesty, and to donate the money collected there for pious works. More specifically, he planned to donate it to the Foundling Home, for which he was a trustee.[81] The priests asked to report to the bishop's advisory board not only refused to go but even threatened to stone the men sent for them." Here ends the first part of Bantysh-Kamensky's story about Ambrose's measures, those of an archbishop obligated through his own measures to ban superstitious practices. The priests were summoned to the consistory to account for their conduct; the priests refused and thereby deprived the archbishop of means for settling the matter appropriately. It is a pity that Bantysh-Kamensky added a purely law-and-order motive: the archbishop wanted to remove the icon because there was no passage at the gates for people or vehicles because of the stairway that had been added.

When the disobedience of the clergy made it impossible for the consistory to conduct inquiries and carry out its intentions, Ambrose looked at the matter from the point of view of hygiene. "Meanwhile," says Bantysh-Kamensky, "the plague grew so virulent in the city that nine hundred and more were dying each day. Since doctors' orders forbade all contact and close assemblages of people, his grace was unable to proceed without discussing means for stopping the popular gatherings near St. Barbara gates with Yeropkin, the only leader left in town. The fear that the common people might turn on them led to the decision to postpone removal of the icon for the time being and, to avoid the money collected at St. Barbara gates from being plundered by factory hands, place the consistory's seal on the boxes. Yeropkin promised to send several soldiers to ensure that this was done in complete safety."

According to Yeropkin's testimony, Ambrose visited him on September 14 and said that he intended to seal the money box at the Bogoliubovo icon because in his judgment the appearance of the image was a hoax concocted by priests who had begun to make great profits from Te Deums. Here something is unclear. The appearance was false, said Ambrose; it was thought up by clergymen from mercenary motives. One must put a stop to something forbidden by law. If this was dangerous, how does it follow from the falsity of the appearance that it was necessary to affix a consistory seal to the money boxes? Bantysh-Kamensky offers this explanation: they decided to seal the boxes in fear that the money might be plundered by the factory workers. But it turns out that a military guard was already posted at the boxes. Be that as it may, this unfortunate instruction concerning the money was the cause of the riot.

According to the report of Field Marshal Saltykov, which he based on the report of Chief of Gendarmes Bakhmetev, on September 15, a Thursday, at eight o'clock in the evening the town tocsin rang out and at the sentry posts along the street barriers the striking of artillery wormscrews was heard. The police chief sent someone to find out what was going on and received a report that a large crowd of rabble was raising a commotion and fighting at the St. Barbara gates. Bakhmetev, accompanied by three dragoons and two hussars, went himself and found that from Ilyinka street to the St. Barbara gates a great crowd of people was standing on both sides of the wall, as many as ten thousand, most of them armed with cudgels. When asked why they had gathered, they answered the gendarme chief that they had come running at the sound of the tocsin, and the tocsin had sounded because six soldiers and the archbishop's secretary had come to take the money given by supplicants from the boxes at the icon of Our Lady of Bogoliubovo. Around the boxes stood the watch from the Moscow garrison, who announced that they would not permit seizure of the boxes without permission from their commander (the commandant's assistant). This led first to a heated argument and then fisticuffs.[82] The villains who wanted to tear down the icon and rob the treasury belonging to the Mother of God were beaten; the people had assembled to stand up for the Holy Virgin Mother to their last breath.

Seeing that he and his convoy of five were in no position to do anything, Bakhmetev went to see Yeropkin at his house on Ostozhenka street.[83] At the Resurrection (Voskresensk) gates he met a mob of about three thousand running with clubs along Tverskaia and Mokhovaia streets and from Hunter's Row[84] under the leadership of a bearded peasant in blue nankeen overalls, who repeatedly shouted at the top of his voice "Fellows, hurry up and make a stand for the Holy Virgin Mother and do not allow them to rob the Mother of God!"

Bakhmetev succeeded in stopping the crowd. Twenty or so men from the crowd stood at his side and took orders from him, and with their help "blue overalls" was seized and put in a sentry box. On Mokhovaia street they seized another bawler with the help of some manorial peasants. Having arrived at Yeropkin's, Bakhmetev heard him advise: "Do whatever you think best, but I can give you neither troops nor support." Returning to the box where "blue overalls" was held, Bakhmetev found that he was gone, and in his place were the men left to guard him, now injured. Somewhat earlier, on his way to Yeropkin's, Bakhmetev had sent a gendarme major to the crowd, demanding that they release into gendarme custody the archbishop's secretary and the detachment that had gone to the icon to get the money, because such villains must be punished publicly, and that to be beaten up by the crowd was not enough. Now the major reported back to Bakhmetev that the crowd not only agreed, but had even asked to do this. But the sentries from the Moscow garrison who stood near the St. Barbara gates said that they could not release the men without orders from their commander, that is, the commandant's assistant. Bakhmetev notofied Yeropkin, who ordered the commandant's assistant or Governor Yushkov to be found as quickly as possible. But even as the carriages and dispatches were going back and forth rumors flew that a crowd of rabble in the Kremlin was plundering the archbishop's home in the Miracles monastery, looking to murder its occupant.[85]

The moment squabbles began between the guards of the Moscow garrison and the archbishop's secretary concerning the money, murmurings against Ambrose were heard in the crowd interfering in the fight. "The archbishop," they cried, "has never shown the proper respect to the Mother of God expected from a man of his rank. But he still knew he could steal the thousand rubles which pious contributors, some of whom gave almost their last copeck, had donated, and he was prepared to do so without hesitation. He is godless. He ought to be killed in front of this very image!"

Aroused by these cries the mob swept into the Kremlin. Ambrose apparently learned about these excesses and threats and left the Miracles for the Donskoy monastery.[86] The crowd, seeking him in the Miracles monastery, stole what it could. Everything else it broke up, smashed, and mutilated. The great wine cellar leased at the Miracles monastery by the merchant Ptitsyn was looted thoroughly, and a drunken binge began. But on the morrow, the 16th, they remembered why they had entered the Kremlin and into the Miracles monastery. Someone told them that the archbishop was at the Donskoy monastery, and a crowd of three hundred descended on it. Ambrose, who learned about the looting of the Miracles monastery, told his nephew Nikolai Bantysh-Kamensky, who was there with him, to write Yeropkin about this and request a passport to leave the city. Instead of a pass Yeropkin sent an officer of the horse guards, who announced that his holiness must change clothes and leave the Donskoy monastery as quickly as possible, and that he, the officer, would wait for him at one end of Prince Trubetskoy's garden, from where he wanted to conduct him to Khoroshevo village, to the Resurrection monastery. While they searched for something to wear and Ambrose changed clothes, and the cart was prepared, they heard noise, cries, and shooting near the monastery. Ambrose went outside to climb into the cart but by this time the crowd had begun to break down the gates of the monastery from all sides. Everyone with Ambrose fled. He headed straight to the large church where mass was being said, joined in, and hoped to hide in the choir behind the iconostasis. But the crowd entered the church and found this refuge. They dragged the poor man out of the church, out of the monastery, and in front of the rear gates murdered him in the most barbarous manner: they beat him with eight stakes for two whole hours until, in the words of an eyewitness, "neither appearance nor likeness remained."

THE UPRISING IS QUELLED

Meanwhile Yeropkin spent the entire day, Friday the 16th, assembling a detachment at his house on the Ostozhenka by bits and pieces. The Velikolutsk Regiment was the principal military force of the Moscow command. But it contained only 350 men, of which 300 were stationed thirty versts from Moscow, away from the plague, leaving only fifty in the city. Yeropkin added to them guards detachments sent from Petersburg, and in this manner the unit reached 130 men. This troop, however small, had two cannon, which guaranteed success against a mob armed with clubs and stones. At 5:30 p.m. Yeropkin and his command advanced into the Kremlin. They seized a clergyman with a cross on the street and forced him to accompany them. When they entered the Kremlin through the Borovitsky[87] gates the detachment was greeted with clubs and brick bats. Yeropkin sent the commander, the crown prince of Georgia, to remonstrate with the insurgents, but he also was met with stones. A similar welcome greeted Brigadier Mamonov, who brought his servants to the Miracles monastery voluntarily and began to reason with the insurgents. They beat him about the head and face. Seeing that admonition was not helping, Yeropkin gave orders to shoot into the mob with cannon and muskets. No fewer than a hundred persons fell from this fire, 249 were taken prisoner, and the remainder scattered. But Yeropkin, wounded in two places by a staff and a rock, exhausted and feverish, was forced to take to his bed and did not participate in further developments.

The next day, Saturday the 17th of September, mobs began at dawn to force their way into the Kremlin through the Savior gates, in which stood Governor Yushkov.[88] The insurgents demanded that their comrades arrested the evening before be returned to them, that the baths be unsealed and the quarantines abolished, and that physicians not be used to make mandatory diagnoses. The evening before, on the 16th, Yeropkin had informed Saltykov about the uprising, and by 9:00 a.m. on the 17th the field marshal was in Moscow. Simultaneously, in accordance with his order of the evening before, the Velikolutsk Regiment—that is, the remaining 300 soldiers—entered Moscow. Saltykov entrusted command of the regiment to Chief of Gendarmes Bakhmetev and ordered him to lead his soldiers onto Red Square and crush the riot. Bakhmetev, after arraying the regiment on the square, said to the surrounding mob: "I advise you to disperse to your homes. If you do not, all of you will be killed." In thirty seconds the square was empty, and with this the riot ended.

The primary cause of the sad events of September 15 and 16 is obvious. This was the lack of military forces, although on the other hand the question naturally arises of why Yeropkin did not begin to assemble troops on the evening of the 15th. Why did he not use the night hours and appear in the Kremlin at dawn on the 16th, and thereby prevent the events at the Donskoy monastery? Be that as it may, the elderly field marshal had every right to complain about insufficient resources and the danger of the situation. "It seems that everything has calmed down," he wrote on September 19. "Nevertheless it is impossible to rest on this hope. The people are drunk—the religious dissenters, the clerks, the manorial serfs. The lords have all scattered to their villages. They left behind idle people who are always in the taverns. I found the Miracles monastery in a sad state: all the windows broken out, feather beds ripped open and the street full of feathers, the icons split. The rioters threatened many, especially the physicians. Although they are raging and threatening to kill many—including me but above all Peter Dmitrievich Yeropkin—their sore point is the quarantines. The people cannot bear that word.

"No one attends the Senate; there were only the two of us. Count Vorontsov writes that in his village people are infected so he went to another one, farther away. Prince Kozlovsky has been released from duty. Pokhvisnev is sick. Yeropkin has become ill and is in bed. The lord presidents (of the colleges) ask no one to do anything, for their members and officials have scattered throughout the countryside;[89] there is no one to carry out orders. Anyone for whom I send answers—I'm in the country. I can do nothing alone, not having a single assistant: the military command is small, the city is large, and the rabble are still numerous enough to do mischief. Among the miscreants apprehended are numerous clerks from almost every college; and soldiers of the colleges, old men of the retired guards battalion who stood watch in the Kremlin, rioted and pillaged more than anyone else, as the architect Bazhenov witnessed; he saw everything from the model house and overheard much talk.[90]

"Now we have received tidings that a crowd of all kind of rabble is gathering on the Pakhra river and wants to march to Moscow,[91] armed with all sorts of weapons, and the drunks scattered into the countryside from here threaten to destroy everything. I am alone in the city and the Senate. I have no assistants and the military command is not large enough. I am surrounded by an infectious disease, subjected to it more than others. Everyone comes running to me. I am compelled to let them leave the city. Each has some need. There is no one to assist me. The gendarme chief alone hurries everywhere, looking into everything; he does not even have time to sleep. I am in no condition to make an exact report to your majesty; I see and hear all sorts of different things. It is impossible to extract obedience from these people without resorting to severe measures."

On September 21 Saltykov wrote that "It is impossible to remain without a commander, for both in Moscow and throughout the district a number of rascals dressed in soldiers' uniforms are visiting crown and economic estates showing the peasants orders allegedly sent by the chancellery of the government and making the priests read them to the people. They are forcing elders and elected officials to pledge that the moment they hear the tocsin in Moscow or the firing of cannon they will run to Moscow with clubs and boar spears. I am leaving the Velikolutsk Regiment in Moscow. The main post is on Red Square with the cannon and there are pickets in key places. If the command were large enough, especially cavalry for patrols, we could put a quick end to this mischief. The organizer of this agitation must be from among the Old Believers because they always have opposed the quarantine, and it is worthy of note that the archepiscopal church was ravaged completely and its sacred vessels broken and scattered." Since the major deficiency involved military force, at the suggestion of the president of the Main Magistracy, Protasov, a watch force was assembled from among the merchants.

GRIGORY ORLOV TAKES COMMAND OF MOSCOW

On the same day, September 21, that Saltykov wrote, "It is impossible to remain without a commander," the empress issued a manifesto sending Count Grigory Orlov to Moscow. "In view of the pitiful condition of our city Moscow and the large number of people dying from the infectious disease," it stated, "we rashly would consider it the duty of our office to be present were it not that our visit under present military circumstances would cause a certain disorder and interference in the vital business of

Count Grigory Grigorevich Orlov

our empire. Therefore, unable to share the danger of the city's inhabitants personally, we deemed it necessary to send an important personage whom we have charged with the authority, upon viewing the need and necessity there, to make all arrangements to save lives and provision the inhabitants adequately. For this task we have selected, on the basis of our confidence in him and his renowned zeal, diligence, and loyalty to us and the fatherland, our quartermaster general and adjutant general, Count Grigory Orlov.[92] We have granted him full authority to undertake whatever the general welfare requires and to dissolve institutions he regards as either inappropriate or useless, and to accomplish whatever he finds conducive to the general good. In sum, we not only instruct one and all to obey and assist him but also instruct all commanders to observe his orders and that he have access in this respect to the Moscow departments of the Senate. We forbid one and all to hinder or obstruct him or his orders for he knows our will, which is to end the suffering of mankind no matter what mortal strength it takes, and enjoys full authority to act without hindrance."

Orlov by his very nature could not have been pleased with his position at court. Nor could he remain satisfied either with his administrative duties as quartermaster general or his activity as a member of the Council. He was attracted to a role in the war, where brilliant victories were being won and where his own brother had burned the Turkish fleet. It had been impossible to leave Petersburg for long while the war lasted but he had not abandoned his dream of commanding a special enterprise which might quickly end the war. Now, when Moscow and all Russia required energetic action to save them from a fearful scourge, Orlov did not want to let slip an occasion to render a great service and acquire a celebrated reputation. On the eve of his departure for Moscow Orlov told the English envoy Lord Cathcart that he was convinced Moscow's chief misfortune consisted in the fear and panic which had seized the upper and lower orders of inhabitants alike, from which cause stemmed the disorder and lack of good management. When Cathcart began to entreat him to postpone his journey, saying that in Moscow he would find not only a lack of good management but also the plague, Orlov answered: "I do not care, plague or no plague, in any event, I am leaving tomorrow. I have waited impatiently for a long time for an opportunity to perform significant service for the empress and the fatherland. Such opportunities come rarely for private citizens and always involve some risk. I hope that just now I have found such an opportunity, and no danger will move me to give it up."

"Plague or no plague," said Orlov. Actually, considerable care had been taken until just before this time in using the word "plague" because of a lack of consensus among the physicians. Doctor Kuhlemann had reported that observation of the sick in the Simonov monastery had confirmed his former opinion that the plague was not present, since no signs other than spots could be found on either the dead or the living that might indicate plague, so he declared that the illness was fever with spots of the worst variety.

On September 28 the Moscow Senate held its first meeting with Count Orlov. The senators present included Rozhnov, Pokhvisnev, Field Marshal Saltykov, Yeropkin, Vsevolozhsky, and a newly named senator who had been an important personage during the two preceding reigns, Dmitry Vasilevich Volkov. Orlov presented the imperial edict authorizing him to preside over the Moscow departments of the Senate and telling one and all to obey him. He announced orally the decision to bring Volkov into the Senate. Governor Yushkov reported that the Mozhaisk gentry had consented to come to Moscow with their servants and a significant number of peasants.[93] The Senate commended them for their zeal; there was no longer need for such daring, however, for order had been restored.

The terms of Orlov's appointment lent him such eminence that Saltykov of course no longer could remain Moscow's commander-in-chief. Catherine had the weakness of not appreciating the significant accomplishments and people of Elizabeth's reign. The victor of Kunersdorf had irritated her by pointing out the danger of applying sanitary measures to Moscow and the need to augment military forces there. It had not been possible to remind Saltykov, as she had Rumiantsev, that the Romans did not ask how many enemy are there, but where they are. The campaigns of a foreign war differed from those of domestic security and maintaining law and order over vast spaces. But the old man offered his own head to Catherine by leaving for the countryside; although his immediate return and quick concentration of troops in Moscow, which brought the unrest to an end, made amends for his initial carelessness, this was not so in the eyes of Catherine, who in a letter to Bielcke directly attributed the murder of Ambrose to Saltykov's absence from the city.

But the question naturally arises about what Saltykov could have done without troops. Could it be suggested seriously that he might have assembled a small unit with cannon and moved into the Kremlin much sooner than the renowned Yeropkin? In her letter to Bielcke Catherine used a curious expression: "Moscow is not a city, but a world of its own." Yet on what subject had Saltykov constantly harped if not his lack of troops? In a letter to Bibikov, Catherine gave full vent to her bias against Saltykov: "The weakness of Field Marshal Saltykov defies understanding, as he did not think it shameful to request leave at the very moment he was needed most. Without awaiting permission he left, one might assume, to amuse himself with his hounds. Meanwhile, fanatics concocted a scheme to awe people with the miracles of the icon over the St. Barbara gates. The crowds of praying rabble were infected all the more easily. While this pilgrimage was happening some 900 people were dying each day. The archbishop and Lieutenant General Yeropkin decided to limit the flow of people to this place gradually, and to this end the archbishop sent some of his people late in the day on September 15 to place a seal on the collection box at that icon. That set off fights, and the regular police turned up short; our mother Moscow is very large. No one was in charge of the city; there was no one to put them down. The chief of gendarmes was found wanting and in some respects even erred. When I realized the utter necessity of sending a responsible person there with full powers, I dis-patched Grand Master of the Ordnance Count Orlov at his own strong urging. Before his arrival everyone was seized by the *terreur panique*, following the example of Count Saltykov (?), and crawled away from the plague into their holes, but now they have returned to their places.... I forgot to say in my letter that the old grumbler, the field marshal, has been retired." In the edict granting the field marshal's retirement Catherine said that, "condescending to his request to retire him she relieved him of all duties, *praising him for his notable service to the predecessors of her majesty.*"

On September 30 Orlov announced in the Senate that it was necessary, first, to see to the livelihood of craftsmen and artisans in the city as necessary; and second, to bring enough vinegar to Moscow to satisfy the needs of the residents. Finally, the people who removed corpses must receive an additional two copecks to their daily wage of six copecks. On October 12 Orlov told the Senate he had learned that there were malicious people who, disregarding the impoverishment in which Muscovites were living, hearkened not to the fear of God but debased themselves by entering the houses of the deceased and stealing what was left of the belongings of these unfortunates. He proposed announcing to one and all that when such godless people and enemies of humanity were discovered committing this crime they would be executed without mercy on the spot where the crime was discovered; the death of even one such malicious spirit could avert sickness and death for innocent people that someone carrying infected things might spread throughout the city. When circumstances were extreme, the measures to counteract them also must be extreme. Four days after this decision the chancellery of the chief of gendarmes reported that a peasant named Timofey Matveev, who belonged to the Imperial Stables Chancellery, two vagabond soldiers of the Main Commissariat, Akutin and Denisov, and the son of a soldier in the life guards named Eremin, not in the army himself, had assembled a band of nine men and robbed three deserted houses. On the basis of the edict of October 12 the chancellery sentenced the criminals to be hanged but the Senate, because the crimes were committed before publication of the edict, sentenced the guilty to the knout and to burying victims of the plague. Furthermore Orlov proposed that since people were conveying the bodies of plague victims without precautions, sitting in the same wagon with the corpses, it be announced that anyone guilty of such rashness be punished—men taken to dig graves, women to attend the sick.

A shelter was set up for orphans whose parents died of plague under the vice president of the College of Manufactures, Sukin.[94] But it proved impossible to shelter more than a hundred children in this home, and almost every day brought more orphans. The Senate ordered Sukin to commandeer the house of the Frenchman, Lyon, built for outings with money collected for that purpose. The Senate justified its order by saying that sheltering orphans was done in the name of society and when the house no longer was needed for orphans it could be used again for outings. Orlov had instructed the treasury earlier to purchase handicraft products in order to provide a livelihood for workers. On October 25 he told the Senate that the city contained numerous people who lacked a trade but made their living by unskilled or manual labor yet under present circumstances could not find even that work. To provide a worthy livelihood for these people and end the idleness responsible for all kinds of mischief it was essential: (1) to raise the rampart of the Treasury College surrounding Moscow and deepen its moat, and to conscript for this all Muscovites willing to work; (2) to make daily payment for this work of fifteen copecks a day for men and ten for women; (3) to supplement this with an additional three copecks daily for all supplying their own tools; (4) to appoint Lieutenant General and Senator Aleksei Petrovich Melgunov as overall supervisor of this work.[95]

PUNISHMENT FOR THE INSURGENTS

Meanwhile an investigation of the rioters seized in the Kremlin was begun. It was entrusted to a special commission of ecclesiastics and laymen under the presidency of the procurator of the Synod office, Rozhnov. On October 4 Rozhnov informed the Senate that one of the insurgents under arrest, Stepan Ivanov, sixteen years old, testified that his former employer, a merchant, had instructed him a week or more before the insurgency that should the tocsin ring in the city he was to run with clubs and staves to a place designated by his employer. Rozhnov asked the Senate whether the boy should be freed because of his youth and truthfulness, and the Senate concurred.

In a letter sent to Bibikov on October 20, Catherine wrote, "The inquest is now under way and it has been discovered clearly that there was neither head nor tail, that the whole event occurred by chance." This view of the event, of course, gained ascendency in Moscow when on November 1 the Senate received the report of the investigative commission. "Some defendants testified that they ran to the Kremlin only after being summoned by police employees at the time of the recent events, but others said that they had heard several days in advance that there would be notices or if they heard the tocsin bell or cannon firing they were to run to the Kremlin, but as to who started these rumors, no one could say. Further questioning proved fruitless, and nothing more was discovered, for the prisoners lapsed into despondency and crossed themselves, and one youth dissolved into tears."

The investigation uncovered the murderers of Ambrose. They were Vasily Andreev, a house servant of Raevsky, Ivan Dmitriev, a Moscow merchant of the second guild and Fedot Parfenev, a ploughman from the cannoneers' suburb of the town of Kashira. The murderers were brought before the Senate, at which time Dmitriev renounced his previous testimony, saying that he had given it out of fear. The chief instigators were not discovered during the investigation. At the meeting of November 4, when one of the senators proposed completing the interrogation of the defendants for whom circumstantial evidence had not been produced, Orlov said: "Although true justice requires that we try to identify the ultimate source of the crime in order that the guilty be punished to the extent of their guilt, on account of the present unfortunate circumstances in Moscow which exposes humanity to death, there is neither the time nor the resources to accomplish this. But there is the fundamental necessity that the criminals who are convicted or confess be punished as quickly as possible, although some will escape. As it is always better that the guilty are not punished than to punish the innocent, this body must reach a verdict and convict the guilty solely on the basis of circumstances and proof now in hand." Because the Senate always agreed with Orlov, thanks to the full powers given him, it consented.

The very next day, November 5, the Senate met to pronounce sentence on the defendants. Senator Volkov spoke first. "The evidence and confessions of prisoners under arrest read to this body concern deeds, all of which are inhumane and violations of law and therefore deserving of strict punishment. Punishment is determined already by the laws of God and men; thus nothing further remains to be done other than pronouncing and carrying out what is defined by laws. But when we examine the violent context of terrible deeds done without warning, expecting to find them rooted in violence, we see clearly that each of the crimes is incomparably heinous and deserving of the most severe punishment. We have seen that our first capital city, the very center of which is a spectacle of holy places and monarchical palaces, instead of reducing raging hearts to sense and reverence, became a place of sacrilegious ignominy. We do not see a robber and murderer who doing evil immediately conceals it and in desperation trembles at the very name of justice, but many people daring to rebel against the laws that might preserve them and, what is worse, revelling in their crimes, in sacrilege, and in the murder of a churchman. We see the world perplexed that this people, normally pious and loyal to their sovereign and the laws, ordinarily strong and glorious, uplifted and everywhere victorious, in an instant could forget itself and turn its hands, terrible to its foes, to suicide. We see the fatherland demanding punishment from the laws of its violent sons. We see the church stained by pastoral blood and crying out for vengeance. Viewing this violent context with horror, we nonetheless feel compassion when the ultimate source of such evil is studied, not to regurgitate a similar poison or because we must expect such misfortunes, but because we see how pernicious to humanity in general are blindness, superstition, and the way private citizens and poor people burn with eager covetousness not for the Creator and the Holy Faith but for a mere ritual or a holy place, disregarding true faith and religion, and how violently but inexorably the most tender and philanthropic heart descends to violence, whereas under mild rule a singular mutual love one for another might have been expected.

"Here we see the soldier Biakov and the factory worker Ilia Afanasiev, each having rejected his cross, that is, his station in life, abandoning himself to deceit and avarice, grubbing with the others gathered there for the money of the Mother of God, who never demands our favor, but seeks only our good in everything. We see these imposters, through their gains, attracting great attention to themselves. We see several clergymen, who nevertheless are totally unworthy of the dignity of the name of their vocation or their own names, despising the people's blindness with loathsome joy before the All-Seeing, setting up a church service in the marketplace and sticking out their hands to receive filthy lucre. We see, even while we sympathize with them, several leaders who, instead of immediately restoring order as the laws command, through weakness abetted the disorder and allowed it to swell to the point that when the late archbishop wanted merely to keep this peaceful gathering of money grubbers from the inevitable plunder of the Biakovs and the Afanasievs the very greed of these people turned legal conduct into robbery and sacrilege. This was likewise the sole accomplishment of all the subsequent evils.

"With this understanding of the event we are judging and its context, we are forced to conclude that the laws must run their harsh course, and the moment then will come to comfort and be comforted. I propose the following: (1) those accused and found guilty of the murder of His Holiness Ambrose should be executed as murderers, the worst among the insurgents; (2) accessories to the murder and participants in robbing the monastery, defiling the holy places, defacing the holy icons, and ransacking the quarantine houses and hospitals, having done so more from unthinking urges than sacreligious intent, are to be subjected to corporal punishment and sent to hard labor as convicts; (3) the soldier Biakov and the factory worker Afanasiev after corporal punishment are to be sent into exile to the Solovetsk monastery[96] as deceivers harmful to society;

(4) the others apprehended, although not convicted of murder and theft, guilty of having been part of a criminal mob, are to be lashed and sent to state labor; (5) those who are left release without punishment. Although they did not confess and there is no proof of their evil deeds, the very fact of their arrest at least indicates suspicion of them. For them, arrest is punishment enough. While satisfying justice, the laws must be observed as well.

"Lieutenant General, Senator and holder of a knightly order, Peter Dmitrievich Yeropkin was the first who, through loyalty to her imperial majesty, love for the fatherland, and courage worthy of his dignity, opposed this violent disorder and restored the initial calm. His noble soul demands no reward for this feat, but our acknowledgement belongs none the less to him. Thus we make this gesture, so that recognition of virtue be virtue's best reward. Thus will we fulfill our duty and satisfy the expectation of the fatherland and the world. We will wash away the spot of guilty blood smeared on the innocent Russian people!

"Knowing the sensitive and humanitarian heart of her imperial majesty and knowing how much she has sympathized with the misfortune of the most sinful criminals, we will dissolve their blood with our tears; and having paid this debt to humanity will be comforted at last that this evil which took place here will serve to remove blindness, extend knowledge and enlightenment, and lend renewed determination to one and all to labor with unflagging zeal for proper upbringing and good manners. In this firm spirit and with omniscient foresight our most august monarch will further her tireless efforts."

Needless to say Senator Melgunov agreed with Volkov but Orlov proposed that the senators settle upon corporal punishment according to the edict of 1754 rather than the death penalty,[97] yet hang two of the convicted by lot. The assembly accepted this sentence for the murderers of Archbishop Ambrose but also decided to apply the death penalty to one of the insurgents and thieves by lot. In doing this they intended to demonstrate the full horror of the crime committed by the rioters apart from the murder of the archbishop.

RESOLUTION OF MOSCOW'S TROUBLES

Concerns about the children orphaned by their parents' death from plague were settled as follows. The Guardianship Council agreed to accept them at the Foundling Home,[98] which had been spared infection thanks to a strict cordon. Orlov's last proposal, made in the Senate on November 7, was that canals be dug from the swamps and streams surrounding Moscow to the Neglinnaia river to increase its flow and provide employment for the surrounding settlements.[99] Another source of employment he suggested was work on the highways from Tula, Kaluga, Kolomenskoe, and other places. On November 17 the Senate heard the edict relieving Count Orlov and appointing as Moscow's commander-in-chief Prince Mikhail Nikitich Volkonsky, who had just returned from Warsaw.[100] At the same meeting it was announced that Yeropkin was to receive the Order of St. Andrew[101] and twenty thousand rubles. He also retired.

In Moscow at this time there were 12,538 houses. Some six thousand of them were infected with plague, and in three thousand every inhabitant died. From April 1771 to the end of February 1772 some 12,565 persons were in hospitals and quarantines at state cost.

We have found a report Orlov wrote about Moscow during the plague. In it, among other things he says that, "It would be very useful were the owners of large factories voluntarily to agree to move them to district towns, for Moscow is not at all suitable for factories. Priests in Moscow must behave better. For them to behave better, they must have a higher standard of living. For their livelihood to improve, their parishes must be larger. And now many of them are deceased. To correct this situation, consulting with the bishops, small parishes must be joined with others. Priests might take turns serving in churches that are farther away. Priests without adequate maintenance have caused much mischief in Moscow. The same is true of the Moscow military guards, the retired garrison soldiers. They are so dissolute they are beyond saving unless they be transferred entirely, for their obedience and discipline are, in a word, like the plague. I saw an example of this when the Velikolutsk soldiers stood guard with them. It was impossible to recognize them as soldiers. Almost all have their own homes, all are traders and no one is responsible for them. They intermingle with the factory workers and other residents of Moscow. Such are the people who live in this place! When you look into the interior of their life and way of thinking your hair stands on end and you are amazed that still more and nastier things have not happened in Moscow."[102]

This was not the first suggestion to move the large factories out of Moscow. On August 31 the procurator general proposed to the Senate in Petersburg that whereas the increase of factories in Moscow was long known to be harmful and consideration had been given to relocating them in other towns, now that an infectious disease had appeared in Moscow both necessity and the security of the city and the realm required their removal, especially since the pestilence began in the factories. The Senate forwarded an edict to the College of Manufactures saying that it was necessary to relocate several factories from Moscow in other towns; to wit, all woolen, sailcloth, sealing wax, stoneware, pin-making, button, wire and brass, instrument, paint, serge, vitriol, chamois and suede, morocco, and all leather working and dye factories. The College of Manufactures might locate them wherever it wished in other towns. Although silk, card, tinsel, raincoat, gold and silver thread, instrument (?), braid, joiners, fan, mirror, chintz and semichintz, flood pipes, bleaching, and brass (?) manufacturies would be permitted to remain, the privileges freeing them from housing their workers would be eliminated.

But the Senate apparently was hasty in this matter and did not think through the obstacles to this measure. Unfortunately it adopted the same thinking a child would use—something unprofitable or undesirable happened in a certain institution under certain conditions, so away with the institution! Most of the factories in Moscow were state-owned and essential for the army and navy. The treasury had suffered great losses when the plague halted all work and now the factories must be brought into production quickly. But there were no people to work. The Admiralty College wondered whether people might be taken from other factories to make up for the shortage of workers in its sailcloth factory. Senator Volkov felt that the Admiralty College's request was contrary to law and justice. Let the Admiralty College provide samples of sailcloth, he suggested, and the needed sailcloth could be produced in privately owned factories without large transfers of workers. The Senate at first concurred, whereupon the procurator general suggested that the matter was extremely important to the public interest. Was it not possible to know beforehand just how many people and which skills the Admiralty required for its Moscow factory, so that the factory might be supplied with a given number of workers. The Senate accepted the procurator general's proposal.

Not until July 1773 did the College of Manufactures respond to the Senate, stating that it was impossible to remove factories outside Moscow. The Senate had to admit that the position of the College of Manufactures had some basis, but it still preferred to stand by its earlier statement that several factories must be removed from Moscow about which, by the way, nothing was said in its previous opinion. It issued a statement that since the factories in question included some that harmed the city because of their bad smell, such as those producing tallow, soap, and the like, which immediately must be moved from the city, it was impossible to list accurately those requiring removal without visual inspection. Following the college's suggestion, Commander-in-Chief Prince Volkonsky was directed to make a general survey jointly with the president of the College of Manufactures to determine which factories harmed the city's inhabitants and should be removed. It then instructed the College of Manufactures not to grant permission to build factories in Moscow in the future without first consulting the Senate.[103]

The issue of relocating factories faded away. But because of the plague another very important measure was introduced throughout the country, prohibition of burying the dead at churches inside towns or locating cemeteries within towns. At the end of 1771 the Synod distributed this edict everywhere.

As remarked above, in Moscow the Guardianship Council sheltered children orphaned when their parents died of the plague. In July 1772 Ivan Ivanovich Betskoy[104] conveyed to the Senate the empress's verbal order to accept at the Moscow Foundling Home young children wandering about the city with no supervision. "Since all children sheltered by the Moscow Foundling Home during the time of the infectious disease were saved from death," wrote Betskoy, "in the future orphans of any status deprived of subsistence and care shall be considered to be perishing and shall enjoy the right of acceptance at the Foundling Home in accord with its charter."

In response the Senate reported to the empress : (1) it vouch-safed to accept verbal edicts solely from senators, the procurator general, the presidents of the first three colleges and the adjutants general of the day— and Betskoy lacked any of these titles; and (2) the new edict changed earlier regulations regarding idle youths and only foundlings and illegitimate babies qualified for the Foundling Home. Betskoy's proposal might lead to abuses by serfs and soldiers, sailors, and other service men who wanted to save their children, the former from their landlords and the latter from service, by entering them at the Foundling Home. Children also might be accepted who ran away from home, as children do, but whose parents had no desire to see them placed in the Foundling Home and would weep over the loss of their children. Landlords would be deprived of their peasants and the realm of its soldiery.

The procurator general feared the bad impression this report might make on the empress and suggested several days later that the Senate might wish to reconsider and accept Betskoy's recommendation for information only. Betskoy had not requested a resolution from the Senate, but merely informed it of his letter to the Foundling Home. But the Senate, in a rare occurrence, adhered to its opinion.

The new commander-in-chief in Moscow began his tenure as usual by dismissing an official who had enjoyed the full confidence of the previous commander-in-chief. Prince Volkonsky wrote the empress at the beginning of 1772 that "Chief of Gendarmes Bakhmetev was found to be careless in his duty and in dealing with unfounded reports and therefore the Executive Commission relieved him of his duties the day before yesterday with my knowledge. This severity is required both by present circumstances and the future to insure that everyone execute the duty entrusted to him and follow orders exactly and without fail." This accusation was completely unfounded, but who could intercede for Bakhmetev in Petersburg?

On February 4, 1772 Volkonsky reported: "For a whole month no one died or was taken ill, but on the 2nd a woman in the house of Major Markov fell sick (with plague). Immediately every precaution was taken. The sick woman was taken to the hospital. The people who had contact with her were quarantined. Her possessions were burned. An order was given to tear down the lodging where she dwelled, and the whole house was locked until lifting of the quarantine." Later it was discovered that the woman suffered merely from a fever. On November 14, 1772 an imperial edict ordered Moscow's government offices to reopen beginning December 1. On November 25 church services were held in Petersburg and Moscow thanking God for bringing an end to the pest plague.

DISCONTENT IN THE GUARDS

Orlov returned to Petersburg in triumph from his civil campaign in Moscow but in the meantime his privileged position continued to cause dissatisfaction in various guards circles. During the first days of the war a captain of the horse guards named Vasily Panov spoke about the condition of the people: everywhere there was dissatisfaction and the war was siphoning money away from the state and sending as much as eight million rubles to other governments. Catherine was intelligent, even stubborn; what she set in motion she finished, and those to whom she gave command she trusted. The mind-set of the gentry was contemptible; the trade in spirits had been abandoned to tax farmers, who alone profited while the houses of many poor landlords were torn apart in the search for illegal spirits. And now the villages were being taken away completely from the gentry. How could the peasants be given freedom? What would the gentry live on? The country yokels all were beating each other up, frequently killing each other, but the guilty merely were sent into exile and given their freedom. Panin and Orlov were getting along poorly.

His fellow officer, Ippolit Stepanov, to whom Panov directed these remarks, asked him: "How is his highness [Grand Duke Paul], and what does he think of the counts [Panin and Orlov]?"[105]

Panov, praising the grand duke, said: "Nikita Ivanovich Panin is teaching him a great deal about everything; it would be unnatural, however, for his highness to treat the Orlovs well: indeed, they did away with his father. Let him grow up, and they will weep like cattle before a wolf. Revenge even now is to be expected because the Panin party is raised high and things could not be better."

Meanwhile many people were gossiping about the observations on the occasion of the transit of Venus.[106] One of the guards officers, Afanasiev, said: "As Venus passes, God will do something; I tell you, it is not passing for nothing."

First Major Zhilin recounted the haughtiness of the present Counts Orlov and other chance favorites towards their predecessors and thereby praised Aleksei Grigorevich Razumovsky and Ivan Ivanovich Shuvalov for treating people so well.[107] These discontented officers were unable to find a "mastermind" to devise a plot and did not know how to proceed without the consent of the grand duke and heir. Ozerov said: "There is no way to avert popular oppression nor can any good be expected until his highness is raised to the throne. It is my misfortune that I am unable to reach him."

Zhilin approached Ozerov and complained that "New laws have ordained freedom for peasants and slaves and have caused confusion among the common people so that many peasants now refuse to obey and insult the gentry. For whom are the laws composed? They are designed solely to oppress the gentry, so that somehow they will decline. Here a war begins, there we see constant conscript levies. No one watches the administrators. Great salaries are paid state officials at the cost of the people's ruin. How long will it last? It is necessary to overthrow her [Catherine]; the tsarevich is old enough."

"Have you heard anything from the great lords?" Ozerov asked him. "Who is one, if not Panin?"

"No," Zhilin answered, "one can place no faith in him! What is needed is a man people can love and give their loyalty to. He is Count Kirill Grigorich [Razumovsky],[108] whom the people love and to whom they entrust their confidence. And he can be persuaded to do it. I am convinced that he will not refuse to act for the good of the fatherland. There are other people as well—Voeikov,[109] a very good minister, and Rumiantsev."

"They aren't even here," objected Ozerov.

"They don't need to be here long," answered Zhilin, "since it can be accomplished more quickly at the Summer Palace. In the Winter Palace there are many nooks, making it impossible to seize whom one must."[110]

They intended to remove Panin and replace him with Voeikov. When a certain officer was arrested because he beat a sergeant in company formation, Ozerov said that the guards were falling into disarray. In former times guards officers could not be arrested without an imperial edict but now the regimental major took such liberties that officers were no longer of one mind and everyone spied on each other. When a company marched past his quarters Ozerov, sitting on the window sill, cried to the soldiers: "Well, fellows, here's to suffering!"

The malcontents never discovered a "mastermind" and the affair was limited to their conversations. But their discussions were passed on, and to try Ozerov and his conversants a commission was formed consisting of Count Nikita Panin, Gendarme General Chicherin,[111] Elagin, and Procurator General Prince Viazemsky, which sentenced the guilty to death. Catherine thereupon resolved in her own hand that "As God himself gave these traitors into my hands it is not mine to judge them, but I leave them their remaining years for repentance and sentence them to the following: Zhilin and Ozerov, after being deprived of all ranks, gentry status, and titles, are to be sent to Nerchinsk for perpetual labor in the silver mines, but not together in the same place; Stepanov and Panov are to be sent to Kamchatka for life, after being deprived of rank and gentry status, to earn a living by their own labors."[112]

BENEVSKY AND HIS CONVICT BAND

Stepanov and Panov were accompanied to Kamchatka by other criminals including the infamous Baturin, who by gazing at the stars had predicted the appearance of the former emperor, and Baron Maurice à la Daré de Beneve (as he signed his name),[113] a Hungarian compelled to flee his homeland for taking the law into his own hands, with his brothers, and who had served in the Polish confederation. In 1768 he was captured by the Russians and released on his word of honor that he would not fight again against Russian troops. Benevsky did not keep his word and was seized for the second time in 1769. He was sent to Kazan along with the captured Swede Wijnbladh, who also served in the confederation. The two escaped from Kazan through Moscow to Petersburg in hopes of escaping abroad by sea, but were recaptured in November 1769 and sent for life to Kamchatka, where they had to support themselves by their own labors.

In July 1770 they were transferred from Okhotsk to a stockade in Kamchatka, Bolsheretsk, which had no more than thirty-five houses. The garrison consisted of seventy cossacks commanded by Captain Grigory Nilov, who was negligent and a drunkard. Also in Bolsheretsk was a former chamber servant of Empress Anna, named Turchaninov, who conceived a plot against Elizabeth in 1742. Another was Semen Gurev, sent in 1762, Khrushchov, and a doctor, Meider.[114] These exiles managed to win to their side one Chulochnikov, the steward of the merchant Kholodilov, and a group of workers, the helmsman Churin, the helmsman's apprentice Bocharov, the priest's son Ustiuzhnikov (who together with the son of Captain Nilov was a pupil of Benevsky), a cossack named Riumin, and several natives of Kamchatka. They told the simple people that Benevsky and the other convicts brought with him were suffering for the sake of Grand Duke Paul Petrovich. Benevsky showed them a green velvet envelope which ostensibly bore the seal of the grand duke and a letter to the Holy Roman emperor stating the grand duke's desire to marry his daughter.

In the spring of 1771 the exiles staged an uprising. They murdered Nilov at night and took over the treasury, two cannon and the military supplies. They seized Bolsheretsk and forced the inhabitants to take the oath to Emperor Paul. On April 30 a group was sent farther down the peninsula to the harbor of Chekavinsk, where the storehouse was looted of its provisions. They seized the state-owned galliot St. Peter, outfitted it for a cruise, renamed it for the emperor, and dubbed themselves the "Assembled Company for the Name of His Imperial Majesty Paul Petrovich."

They composed a proclamation to the Senate that Paul Petrovich had been deprived of the throne illegally and that the destructive Polish war was being waged solely for the benefit of Poniatowski. They claimed that trade in spirits and salt had been farmed out to a favored few; that villages were confiscated from monasteries to educate illegitimate children while legitimate children remained without care; that the deputies named to compose a law code were deprived of discussion by an oppressive instruction; and that extraordinary tribute had been exacted from the people.[115] The proclamation continued by saying that quitrents were required from the disabled and young as well as the healthy; that for gross injustices judges merely assessed fines in money, whereas if they accepted anything from a suitor for a just decision, they were excluded from humanity; that only the tsarina's favorites had access to the gold and silver being mined; that the people stagnated in ignorance and suffering; and that no one was rewarded for true, loyal service. The insurgents said they had wanted to give counsel to thirty-three fur traders unjustly condemned to work without pay for their comrade, Kholodilov. This brought on them the wrath of Captain Nilov, who ordered their arrest. This forced both them and the men being punished to declare their loyalty to the legal sovereign [i.e., Paul], whereupon they went into action, arrested Nilov (who fell into paralysis from fear and drunkenness) and in his place chose Benevsky.

Benevsky and his comrades went to sea, hugging the coastline and setting their course along the Kurile Islands. On July 7 they approached the coast of Japan but the Japanese allowed them neither to land nor to reach the open sea. Then Benevsky opened the way to sea with a cannon shot. On August 7 they reached the island of Formosa where three of their comrades were murdered by the inhabitants, among them Panov. Benevsky repaid the Formosans by destroying a boat with islanders aboard and by burning houses in the vicinity of the bay. On the coast of China the sailors were received amicably. On September 12 they came to the Portuguese colony of Macao. Here only Benevsky, speaking in Latin, could plead their case to the governor. He lived in the governor's house, sold him the galliot as though it were his own boat, and declared that his native land was Hungary, to which he must return. He ordered the Russians to call themselves Hungarians. He forbade them to pray before icons. He had an argument with Wijnbladh and Stepanov and slandered the Russians, accusing them of plotting an uprising to take over the city. The whole gang was arrested and thrown into jail and thus obliged to submit to Benevsky. Only Stepanov demurred, declaring that he would sooner remain in prison than give his signature in submission to Benevsky or in loyalty to the Holy Roman emperor. Fifteen of the Russians fell victim to Macao's climate, among them Turchaninov.

For the return to Europe of the survivors Benevsky hired two French frigates which set sail in January 1772. During the voyage Baturin died. Finally the travellers reached the coast of France and disembarked at Port Louis. Benevsky went to Paris with an idea for conquering the island of Formosa, but instead of Formosa the French government pointed him toward Madagascar. Meanwhile the Russians arrived on foot in Paris from Port Louis and requested the Russian resident, Khotinsky, to intercede with the sovereign for their pardon. Forwarding Khotinsky's letter to the procurator general, Catherine wrote on October 2: "I have promised them a pardon, which seems fitting, since they have been punished sufficiently for their sins. Clearly a Rusak loves his Rus', and their faith in me and my mercy could not help but touch my heart." All returned to Russia and were settled in Siberian towns as free men.

PLOTS IN THE GUARDS

While Benevsky's brothers-in-arms were requesting permission to return to Russia, an investigation was being conducted in Petersburg into rumors spreading among the guards. Private Isakov told private Zhikharev that he had heard in camp the year before from many soldiers of the Preobrazhensky Regiment that they had designs upon the grand duke. Men in the ninth company wanted to steal cartridges and were not permitted to take more than five each into the palace. Would there be a revolution on St. Peter's Day,[116] wondered the soldiers, and would his highness be in camp to accept the throne? If not, would Count Orlov be there, and with spirits laid by for the soldiers to drink on St. Peter's Day? Zhikharev passed these rumors to private Karpov, who told Corporal Olovenikov, who informed his cousin, Second Lieutenant Selekhov, openly proposing that Grand Duke Paul Petrovich be put on the throne. The soldiers would be supportive, he said, first because they were being beaten without cause, second because they had designs upon the grand duke, and finally because Orlov wanted to become emperor.

Olovenikov had made similar representations to corporals Podgornov and Chufarovsky, who in league with Selekhov agreed to act. They approached others and discussed how to get the grand duke out of Tsarskoe Selo and what to do with Catherine—to force her to become a nun or leave her alone. Olovenikov and Selekhov thought that if Paul Petrovich would not agree to accept the throne he should be killed along with his mother. The people would be told that Catherine killed Paul because she did not love him, and that she perished in an act of vengeance. Thereupon a new tsar acceptable to the soldiers would be chosen. To be sure, Olovenikov aspired to the crown and had quarreled with his comrades about the future tsardom. Olovenikov said that he would be tsar, Podgornov would be master of ordnance, his brother would be procurator general, and Karpov would be adjutant general. Podgornov replied: "When it is possible for you to be a tsar, I will be one too." Then they rattled on about the need to choose Master of Heraldry Prince Mikhail Mikhailovich Shcherbatov as tsar because he was an honest, intelligent, and good man.[117]

On May 27 Isakov and Karpov went to Olovenikov and said: "Would you be willing to go public with your plan? Grenadier Filippov wanted to do so with the grenadiers, so go speak with them." Olovenikov went to the appointed place, where he met grenadiers Filippov, Murzin, and Mikhailo Ivanov. Olovenikov led them behind the horse guards stables to the bank of the Neva where Ivanov said to him: "So why all the empty chatter? Let's get to the point as to why we came here."

Olovenikov said: "Isakov has been telling me that he heard rumors in the palace that the entire guards will be placed in army regiments and replaced by grenadiers. Are we to wait for this? If we permit it to happen, it will be difficult to oppose then. Orlov is probably behind this and has left (for Focsani) in order to name himself prince of Moldavia or even emperor."

The grenadiers replied: "This very well may happen, but maybe he will not pull it off and we will make his highness emperor all the sooner."

How should we begin this action?" asked Ivanov. "We do not see a straight road!"

"It is true," Olovenikov answered, "that we don't see a straight road, but Filippov here has been saying that he knows Bariatinsky and has promised to go ask him about the attitude of his highness."

Ivanov added: "I know Bariatinsky too, so I will go see him. Should his highness consent, we could assemble about three hundred men, tell them our plans, and they will accompany us. We could send half to seize the roads and the other half to his highness."

"Those are trifles," said Olovenikov, "don't try to guess what will happen beforehand."

But Karpov continued to speculate. "Well, suppose his highness agrees to this; what will we do with the monarch?"

"We have no alternative but to leave her alone."

Karpov queried: "Would it not be better to shut her in a convent?"

"It is impossible to do that," Olovenikov retorted, "it is a matter for his highness. What do you say, brothers, do you think we can take his highness from Tsarskoe Selo?"

Karpov suggested a way. "Here is how we can get him. When his highness goes out for a walk we will have fifty or a hundred men there. We can bring him to our regiment here. And as we bring him, we can place another hundred fifty men near the Middle arm [the middle of three roads leading out of the city] so that no one can leave Petersburg."

Olovenikov approved this and the grenadiers said that the next step was to approach Prince Bariatinsky. Actually, Mikhailo Ivanov, Shmelev, and Aleksei Filippov did go to Chamberlain Prince Bariatinsky, but with a different purpose. "A musketeer in our regiment named Isakov," they told the prince, "approached us and told us of a plot to place the grand duke on the throne, but we are now informing your excellency about it. Tell us where to report it."

"Come, take a seat," Bariatinsky answered them. "God be with you. I am listening."

An inquest began. Olovenikov described in his own hand his conversation with Selekhov about the grand duke, the empress, and the selection of a new emperor. If the grand duke would not agree to take the throne he was to be murdered first, then the monarch, and the people were to be told that the empress had murdered the grand duke because she did not love him and she had been murdered in an act of revenge. Thereupon some one acceptable to the soldiers was to be selected tsar. Olovenikov had shared this idea with Podgornov, Chufarovsky, Karpov, and Zhikharev. Selekhov had asked Olovenikov: "And who might be elevated?"

"What do you mean, who?" Olovenikov replied. "It will be the one of us who tries hardest to get it."

Selekhov laughed and said, "So I think that will be you."

"So what if it is me?" shot back Olovenikov.

"You fool!" said Selekhov. "Do you really think someone like you is cut out be be tsar? Look at yourself, at what you are. You don't know how to talk and you certainly don't have ideas. Will being a tsar change such a fool? Even if all the guards agreed there are still two armies. What will they do with us then and later?"

Olovenikov shrugged. "Well, if the guards have taken the oath here, the army will begin to realize what it must do."

According to Karpov's testimony Olovenikov had said of Prince Shcherbatov: "He is such proud canaille, already conditioned to pomp and luxury. How could he be selected? He knows nothing of the soldiers' or peasants' needs and will think that everyone has been created for him."

According to Ivanov's testimony, Isakov said, "Put the empress in a convent, although she has done nothing bad. Orlov has done all the bad things; he turns everything to his own use. Now he has gone to the army to persuade the soldiers to take the oath to him. When they take the oath he will be tsar and bring the Petersburg Regiment here and transfer us, the entire guards, away from here."

While this case was proceeding, on June 2 Catherine wrote to Procurator General Prince Viazemsky: "I find this gang to be of the type that clearly must be eliminated to the last man in order to purge the guards this time as thoroughly as possible and extinguish the root of the evil, while maintaining moderation and humanity. But to ease the task of bothering with and taking confession from so many people I am offering you Preobrazhensky Major Maslov and Head Procurator Vsevolodsky to assist in the investigation." Later Catherine wrote Viazemsky: "Tell Chicherin (the gendarme chief) that if rumors are heard in the city that many soldiers are being arrested he is to think up some nonsense and release it in order to maintain confidence, or say whatever comes to mind."

The empress was struck by the youth of the men who had been discussing a coup. "I read all their papers," she wrote Viazemsky, "and am amazed that such young fellows fell into such dissolute affairs. Selekhov is the oldest, and he is twenty-two. The others really shouldn't be beaten except with rods. One is seventeen and another eighteen." The sentence was to punish Olovenikov with the knout and send him to Nerchinsk for life at heavy labor. Selekhov was to run the gauntlet twice and be sent as a soldier to a remote Siberian garrison. Because of their youth corporals Podgornov and Chufarovsky were to be beaten with rods secretly and sent to Siberian regiments as soldiers. The others were to be beaten with whips and sent in perpetuity to Nerchinsk.

ORLOV'S FATE

Even as these low-ranking men grown sufficiently courageous to make plans against the great Orlov perished in the desolate Siberian expanses, the favorite was returning to Petersburg with a new, heroic distinction: not only was he a hero as victor and conqueror, but the hero who restored calm to the great old capital and thus to the entire realm. True, Orlov, like Suvorov and Peter Panin later, was anticipated by events, but in the moment of liberation from danger no one thought much about that, and the official story which put Orlov in the foreground has retained its currency until recently. It was to Catherine's advantage under the circumstances to extol her favorite to the skies: what people these were whom she gave to Russia! A medal was struck; triumphal gates were erected. On one side of the medal was a portrait of Orlov and on the other a likeness of Curtius leaping into the abyss.[118] The inscription read, "Russia also has such a son." But Orlov told Catherine, "The inscription ought to be changed for it is insulting to other sons of the fatherland." Another in-scription then appeared: "Russia also has such sons."

It is understandable that Catherine had to support Orlov by every means, for the instinct of self-preservation alone had united their fates closely. The first blows on behalf of independent rule for Paul would have showered down on Orlov. Orlov was a superior sort of man, capable of saving the realm, and in happier times Catherine had been convinced of this and prepared to support him passionately in anything. But now that day had passed: Catherine had had time to study Orlov and, most importantly, she had had time to cool towards him.[119] She found herself in a most precarious and difficult situation. Although she no longer was passionately convinced that Orlov could do everything, it was frightening to admit it. It was frightening to her heart and frightening to her political circumstances, for Orlov was more than just anybody. He was necessary for stifling all intrigues on behalf of an independent Paul.

Catherine had begun earlier to review various aspects of Orlov's character in letters to her friends. This was a sad development which showed that she no longer had a relationship with him that did not permit her to review his character and abilities. Why did she undertake this review? Apparently to praise Orlov, but primarily to justify herself. Here lay the beginning of the estrangement. She realized that Orlov was a man of unusual valor, although undistinguished for the quality of his mind or education. She had thought he would work to complete his education, but she was mistaken. He was unable to help her retain her hold on the power he had helped her acquire. The main things that could be said on Orlov's behalf were that he had good intentions and was patriotic. But he was unable to rule or make important decisions of state. He was capable only of sitting at the head of a faction, supported and pushed by others. In a letter to her friend Frau Bielcke Catherine outlined Orlov's character at the time she sent him to the Bucharest congress.

"Count Orlov," she wrote, "who is without exaggeration the best looking man of his time, must really seem an angel in the presence of those vile Turkish beards. His retinue is brilliant and hand-picked, and my envoy loves splendor and brilliance. But I would wager that his person distresses everyone around him. This envoy is an amazing man. Nature has so magnificently endowed him with mind, heart, and spirit that nothing is lacking. Everything is natural and everything is good. But mother Nature also has spoiled him, for diligence is more difficult for him than anything on earth. For thirty years nothing has been able to force him to it. Despite this, it is remarkable how much he knows. His natural insight is so broad that, hearing about something for the first time, he grasps its strong and weak points and retains them longer than the person who introduced him to the matter."[120]

This praise, frightfully exaggerated, was elicited by Orlov's decline, when it was clear that nothing could be done with him. But this was not the important thing. She began to feel the burden of Orlov as a man; the relationships of 1768 were past, yet other circumstances alone prevented a break with a man who gave sufficient cause for it. It looked as though it would be easy for Orlov's enemies to remove him politically, but he was a powerful man and a long struggle loomed ahead.

Orlov long had languished under the burden of inactivity. The laurels of Rumiantsev and his own brother tormented him. His trip to Moscow merely irritated him, and he wanted some new undertaking. This would be dangerous for his enemies, but on the other hand they understood how easy it would be to estrange Catherine during his absence, for they saw full well that the crux of the matter was that he was bored.

Major General Grigory Alexandrovich Potemkin

With unaccustomed splendor and a brilliant entourage Orlov was sent to Bucharest,[121] and there he had to collide with the foremost military authority of the time, Rumiantsev, which was an advantage for his enemies. We have seen that in the Council Orlov constantly favored decisive measures which might end the war more quickly, owing to which there arose the view that Rumiantsev was slow but that there existed a man who might decide the campaign with one blow. This opinion, need it be said, offended Rumiantsev, and enmity existed already between Rumiantsev and Aleksei Orlov, the victor of Chesme. The recriminations and indisposition had begun long before, and Orlov constantly criticized Rumiantsev for his inactivity. This accounts for the close bond between Panin and Rumiantsev in their similar relations with Orlov, as was the case with others who were close to Panin and Rumiantsev such as, apparently, Volkonsky and Potemkin. Volkonsky, who had drifted away from Rumiantsev, again developed a fond relationship with him.

Volkonsky's qualities have been discussed but we have encountered Potemkin only in passing. His character has been examined at length. He was a gifted man, but his gifts alone could not guide him to worthy goals because of the fearful avarice and ambition nourished by the precariousness of his situation. From childhood his first dream had been of playing a principal role. A Smolensk gentryman without great wealth, he attended Moscow University but soon abandoned scholarship because it did not promise rapid advancement. Religious interests, which had great influence especially then in Moscow, occupied Potemkin next; he would not have minded being a pastor of a church and moving up from there. Thus he involved himself in ecclesiastical questions and drew close to the archbishops, who could expect much from a gifted young man in advancing their cause.

A Russian gentryman had one other alternative—the military. Potemkin entered the guards and participated in the coup of June 28, but unfortunately in a secondary role when Orlov assumed the principal position. Why had Potemkin not taken it? He was stronger than Orlov and more gifted. Although he did not succeed the first time, it might be easy to succeed the second. Patience and intrigue overcome everything, especially in view of Orlov's awkward abilities. Catherine was flattered by the attentions of the other athlete of her retinue of June 28. She needed to woo him. Naturally the Orlovs frowned, but Catherine managed to preserve peace among her friends. The clashes between Orlov and the Panins, the leading ministers of the realm, had been much sharper, particularly as regards formation of the Imperial Council. This occasion revealed the differences in their outlooks, although Orlov did not always observe the necessary caution, intimating that Russian policy need not be strongly pro-Prussian.

Now passion had burned out in Orlov. He had lived long at the side of a woman; he had taken care of her, but to what end? Most people had no idea who this mighty hero was, the man they so celebrated, the man who had saved the fatherland. Orlov had proved himself a ruler in Moscow. Now his was the opportunity to become a diplomat, but this was supposed to lead also to military command. He departed with the idea of taking the troops from the indecisive Rumiantsev and pushing across the Danube directly toward Constantinople. A grave danger threatened Rumiantsev, and he all the more readily joined forces with the Panins.

Meanwhile in Petersburg no one was dozing. It was necessary to replace Orlov the man and deliver a decisive blow. This stroke appeared in the guise of the kindliest, the handsomest but the emptiest officer, Vasilchikov.[122] Everyone was amazed but Catherine perhaps most of all when, having thought the matter over, she surveyed her new company—Vasilchikov instead of Orlov, and Panin preeminent!

She had never liked Panin after the coup of June 28 although sometimes she drew near to him and sometimes was estranged. Their closest relationship was evoked by the Polish partition, during which Catherine grew convinced that her minister somehow had unusual political abilities. With the worsening of the Polish situation the relationship between Panin and the empress also worsened. But the most serious blow came when Count Peter Panin expressed his dissatisfaction too sharply when Bendery was taken. He retired, continuing to criticize Catherine's policies, and Nikita also grew angry and would have retired forthwith had his friend the Danish minister, Struisberg, not bolstered him.[123]

NOTES

Additional information on personalities and topics found in the text and notes is available in Joseph L. Wieczynski, ed., *The Modern Encyclopedia of Russian and Soviet History* (MERSH); Harry B. Weber, ed., *The Modern Encyclopedia of Russian and Soviet Literatures (Including Non-Russian and Emigre Literatures)* (MERSL); David R. Jones, ed., *The Military-Naval Encyclopedia of Russia and the Soviet Union* (MNERSU); Paul D. Steeves, *The Modern Encyclopedia of Religions in Russia and the Soviet Union* (MERRSU), all published by Academic International Press.

CHAPTER I

1. Turkey declared war on Russia on September 25, 1768 after Russian cossacks violated the Turkish border while in hot pursuit of Polish troops. For some time France had been encouraging Turkey, also known as the Ottoman Porte, to declare war on Russia in order to blunt Russia's activist foreign policy which sought to dominate two other countries where France also had interests, Poland and Sweden. The first three years of the war went much better for Russia than Turkey. Russia won several notable victories in Bessarabia (also called Moldavia and Wallachia), its navy controlled the Aegean Sea and eastern Mediterranean, and Russia occupied the Crimean peninsula. None of these victories in themselves seemed to bring Russia any closer to peace. The good services of the ambassador of Russia's ally, Prussia, in Constantinople helped sway Turkey toward peace. Two weeks before the end of 1771 the ambassador reported that the Porte was prepared to send envoys to peace talks at Jassy if Catherine II (ruled 1762–1796) would agree to discuss returning the territories Russia had occupied during the war. This raised the hopes for peace during the new year of 1772.

2. Nikita Ivanovich Panin (1718–1783) served as minister to Denmark (1747–1748) and Sweden (1748–1760). In 1760 he was given charge over the education and upbringing of Grand Duke Paul Petrovich (1754–1801), the son of the future Peter III (1728–1762) and Catherine II. Panin held this post until Paul achieved his majority in 1772. Once back in Russia he gained influence over the future empress, Catherine, who named him to head the College of Foreign Affairs (1763–1780). Throughout the 1760s Catherine followed the Northern policy advocated by Panin, anchored by an alliance with Prussia. Panin's views were opposed by the faction led by the Orlovs, whose orientation was southerly,

grounded in friendship with the Austro-Hungarian empire of the Hapsburgs. The events covered in this volume had much to do with Catherine's shifting orientation from Panin's Northern accord to the southern alliance. On Panin and the conflict of party interests see David L. Ransel, *The Politics of Catherinian Russia. The Panin Party* (New Haven, 1975); on the Northern alliance see Note 51 of this chapter and David M. Griffiths, "The Rise and Fall of the Northern System. Court Politics and Foreign Policy in the First Half of Catherine II's Reign," *Canadian Slavic Studies*, IV (1970), 547–569.

The Council, sometimes referred to as the Imperial or Military Council, was constituted on January 22, 1769 to help Catherine shape military strategy and diplomatic initiatives during the war with Turkey. Its seven original members included Count Zakhar Grigorevich Chernyshev (vice president of the War College), Prince Alexander Mikhailovich Golitsyn (field marshal; commander of the First Army in 1768–1769), Count Grigory Grigorevich Orlov (Catherine's long-time favorite), Counts Nikita and Peter Ivanovich Panin (the latter a field marshal and commander of the Second Army until late 1770), Count Kirill Grigorevich Razumovsky (formerly viceroy of the Ukraine, or Little Russia), and Prince Alexander Alexandrovich Viazemsky (procurator general of the Governing Senate). It met twice weekly with the empress generally in attendance. After the war's end Catherine continued to use the Council as an advisory body until the end of her reign.

3.   Prince Wenzel Anton von Kaunitz-Reitberg (1711–1794) began directing Austrian foreign policy in 1753, although five years earlier he began the reorientation of foreign policy that culminated in the so-called diplomatic revolution of 1756. His influence was also great in domestic affairs. The dual monarchy of mother and son, Maria Theresa and Joseph II, from 1765–1780, can actually be seen as a triangle of power, with Kaunitz at the third point. As Russian successes mounted in the war against Turkey, Kaunitz began to fear Russian domination over the Balkans or even its expansion to Austria's borders. How to check Russia and further Austria's own aims stymied Austria's rulers throughout 1770 and 1771. On Austria's role in the war generally see Karl A. Roider Jr., *Austria's Eastern Question 1700–1790* (Princeton, 1982).

Russia's initial condition for peace was access for commercial and naval vessels on the Black Sea. Following the occupation of the Crimea early in 1771 it added an independent Crimean Tatar khanate as a second term. Less important to Russia was its attempt to establish its protection over Christian areas in the Caucasus. In exchange for these Turkish concessions Russia offered to evacuate Moldavia and Wallachia, occupied early in the war, restoring them to the Porte.

4.   Austria first offered its services as intermediary between Russia and Turkey in 1770. On July 6, 1771 Austria and Turkey signed a secret treaty in Constantinople by which Austria promised either diplomatic or military aid to help Turkey regain territory and fortresses occupied by Russia during the war that began in 1768. Austria also would try to obtain a just peace for the Porte. In return, the Porte was to pay Austria a subsidy in excess of eleven million gulden (or

20,000 purses of 500 piasters) in installments, cede Little Moldavia, adjacent to Transylvania, and provide most-favored nation commercial rights to Austrian subjects. The treaty was to go into effect only if Russia refused to retreat from its harsh peace demands. Austria's involvement caused Russia to concentrate its campaigns of 1771 on the Crimea rather than in the Danube basin, where there was a greater chance of conflict with Austria. See Karl A. Roider Jr., *Baron Thugut and Austria's Response to the French Revolution* (Princeton, 1987).

5. Grigory Grigorevich Orlov (1734–1783) was the second of five brothers in a family that rose to prominence under Peter I. Noted for his size and strength, he also displayed remarkable courage under fire at Zorndorf in the Seven Years War, where he was wounded three times. He met Catherine when he accompanied the captured adjutant of Frederick II, Count Schwerin, to Petersburg in 1758. When he became intimate with Catherine in 1760 a place was found for him in the Izmailovsky Guards and he became paymaster of artillery. Orlov benefitted enormously from Catherine's coup, having been one of its organizers. He was promoted to major general, made gentleman of the chamber, given the title of count, awarded the Order of St. Alexander Nevsky, made master of ordnance, director-general of engineers, and chief of cavalry. A member of the Council from its origin, he was kept from the front during the war by Catherine. Instead she used him to restore order to Moscow after the riot there in September 1771 (see Chapter III, pp. 235 ff). Next he was sent to negotiate peace at Focsani. While there he was supplanted in Catherine's affections by Alexander Vasilchikov. He tried to regain his favored position with Catherine but even the gift of the Orlov diamond could not turn the trick. Orlov went abroad in 1775. After his return he married his niece. She was ill with tuberculosis. The couple went abroad for her health in 1780. Two years later she died and he slid into insanity. His brothers settled him on one of his estates, where he died a few months later.

6. Count Peter Alexandrovich Rumiantsev (1725–1796) was a career army officer, highly decorated for service in the Seven Years War, especially the victory at Kolberg in 1761. Peter III named him general-in-chief in 1762. He presided over the board that administered Little Russia after its vice-regency was abolished in 1764. When the war with Turkey broke out, he and Peter Panin were the logical choices as commander-in-chief. Neither got the post, which went to a compromise candidate, Field Marshal A. M. Golitsyn (1718–1783). Even though Golitsyn took Jassy and Khotin, within a year Rumiantsev replaced him as commander of the First Army (and Panin received the Second). On July 7, 1770, after crossing the Pruth river, Rumiantsev with 37,000 men crushed a Turkish force of 80,000 at the confluence of the Larga and Pruth rivers. Pursuing the fleeing enemy, Rumiantsev with only 25,000 men caught the entire army of the grand vizier— 150,000 strong—at Lake Kagul on the Pruth three weeks later and routed it (July 21). These two victories of Larga and Kagul assured his fame; Catherine promoted him from general to field marshal. In 1771 the First Army engaged in little fighting as the theater of war shifted to the Crimea. Rumiantsev was rumored to have been an illegitimate son of Peter I.

7. Because the Austro-Turkish treaty was kept secret, Russia could not be certain of the measure of support Austria was willing to provide the Porte. In fact, the Austrians and Turks were discussing that very issue: which acts on Russia's part might give Austria cause to enter the war on Turkey's side. The 1771 agreement between Vienna and Constantinople called vaguely for either diplomatic or military intervention. By June 1772 Austria made it clear that its support would extend only to the conference table, not the battlefield.

8. Joseph II (1740–1790) co-ruled with his mother Maria Theresa (in German, Maria Theresia) from 1765–1780, having become Holy Roman emperor upon the death of his father Francis. Maria Theresa's conservative Catholicism and Joseph's enlightened humanitarianism clashed constantly. The empress-queen relied upon Kaunitz—similar to Joseph in basic outlook but of Maria Theresa's generation—to keep her energetic son in check.

9. A partition of Poland was first suggested by Prussia's monarch Frederick II (ruled 1740–1786) to Nikita Panin in February 1769. Frederick wanted Polish Prussia and the bishopric of Warmia and protectorate status over Dantzig. He proposed that Austria be offered Zips and part of Galicia. Undaunted by Panin's lack of interest, Frederick II made similar representations to Austria in May 1770. Austria actually occupied the Polish county of Sandec in December 1770, claiming that it belonged to Hungary's crown lands. Frederick's brother Prince Henry revived the idea of partition during his visit to Petersburg from September 1770 to February 1771. By the latter date Panin was agreed in principle to a scheme that might reward Russian military victories against Turkey with Polish territory, since the Turks were proving to be intractible regarding Russia's peace terms. Prussian subsidies to Russia likewise could be repaid with Polish territories. Austria would have to be included in a partition of Poland in order to maintain the proper balance among the powers. But Austria coveted certain Turkish lands more than Polish. Thus Kaunitz's dilemma. On these points see Isabel de Madariaga, *Russia in the Age of Catherine the Great* (New Haven, 1981), pp. 221–225.

10. Silesia was the province invaded by the young Frederick II in 1740, precipitating the War of the Austrian Succession (1740–1748). The treaties ending the war awarded him Lower Silesia. Thereafter Prince Kaunitz doggedly sought a way to regain the province. These revanchist aims played no small part in causing the diplomatic revolution of 1756 and the ensuing Seven Years War (1756–1763). After that war as well Frederick retained Silesia, but Kaunitz continued his life-long quest—unfulfilled—to regain it for Austria.

11. Forming the core of Panin's beloved Northern system, Russia and Prussia signed a defensive treaty on March 31, 1764 guaranteeing each other's possessions, including Russia's claims to Holstein. The guarantee was backed by pledges to provide each other with troops in the event of war with a third power. Valid for eight years, the treaty contained several secret clauses which eventually proved to be important. If the Porte attacked Russia, Prussia could substitute a subsidy of four hundred thousand rubles for military aid. Both states guaranteed the constitutions of Poland and Sweden, agreeing to concerted action if the form of

government in either country were threatened, including the use of arms in Poland. Following the outbreak of Russia's war with Turkey, the treaty was updated on October 12, 1769. Threats to Sweden's fundamental constitution (but not minor adjustments) were now liable to be met with armed intervention in concert by Prussia and Russia. The original treaty was due to expire in 1772. Frederick was determined to gain its extension whether or not Panin retained his powerful position. He also knew that he could bend Russia more easily to a partition of Poland while the war with Turkey continued than after its end, because Russia was dependent upon his subsidies and thus amenable to his suggestions. By finally agreeing to drop his own claims to Dantzig, Frederick gained Russian commitment to partition Poland. All that remained now was to gain Austria's consent.

12. Alfred, Ritter von Arneth, *Maria Theresias letzte Regierungszeit* (Volumes 7–10 of *Geschichte Maria Theresias* (Vienna, 1863–1876), VIII (II), 338–350. (Soloviev's note)

13. Arneth, ed., *Maria Theresia und Joseph II. Ihre Correspondenz sammt Briefen Josephs an seinen Bruder Leopold* (3 vols., Vienna, 1857), I, 36. (Soloviev's note)

14. Arneth, ed., *Maria Theresia und Joseph II*, I, 361–363. (Soloviev's note)

15. Baron (Freiherr) Franz Maria von Thugut (1739–1818) was appointed Austrian resident in Constantinople in 1769. He negotiated the Austrian-Turkish convention of 1771, for which feat Kaunitz had him promoted from resident to internuntius. Through him Austria extended its mediation in the Russo-Turkish war, although at Russian insistence he was excluded from the peace talks at Focsani. He was awarded his baronage in connection with the peace of Kuchuk-Kainardji which ended the war in 1774, retiring from his post immediately before the treaty's signing. Eventually he headed Austria's foreign ministry (1794–1801).

16. Sultan Mustafa III (1717–1774) took the throne in 1757 as the twenty-sixth sultan. His father, Ahmet III (1673–1736; sultan 1703–1730), was his model for an opulent reign emphasizing culture and intellectual life. The war with Russia assured that his would be remembered as an unpopular reign. See Norman Itkowitz and Max Mote, eds. and trans., *Mubadele—An Ottoman-Russian Exchange of Ambassadors* (Chicago, 1970), pp. 209–210, 219.

17. Although Soloviev concentrates in the next few paragraphs on the Turkish question, the "good news" from Vienna also had to do with Poland. Prince Kaunitz won Joseph II to his view of continuing to mediate peace between Russia and Turkey while joining with Russia and Prussia in partitioning Poland. See also Note 20 of this chapter.

18. These preparations were made at Kaunitz's advice. Arneth, *Maria Theresias letzte Regierungszeit*, II, 439–455. (Soloviev's note)

19. Aleksei Mikhailovich Obreskov (1718–1787) spent most of his career in the diplomatic service dealing with Turkey, being posted there almost continuously after 1751. Imprisoned in the Fortress of Seven Towers upon Turkey's declaration of war against Russia in 1768 he languished there until 1771, when Prussian and Austrian mediation secured his release. After participating in the

inconclusive negotiations at Focsani and Bucharest, he helped prepare the Treaty of Kuchuk-Kainardji. See E. I. Druzhinina, "Russkii diplomat A. M. Obreskov," *Istoricheskie zapiski*, XL (Moscow, 1952).

20. Austria and Russia agreed in principle to discuss a three-way partition of Poland on February 1, 1772. Immediately thereafter Russia and Prussia signed a convention too, although it was backdated to January 4 to give the appearance that it had preceeded the Russian-Austrian convention. The three states together signed a preliminary agreement on March 7. Austrian foot-dragging prevented the final agreement among the three states from being signed until August 5. See Madariaga, *Russia in the Age of Catherine*, p. 225.

21. Located along the Terek river and its tributaries, to the northwest of Georgia, the Kabardas were the homeland of a people who called themselves the Adyge. Their ties with Russia dated from the sixteenth century, when Muscovy first contemplated their annexation. At one time Christian, the Adyge were thoroughly Islamicised by the seventeenth century.

22. The matter of Georgia was extremely complex. Rarely had there been a single Christian kingdom in Georgia, in part because there was no single Georgian nation but rather a variety of peoples; their political and cultural identities were grouped traditionally into Eastern Georgia, or Kakheti, and Western Georgia, or Imereti. For some time prior to Catherine's era Eastern Georgia was under relentless pressure from the Safavi dynasty of Persia; in the seventeenth century thousands of Georgians were forcibly relocated into Iran. The Ottoman Turk "slave tribute" from Western Georgia, also called Mingrelia, was at least less capricious. The levies included both young men and young women; the service of Georgian slaves was much esteemed in Turkey.

After the middle of the eighteenth century both Eastern and Western Georgia won a greater measure of freedom from their respective oppressors. Tsar Heraclius (Irakli) restored the fortunes of Eastern Georgia and King Solomon strengthened Western Georgia. The exaction of Christian virgins so deplored by Russia's government was probably more a result of incursions by the Lazghi than of systematic taxation by either Turks or Persians. The Lazghi lived to the northeast of Georgia, towards Daghestan. In fact, their leaders included Christian Armenians and even renegade Georgian princes. The Lazghi were particularly troublesome to Tsar Heraclius. The overtly sexual association of rapine with the powerlessness of Georgia's political subjugation made a good rallying cry, if it did overly simplify complex political and cultural relationships in the Transcaucasus.

In 1770 Catherine sent the swashbuckling General Todtleben across the Caucasus mountains to aid the two Georgian kingdoms. His campaigning there was inconclusive. When the Pugachev rebellion broke out two years later, Russian troops were withdrawn.

23. The Treaty of Belgrade (September 7, 1739) ended a Russo-Turkish war begun in 1735. Its immediate causes were disputes over frontiers in the Kabardas and the Kuban, Tatar raids on Russian border areas, and Turkish dissatisfaction with growing Russian influence in Poland. Early in the war Russia invaded the

Crimea, sacking its capital, Bakhchisarai. It also captured the fortresses of Kinburn, Azov, and Ochakov. Later campaigns proved costly and ineffective. In 1739, just as Russia's ally Austria (committed to the war by treaty with Russia) was concluding a separate peace with Turkey, a Russian army took Khotin and Jassy in Moldavia. Russia's exhaustion compelled it to agree to peace. Russia retained Azov, but the fortress was dismantled. Russia could build no fortifications along the coastline and could trade only in Turkish ships. An English translation of the full treaty may be found in Fred L. Israel, ed., *Major Peace Treaties of Modern History, 1648–1967*. Commentary by Emanuel Chill, introductory essay by Arnold Toynbee (4 vols., New York, 1967), I, 897–911.

24.   Johanna Dorothea Bielcke enjoyed an extensive correspondence with Catherine throughout the 1770s, candid on both governmental and personal matters. Frau Bielcke, an old friend of Catherine's mother, lived in Hamburg, where she held a salon reminiscent of those in Paris.

25.   Soloviev quotes the same passage again near the end of this volume (Chapter III, p. 258), commenting that Catherine already must have been evaluating critically her relationship with Orlov. In fact, it was rumored that she discovered his affair with a teen-aged niece on the very day he left Petersburg for Focsani. As Soloviev indicates, Catherine herself at this point may have needed persuading of Orlov's wonderful qualities.

26.   Prussia's envoy was Major J. C. von Zegelin; Austria was represented by Thugut. Osman-effendi was a former reis-effendi, the official who controlled the central administrative apparatus of the Ottoman empire, including finances. During this era the reis-effendi was also gaining control over foreign policy; under Sultan Mahmud II (son of Abdul Hamid, ruled 1808–1839) the office of the reis-effendi became the office of foreign affairs.

27.   In Islam there is no division between the lawgiver and the priest; law and religion are one. The Ottoman civil service evolved from the specialists trained in Constantinople in law and theology, the *ulema*. The sultan ruled, but the supreme authority in spiritual matters was the grand mufti, who likewise was guardian of the fundamental law (kanoun namé). Before making any important decision the sultan consulted the grand mufti. For a brief overview of the structure of Ottoman government see Geoffrey Treasure, *The Making of Modern Europe, 1648–1780* (London, 1985), pp. 602–608.

28.   Gustavus III (1746–1792) was the son of King Adolphus Frederick (an uncle of Catherine II) and Louisa Ulrica (sister of Frederick II). Educated by Carl Gustaf Tessin and Carl Frederick Scheffer, he was married to the daughter of Denmark's King Frederick V, Sophia Magdalena. Gustavus first tried to strengthen the crown by reforming the Riksdag (parliament) in 1768, while his father was still on the throne. The attempt failed.

Gustavus was in Paris when his father died. France's foreign minister, the duke de Choiseul, agreed to reinstate French subsidies to Sweden if Gustavus would strengthen the throne. To assist in these matters, France transferred Charles

Gravier, count of Vergennes (1717–1787), its ambassador to Turkey, to Stock-holm. On his way home, Gustavus stopped to see his uncle Frederick II in Berlin. The king of Prussia warned him not to tamper with Sweden's constitution, which he, Denmark, and Russia were sworn to uphold. Despite this warning, events in Sweden took such a turn that on August 18, 1772 Gustavus arrested the leaders of the four estates in the Swedish Riksdag and suspended the constitution of 1720, which had reduced greatly the power of the king. His more autocratic regime last-ed until his assassination. The revolution in Sweden is discussed on pp. 54–60.

29. Kerch and Yenikale sat on either side of the Kerch straits leading from the Sea of Azov (and the Don river basin) to the Black Sea. In 1771 Russia be-gan demanding the right to station garrisons in both places. At Focsani Russia insisted on cession of the entire coastline of the Sea of Azov, presumably includ-ing both towns; at Bucharest the towns were specifically enumerated in the Rus-sian demands. Late in 1773 Catherine agreed to concede them for Kinburn and Ochakov, two fortresses circumscribing the bay into which the Dnieper and Bug rivers emptied, along with the coastline between the rivers. Russia won both Kerch and Yenikale in the treaty ending the war.

30. The treaty is discussed in Chapter II, pp. 166–175.

31. The Treaty of the Pruth (July 12, 1711) ended Peter the Great's ignomini-ous campaign into Moldavia begun the previous year. After his defeat by Peter at Poltava on June 27, 1709 Charles XII of Sweden fled to Constantinople. Peter insisted that Sultan Ahmet III hand him over to Russia, threatening war should the Turks not do so. Ahmet declared war in November 1710. The following spring Peter invaded with 40,000 men, but soon found himself backed against the Pruth river by a superior Turkish force. Annihilation of Russia's army was pre-vented when the future Catherine I, who accompanied Peter on the campaign, ar-ranged a gift of valuable gems to the grand vizier, inducing him to accept Peter's offer of peace. Among Russia's concessions was the cession of Azov, won hardly a decade earlier from Turkey, and the razing of several other fortresses. Russia's disappointment in the Treaty of Belgrade of 1739 (see Note 23 above) stemmed from the huge human cost of the war—more than a hundred thousand lives lost— and the disappointment of military failures after initial success.

32. Count Alexander Ippolitovich Dmitriev-Mamonov in his review (*Russkii arkhiv*, No. 12 (1877), pp. 395–396) of Jean Henri de Castera, *The Life of Cather-ine II, Empress of Russia*, alleges that Rumiantsev told Orlov that he thought he (Rumiantsev) had the right to continue the negotiations personally and forbade Orlov to erect any obstacles that might damage Russia's advantage or dignity. In answer Orlov is supposed to have threatened to have Rumiantsev relieved of his command and even hanged. Rumiantsev in turn threatened to expel Orlov from Focsani and from the army. Allegedly it took enormous effort to prevent the conflict from reaching crisis proportions and it was resolved in an unheard-of way: Osman-effendi, the enemy envoy, used his mediation to restore harmony between Rumiantsev and Orlov. In response to these allegations, first we should

note that Rumiantsev was not in Focsani during the negotiations and thus Osman-effendi could not have mediated. We would reject allegations of any collision at all between Orlov and Rumiantsev had one not occurred in Jassy, where Orlov went upon leaving Focsani and where Rumiantsev had his headquarters. The latter desired peace and opposed a "new blow," that is, the crossing of the Danube, while Orlov always favored a "blow" which might lead to peace on all of Russia's terms. (Soloviev's note)

33. The plague and its consequences are treated at greater length in Chapter III, pp. 215–248.

34. Khan Sahib-Girey (Sahip-Giray, Salip Girey) was elected khan in 1772. His family, the Gireys, had ruled the Crimea since the fifteenth century. Descended from Genghis Khan, the Gireys acknowledged Ottoman suzerainty in exchange for assistance in driving Genoese merchants from their territory. Much of the tribal aristocracy, however, preferred independence. Russia turned to these internal opponents of Turkish overlordship when occupying the Crimea militarily in 1770–1771. At that time Khan Selim-Girey fled to Turkey. In electing a new khan the tribal leaders bypassed the hand-picked candidate of the Ottomans for Sahib-Girey, who placed himself under Russian protection, but whose political position was quite weak owing to the deep rifts between the pro-Ottoman and pro-independence (pro-Russian) factions. It was a balancing act difficult to perform. Russian high-handedness gradually forced him to become disenchanted with Russian patronage. During a coup against him in 1777 he fled to Turkey. See Alan Fisher, *The Crimean Tatars* (Stanford, 1978) and Itkowitz and Mote, *Mubadele*, pp. 44–45.

35. The capital of the Crimea, Bakhchisarai, was located inland from the southwestern tip of the peninsula. The second largest city in the Crimea, it had at this time 30 mosques, two synagogues, a Greek church and an Armenian church. Its palace, a copy of Topkapi palace in Constantinople, had been rebuilt after Russian troops burned it in the 1730s.

36. The Nogay Tatars originally lived in the area between the Dniester and the Danube. During the war with Turkey the Russians persuaded them to leave these lands for the Kuban, to the east of the Sea of Azov. There had always been some question as to whether and how much allegiance they owed to the khan of the Girey horde.

37. By tradition the heir apparent (kalga, kalkay) to the khanship of the Crimea was a brother of the current khan. Russia could gain further influence over the Tatars by currying favor with him—a practice which traditionally the Ottomans had followed and which Russia now imitated.

38. In 1764, upon the initiative of Ivan Ivanovich Betskoy (see Chapter III, Note 102), Catherine opened the Educational Society for Well-born Girls, otherwise known as Smolny Institute, in the building of the Resurrection convent. Here the daughters aged 6–18 of the gentry could study divine law, French, arithmetic, drawing, history, geography, rhetoric, music, dancing, handwork, and home economics. A second school was opened there the following year for girls of all

other social backgrounds except serfs. Catherine took great pride in these institutions and seized every advantage to show off the pupils there.

39. On Prince Mikhail Nikitich Volkonsky, see Chapter III, Note 98.

40. Godefroy, Baron van Swieten (1734–1803), Belgian by birth, was the son of Maria Theresa's personal physician. He was Austria's minister to Berlin from 1768–1776 and later served as court librarian in Vienna.

41. Adolf Beer, *Friedrich II und van Swieten. Berichte über die zwischen Österreich und Preusen geführten Verhandlungen, die erste Theilung Polens betreffend* (Leipzig, 1874), p. 55. (Soloviev's note)

42. Prince Dmitry Mikhailovich Golitsyn (1721–1793), after a year of service in France, became Russia's ambassador to Vienna in 1764, remaining there until 1792. As a philanthropist, he also founded a hospital in Moscow.

43. Beer, p. 66. (Soloviev's note)

44. Frederick's sarcasm refers to the outward act of conversion to Islam. The Austrians had drawn so close to the Turks, he implies, that they could be accused of having submitted to this rite.

45. Soloviev presumably is referring to the Russo-Turkish war of 1735–1739 in which Austria participated as a Russian ally. For fuller explication of relations at that time see Roider, *Austria's Eastern Question*, Chapter 5.

46. See Note 20 above.

47. Maximilian Wolfgang Duncker, *Aus der Zeit Friedrichs des Grossen und Friedrich Wilhelms III. Abhandlung zur preussischen Geschichte von Max Duncker* (Leipzig, 1876), p. 255. (Soloviev's note)

48. See, for example, Adolf Beer, *Die erste Theilung Polens* (3 vols. in 1; Vienna, 1873), II, 164, and Arneth, *Maria Theresias letzte Regierungszeit*, II, 369. (Soloviev's note)

49. Arneth, ed., *Maria Theresia und Joseph II*, I, 367–368. (Soloviev's note) The Polish province alluded to was the county of Spics (Zips); see Note 79 below.

50. Empress Elizabeth of Russia (reigned 1741–1762) followed the Austrian alliance of her predecessors on the throne, renewing it in 1746. Russia and Austria were allied in numerous wars, most recently the Seven Years War. When Elizabeth died at the end of 1761 her Prussophile nephew Peter III reversed Russia's orientation, abandoning the Austrian alliance in 1762 for a Prussian. Catherine II after her coup did not alter this turnabout, following Panin's Northern policy. Austria did not give up hope of restoring the earlier relationship with Russia.

51. The Northern accord or alliance came into existence in the aftermath of the Seven Years War. It was Nikita Panin's idea. He divided northern Europe into "active" powers—Russia, Prussia, the United Kingdom, and Denmark—and "passive" powers—Sweden, Poland, and Saxony—to be safeguarded by the former. The alliance featured bilateral treaties with the other active powers. The treaty of 1764 with Prussia called for a common policy between Prussia and Russia in Sweden and Poland in order to prevent constitutional changes and to take up the cause of Poland's religious dissidents. Russia and Denmark signed a treaty in 1765. Britain proved more recalcitrant, agreeing only to a commercial treaty in

1766. The alliance began to unravel with the Polish rebellion of the mid-1760s and Russia's Turkish war. Prussia renewed its alliance with Russia in 1769 and 1772, but sought compensation in Poland for Russian victories against Turkey. The Northern alliance was thoroughly discredited when Russia used France's failure to support Austria in Bavaria in 1777–1778 to move closer to the Hapsburg empire, and when Russia and Britain found themselves opposing each other on the matter of neutrality on the high seas in 1780. See David M. Griffiths, "The Rise and Fall of the Northern System," *Canadian Slavic Studies*, IV, 547–569.

52. Maximilian Joseph, the childless elector of Bavaria, was quite old; he died at the end of 1777. His lands were claimed by the elector palatine, Charles Theodore. Joseph II of Austria supported this claim, in exchange for which Joseph expected to receive a slice of Bavaria. But Frederick II had his own candidate for the inheritance, Charles of Zweibrücken. After Maximilian Joseph died Austria sent troops into Bavaria, whereupon Frederick dispatched an army to Bohemia. Joseph expected France to come to his aid, but France could offer only money since it had just committed itself to help the American colonies against England. In the end Charles Theodore got Bavaria, Joseph won only a tiny piece of it, and Frederick was promised Ansbach and Bayreuth when their childless ruler died (Treaty of Teschen, May 1779).

53. Galicia, presumably named for Gauls who once conquered it, comprised the southwesternmost part of Poland along the left bank of the upper Vistula. As generally understood, it incorporated the southern part of Red, or Chervonnaia, Russia, in southern Poland. Chervonnaia Russia lay to the west of Volhynia and Podolia. At its center was the city of Lemberg (Lwow, Lwiw, Lvov). The upper reaches of the Northern Bug and the Dniester rivers lay within Red Russia. These territories had been Polish since medieval times.

54. Beer, *Friedrich II und van Swieten*, p. 71. (Soloviev's note)

55. Emmanuel-Armand de Vigneret, the duke d'Aiguillon (1720–1782), succeeded the duke de Choiseul (1719–1785), an able and energetic minister who directed foreign affairs, the army and navy, and much else from 1758–1770. Choiseul owed his appointment to Mme. de Pompadour, Louis XV's mistress (1721–1764), but outlasted her. Coming to power during the dark days after the loss of Canada, he based his foreign policy upon the Austrian alliance and a family compact with Spain. He fell from power in late 1770 by backing Spain too vigorously in a quarrel with England over ownership of the Falkland Islands. D'Aiguillon, former royal governor of Brittany and much less competent than Choiseul, was appointed secretary of state for foreign affairs in 1771 after a six-month struggle, upon recommendation of King Louis XV's new mistress, Mme. Du Barry (1743–1793). D'Aiguillon lasted out the remainder of Louis XV's reign, being replaced by Count Vergennes only after the accession of Louis XVI in 1774. Soloviev's summary of French foreign policy may be found on pp. 45–47; he quotes N. I. Panin's assessment of both Choiseul and d'Aiguillon on pp. 150–151.

56. Friedrich Ludwig Georg von Raumer, *Beiträge zur neueren Geschichte aus dem Britischen Museum und Reichsarchive* (5 vols., Leipzig, 1836–1839), IV, 493. (Soloviev's note)

57. Frederick II, *Oeuvres de Frédéric le Grand* (31 vols. in 33, Berlin, 1846–1857), XXVI, 359. (Soloviev's note)

58. Arneth, ed., *Maria Theresia und Joseph II*, I, 369–373. (Soloviev's note)

59. Under Poland's unusual form of government a group of nobles who had a grievance against the government could form themselves into a confederation by taking an oath to see the injustice righted or fight to the death in the attempt. The confederation lasted until it won its case or it was defeated in battle, whereupon the oath-takers were freed from their oath. In this case the reference is to the Confederation of Bar, so named for the small fortress in Podolia where it was formed in February 1768. Independent of and opposed to King Stanislaw Augustus, the confederates won several battles against Russian troops and were the precipitating cause of Russia's war with Turkey when Russian forces in hot pursuit chased some of them across the Turkish border and destroyed several Turkish villages. The confederates undertook their own diplomacy as well, functioning as an alternative government to the king. In 1770 the movement became a general confederacy and the confederates moved their government offices to Hungary. General Dumouriez (see Note 88 below, this chapter) took over as commander-in-chief of their troops. The last confederate armed resistance ended in 1776.

60. Alexander Vasilevich Suvorov (1729–1800) began his long military career in the 1750s. He served under General Ivan Ivanovich Weimarn (1722–1792) against the confederates in Poland from 1768–1772, taking the fortress of Cracow in 1772. In 1773 he asked to serve under Field Marshal Rumiantsev in the First Army. In the same year he participated with distinction in the crossings of the Danube and the victory at Turtukai. The maneuvers and victories of troops under his command helped bring the peace in 1774. Later that year he helped convey the rebel Pugachev to Moscow. After 1774 Suvorov commanded troops in various parts of the empire. Promoted to general-in-chief in 1786, he took Kinburn and Ochakov fortresses in the second Turkish war. Following the second partition of Poland in 1794, he commanded the Russian troops which defeated the Polish national uprising. When Emperor Paul came to the throne Suvorov at first was exiled, but later commanded the Russian army in Italy and Switzerland in 1799. He is celebrated as one of Russia's greatest military commanders.

61. General Alexander Ilich Bibikov (1729–1774) began service in the Russian army in 1746. In the Seven Years War he commanded the troops that took Frankfurt-an-der-Oder, ending the war as a major general. While abroad he became acquainted with the Panin brothers. After Catherine II came to power she entrusted Bibikov with the task of conducting the duke of Brunswick, father of the unfortunate former Ivan VI, out of Russia. In 1765 he commanded one of the two Russian forces that occupied Poland when disturbances broke out following the election of Stanislaw Poniatowski as king. When the commission to draft a new law code was called in 1767, Bibikov was selected as its marshal. He played an active role in its deliberations while still commanding Russian troops in Poland. He apparently did not favor the war with Poland, which perhaps helps explain the hostility Caspar Saldern felt for him (see pp. 39–40). Bibikov did not like Saldern either, and was pleased when he was replaced as ambassador.

62. Avram Ivanovich Romanius, or Romanus (17??–1799) entered Russian military service in 1735. Descended from the minor Austrian nobility, he rose very slowly through the ranks. The Seven Years War boosted his career considerably; he ended it as a major general. In 1768–1769 Romanius served in Little Russia with Rumiantsev. By 1771 he commanded troops in Lithuania and Poland, with headquarters in Lublin.

63. Dantzig (or Danzig), the modern Gdansk, was a largely German city at the mouth of the Vistula (Visla) river, valuable because it controlled most of Poland's foreign trade, confined to the Vistula and its tributaries. Thorn (Polish Torun) was a river town some 120 miles up the Vistula from Dantzig.

64. Beer, *Die erste Theilung Polens*, II, 182. (Soloviev's note)

65. Fedor Fedorovich (Thedor T.) Martens, ed., *Sobranie traktatov i konventsii, zakliuchennykh Rossieiu s inostrannymi derzhavami* (Recueil des traités et conventions conclus par la Russie avec les puissances étrangères, 15 vols., St. Petersburg, 1875), II, 24–29. (Soloviev's note)

66. Prussian troops moved to the Polish border in October 1769, opposite Warmia. In the summer of 1770 they occupied Dantzig, but withdrew after being paid a substantial sum of money. Frederick seems to have used the occupation to recruit men for his army. By the fall of 1770 Prussian troops began occupying Polish Prussia with impunity. A Russian army already occupied much of Poland and Austrians were establishing cordons in southern Poland. Frederick insisted that the Poles pay for his occupation of their lands, exacting provisions and supplies for his troops from the local population.

67. Baron Caspar Saldern (1711–1788), a native of Holstein, began his career in his native land. His penchant for intrigues soon made it necessary for him to flee. He went to Russia, where Grand Duke Peter helped him launch a new career in Russian service. In 1761–1762 he participated in talks with Denmark concerning the future status of Schleswig. He survived Peter's fall and became close to N. I. Panin during the 1760s, participating in the education of Grand Duke Paul. He travelled again to Denmark in 1766 in diplomatic service, stopping on the way in Poland and Berlin. In the latter city he had two audiences with Frederick II, who took an intense dislike to him. Late in 1766 he secured Danish consent to a preliminary agreement on Holstein: Russia's ruling house would drop all claims to the county, consigning it to Denmark, in exchange for the latter state dropping its claims to Oldenburg and Delmenhorst, ancestral lands of Peter III's father. The agreement would not become final until signed by Grand Duke Paul of Russia, still a minor in 1766. In 1771 Panin arranged for Saldern to replace Mikhail Nikitich Volkonsky as ambassador to Poland, but Saldern revealed few diplomatic skills. Bribing, extorting, generally pushing the Poles around, Saldern held that post only until August 1772. Back in Russia he became involved in a bizarre scheme apparently to raise Paul to the throne. Panin quickly sniffed it out and squashed it before it could ruin his own career. After helping early in 1773 to negotiate the final treaty on the return of his native duchy of Holstein to Denmark (Paul dropping his claims), Saldern carried the treaty to Copenhagen. Thus

removed from Russia, he never returned. On Saldern see Otto Brandt, *Caspar von Saldern und die Nordeuropäische politik im Zeitalter Katharinas II* (Erlangen, 1932).

68. The Czartoryski family, known in eighteenth-century Poland simply as "the Family," dominated that country's political system. Descended from the grand dukes of Lithuania, the Czartoryskis under King Augustus III (reigned 1733–1763) held the posts of military commander (voevoda) of Ruthenia and chancellor of Lithuania. At the end of his reign they favored an end to the Saxon dynasty and, supported by Catherine II, put up their own candidate for the throne. They favored Prince August Czartoryski but Catherine preferred his nephew, Stanislaw Poniatowski (his mother was a Czartoryski). They controlled Poniatowski's election as King Stanislaw Augustus and then sought to reform the country. Catherine, however, wanted to bring Poland fully under Russia's control, and soon broke the power of the family. For a few years the Czartoryskis tried to work their influence under Russian domination, but by 1768 they began openly to oppose Russian control, adopting a pro-French attitude. Thus at the time discussed here they were seen by Russia as opponents. See M. Kukiel, *Czartoryski and European Unity, 1770–1861* (Princeton, 1955), pp. 4–6.

69. Saldern refers to the kidnapping of Stanislaw in November 1771 by men loyal to the confederation. Whether they planned to hold him for ransom or to try and execute him as a traitor to Poland remains open to conjecture. Within hours he managed to escape by bribing his captors.

70. The Russian-Polish treaty of February 1768 led immediately to the Confederation of Bar. The Poles had resisted making the treaty at all. An earlier treaty signed in 1762 but never implemented raised the same issues that dominated the agenda in 1768: the elective kingship and the rights of religious dissidents. Russia insisted upon full equality and civil rights under Polish law for Protestants (some 200,000 people) and Orthodox Christians (600,000 people) in Poland. The outrage of Catholic church leaders to these provisions knew no bounds. Even to bring the Diet to hear the proposed treaty Russia had to arrest and exile to Russia several leading spokesmen of the opposing side. The concessions referred to by Saldern had to do with the dissidents abandoning claims to representation in the Senate and holding high state office in exchange for the right to worship freely and publicly. See Herbert H. Kaplan, *The First Partition of Poland* (New York, 1962), pp. 5–6, 88–90, 129.

71. In addition to the legislation stripping dissidents of access to political power and of religious freedoms, crowds of Catholic Poles frequently attacked dissidents and their places of worship, work and domicile. These acts were especially virulent in the 1720s and 1730s, so much so that several European states discussed the possibility of a union of Protestant and Orthodox countries to place pressure on Poland to limit these popular attacks on non-Catholics. It should be noted that Jews, although technically not included among the dissidents, suffered equally if not more from religious intolerance during this period.

72. The liberum veto was thought by the lesser Polish nobility to protect its rights and freedoms. As the liberum veto had evolved since the sixteenth century, any single member of a Diet by voting against a piece of legislation could defeat it and adjourn the Diet as well. In mid-eighteenth century the Czartoryski family worked to limit the liberum veto without success. Of course it suited well the interests of any foreign state, not just Russia, with sufficient interest (and money) in influencing Polish politics.

73. See Note 20 above.

74. Stanislaw Lubomirski (1720–1783) was marshal of the 1766 Diet. Michael-Casimir Oginski (1731–1803) had a distinguished career in both military and civil service. During this period he was hetman of Lithuania. In the confederations that sprang up against Russia after the forced signing of the 1768 treaty between Russia and Poland he at first won several victories in the field. With Russia's crushing of all opposition, Oginski's properties and goods were confiscated and he was exiled until 1776. Prince Michael-Frederick Czartoryski (1695–1775) headed "the Family" and served as chancellor of Lithuania at the time. He was the grandfather of King Stanislaw.

75. The clash between Frederick II and Saldern dated from 1766, when Frederick took an intense dislike to the diplomat during Saldern's two audiences with him.

76. Beer, *Friedrich II und van Swieten*, p. 21. (Soloviev's note)

77. Baron Karl Emerich Rewiczki (1737–1793) was an accomplished linguist and bibliophile. Named ambassador extraordinary to Warsaw by Empress Maria Theresa, Rewiczki appears as a minor player in Soloviev's account. Indeed he may have been more interested in collecting books than in policy. Rewiczki later was transferred to Berlin by Emperor Joseph. In the mid-1780s he became ambassador to England. In 1790 he refused yet another transfer, to Naples, and went into retirement after selling his substantial library to Lord Spencer.

78. Baron Otto Magnus Stackelberg (1736–1800), descended from the German nobility of Livonia, began his diplomatic career as an envoy to Spain. In 1772 he was posted as Russia's ambassador to Poland upon the advice of Frederick the Great. Of the three ambassadors of the partitioning powers, Stackelberg clearly played the leading role. It was he who announced the declaration of partition to the Poles and he who pushed through the Diet the particular form of government that Russia wanted Poland to have, including the Permanent Council. Polish patriots hated him, but he served his court capably. Stackelberg helped to complete a commercial agreement between Poland and Prussia in 1775, and worked to draw Russia and Austria closer together. For the latter service Joseph II made him a prince of the empire. Stackelberg held his post as ambassador to Poland until 1790.

79. The southern Polish county of Spics (Zips in German) lay south of the Carpathians and geographically, at least, seemed to fit better into Austria than Poland. The first seizure of Polish territory was made by Austria even though it seemed to be the most recalcitrant about the partition, owing to the Catholic faith

shared with Poland, memories of Polish assistance in Vienna's hour of need against Ottoman expansion in the 1680s, and Austrian antipathy toward Poland's two enemies, Russia and Prussia.

80. The Polish Diet, dating from the sixteenth century, had two chambers, the Senate and the Chamber of Deputies. The 140 senators comprised the top officials of church, state, and military command. The king was a member but not the presiding officer, who was an elected marshal. The lower chamber had two delegates from each local diet and two from Cracow. It too was chaired by a marshal. The two houses were required constitutionally to meet in joint session periodically. Ordinary Diets met every two years, extraordinary Diets dealt with specific issues, and convocational Diets elected kings. Because only nobles were eligible for the local diets, the Diet also had an exclusively noble membership. Poles considered the local diets to be a higher power than the Diet. The general structure of Poland's government is outlined in Norman Davies, *God's Playground. A History of Poland* (2 vols., Oxford, 1981). Vol. I: *The Origins to 1795*, especially pp. 529–534.

81. In the political struggles of the mid-1760s in Poland the Branicki clan was identified with the anti-Russian party, together with the Radziwills and others. The elderly head of the family, Jan Branicki, was nominated as an anti-Russian candidate for the throne when Stanislaw Poniatowski was chosen. On Frantiszek Branicki, see Chapter II, Note 80.

82. The marriage of the Austrian grand duchess, Marie Antoinette, youngest child of Maria Theresa, to the future French king, Louis XVI, was the last triumph of Choiseul's foreign policy. The wedding actually took place after the foreign minister's fall.

83. Nikolai Konstantinovich Khotinsky (1727–18??) lived in Paris from 1756. In 1765 he was appointed Russian envoy to Spain, then filled the same position in France in 1767–1773.

84. The first conscription for the Turkish war, in 1768, took one man out of every three hundred. Thereafter the ratio of men drafted in the annual levies was reduced until in 1773 one out of one hundred was being taken. See Chapter II, Note 8.

85. Soloviev referred to the islands in the Aegean Sea with largely Greek populations as the Greek islands or the archipelago islands. A Russian fleet first visited the Aegean early in 1770. On June 24–25 of that year the fleet commanded by Aleksei Orlov annihilated the Turkish navy in Chesme harbor, opposite the island of Chios.

86. To help finance the war Catherine created in both Moscow and Petersburg a Bank of State Assignats in 1769 issuing paper bills in large denominations (see p. 194 below). The experiment reminded Aiguillon of France's own disastrous experience with John Law's Royal Bank following the War of Spanish Succession, which ended in the "Mississippi Bubble," the crash of the bank, Law's flight from France, and persistent suspicion thereafter in France of creative government financing.

87. Arneth, *Maria Theresias letzte Regierungszeit*, II, 360. (Soloviev's note)

88. Charles-François Duperrier Dumouriez (1739–1823), the brother-in-law of Madame Du Barry, was France's secret agent in Poland in the late 1760s and early 1770s. He apparently had arranged for a joint invasion of Russia by Polish and Turkish troops when his patron, the duke de Choiseul, fell from power in France. Upon his return there Dumouriez was imprisoned in the Bastille for six months, released only when Louis XVI ascended to the throne. Later he won both fame and infamy as a commander in the first of France's wars during the revolution.

89. Edgard Boutaric, ed., *Correspondance secrète inédite de Louis XV sur la politique étrangère* (Paris, 1866), pp. 160, 425, 430, 436. (Soloviev's note)

90. Arneth and Auguste Geffroy, *Marie Antoinette. Correspondance secrète entre Marie-Thérèse et de Mercy-Argenteau* (3 vols., Paris, 1874–75), I, 298, 305, 307, 352. (Soloviev's note)

91. François Michel Durand de Distroff (1714–1778), a jurist, served as secretary to the French ambassador at the peace talks at Aix-la-Chapelle in 1748. Thereafter he was chargé d'affaires in London (1749–1751) and The Hague (1751–1752) before serving as French minister to Poland in 1754–1762. After a brief stint in the foreign ministry in Paris he held posts successively as minister to England (1766–1770) and Austria (1770–1772) before his assignment to Petersburg in 1772. In 1775 he returned to France as a state councillor. The posting in Russia was especially sensitive because of the wide range of issues dividing the two countries.

92. Count Ivan Andreevich Osterman(n) (1725–1811) was a son of Count Andrei Ivanovich Ostermann, whom Peter I brought into Russian service. A promising career for the younger Ostermann seemingly was cut short when his father fell from power at the time of Empress Elizabeth's coup. In subsequent years he travelled abroad, learning numerous languages. In 1757 he found service in the Russian embassy in Paris. When Nikita Panin left his post as ambassador to Sweden, Ostermann was hand-picked to replace him. He spent fourteen years in Stockholm. His skills were particularly instrumental in dissuading Gustavus III from waging war on Russia in 1772–1773. In August 1774 Ostermann was invited to Petersburg to work on the staff of Vice Chancellor A. M. Golitsyn. In 1781 Catherine made him a senator, essentially turning over to him the direction of Russia's foreign affairs; with Panin's death in 1783 this was formalized in the rank of vice chancellor. Paul made him chancellor of Russia. He retired from service in 1797.

93. Gustavus' projected trip to Finland, a delicate event, was intended to underscore his independence (if not scorn) of Russia by approaching so near its border while at the same time ensuring that Russia, informed of the journey beforehand, not take it as a provocation.

94. In Sweden the membership of the Senate was supposed to reflect the proportionate share of representation of the two parties, Caps and Hats, in the top

three estates of the Riksdag (parliament). After each election the Senate's composition was changed by dropping members from one party and adding those from the other. The names of those whose seats changed, as well as the overall number changed, was agreed upon beforehand in articles of composition. Robert Nisbet Bain, *Gustavus III and His Contemporaries, 1746–1792. An Overlooked Chapter of Eighteenth Century History* (2 vols., London, 1894), I, 77.

95. The son of the president of the Dijon parlement, Vergennes started his diplomatic career in Lisbon in the 1740s. In the 1750s he served in western Germany in various posts. After serving in Constantinople he was named ambassador to Stockholm in 1771, where he supported Gustavus III's coup. In 1774 upon the accession of Louis XVI Vergennes became France's foreign minister. As foreign minister after 1774 he followed a policy of friendship with Austria and animus toward England. He brought France to the side of the American colonists rebelling against Britain and urged Catherine to organize a league of armed neutrality. In 1781 he also became chief of the council of finance.

96. Under the constitution of 1720 Sweden's king had almost no power. The Secret Committee had supreme executive, judicial, and legislative powers. It controlled foreign policy, administered justice, created and deposed all ministries, and prepared bills for the Riksdag. The latter institution was composed of four estates, the nobles, the clergy, the burgesses, and the peasantry. The Secret Committee comprised fifty nobles, twenty-five clergymen, and twenty-five burgesses (townsmen). When the Riksdag was not in session its executive power lay with the Senate, nominally chaired by the king. The king's impotence was so total that, to cite one example, he could create peers only once in his reign, at his coronation. Bain, *Gustavus III*, I, 5–6.

97. Sveaborg fortress, begun in the 1750s as Sweden's main defensive bulwark against Russia, sits on several islands at the entrance to the harbor of Helsinki, Finland. It was the idea of a Swedish nobleman from Finland, Col. Jakob Magnus Sprengtporten, to initiate the coup on behalf of King Gustavus by rallying the Sveaborg troops to his cause. This he did, but unfavorable winds prevented him from arriving in Stockholm with the troops in time to help with the coup.

98. Norrköping was a small port town some 115 miles southwest of Stockholm in Ostrogothland (Östergötland). According to the plan, the superintendant of forests, Johan Kristoffer Toll, was supposed to win over the garrison there. Then the king's brother, Prince Charles, would gather other troops in southern Sweden, ostensibly to put down this rebellion, but in reality to join forces with it. Before all this could be accomplished word of the plot reached the Council, forcing Gustavus to act on his own. He rallied the officers of his bodyguard, arrested recalcitrant members of the Riksdag, and rewrote the constitution.

99. The "so-called Intoxicated Garden" was undoubtedly Haga Park, a retreat favored by Gustavus, where he built several pavilions. The park is within the modern city limits of Stockholm.

100. A somewhat dated account of the background and consequences of Gustavus' coup, from a different perspective, is found in Bain, *Gustavus III*, I, 81–159.

101. Louisa (Swedish Lovisa) Ulrica, Frederick II's sister, was married to Sweden's King Adolphus Frederick. At the beginning of the Seven Years War she masterminded an attempt to strengthen the crown. Her coup failed, the crown was humiliated, and Sweden went to war against her brother. The Caps (generally pro-Russian in their outlook) favored the war; after its end the Hats gained the majority in the Riksdag.

102. Auguste Geffroy, *Gustave III et la cour de France, Suivi d'une étude critique sur Marie-Antoinette et Louis XVI apocryphes* (2 vols., Paris, 1867), I, 154–168. (Soloviev's note)

103. A treaty was signed in autumn 1769 among Prussia, Denmark and Russia to guarantee the Swedish constitution. At that time Denmark's Count Bernstorff and Russia's Nikita Panin had feared that the return to power of the Hats would permit a strong monarchy in Sweden and sought to prevent it.

104. Frederick refers here to Count Arvid Bernhard Horn, the architect of elective kingship in Sweden. It was he who increased the power of the Riksdag and Secret Committee in the constitution of 1720, thereby weakening the central government. Count Horn is often regarded as having played a role in Sweden analogous to that of Robert Walpole in England.

105. Frederick II, *Oeuvres*, XXVI, 359–360. (Soloviev's note)

106. The Swedish Constitution of 1720, while it restored the hereditary monarchy dissolved in the short-lived constitution of 1719, so limited the kingship that the era between 1719–1720 and 1772 is termed in Sweden the Age of Liberty, when the state was dominated by the legislative rather than the executive branch. See Michael Roberts, *The Age of Liberty. Sweden 1719–1772* (Cambridge, 1986).

107. Scania (Skåne), the southernmost province of Sweden, was where Prince Charles, the king's brother, planned to rally troops in support of Gustavus's coup. Christianstad was one of the two counties in the province. See also Note 98 above.

108. Located on the southern shore of the Baltic Sea, Pomerania lay immediately to the east of Mecklenburg and north of Brandenburg. Western Pomerania was awarded to Sweden in the Peace of Westphalia. After 1720 Sweden retained only the coastline west of the Peene river, not surrendering it until 1815. Sweden counted upon Prussian assistance to defend this small territory.

109. Ivan Ivanovich (Johann) Mestmakher (1733–1803) was Russia's envoy to Denmark in 1770–1772. He later served in Lübeck (1774–1784), Courland (1784–1789) and Saxony (1790–1799). He was made a baron in 1777.

Denmark's King Christian VII probably would be diagnosed today as schizophrenic. His wife, Caroline Matilda, was a sister of George III of Great Britain. The king's physician, Dr. Johann Friedrich Struensee, a Holsteiner, gained extraordinary power over the king, perhaps by the use of drugs. He also treated Crown

Prince Frederick successfully. By 1770 Struensee and the queen were lovers. They conspired to dismiss the holdover foreign minister from the previous reign, the highly respected Count Johann Hartwig Bernstorff. By July 1771 Struensee was virtual dictator over Denmark. His was a liberalizing and energetic rule, abolishing censorship, relaxing the moral climate, encouraging the support of the peasantry. In less than two years in power he promulgated more than a thousand laws. He also lavished expenses on entertainments and restored to court life several exiles, including his good friend Count Enevold Brandt. In January 1772 his dictatorship ended suddenly, as Soloviev describes below, in a plot masterminded by the queen mother.

110. Johann Hartwig Bernstorff, foreign minister between 1751–1770, when he was dismissed by Dr. Struensee, followed an enlightened policy of diplomatic neutrality within an overall framework of amity with Russia, whose ruling house had close family ties with the house of Oldenburg. Like Russia, Bernstorff also wished to keep the monarchy weak in Sweden. He helped negotiate the Holstein-Oldenburg exchange treaty, signed in 1767, by which Tsarevich Paul renounced his claims to Holstein.

111. Count Adolph Sigfried Osten (1726–1797), although from Pomerania, served the Danish crown loyally for many years. Sent on diplomatic service to Petersburg in 1755, he became Danish ambassador there in 1757. In addition to his skillful diplomacy, he served as a go-between in the affair of the future Catherine II and Stanislaw Poniatowski. In 1761 he was transferred briefly to Warsaw. The brief reign of Peter III was tense for the Danish ambassador because of the emperor's transparent plan to invade Denmark for the sake of his contested inheritance of Gottorp. Catherine's accession brought warmer relations. In 1766–1770 Osten served as ambassador to Naples, then returned to Copenhagen as foreign minister and director of the Sound tolls. His task was made much more difficult by Struensee's rise to influence. Just over a year after the latter's fall Osten surrendered his posts as well; he enjoyed little support either among Danes or from foreign states. Thereafter he served as a local prefect and finally on the supreme court.

112. Count Carl Schack Rantzau-Ascheberg (1717–1789), a career military officer, rose to major general by 1756. In 1762 he was sent as messenger extraordinary to Petersburg to discuss the differences between the two states. He succeeded only in irritating Peter III. In the latter 1760s he commanded all Danish troops in Norway. Struensee, who had met him some years before, brought him onto the state council late in 1770. His relations with Struensee were not wholly friendly, and he participated in the coup that brought down the latter. In particular, he was in charge of the imprisonment of Queen Caroline Matilda. He served thereafter as general-of-infantry, resigning from the state council at Russia's request in July 1772. Catherine did not want him as foreign minister because he lacked skill and experience as a diplomat (he appears to have been heavy-handed and dull-witted) and because he had not proved himself a friend of Russia.

113. Count Bernstorff was a native of Hannover and Dr. Struensee a physician from the Altona quarter of Hamburg. Danes could rightly feel that their affairs had been in the hands of foreigners for a number of years.

114. The domestic counterpart to Bernstorff's foreign policy was strict mercantilism. This led to prosperity, but at the expense of the accumulation of a large state debt. Furthermore, many of those who profited most from the state-sponsored enterprises were German merchants recently come to Denmark. Peasants felt the heavier load of taxation. Danish complaints thus were understandable.

115. Indeed, the entire situation in Denmark recalled Catherine's own history. Catherine's husband Peter III also was emotionally unbalanced. Catherine also had a lover. Had Catherine's coup failed, Grigory Orlov could well have been in the same situation as Dr. Struensee. Catherine likewise was averse to the death penalty and strongly convinced that punishment should be executed only after a fair trial. She expressed these views in her Great Nakaz of 1767, available in an English translation of 1768 in W.F. Reddaway, ed., *Documents of Catherine the Great. The Correspondence with Voltaire and the Instructions of 1767* (Cambridge, 1931), pp. 216–293.

116. Joachim Otto Schack-Rathlou (1728–1800) rose quickly in Denmark's civil service to be a judge on the supreme court by 1759. He became a close advisor to Count Bernstorff the elder in the 1760s, serving first as ambassador to Sweden and then at the head of the finance college and on the general toll council. When Struensee took over the reins of government he retired briefly. After the overthrow of Struensee he became a member of the State Council, one of the most influential men in the government. His name is associated with the settlement of the Holstein question with Russia, as well as with the law on citizenship of 1776. He was one of the reformers of the following decade who set the agenda for social equality that Denmark has followed ever since.

117. Charles Schaw, Lord Cathcart, the ninth Baron Cathcart, represented Britain in Russia in 1768–1771. His expulsion resulted from confusion between the two courts over the matter of upgrading the rank of diplomatic representation. The elder Pitt in his last ministry hoped to draw closer to Russia through a stronger Northern alliance. His plan to send a full ambassador to Petersburg in 1768 forced Catherine to reciprocate by withdrawing Aleksei Semenovich Musin-Pushkin (1730–1817), the minister who had served in London since 1765, in favor of the full ambassador Ivan Grigorevich Chernyshev (1726–1797), whose brother Zakhar served on the Council. The English ambassador was never actually sent, so after a year Catherine reinstated Musin-Pushkin. Cathcart, meanwhile, had been appointed ambassador from England; when Russia downgraded its embassy, England followed suit. Musin-Pushkin was posted earlier as resident in Dantzig (1757–1760). Leaving England in 1779, he finished his diplomatic career in the Netherlands (1779) and Sweden (1779–1784).

118. Robert Gunning (1731–1816) moved successively from Denmark (1761–1771) to Prussia (1771–1772) to Russia (1772–1775). He arrived in Russia

to offer British mediation in the war with Turkey and to try to safeguard Poland's liberties. He also used whatever influence he had in Russia to defeat Prussia's designs on Dantzig. One of his last major efforts in Russia—unsuccessful in the end—was to hire units from Catherine's army to fight against the American colonists.

119. White Russia (Belorossiia, sometimes spelled Byelorussia) lies between Great Russia and Poland and comprised the territories taken in the first partition of Poland. Little Russia (Malorossiia) is otherwise known as the Ukraine.

120. The reference here is to the so-called union of Little Russia with Great Russia, or the union of the Ukraine with Muscovy, brought about by the Zaporozhian Cossack hetman, Bogdan Khmelnitsky. When the Poles severely limited the number of men who could register as cossacks, Khmelnitsky in 1651 offered Tsar Alexis Mikhailovich his allegiance. For various reasons Muscovy delayed accepting the offer until early 1654. War with Poland ensued, in which Muscovy reconquered Smolensk. The armistice of Andrusovo ending the war partitioned the Ukraine, with Muscovy receiving only the left bank of the Dnieper. The areas remained points of dispute between Muscovy and Poland for the remainder of the seventeenth century; Russia did not gain as extensive a control over Little Russia then as Soloviev seems to assume here.

121. Raumer, *Beiträge zur neuern Geschichte*, IV, 515. (Soloviev's note)

122. Frederick II, *Oeuvres*, XXVI, 361. (Soloviev's note)

CHAPTER II

1. Count Aleksei Grigorevich Orlov (1737–1807) was the middle of five brothers, next younger than Grigory. He was enrolled in the Preobrazhensky Guards in 1749. His role was central to Catherine's coup in 1762 and a week later it was he who strangled Peter III. Rewarded handsomely (major general rank, the title of count, second-major in his guards regiment), Orlov played a slight role thereafter in political life. In Italy for his health when the war with Turkey broke out, he proposed a Mediterranean navy to interdict Turkish communications by sea. In January 1769 he received command of this fleet. In 1770 this force overran the Pelopponesus, and on June 24–26 decimated the Turkish navy at Chesme. In November of that year Orlov returned briefly to Italy, then Petersburg and back to the fleet in a month's time. During the peace talks at Focsani the fleet remained in port, even though the Turks used the hiatus to resupply their forces by sea. In September 1772 the navy stalked the coasts of Egypt, Palestine and Anatolia. Again at the end of 1773 Orlov returned to Petersburg. In 1774 he resumed his life in Italy. While there he persuaded the infamous Princess Tarakanova to board ship for Russia. Eventually he settled down on the family estates to breed horses. He was humiliated by Paul in 1796 when forced to walk, bearing a crown, in front of the carriage holding the remains of Peter III in the procession from the Alexander Nevsky monastery to the Peter and Paul cathedral for reburial beside Catherine.

2. General Ivan Petrovich Saltykov (1730–1805) was the son of Peter Semenovich. He saw action in the Seven Years War, climbing to major general rank in 1761. Present at the taking of Khotin in 1769, he was awarded almost every order Russia had for service in the war with Turkey. In the 1780s he was governor general of Kostroma and Vladimir. Saltykov fought in the Caucasus in the second Turkish war, then against Sweden in 1790. Under Paul he was governor of Kiev, then inspector general of cavalry. In 1797 he was made governor general of Moscow, finally retiring in 1804.

Soloviev treats Grigory Alexeevich Potemkin (1739–1791) in greater detail at the end of Chapter III. Potemkin attended the University of Moscow and enrolled in the Horse Guards while young. He saw no action in the Seven Years War yet found a source of promotion by supporting Catherine's coup. In the 1760s he worked in the Synod (he had considered a career in the church as a youth, and again contemplated it now). He found a staff position with Golitsyn's army in the war against Turkey, then served as an aide to Rumiantsev. By 1773 he held the rank of lieutenant general and was considered one of Russia's finest cavalry commanders. Catherine called him to Petersburg to be her favorite in March 1774. By 1776 the affair was cooling, and Potemkin turned to politics, remaining per-haps Catherine's most trusted advisor for the rest of his life. He became virtual vice-regent of the south, formally the governor general of New Russia, Azov, and Astrakhan. He integrated the Crimea into the empire after its annexation in 1784. The "Greek Project" was largely his. His life is the subject of George Soloveytchik, *Potemkin. Soldier, Statesman, Lover and Consort of Catherine of Russia* (New York, 1947).

Otto Adolf Weissmann von Weissenstein (17??–1773), descended from the Livonian nobility, saw extensive action in the Seven Years War. In 1768 he commanded the Belozersk Infantry Regiment, whose troops crossed the Polish-Turkish border at Balta and precipitated the war with the Ottomans. Present at the victories of Larga and Kagul, he was killed in June 1773 near Kuchuk-Kainardji.

3. See Chapter I, Note 54.

4. Bibikov was transferred with several regiments to join Rumiantsev, but while he was on his way his command was diverted against Pugachev (November 1773). Bibikov set up a secret commission to investigate the nature of the rebellion. While pursuing Pugachev in April 1774, Bibikov died.

5. Catherine had the obelisk erected on the grounds of her summer palace at Tsarskoe Selo, the modern Pushkin, to the right (south) of the main building as one faces the formal garden, where it still can be seen. Designed by the architect Antonio Rinaldi, it was the first of the Turkish monuments to be erected there. Eventually a small garden was built around it. Its inscription reads "In memory of the victory on the river Kagul in Moldavia, July 21, 1770. Through the leadership of General Count Peter Rumiantsev a Russian Army numbering seventeen thousand turned to flight as far as the river Danube the Turkish Vizier Galil Bey with a force of one-and-a-half hundred thousand."

6. The letter was written before Rumiantsev crossed to the right bank of the Danube, probably to convince the field marshal to make the crossing. (Soloviev's note)

7. The allusion is to Orlov's brother, Count Aleksei Orlov, who had titular command of Russian naval forces in the Mediterranean and Aegean seas.

8. This was indeed the sixth recruitment levy since 1767. A recent tabulation indicates that the first five levies called up 323,360 men (Madariaga, *Russia in the Age of Catherine the Great*, p. 233). The complexities of Russia's recruitment system are summarized in John L. H. Keep, *Soldiers of the Tsar. Army and Society in Russia 1462–1874* (Oxford, 1985), especially pp. 144–153, and Arcadius Kahan, *The Plow, the Hammer and the Knout. An Economic History of Eighteenth-Century Russia* (Chicago, 1986), pp. 7-10.

9. See Chapter I, Note 29.

10. Soloviev was not beyond commenting editorially on the views of the various people whose opinions he incorporated into his text. This question mark indicates incredulity that Chernyshev could have expressed such an opinion. Apparently Soloviev had no idea why Chernyshev might have thought the acquisition of Kinburn and Ochakov "more harmful than useful." The next short paragraph contains similar evaluation of N. I. Panin, who seems not to have been paying attention at the Council's session.

11. Peter I created the position of procurator general in 1722 as a means of controlling the Senate. The procurator general could propose new legislation to deal with problems (senators could not) and he controlled a vast patronage system. Under Catherine the position became extremely powerful. Her long-time procurator general, Prince Alexander Alexeevich Viazemsky (1727–1793), had been chief of staff to Rumiantsev during the Seven Years War. Appointed as procurator general in 1764, he soon gained control over the secret police (1765) and two years later headed the commission to draft a new legal code. He was a member of Catherine's Council and later drew up a reform of finances. He held the post of procurator general until his retirement a few months before his death.

12. Located on the western coastline of the Black Sea halfway from the mouths of the Danube to Constantinople, Varna was the key fortress for the defense of both land and sea approaches to Turkey's capital. To take Varna was to bring the war directly into the sultan's back yard.

13. After the breakup of the Bucharest negotiations in March 1773 Zegelin served as unofficial intermediary between the Russians and the Turks.

14. Kronstadt served a double purpose. As a fortress on the eastern end of Kotlin Island, located some 14 miles west of Petersburg, it protected Russia's capital from attacks by sea. Secondly, because of sandbars at the mouth of the Neva river, fully-laden ships of the largest draft could not sail into the city itself. Instead a commercial harbor was built at Kronstadt and goods were carried to and from the city on lighters.

15. All judges in Islam were graduates of the higher schools (medreses) where they studied law and theology, which were seen as one. Even in areas where

the political power of the sultans was dubious, the judges (kadis) were hierarchically arranged to culminate in the chief judge (kadiesker). There was one kadiesker for Europe and one for Asia. The jurists (muftis), also graduates of higher schools, functioned as courts of appeals. The highest-ranking mufti was the grand mufti of Constantinople (Sheik al-Islam), discussed in Chapter I, Note 27.

16. Baron Karl Karlovich Ungern-Sternberg (1730–1799) eventually rose to the rank of general-of-infantry, adjutant general of the army, and governor of Petersburg. Prince Yuri Vladimirovich Dolgoruky (or Dolgorukov, 1740–1830), registered in service at age nine, was wounded at the battle of Gross Jägersdorf when only 17. He commanded a regiment in the battle of Zorndorf. At the time of the election of Poniatowski as king of Poland Dolgoruky commanded Russian troops sent to Poland to keep the peace. By 1767 he was a major general and major of the Preobrazhensky Regiment. He wanted to serve with Rumiantsev in the war with Turkey, but was sent to Montenegro for the first two years of the war; unable to raise the population there to revolt, by 1773 he was serving under Rumiantsev. He and his brother Vasily (1738–1784) covered themselves with glory at Kagul. After the war Prince Yuri Vladimirovich was posted to Kharkov province, and in the second Turkish war he commanded the troops that defended Ochakov.

17. A traditional symbol of rank among the Turks was the horsetail; the higher an official's rank, the more horsetails he was entitled to. They were mounted on poles under a ball. Pasha was the title denoting membership in the divan, or state council. Pashas served dual roles as civil administrators and military commanders over large areas. A pasha of three horse tails, or three-tailed pasha, was a very high-ranking official.

18. Lieutenant general Fedor Ivanovich Glebov (1734–1799) served under his father in resettling Serbs in southern Russia in the 1750s. In the Seven Years War he saw action first as a volunteer in the French army, then entered Berlin with General Todtleben's forces in 1760. In the Turkish war he was at Khotin in 1769 with Golitsyn, fought under Rumiantsev, and then served under Bruce. September 1771 saw him commanding a corps at Brailov. In May 1772 he went on leave for a year, returning as a lieutenant general to fight at Silistra in June 1774. The following year he commanded Russia's troops in Poland. He was named a senator in 1781 and full general in 1782.

19. Prince Vasily Mikhailovich Dolgoruky-Krymsky (1722–1782) fought his first war against Turkey in 1735–1739. He commanded Russia's Second Army that took the Crimea in 1771. He retired in 1779 when he was not promoted field marshal, but consented to command Moscow in 1780–1782. Apparently he was a rather ineffective general, despite his honors.

20. Not the least of Catherine's agitation had to do with Grigory Potemkin, commander of the Russian troops facing Silistra. Unhappy with her personal domestic arrangements, Catherine apparently at this moment was deciding to invite Potemkin to Petersburg. She had noticed him several years before, but was still in love with Orlov at the time. Only two or three weeks after writing this note to Rumiantsev she sent Potemkin her polite invitation. Within two months he was her inseparable companion.

21. Little is known about Captain Mikhail Timofeevich Koniaev, other than that he retired in 1782.

22. Captain Mikhail Gavrilovich Kozhukhov (1730–18??) captured two Turkish galleys with crews and guns at Beirut.

23. Admiral Grigory Andreevich Spiridov (1713–1788) commanded his first ship in 1730 on the Caspian and saw action against the Turks on that sea a few years later. He gained considerable experience sailing several times from Archangel to the Baltic in the 1740s. He commanded various ships in the Baltic during the Seven Years War and in 1765 was given command over Kronstadt. He took the Russian fleet to the Mediterranean in 1769 and was its real commander, Aleksei Orlov having been given nominal command. He retired in 1773.

24. This action was referred to above on page 97 when the Council discussed whether commerce might be interdicted once again.

25. Admiral Samuel Karlovich Greig (1735–1788), a Scot, sought service in Russia in 1764. He captained several ships in the Baltic in the 1760s and then served under Spiridov on the voyage from the Baltic to the Mediterranean in 1769. A part of the expeditionary force until 1773, he saw action at Chesme and elsewhere. In late 1773 he returned to Petersburg. As a vice admiral in the 1770s and 1780s he helped improve the quality of the Russian navy. He became ill and died while fighting the Swedes in 1788.

26. Grigory Orlov had been forbidden to attend official functions from mid-September 1772 until May 1773, except for a brief period late in 1772. He then participated fully in affairs until May 1774, when he retired permanently from politics.

27. Orlov had every right to be touchy on this point. Without British officers the Russian fleet would have had little success in the Mediterranean and Aegean. They included Greig, Elphinstone, MacKenzie, and Dugdale (the lieutenant who single-handedly sailed the first fireship into the Turkish fleet at Chesme). Orlov himself was no navy man, even if he did hold titular command over the fleet.

28. See Chapter I, pp. 17–18.

29. Genghis Khan (1162–1227) unified the Mongolian tribes and built the great Mongol/Tatar empire encompassing much of Eurasia. Tamerlane (1336–1405), son of the first man of his clan to convert to Islam, was both scholar and warrior. His empire, a successor state to the great Mongol empire, extended from Russia to India, from Siberia to Egypt. He crushed the Ottoman Turks in battle (1402). His capital was at Samarkand. The Timurid dynasties (Persian, Afghan, Indian) were descended from him.

30. Many members of the Girey clan, including two former khans, had emigrated to Constantinople, where they owned a large urban estate. They continually urged the Porte to greater action on behalf of the Crimea.

31. Stanislaw here reminds Catherine of their passionate love affair lasting from late 1755 to summer 1758, while Poniatowski was in Petersburg in the entourage of the English envoy Charles Hanbury-Williams. After Catherine took the throne Poniatowski proposed marriage in 1763, but by then Catherine was enamored of Orlov.

32. During the scuffling that occurred on the occasion of Stanislaw's kidnapping in November 1771 the king was slashed across one cheek.

33. The local diets (sejmiki in Polish) met in advance of the national Diet in order to select the delegates to it. It was much easier to control the Diet if some control could be gained over the very selection process of its membership.

34. The liberum veto meant that a Diet had to achieve unanimity in order to accomplish anything. A confederation, on the other hand, expressed its will through a simple majority. Technically the Diet and the confederation were two different institutions, but it was not uncommon to refer to the latter as a confederated Diet, as Catherine's instructions do here.

35. The German state of Saxony provided the two Polish kings immediately prior to Stanislaw Augustus (Augustus II and Augustus III). Not having a suitable adult male candidate in 1764, they could not realistically oppose Russia's nomination of Poniatowski. Instead, in light of Russia's earlier support of Augustus II and III, the Saxon party threw its support behind Russia's policy in Poland during this period.

36. Before partition the crown's lands comprised about one-sixth of the total in Poland. Because it was uncertain how many of those estates (and their income) were in partitioned provinces, the ministers were to ensure that enough remained for the king to have what might be deemed a sufficient landed income. Crown estates (starostwo in Polish, often rendered as starosty in English) traditionally were distributed by Poland's kings in exchange for special services. On this occasion those estates remaining were to be parcelled out to the nobility on a basis that prevented any one family from enriching itself at the expense of others.

37. During the Diet of 1768, called by the Russian ambassador Prince Nikolai Vasilevich Repnin to deal with the issues of the liberum veto and the dissidents, several traditionalist Catholic opponents to Russia's designs emerged. Their leader was the senator and bishop of Cracow, Cajetan Sołtyk. After several months of political sparring with Repnin, inciting Poles to opposition to any rights for dissidents, Sołtyk was arrested in October on orders from the Russian ambassador. With him were arrested three other senators, his allies Joseph Zaluski, the bishop of Kiev, Waclaw Rzewuski, the governor of Cracow, and Rzewuski's son, Seweryn, a military commander. All four were taken to Kaluga in chains where they were held until early 1773.

38. Adam Poninski (1732–1798), the marshal of this particular Diet, had been bought by the Russians to such an extent that he was obliged to work the will of Stackelberg in every instance. Tadeusz Rejtan (1746–1780) was never able to come to terms with the first partition. When it was accepted by the Diet he went into a frenzy, tearing his clothing and throwing himself on the floor of the chamber, accusing them of playing Judas to Poland. Seven years later he committed suicide. By tradition Rejtan could have cried either "Veto!" (I deny) or "Nie pozwalam!" (I do not allow it). Shouting it once would have produced only a delay in the agenda, but doing so three days running brought matters to a standstill.

39. Antony Kazimierz Ostrowski (1713–1784), bishop of Kujawy, was in the delegation that signed the treaty negotiated by Repnin in 1766 dealing with

dissidents. He was seen in Poland as a friend of Russia. Later he became archbishop of Gniezno and primate of Poland.

40. Mme. Marie-Thérèse Geoffrin, née Rodet (1699–1777), hosted one of the choicest salons in Paris during the heyday of that institution, the 1740s and 1750s. Hers in particular was associated with the encylopedists. At one time or another she played hostess to virtually every famous visitor to Paris during this era, including the future kings Gustavus III of Sweden and Stanislaw Augustus of Poland. She sometimes paid the debts of the latter during his stay in Paris. He called her "Maman" (Mama). In 1766, following his election as king of Poland, she visited Warsaw upon his invitation. She counted Catherine II as well as Stanislaw among her regular correspondents.

41. The river called here the Podorze, usually called the Seret, did not even flow through Poland. Its upper reaches bisected Bukovina, the farthest northwest province of Turkey. In the end Austria's share did reach the Sbrucz, a tributary of the Dniester marking the eastern boundary of Austria's share of the partition.

42. Prince Vladimir Sergeevich Dolgoruky (1720–1803) was born in France, where his father was a Russian diplomat. He grew up there and in Constantinople, to which his father later was transferred. In 1762 he was one of those who brought troops over to Catherine's side in her coup against her husband, for which Dolgoruky was rewarded with the rank of colonel. He was posted to the important ambassadorial post at Berlin, where he remained Russia's representative for twenty-five years.

43. See Chapter I, Note 74.

44. Uniat churches were Orthodox in ritual and rite, Catholic in administration. Their name comes from the Union of Brest (1596). The majority of Russian Orthodox never recognized the union. The government of Poland, which did, thereafter persecuted the Orthodox churches within its borders. Perejaslaw was located on Russian soil across the Dnieper from Polish territory, downstream from Kiev.

45. The Permanent Council itself was a creation of Russia imposed upon Poland in the new constitution of 1773. It consisted of thirty-six members elected every two years by the Diet and chaired by the king. It functioned as the government between Diets.

46. Frederick refers here to his meeting at Neisse with Count Dietrichstein, recounted in Chapter I, pp. 34–35.

47. Abbé Charles Irénée Castel de Saint-Pierre, writing at the end of the War of Spanish Succession, questioned the value of war in his *Project of Permanent Peace*, published in 1719.

48. Frederick was unhappy that England signed the separate Treaty of Paris on February 10, 1763 ending its participation in the Seven Years War, which it fought primarily against France. England supplanted France in much of North America and the West Indies, as well as on the coasts of western Africa and India. Prussia at the Peace of Hubertusburg (February 15, 1763; both dates New Style) had to be satisfied with a return to the status quo ante bellum.

49. The Peace of Aix-la-Chapelle ended the War of the Austrian Succession in 1748. Its English text is published in Israel, ed., *Major Peace Treaties*, I, 269–304. King George of England was dissatisfied with Austria's performance in helping protect his interests in Hanover; England eventually abandoned its Austrian alliance for one with Prussia, signed at Westminster in January 1756.

50. Golitsyn is speaking about the Nogay Tatars, discussed in Chapter I, Note 36.

51. By this reference Golitsyn meant of course France.

52. Major General Prince Ivan Sergeevich Bariatinsky (1740–1811) was enrolled in the Izmailovsky Guards Regiment as a child. In the Seven Years War he saw action at Zorndorf before serving as an adjutant to Peter III. Ordered to arrest Catherine during her coup in June 1762, he delayed doing so and thus did not incur her wrath when she won. He was assigned to be a companion to Catherine's son Paul not as tutor but as friend. By 1779 he held the rank of lieutenant general. Appointed ambassador to Paris in 1773, he served there until 1783, representing Russia in France during the era when Count Vergennes sought a rapprochement with Russia. Soloviev used the variant spelling Boriatinsky for his surname.

53. Russia might have exercised considerable influence had it not abandoned the principal role which it played under Empress Elizabeth. (Soloviev's note)

54. Beer, *Die erste Theilung Polens*, II, 255. (Soloviev's note)

55. After numerous invitations from Catherine, Denis Diderot came to visit her in Petersburg in 1773. She fully patronized him by this time, having purchased his library for a large sum and then hired him as librarian. Diderot spent the six winter months in Russia, often dining with Catherine and engaging in conversations with her regarding political, social and aesthetic philosophies.

56. Charles, duke of Södermanland (1748–1818), was the younger brother of King Gustavus III. Lazy and indulgent, he was also one of Sweden's leading Freemasons. He alternately supported and opposed his older brother. From 1792–1796 he was regent for King Gustavus Adolphus IV; he finally reigned as Charles XIII in 1809–1818.

57. Count Hans Henry von Lieven (1703–1781) was supreme marshal in 1772, having been governor general of Pomerania and chancellor. Carl Frederick Scheffer (1715–1786) was a political theoretician and Hat politician, and therefore an opponent of Russian control over Sweden's foreign affairs and constitution; the ambassador to France in the 1740s, he was driven out of the council in 1761. Frederick Axel von Fersen (1719–1794) was marshal of the Riksdag in 1760 and a former general in Pomerania; he was a member of the state council from August 1772–March 1773. Baron Christopher Falkengréen (1722–1789) was at this time a vice admiral in charge of the commissariat; he entered the state council in May 1772.

58. The name Estland referred to Estonia, a duchy under Swedish rule before the Great Northern War. The name of the military unit was retained even though the territory had been lost.

59. By the second half of the eighteenth century galleys were obsolete everywhere except in the Baltic. Their use had already declined by the end of the

seventeenth century in the Mediterranean. Peter the Great used them to good effect against Sweden in the battle of Hangö in 1715. Amongst the many rocky islands and the broken shoreline of western Finland, in particular, galleys were much more maneuverable than sailing vessels.

60. The oft-proposed visit by Gustavus did not take place until the summer of 1777, when he visited Petersburg incognito as the duke of Gotland. Gustavus and Catherine, although first cousins, were sixteen years apart in age and too much alike in ambition to be good friends.

61. Ivan Matveevich Simolin (1720–1799) went to work in the College of Foreign Affairs in 1743. He was part of the delegation sent to fetch the future Peter III to Russia in 1744. He was posted in Copenhagen (1744–1757), Vienna (1757–1758), the German diet in Regensburg (1762–1771), then ambassador to Denmark (1772–1775), Sweden (1775–1779), Great Britain (1779–1784), and France (1784–1792).

62. Immediately after coming to the throne, Catherine defended her son's inheritance of Holstein. As Panin developed his Northern policy he persuaded her that it would be in Russia's interest to concede the duchy to Denmark in order to gain a Danish alliance. The alliance was signed on February 28, 1765. In the inheritance settlement, signed on April 11, 1767, Paul agreed to renounce his claims to Holstein in exchange for Denmark recognizing control of the counties of Oldenburg and Delmenhorst by a junior branch of the Holstein-Gottorp family. This agreement was to go into effect when Paul achieved his majority.

63. The French envoy to Denmark from 1766–1774, Paul, marquis de Blosset (1728–178?), had served earlier in England (1764–1765) and Florence (1765–1766), and after his stint in Denmark was posted to Portugal (1775–1778) before finishing his career in the ministry of foreign affairs at Versailles. Osten's dealings with the French ambassador obviously made him suspect to Catherine.

64. See Chapter I, Note 117.

65. Count Andreas Peter Bernstorff (1735–1797) became a member of the council of state in 1773. Forced out in 1780 because of Russian anger with his failure to lend sufficient support on the issue of armed neutrality, he headed the government from 1784–1797, during which time serfdom was abolished, free trade policies implemented, and the basis laid in enlightened social legislation for modern Denmark.

66. The Lord Suffolk with whom Musin-Pushkin spoke was Henry Howard, 12th duke of Suffolk (1739–1779), England's secretary of state from 1771–1777, the leader of the Grenville faction after Grenville's death in 1770.

67. Emelian Pugachev (1742–1775) fought in the Seven Years War and served in Poland in the late 1760s before deserting the army. In 1772 along the Yaik river he took advantage of a disturbance among the cossacks and others to mount a grave challenge to Catherine's power. Claiming to be Peter III, he roused disgruntled peasants, Tatars, Kalmyk tribesmen, and industrial workers in the Urals. He attacked Orenburg unsuccessfully in 1773 and by mid-1774 had ranged into the Urals and as far northwest as Kazan, occupying the entire city except for

its kremlin. Under attack by the Russian army, he then moved south along the Volga toward his native land on the Don river. Captured late in 1774, he was taken to Moscow and executed in 1775. The story of his uprising is told in John T. Alexander, *Emperor of the Cossacks* (Lawrence, Kan., 1973).

68. Sultan Abdul-Hamid I (1725–1789) succeeded his brother on January 21, 1774 as twenty-seventh Ottoman sultan. For information on Sultan Mustafa III, see Chapter I, Note 16.

69. Mussin-Zade Pasha (17??–1774) was grand vizier when the war with Russia broke out in 1768. Alone of the members of the divan he opposed it, for which he lost his post. However, he performed so well in defending the Morea (Pelopponesus) against the Russian-sponsored Greek uprising in 1770 that he was promoted again to grand vizier (commander-in-chief of the armed forces) in late 1772. When Mustafa III died Mussin-Zade was retained by Abdul-Hamid. The peace of Kuchuk-Kainardji was laid to his charge; when news of it reached Constantinople he was immediately recalled. He died from being poisoned while enroute to the capital.

70. Lieutenant General Mikhail Fedotovich Kamensky (1738–1809) was the rare Russian army officer who saw no combat in the Seven Years War, although he was attached to the French army. A friend of Tsarevich Paul, he was sent to Prussia in 1765 to learn from their methods of training artillery units. While there, his career was enhanced when he came to the attention of Frederick II. A major general by 1766, he served under A. M. Golitsyn and P. I. Panin early in the war with Turkey, then under Rumiantsev in 1772. In 1774 he commanded the left flank of the army. After the war he served as governor general of Riazan and Tambov (1783–1785). Promoted to field marshal in 1797, he was murdered by his own peasants in 1809.

71. Prince Nikolai Vasilevich Repnin (1734–1801) advanced through the Preobrazhensky Regiment and was promoted rapidly during the Seven Years War, ending it as a major general. Named minister to Prussia in 1762, he blundered badly and was withdrawn, being posted next to Poland in 1764. His heavy-handed tactics offended the Poles, although he did force through the election of Stanislaw as king and the concession on dissidents in 1766. His difficulty in getting along with people surfaced in his next appointment as well, under Rumiantsev in the war with Turkey (1770). Dismissed from his command, he travelled in Western Europe for a time, returning to Russia to help negotiate the peace at Kuchuk-Kainardji. In 1775 he became the ambassador to Constantinople. Later Repnin served as governor and governor general in various provinces and governments.

72. An English translation of the treaty, dated July 10, 1774, is found in Israel, ed., *Major Peace Treaties*, II, 913–929. Ironically this treaty, the most humiliating ever signed by Ottoman Turkey, fell on the same day as Russia's humiliating Treaty of the Pruth signed in 1711.

73. Seraskir was a title meaning commander-in-chief or minister of war. Peter Petrovich Veselitsky was Russia's first envoy to an independent Crimea, serving 1772–1775.

74. Khristofor Ivanovich Peterson (1732–1789), descended from Holstein-ers, was sent to Constantinople the first time in 1763 to serve on the embassy staff. He participated in the negotiations at Focsani and Bucharest. In 1771 he command-ed troops under Wittgenstein and Potemkin at Bendery, and in 1772–1774 par-ticipated in many Danubian actions. In 1774 Peterson escorted the Ottoman envoys to Kuchuk-Kainardji. In September of that year he received his posting to Con-stantinople and exchanged ratifications of the treaties in January 1775. He served later as a diplomat in Dantzig and Munich, where he died.

75. Austria's Emperor Joseph continued to covet Bukovina, or upper Molda-via, because it provided the best communications with the Galician lands recently ceded by Poland. Joseph also coveted Little Moldavia, particularly the city of Orsovo on the Danube. At his behest Prince Kaunitz instructed Thugut to try to acquire them by negotiation from the Turks. It was clear that the Turks would refuse to cede Little Moldavia because it had a partially Muslim population and contained mosques. As for Bukovina, it had been occupied throughout the war by Russian troops. Austria therefore sought to negotiate permission from the Rus-sians to occupy Bukovina as the Russians withdrew their forces in conformity with the agreement at Kuchuk-Kainardji. The arrangements were kept secret and not conducted between the governments but by generals in the field. For their cooperation, Rumiantsev and his staff received valuable gifts from their Austrian counterparts. In August 1774 Austrian troops replaced the withdrawing Russians. By separate agreement in May 1775 Turkey officially recognized Bukovina as Austrian.

76. Peter Vasilevich Zavadovsky (1738–1812) later became Catherine's fa-vorite, picked for that role by Potemkin after his and Catherine's ardor cooled; Zavadovsky lasted less than a year in that position. Egor (Georg) Fedotovich Asch (1727–1807) was the army's doctor. Velda and Prince Andrei Nikolaich have not been identified.

77. The Nogay Tatars, led by Djan-Mambet-bey (alternatively Can Membet Bey), at first did whatever the Russians wanted, moving from their homelands to the Kuban. Not all elements within the nation were loyal to him, however, feeling that Djan-Mambet-bey had sold out his Crimean kinsmen. Now they desired either submission to the Crimean khan or even vassalage under the Ottomans.

78. Shagin-Girey's opportunity came quite soon. Khan Sahib-Girey fled to Constantinople at the end of 1774, following the invasion of the Crimea by former Khan Devlet-Girey, now backed unofficially by the Ottomans. At first Catherine recognized Devlet, especially after he freed Veselitsky, who had been placed under arrest by Sahib-Girey. But by July 1775 Devlet was approaching the Turks with the possibility of the Crimea becoming an Ottoman vassal once again. Using the Nogay hordes as a power base, Shagin-Girey invaded the Crimea. In March 1777 Devlet-Girey abdicated.

79. See above in this chapter, pp. 126–127.

80. The supreme commander, Hetman Frantiszek-Ksavery Branicki (1731–1819), was trusted deeply by King Stanislaw because of his previous service as

go-between in Poniatowski's affair with Catherine in Petersburg in 1757–1758. In the Diet of 1767–1768 he helped confirm the rights of dissidents. He fought against the Confederation of Bar. By sending him to Petersburg the king was reminding Catherine of the affection they formerly shared. Nothing availing in Petersburg Branicki was sent to Paris, again without effect. In 1774 he returned to Petersburg to ask relief from excessive territorial demands by Prussia. In 1781 Branicki married one of the Engelhardt sisters, nieces of Potemkin.

81. By this term Stackelberg undoubtedly meant the Permanent Council. It was a new institution whose name he simply misstated. There was no "National Council" in Poland.

82. See above in this chapter, p. 134.

83. Stanislas Konarski (1700–1773) was the greatest Polish political thinker of his day. In the 1720s he spent time in France, where he came under the influence of Montesquieu's ideas. A Piarist father, he had a life-long interest in education (Piarists traditionally specialized in elementary education) and in 1740 he opened his "collegium nobilium," a high school for noble boys which became a model for Poland. In 1760 he published A Way to Effective Counsels and in 1761–1763 the four-volume On the Effective Conduct of Debates. Together these were the most influential political treatises written in eighteenth-century Poland. In the latter work he attacked the liberum veto and called for the creation of a permanent council drawn from both houses of the Diet.

84. The rebellion led by Emelian Pugachev.

85. Both rivers are tributaries of the Oder. The Netze lies farther to the north. In the end, Frederick's border lay closer to the Netze than the Warta, but between them.

86. As remarked earlier (this chapter, Note 80), Branicki served as a go-between for Catherine and Stanislaw Poniatowski at the time of their love affair in Petersburg in the late 1750s, on at least one occasion (according to Catherine's own notes) arranging the logistics for a liaison.

87. Beer, Friedrich II und van Swieten, pp. 116–137; Beer, Die erste Theilung Polens, II, 276 ff; and Arneth, Maria Theresia's letzte Regierungszeit, II, 492 ff. (Soloviev's note)

88. Raumer, Beiträge zur neueren Geschichte, V, 32. (Soloviev's note)

89. What Soloviev calls Frederick's "Political Catechism" is generally known as his "Political Testament," the title of a work he published in 1752 in which he likened Poland to "an artichoke ready to be consumed leaf by leaf." He himself borrowed the metaphor, but it suited his view of Poland as a territory with no natural definition, which might be devoured piecemeal by its neighbors.

90. The letter "F" in Russian looks like the Greek letter Phi (Φ). Catherine imagines herself with hands on hips, doing nothing and receiving praise for it.

91. Alexander Stakhievich Stakhiev (1724–1794), the son of a priest, entered the College of Foreign Affairs in 1744. In 1745 he was sent to Stockholm, where he remained for twenty years, serving at first under other ambassadors (including

Nikita Panin in the 1750s) before finally being Russia's ambassador to Sweden in 1774–1775. He was posted next to Turkey (1776–1781) before returning to Petersburg to finish his career in the College of Foreign Affairs. He also served two years as Russian secretary of the Free Economic Society.

92. Oranienbaum, the modern Lomonosov, was an estate built by Prince Menshikov, Peter the Great's associate. After his disgrace it reverted to the crown and was rebuilt extensively by the architects Rastrelli and Rinaldi in mid-century. Peter III used it periodically and Catherine had the so-called Chinese Palace (for some of its interior decor) built in the 1760s. It was a summer retreat fronting on the Gulf of Finland approximately 26 miles west of Petersburg, seven miles west of Peterhof.

CHAPTER III

1. The Governing Senate was established by Peter I in 1710 to administer Russia in his absence (during the campaign on the Pruth). He retained it after his return, giving it administrative, legislative, and judicial responsibilities. Under succeeding rulers the Senate fell into disuse until revived by Empress Elizabeth, Peter's daughter. The Senate interpreted the laws and served as final court of appeal. Catherine II in 1763 divided it into six departments, four in Petersburg and two in Moscow. This division lasted until the early 1780s, when the Moscow departments were closed down. The departments divided the Senate's work functionally.

2. In 1764 Catherine named as procurator general—the official with responsibility for the administrative functioning of the Senate—Prince Alexander Alexandrovich Viazemsky, who held the post until 1792. In the early years of her reign Catherine placed much reliance upon the Senate, but the creation of the Council in 1769 indicated that she would place more power thereafter into the hands of other institutions. Later reforms bore out this intent.

3. This story Soloviev tells in detail in an earlier volume (XIII, 429 of the Soviet edition).

4. In eighteenth-century Russia the word *ekspeditsiia* (as in "Moscow Secret Ekspeditsiia") referred to a special chancellery assigned a particular investigative task. Because it frequently had to travel to distant locations in order to accomplish its work, it is sometimes called in English an "expedition." The Treasury College, the *Kamerkollegium*, had responsibilities over the collection of revenue but not its dispersal. For this reason the designation is sometimes rendered in English as "Revenue College." The reader wanting an overview of the Russian governmental structure at this time should see John P. LeDonne, *Ruling Russia. Politics and Administration in the Age of Absolutism, 1762–1796* (Princeton, 1984).

5. A government (Russian *guberniia*) was a territorial administrative unit introduced by Peter I. By Catherine's time there were some 50 governments in

Russia, some of them subdivided into provinces. All were subdivided into districts (uezdys). Governors were usually military men of general's rank. They had considerable power, being appointed by the empress after screening by the First Department of the Senate. There was no set term of office.

Orenburg was the southeastern-most province of the empire, lying on the border with the Central Asian steppes; Ufa, nearly 200 miles to the north, was administrative capital of a territory (*okrug*) within Orenburg province.

6. The Holy Synod, another of Peter the Great's creations, dated from 1721. The Synod replaced the earlier patriarchate. Like the colleges of secular administration, it was headed by a committee. Its chairman was designated the high procurator of the Holy Synod.

7. The following anecdote is indicative of the persistence of pre-Christian belief. Ustiug and Yarensk were in the far northeast of European Russia, bordering on areas where shamanistic religion still held sway. Soloviev noted that there was a remarkable similarity between the testimony of these sorcerers about their relationships with the devil and the testimony of their counterparts in Western Europe one and two centuries earlier; for example, they too kissed the devil's feet and scattered worms to the winds, resulting in hysteria.

8. The Main Magistracy as established by Peter I had two functions: to serve as a judicial court and administrative body for merchants, tradesmen and craftsmen in Petersburg, and to be a court of appeals for magistracies of all other towns in Russia. Under successive rulers the Main Magistracy continued to have both assignments until 1775, when Petersburg's magistracy was made similar to others in large towns. A different court of appeals was instituted. The Main Magistracy was abolished in 1782.

9. Jakob Sievers (1731–1808), descended from the German landowning class of Estonia, entered Russian service at age 13 in the College of Foreign Affairs. Starting in 1747 he served in the diplomatic corps in Denmark and England until 1756, when he transferred to the army. A general by 1761, he took leave to recover from wounds, travelling in Italy. Catherine chose him as governor of Novgorod in 1764. Holding that post until 1781, Sievers was perhaps the preeminent governor of his day. Catherine consulted with him on numerous issues and projected reforms. As Soloviev notes, he had a reputation as a creative, effective and fair-minded administrator. He is the subject of Robert E. Jones, *Provincial Development in Russia. Catherine II and Jacob Sievers* (New Brunswick, N.J., 1984).

10. Count George Browne (1698–1792), born in Ireland, entered the Russian army in 1730. He fought in all the wars from then until the 1760s—against Poland and Turkey in the 1730s, against Sweden in the early 1740s, in the Seven Years War. In 1762 he became governor general of Riga, a post he retained for the remainder of his life. He was made a count in 1774.

11. These coastal governments on the Baltic Sea and Gulf of Finland traditionally had conducted their business in German (Riga and Reval—modern

Tallinn) or Swedish (Vyborg). All three areas—Livonia, Estonia, and Russian Finland respectively—retained most of their institutions of local government when they came under Russian control during the reign of Peter the Great. The attempt to acquire administrative staffs literate in Russian was part of the effort to systematize and standardize the government, typifying the reign of Catherine II.

12. Soloviev calls the area "Belorussia," literally White Russia. The area began to be seen as a distinct linguistic region between Great Russia (Muscovy) and Poland in the sixteenth and seventeenth centuries. Soloviev is enumerating here the territories acquired in the first partition of Poland discussed in the previous two chapters.

13. Mikhail Nikitich Krechetnikov (1729–1793), governor of Pskov, negotiated the final boundary between Poland and Russia after the first partition. In 1775 he became governor of the new province of Tver, then of Tula, Kaluga, and Riazan. In 1789 he commanded Russia's troops against Sweden, before serving under Kakhovsky in Poland following the second partition. Count Mikhail Vasilevich Kakhovsky (1734–1800), had a distinguished military career before being named governor of Mogilev. In 1779 he joined the War College. He fought the Turks in the Caucasus during the second Turkish war before commanding Russian troops in Poland at the time of the second partition.

14. The colleges, modelled on the Swedish pattern, were Peter the Great's attempt to distinguish functional divisions of administration. By the time of Catherine's reign there were twelve colleges: Audits (Revizion), Commerce, Economy, Foreign Affairs, Hereditary Estates (Votchina), Justice, Manufactures, Medicine, Mines, Treasury (Kamer), Ukrainian and War; the Admiralty and the Holy Synod, although not called colleges, were structured essentially the same way. Other offices roughly equivalent to colleges included the Main Magistracy and Office of State Accounts (Statskontora).

15. Originally a *voevoda* was a military commander. By the seventeenth century the term also applied to the administrator of a district and later, after the designation was introduced, a province. Thus he was the central government's representative, with both administrative and police functions, and serving a fixed term. In 1760 that term was reduced from five years to two; in 1764 the post was made elective by the local nobility.

16. To help finance the war with Turkey, at the end of December 1769 Catherine authorized two state assignat banks, one in Petersburg and the other in Moscow, to print paper money redeemable on demand. The idea for doing this was first approved in 1762 by Peter III but abandoned by Catherine immediately after her accession to the throne. Now she printed notes valued at 25, 50, 75, and 100 rubles. They could be redeemed in copper money. Because it proved far too easy to counterfeit the 75-ruble notes by changing the "2" on a 25-ruble note to a "7," the 75-ruble note was discontinued in 1771. Some 20 million rubles worth of assignats were issued by the end of the war.

17. The case is described in detail in Peter Bartenev, ed., *Osmnadtsatyi vek. Istoricheskii sbornik* (The Eighteenth Century. An Historical Collection) (4 vols., Moscow, 1868–1869), I, 69–73.

18. The Bank for the Gentry was established in 1754 to lend money to nobles on the surety of serf-ownership. Loans were made in denominations of five hundred rubles up to ten thousand. The initial capitalization of three-fourths of a million rubles was lent out within a year. The ceiling was raised several times; by 1775 some 4.3 million rubles were outstanding as loans. The value of serfs as collateral was set initially at ten rubles each, then raised by degrees. Obviously it was difficult either to count the collateral or to check records of land ownership.

19. Both were economic advisors inherited from Peter III. Dmitry Vasilevich Volkov (1718–1785) served as secretary to the conference that conducted the Seven Years War. In 1760 he first proposed freeing the grain trade from restrictions. He was a close advisor to Peter III, with him when he was arrested. Marking his administrative ability but showing her displeasure with him all the same, Catherine made him vice governor, then governor of Orenburg government from October 1762 to April 1764. On the latter date she appointed him president of the College of Manufactures (until 1777). With Teplov he designed the special taxes for the duration of the war with Turkey; in 1771 Catherine had the two of them research European legislation regarding quarantines and other policies against plague. Grigory Orlov insisted that Volkov accompany him to Moscow to fight the consequences of plague there. Volkov remained in Moscow a year and received the Order of St. Alexander Nevsky for his efforts. Later he served as governor general of Smolensk and Belgorod when the provincial reform was instituted there (1776–1777). His last post, until he retired in 1782, was as chief of gendarmes in Petersburg.

Grigory Nikolaevich Teplov (1717–1779) may have been the illegitimate son of Archbishop Feofan Prokopovich, who took an inordinate interest in his education at the Alexander Nevsky monastery school which Feofan established. With his education polished in Germany (he became a disciple of Christian Wolff), Teplov returned to Russia in 1736 to work at the Academy of Sciences. He was chosen to educate Kirill Grigorevich Razumovsky, travelling with him in Western Europe for three years. When Razumovsky was named to head the Academy of Sciences in 1746, Teplov did the real work. The same could be said of the vice-regency of Little Russia from 1751–1764. Teplov in fact wrote the proposal for abolishing the vice-regency. Somewhat under suspicion during Peter III's reign, Teplov was close to Nikita Panin. In Catherine's first years he served in numerous capacities: as her secretary, as author of the instruction on church lands, on the Commission on Education, in the Free Economic Society, and finally in 1768 as a senator. He helped draft the commercial treaty with England in 1766. Perhaps his greatest intellectual contribution was as a theoretician on the commerce commission in 1763–1779.

20. The General War Commissariat, located in Moscow, was the most important financial agency in Russia. It collected the soul tax, the single greatest

source of revenue in the empire, and was responsible for disbursing funds to the army. The chief of the General War Commissariat (General krigs-kommisar) at this time was Alexander Ivanovich Glebov, from 1772 to 1790.

21. Andrei Nikitich Kvashnin-Samarin (?–1775) served as governor of Kazan from 1766–1772; Senator Count Ivan Larionovich Vorontsov (1719–1786), less well-known than his brothers, cousins, and nephews and nieces in the Vorontsov family, was a member of the commission on church lands in 1762 and eventually rose to the rank of lieutenant general.

22. Count Johann Ernst Münnich (1707–1788) was banished to Vologda with his father in 1743. Returning to the capital in 1763, he served as president of the Commerce College in 1763–1773, member of the Commission on Commerce from 1763–1779, and director of the Main Chancellery for Customs Duties from 1763–1784.

23. Before 1763 the collection of customs revenues was farmed out. In that year responsibility was put in the hands of the Main Chancellery for Customs Duties, located in Petersburg. Once goods passed through customs at border towns there were no further checks to see that duties had been paid. Smuggling was considered to be a significant problem by the chancellery; this proposal by Münnich would subject merchants to inspections at the place where they unpacked their wares and began selling them.

24. According to the figures published recently by Arcadius Kahan, nearly two and a half million rubles were collected per year during the 1760s, rising to more than three million annually in the first half of the 1770s. See Kahan, *The Plow, the Hammer and the Knout*, pp. 241–246.

25. The Senate took up this matter on September 9, 1774, according to Soloviev. The manifesto revoking the extraordinary taxes was promulgated on March 17, 1775. Some of the taxes now lifted, such as the tax on benches in Russian bath houses, predated the wartime exactions.

26. Since the time of Peter I the state had been concerned about the excess of clergy, opposing the practice of a single small parish sharing two or three priests, since none of them could earn a decent living. Furthermore, the sons (and daughters) who did not take holy orders were seen as potential thieves and worse. For these reasons excess churchmen and sons had been conscripted into the army during time of need since the Great Northern War. When Catherine ordered this conscription in 1769 the Synod produced figures indicating that some 13,000 clerical positions were vacant. In spite of that, the army took even those seminarians who were not already enrolled when the decree was published. In all, some 9,000 sons of churchmen were conscripted during the war. See Gregory L. Freeze, *The Russian Levites. Parish Clergy in the Eighteenth Century* (Cambridge, 1977), pp. 37–40.

27. The Old Believers were spiritual descendants of those who rejected the reforms introduced by Patriarch Nikon. In church councils of 1654 and again in

1666–1667 the opposition to reforms was condemned. Led by such churchmen as Archpriest Avvakum the Old Believers persisted in holding to elements of ritual and liturgy that scholars had deemed to be latter-day corruptions.

28. The castration heresy grew out of another sect, the khlysty. The latter group, dating from mid-seventeenth century (that is, from just before the Nikonian reforms), sought closer communion with God through ecstatic mysteries. Each participant could share in the divine, or become one with the in-dwelling Christ, through mortification of the flesh, prayer, and singing. Their anticipation of becoming "christs" (khristy) was transformed by their critics into their use of instruments of flagellation (khlysty, whips). Carrying these notions of self-abnegation and the mortification of the flesh to an extreme, the castrators (skoptsy) took literally Jesus' teaching that some made themselves eunuchs for the sake of the Kingdom of Heaven. Appearing in the 1760s and 1770s, the heresy was treated as especially pernicious by both church and state. Despite the most vigilant efforts to eradicate it, the sect endured into the twentieth century.

29. Russian convicts normally were sent to hard labor at any of several points in remote areas of the empire. One of the most notorious places was the silver mining complex near Nerchinsk, 300 miles east of Lake Baikal in farther Siberia.

30. Inability to engage in sexual relations was one of the justifications for annulling a marriage according to canon law.

31. Yakov Illarionovich Brandt (172?–1774) was a member of the Ukrainian College in 1764, named as governor of New Russia in 1765, and Kazan in 1772. He held Pugachev under arrest in May 1773, but the cossack escaped. Brandt was killed when Pugachev's forces took Kazan in June 1774.

32. Catherine's Great Nakaz, or Great Instruction, expressed her political philosophy. She spent some two years writing it at odd hours, drawing heavily from Montesquieu and Beccaria. The version published on July 30, 1767 for the instruction of the commission to draft a new law code was only about half the length of her original, pared down by her advisors. The Nakaz immediately was translated into most major European languages (see Chapter I, Note 116). In later years Catherine moved away in practice from the liberal philosophy it espoused.

33. Zhukov, the military commander of Penza, was convicted in Elizabeth's reign of assault and theft. Before he was sentenced his wife and teenaged daughter were murdered by some of his serfs, under instructions from his own son and daughter-in-law and her mother. Elizabeth long pondered their sentence without decision. Finally in 1766 Catherine, having inherited the case, turned to bishops Dmitry of Novgorod, Innocent of Pskov and Gabriel of Tver for advice. They recommended public confession under humiliating circumstances for the Zhukovs, in order first to win pardon for their souls. The ceremonies were conducted at four churches in Moscow on four different days during Lent in 1766. After their humiliation and public confession, they were sentenced to long terms at hard labor in various places.

34. The Second Department of the Senate, located in Petersburg, had responsibility for judicial appeals, including criminal cases. The Sixth Department, housed in Moscow, handled judicial cases for Moscow and territories south of Moscow, but those cases too went on appeal to the Second Department in Petersburg.

35. Catherine was not the first Russian ruler of her century to set up a commission to draft a new law code, but her attempt certainly was the most celebrated. In a manifesto of December 1766 she called together an elective commission comprising representatives of most social groups recognized by the state. At the end of July 1767 she issued her Great Nakaz as an instruction for them. The commission met both in plenary session and in various committees working on specific legislative problems. In December 1768 it was adjourned as a body because so many of its members were in military service and essential for the war against Turkey. It never met again as a body, although various committees continued to meet until 1774 and the staff to draw salary until 1796.

36. The single homestead holders (odnodvortsy) were descended from military servitors settled on the steppe frontiers in the sixteenth and seventeenth centuries. In exchange for military service they were given small allotments of land, generally a single homestead. Not really nobles nor actually peasants, the majority of them gradually declined into the ranks of crown peasants as the military frontier moved farther from where they lived. In the eighteenth century they paid the soul tax like peasants but continued to argue, generally unsuccessfully, for higher status.

37. On February 19, 1762 Peter III issued a manifesto freeing the Russian nobility from state service in time of peace. While historians have debated the motivation and significance of this edict, its results are clear. Large numbers of nobles departed state service, forcing Catherine to embrace a new definition of noble service in her reforms of 1775 and 1785. This topic is discussed at length in Marc Raeff, *Origins of the Russian Intelligentsia. The Eighteenth-Century Nobility* (New York, 1966).

38. The state imposed levies of young noblemen to generate non-commissioned officers for the military, particularly for the militia. Only vaguely analagous to the levy on peasants, this selection was made by lot.

39. Assigned (pripisnye) peasants were state peasants sent from their villages to be attached to an industrial enterprise or mining operation. This form of service was first introduced to provide manpower for state-owned enterprises, but Peter I quickly saw its utility in privately-owned manufactories as well, especially when the enterprise owners had no legal right to own serfs. Throughout the century most mining operations, particularly those in the Urals, were worked entirely by assigned peasants.

40. At issue was whether to change the primary residence of the peasants. If simply assigned to work at the mines they would remain agricultural peasants

who travelled back and forth at stated times annually to work part of the year in agriculture and part in the mines. If sent to the mines to live they and their households would still earn their sustenance from agriculture, but at a new village adjacent to the mines. Their status would not change.

41. Soloviev apparently based his discussion of the peasant uprising on the papers of Governor Jakob Sievers. Because those papers yield only a partial picture of the event, a brief outline is worth presenting. The uprising involved some 40,000 men who fulfilled labor requirements as assigned peasants in Karelia at the Voitsk iron mines, the Petrovsk cannon foundries, and the newly opened Tivdia marble quarries (for the construction of St. Isaac's cathedral in Petersburg). Already unhappy with conditions of labor, the peasants were further angered by the increase of a ruble in the soul tax announced on May 27, 1769 from 1 ruble 70 copecks to 2 rubles 70 copecks. The peasants were permitted to pay one ruble in cash and the remainder in labor. They preferred paying as much as possible in cash in order to reduce the hated labor obligation.

When Vasily Nazimov came from the Office of Mines to explain the new tax, for some reason he told the peasants that they could pay two rubles in cash, performing labor only for 70 copecks. Among those who spread the word about this new method of payment were Emelian Kalistratov, a peasant from Kizhi administrative territory, and Kliment Sobolev from Tolvuisk village. Many peasants apparently took this relaxation in regulations as proof that they no longer had to carry out their labor obligations at all. Many refused to work from then on. A delegation of peasants was sent to the Mining College in Petersburg to ascertain the exact nature of their obligations. While they were gone the strike spread to virtually all the enterprises in the region using assigned labor. The Mining College reported to the Senate that the peasants not only refused to carry out new obligations but were refusing even to do their traditional work of supplying firewood and coal for the industrial enterprises.

In a show of force the government arrested the leaders of the petitioners, including Kalistratov, and attempted to lay hands on the ringleaders in order to beat them, but the peasants refused to turn their leaders over to the authorities. In spring 1770 an investigative commission under Colonel Christopher Winter was sent to the Lake Onega region.

The investigative commission decided to conduct its work in Petrovsk. In June more than a thousand peasant representatives came to demonstrate their solidarity, and their written statement was signed by more than five hundred of them. The peasants continued to refuse to carry out their assigned work. More spokesmen were sent to Petersburg, where they delivered their complaint to Catherine's state secretary.

In January 1771 Major General Demian Grigorevich Lykoshin, now head of the investigative commission, persuaded, cajoled, and threatened about half of the striking peasants to return to work, but those living around Kizhi refused. In February the peasant petitioner Kliment Alexeevich Sobolev returned from

Petersburg, affirming that Catherine had not yet but soon would satisfy their demands. Visiting many of the villages in a span of two weeks, he raised funds for another trip to Petersburg, together with 30 other petitioners.

General Lykoshin hoped to forestall this adventure by sending a detachment to arrest Sobolev. He was actually seized, but the tocsin was sounded and the outnumbered troops were forced to release him. Sobolev and his band of petitioners went to Petersburg where Sobolev evaded arrest for two months, managing to submit the petition to one of the government agencies. Meanwhile the peasants in the area of Kizhi continued to hold district-wide assemblies. This grass-roots democratic tendency reached its greatest extent in March 1771 when some 5,000 delegates came together to discuss what to do in the face of a threatening military action against them.

The punitive expedition sent against them, commanded by Captain Lamsdorff, had instructions to arrest the ringleaders and read once again the order from General Lykoshin to return to work. The troops were met by more than five thousand peasants, many of them armed. The outnumbered Lamsdorff, rather than forcing the issue, decided to withdraw. The peasants then began to fortify Kizhi for a defense.

Catherine was concerned by now that the disturbance would spread to other areas of the empire. Indeed, echoes were being heard. In April she sent Junior Captain Matvei Rzhevsky of the Semenovsky Guards Regiment with an ultimatum. Again, the peasants in some areas capitulated, but not those on the far side of Lake Onega, in the vicinity of Kizhi. At the end of June General Lykoshin sent a second punitive exedition under Colonel Prince Alexander Urusov, consisting of three infantry companies and an artillery battery of two cannons. Urusov assembled two thousand men in the churchyard and ordered them to sign an agreement to return to work. They were surrounded on three sides by the infantry. Lake Onega was behind them. The two cannon were pointing out at them from the church doors and loaded in full view of them. They refused to comply. Urusov gave the order to fire; five men were killed. The peasants refused to flinch, saying that they were prepared to die one after the other. But when grapeshot was loaded into the cannon, again before their very eyes, they saw the futility of further resistance. This action on July 1 broke the strike, and peasants everywhere in the region returned to work.

Four men, including Kalistratov and Sobolev, were sentenced to be hanged, later reduced in the cases of all but Kalistratov to 100 lashes by the knout, the slitting of nostrils, and branding with the letters REB for "rebel" on their foreheads and cheeks. Others were handed less severe sentences, including the slitting of nostrils, hard labor, and resettlement in Siberia. The vast majority of peasant males were sentenced to be beaten with sticks. Some 80 additional recruits were taken for the army from among their number, and they were forced to pay 8,000 rubles for the expenses of the investigative commission and several hundred rubles for other expenses.

42. Ivan Nazarov(ich) Elagin, a judicial councillor (nadvornyi sovetnik) of the Mining College, was in charge of finding iron and copper ores in the Lopsia district. On a trip to Petersburg he expressed sentiments sympathetic to the peasants' complaints on several occasions, inviting petitioners in Petrovsk to visit his lodgings, promising to take up their case in Petersburg. He was arrested later but released after the investigation was completed. His role is discussed in Ya. Balagurov, *Kizhskoe vosstanie 1769–1771 gg.* (The Kizhi Uprising of 1769–1771) (Petrozavodsk, 1951).

43. State Councillor Peter Nikolaevich Kozhin (172?–1805) served after 1762 on the commission to build St. Isaac's cathedral in Petersburg. In charge of gathering building materials, he travelled widely throughout the empire in search of high-quality building stone. It was his idea to exploit the Tivdia quarries. He was made a state councillor in 1768. In 1772 he was named to the commission for building Petersburg, Moscow and other towns. He drew up the comprehensive plan for the reconstruction of Moscow in 1775.

44. The College of Church Landed Property (kollegiia ekonomii) was established in 1726 to administer ecclesiastical estates. Initially under the control of the Synod, the college was put firmly but briefly under lay leadership in 1738. Elizabeth abolished the college for a decade but restored it in 1757, ostensibly because of repeated disturbances by harshly-administered ecclesiastical peasants in the 1740s and 1750s. Peter III secularized church lands entirely. Catherine II, after initially undoing this act and facing massive peasant unrest as a result, confirmed Peter's decision in 1764. Thereafter the peasants under the jurisdiction of the college became known as "economic" peasants. The estates containing economic peasants were a principal source from which Catherine drew the lands she distributed to favorites and distinguished servants of the empire.

45. The Demidov family were the lords of Russia's iron mining throughout the eighteenth century. Nikita and Akinfy Demidov, father and son, built the family's fortune with government contracts for wrought and bar iron. After moving from Tula to the Urals they owned numerous mines, foundries, and manufactories, producing more than all other privately-owned iron producers together and more than all state-owned enterprises combined. Their products were floated to market down the river systems to the Volga, then hauled upstream to Moscow or, predominantly, downstream once more to Petersburg for export. On the Demidovs' operations see Hugh D. Hudson Jr., *The Rise of the Demidov Family and the Russian Iron Industry in the Eighteenth Century* (Newtonville, Mass., 1986).

46. In the mid-1760s more than 20,000 foreign colonists from Germany were settled along the Volga and its tributaries in the vicinity of Saratov. Some also were settled in the valley of the Medveditsa river, which flows parallel to the Volga and empties into the Don. This is steppe country, and the supply of lumber was troublesome from the beginning. The whole question of foreign colonists in Russia is dealt with ably in Roger P. Bartlett, *Human Capital. The Settlement of Foreigners in Russia 1762–1804* (Cambridge, 1979).

47. Magistracies, introduced by Peter the Great, functioned as the administrative bodies and courts for merchants, tradesmen, and artisans living in Russian towns. Magistracies were composed of burgomasters (from one to four, depending on the size of the town) and councillors (one or two, depending on size). The magistracy was renamed *ratusha* (from the German *Rathaus*; the entire apparatus clearly was derived from Baltic precedents) in 1727. The original name of magistracy was restored under Empress Elizabeth. Later Catherine II modified the role of the magistracy in her urban reforms of 1775 and 1785, giving it jurisdiction over judicial matters only.

Tax-farming had characterized the collection of revenues in Russia before Catherine's reign. Opposed to it in principle, she gradually abandoned the practice. She retained it in some instances, such as the vodka tax, where no other system seemed easily workable.

48. The Main Magistracy Regulation was drawn up in 1721 for governing Russia's towns. Together with the instruction issued three years later it became the basis for urban administration. In 1727 the Main Magistracy was dissolved, but it was revived in 1732. It lost its significance with the urban administrative reforms of Catherine II in 1775 and was disbanded in 1782. The Main Magistracy in Petersburg oversaw the activities of all other town magistracies in the empire.

49. Andrei Matveevich Fliverk (Heinrich Mathias Flüwerk, 1705–1783) was governor of Belgorod in 1767–1781. He held the title of privy councillor.

50. The Settlement Ukraine (Slobodsk-Ukraine) was an area in southern Russia settled in the seventeenth and eighteenth centuries by peasants and cossacks from Poland. Their settlements were called "slobody," hence the name. Slobodsk-Ukraine encompassed the lands surrounding Kharkov, Kursk, and Voronezh as well as the Donets river valley. The area was incorporated into the empire in 1765 as a territory with this name.

51. The story which follows on the next thirty-three pages is told in even greater detail in John T. Alexander, *Bubonic Plague in Early Modern Russia. Public Health and Urban Disaster* (Baltimore, 1980).

52. The plague first affected Russian soldiers in 1769. They apparently carried it across the Russian border sometime between June and August 1770.

53. Lefortovo lay at the eastern fringe of Moscow on the Yauza river. It was named for one of Peter I's foreign mentors, François Lefort. Formerly it was called the Foreigners' or German Suburb. The army hospital was founded in 1706–1707 and faced toward Moscow on the bank above the Yauza.

54. Afanasy Filimonovich Shafonsky (1740–1811) had been physician for German colonists along the Volga and a field doctor in the army before taking over as senior physician at the army hospital in Lefortovo in 1769. He served on the plague commission from 1771–1775, then was Moscow city physician from 1776–1781. He then left the practice of medicine and served as a judge in Chernigov government until his death.

The Medical Office was the Moscow branch of the Medical College in Petersburg. After 1763 it was administered by the Moscow city physician, a post held after 1765 by Dr. Andrei Andreevich (Franz Andreas) Rinder (1714–1771).

55. Count Peter Semenovich Saltykov (1698–1772) rose to prominence under Empress Anna, receiving his title of count in 1733. He led Russia's troops against Poland in 1733–1735 and Sweden in 1742. In 1759 Saltykov commanded Russia's troops against Prussia, winning the battle of Kunersdorf and with it the rank of field marshal. He retired in 1760 after falling out with Empress Elizabeth. His befriending of the young Catherine stood him in good stead after she became empress, and he reentered service in 1762, becoming governor of Moscow the following year.

56. Eighteenth-century medicine was baffled by the plague. There was no distinction between pneumonic and bubonic plague, and the causes of plague remained undiscovered until the end of the nineteenth century. It is not surprising therefore that specialists a hundred years earlier disgreed even on to what to call the disease. The term used in the sources is literally "pest plague."

Of the doctors mentioned here, Johann Friedrich Erasmus (172?–1777), Peter Dmitrievich Veniaminov (Soloviev writes it Venemianov) (1733–1775), and Semen Gerasimovich Zybelin (1735–1802) taught in the Moscow University medical faculty; Charles de Mertens supervised medical care at the Foundling Home. Georg (later Baron) von Asch (1727–1807) was a member of the Medical College, and Kassian Osipovich Yagolsky (sometimes Yagelsky, 17??–1774) taught at the Moscow surgical school. Johann Kuhlemann was the main doctor at the Pavlovsk hospital in Moscow. The exact nature of Grigory Shkiadan's duties is not known.

57. The Big Woolen Court was a two-story brick textile mill located across the Moscow river from the Kremlin near the Stone bridge, which connected the southwestern corner of the Kremlin with the river's southern bank. The Big Woolen Court, which dated from 1705, was the largest woolen textile mill in Russia and produced uniforms for the army. It employed more than three thousand assigned peasant workers. The Stone bridge (usually called the Great Stone bridge), consisting of eight arches, was built at the end of the seventeenth century.

58. The St. Nicholas on the Ugresha monastery was founded by Prince Dmitry Donskoy in 1380 upon his return to Moscow in gratitude to God and St. Nicholas the Miracle Worker for his victory over the Mongols earlier that year. He is supposed to have seen a vision over some trees at this spot by the river and said, "All my sins are forgiven" (Sia vsia ugresha serdtse moe), for which reason the monastery became known this way.

59. Doctor Gustavus Orraeus (17??–1811), a native of Russian Finland, received the first M.D. degree awarded by the Medical College in 1768. He was Moscow city physician from 1772–1776 and later wrote a scientific treatise on the plague, published in Petersburg in Latin in 1784. Staff doctor Christian Grave served in the army for thirty-eight years before retiring in 1771 to Moscow—just in time to fight the plague there.

60. It was generally assumed that fires had some effect in reducing the spread of the plague by cleansing the air. Similarly, vinegar, often combined with sweet-smelling herbs, was used as a disinfectant.

61. Ivan Ivanovich Yushkov (1728–1781) was governor of Moscow government. Earlier he served on Elizabeth's 1754 commission to compose a new legal code.

62. Count Jacob Alexandrovich Bruce (1732–1791) was married to Rumiantsev's sister. He served directly under his brother-in-law at Larga and Kagul, but thereafter lost his command for not pursuing the enemy with sufficient enthusiasm. He was transferred to Kiev and then Petersburg, where in 1771 he was placed in charge of defending the city against the plague. His system of quarantines did the job. Next he commanded Russian troops in Finland during the threat of war with Sweden in 1773. He succeeded Jakob Sievers as governor of Novgorod in 1782, and when the posts of governor general of Petersburg and of Moscow became open almost simultaneously in 1784, he was named to both.

63. Catherine handed these duties to Yeropkin (1724–1805) on March 25, 1771. He had full charge thereafter of anti-plague measures in Moscow. Richly rewarded for his role, he returned as administrator years later to become governor general of Moscow in 1786–1790.

64. The White wall (Belyi gorod) referred in Russian both to the wall itself and to the large part of Moscow it enclosed (White town or quarter). As Moscow expanded, several different walls were built. At the city's center was the triangular Kremlin. East of the Kremlin, starting from Red Square, was Kitaigorod, or the Kitai quarter, which added to the Kremlin made a rather pie-shaped city. The White wall surrounded this area, standing where the boulevard ring streets now run. Outside the White wall, again at some distance, lay the Earthen rampart, in a large circle now cleared where the garden ring runs today. Underground is the metro's circle line. Only the Earthen rampart extended to the south bank of the Moscow river. More information on eighteenth-century Moscow can be found in Albert J. Schmidt, *The Architecture and Planning of Classical Moscow. A Cultural History* (Philadelphia, 1989).

65. The Simonov monastery, downstream from the Kremlin on the left bank of the Moscow river, was founded in 1370. The Danilov was nearly a century older, having been established by Prince Daniel Alexandrovich, the first prince of Moscow, in 1280. It lay across the river from the Simonov and slightly downstream. The Pokrovsk was founded in 1635 by the first Romanov tsar, Michael Fedorovich. It was east of the city near the Vvedensky hills, outside the Earthen rampart.

66. Mikhail Grigorevich Sobakin, also spelled Sabakin (17??–1773), represented the College of Foreign Affairs in the commission to compile a new law code in 1767.

67. Moscow's medical council was an informal group of physicians, already mentioned in the text, who consulted together on diagnosis, treatment, and possible measures to safeguard public health.

68. Moscow's senators numbered at least eight: Prince Stepan Alexeevich Kozlovsky, Mikhail Semenovich Pokhvisnev, Rozhnov, and Vsevolod Alexeevich Vsevolozhsky (1738–1797), as well as Saltykov, Sobakin, Ivan Vorontsov, and Yeropkin. Later Dmitry Volkov was added to their number.

69. The Treasury College rampart was erected during the reign of Elizabeth well outside the city itself as the toll barrier for Moscow city, replacing an earlier wooden wall erected by the sellers of spirits from toll gate to toll gate. The rampart encompassed many villages and outlying monasteries in addition to the city itself.

70. Preobrazhenskoe (Transfiguration) village lay northeast of Moscow on the Yauza river, just inside the Treasury College rampart. This was where Peter I spent much time as a youth. Russia's first guards regiment was named for the village. It was an outgrowth of his youthful play regiment of the same name. The Preobrazhensky Regiment dated its founding (somewhat inaccurately) to 1683.

71. Metropolitan Timothy (Tikhon Ivanovich Shcherbak or Shcherbatsky), (1698–1767) was metropolitan of Kiev from 1748–1757, then Moscow from 1757–1767. He was metropolitan of Moscow and Kaluga from 1764.

72. Ambrose's father, Stepan Konstantinovich Zertis, was a local official in the village of Soroka. He emigrated into Little Russia in 1691 and served as translator for the supreme commanders (hetmans) there. His son Andrei Zertis received his surname from his maternal uncle Vladimir Kamensky, who was archimandrite of the Pozhinsk Mother of God monastery. Andrei, whose monastic name was Ambrose, was born in 1708. (Soloviev's note)

73. The parish clergy are assumed to have been almost universally poor. Few churches were endowed, so most parish, or white (monastic clergy were called black) clergy had to live off their stipends and their land allotments. These landholdings were often smaller in reality than in prescription. Some churches provided such little income that they had trouble keeping staffed. See Freeze, *Russian Levites*, Chapter 5.

74. The bishop's council or consistory was instituted by the Synod under Peter I to help run the diocese. It had disciplinary as well as administrative powers.

75. Crossroads priests had no parish church of their own, so stood in the crossroads offering their services in sacraments and rites. They tended to congregate in Moscow, and especially at the Spassky crossing, where a bridge led from Red Square into the Kremlin through the Spassky (Saviour) gates, the one with the clock over it. Bishop Ambrose first forbade churchmen to stand there in February 1768, when he had been archbishop for only a month.

76. Elderly people in Moscow were spreading rumors that when Ambrose was archimandrite of the Resurrection monastery (New Jerusalem) he mistreated the monastery's peasants. Because of the general dislike for him he was sent to Moscow and subsequently became involved in the events of 1771. (Soloviev's note)

77. The St. Barbara gates in the Kitai quarter wall east of the Kremlin originally permitted Varvarka street, originating in Red Square, to exit the city.

Above the gates in the wall was the icon of the Bogoliubovo Mother of God, so named because it was patterned after an earlier icon associated with the place outside Vladimir where Prince Andrei Yurevich, the son of Moscow's founder, had his palace in the twelfth century—Bogoliubovo.

78. The Ecclesiastical Statute (Ecclesiastical Regulation, Spiritual Regulation) was issued by Peter I in 1722 for administering the church. Its text is available in English in A. V. Miller, trans. and ed., *The Spiritual Regulation of Peter the Great* (Seattle, 1972).

79. Nikolai Nikolaevich Bantysh-Kamensky (1737–1814) kept the Moscow archive of the College of Foreign Affairs. His parents came from Moldavia, where his grandmother was a cousin of Prince Dmitry Cantemir. His mother was Archbishop Ambrose's sister. He barely escaped being murdered in the riot. Beginning in 1766 he published numerous historical works, some from archives and others compiled by himself. He received his archival training from Gerhard Friedrich Müller, the greatest compiler of historical materials in eighteenth-century Russia.

80. The archbishop did not want to move the icon to the nearest church, the church of All Saints, but to the church of Sts. Cyrus and John. The latter was built at the empress' expense since the translation of the remains of those two saints was celebrated on June 28, the day that Catherine gained the throne. By Soloviev's time the church, because it had no parish, had been redesignated the Serbian Guest House.

81. The Foundling Home, established in 1764 by I.I. Betskoy, was housed nearby on the bank of the Moscow river, just outside the Kitai quarter, in a large two-story building. Ambrose's support of the Foundling Home further underlines his enlightened leadership.

82. An anonymous account by an author who was close to the action says in part, "The watchmen set by the people themselves did not take any money (which contradicts Bakhmetev's categorical assertion that the guards came from the Moscow garrison); they tied up the secretary and placed him under guard, but an argument began with the troops." The author was a learned man. Speaking about the senators leaving Moscow, he said, "The *patres conscripti* themselves scattered to their villages." Concerning Ambrose's decree about the money the author of the account said, "It is true that his holiness behaved somewhat crudely and heedlessly in this matter." (Soloviev's note)

83. To give the events he was describing in the text an even greater immediacy for his readers, Soloviev noted that in the 1870s the Commercial School building stood on the same spot.

84. Tver street was the former name of Gorky street, although the modern avenue is much broader; Tver street ran northwest from the Iversky gates at the northern end of Red Square. Mokhavaia street and Hunter's Row were opposite ends of the same street running along the Neglinnaya river on the bank opposite the Kremlin.

85. The Miracles (Chudovo) monastery was located behind the Savior (Spassky) gates into the Kremlin, on Tsar's Square. Founded in 1365, it was the official seat of the archbishop of Moscow.

86. The Donskoy monastery was located at the Kaluga gates to the city, several miles south of the Kremlin and across the Moscow river. It was established in 1591 at the spot where the Crimean Khan Kaza-Girey was defeated in an attempt to raid Moscow. The large cathedral, the Donskoy Mother of God, was built in 1684–1698.

87. The Borovitsky gates are the westernmost entrance to the Kremlin, above the Neglinnaia river (now encased in a pipe) near the Water Tower.

88. That is, from the southwestern corner of Red Square.

89. Most of the colleges had at least an office in Moscow. The ones with their principal office there and a subsidiary office (kontora) in Petersburg included Justice and Hereditary Estates. Their lord presidents told everyone to stay home from work.

90. Vasily Ivanovich Bazhenov (1737–1799) was one of Russia's leading architects. Trained by Prince Dmitry Vasilevich Ukhtomsky, Bazhenov introduced classicism to the city of Moscow. The use of model houses dated from Peter the Great's time. They emphasized the facade, leaving interior appointments to individual taste. By the end of the eighteenth century the use of model house facades had revitalized the appearance of central Moscow. Several albums of model facades were in print by the early nineteenth century. See Schmidt, *The Architecture and Planning of Classical Moscow.*

91. The Pakhra river was due south of Moscow at a distance of some 16 miles or 25 kilometers.

92. Orlov held the title of grand master of the Ordnance from 1765 to his death in 1783, meaning that at least titularly he commanded Russia's artillery and engineer corps. The adjutant general was a personal servitor of the ruler; Catherine usually presented the title to her current favorite.

93. Mozhaisk was located upstream from Moscow on the Moscow river in the southwestern corner of Moscow province.

94. Vice President (1766–1772) of the College of Manufactures Fedor Sukin was charged in 1773 with heading a conspiracy to counterfeit assignats. His own guilt was not proven, but he was exiled for life to Orenburg for not denouncing colleagues involved in counterfeiting.

95. Senator Aleksei Petrovich Melgunov (1722–1788) was a member of Peter III's informal council who remained loyal to Peter III and therefore distant at first from Catherine. Yet in 1764 he was named commander of New Russia and a year later president of the Treasury College (to 1777). In the 1760s he served in Moscow's Fifth Department of the Senate, later in Petersburg's First Department. Later he was appointed governor general of Yaroslavl and Vologda.

96. The Solovetsk monastery on the islands of the same name in the White Sea, 600 miles north of Moscow, was founded in 1436 by Sts. Savva and Zosima.

Used as a place of imprisonment as early as the sixteenth century, it was also a fortress where in the late seventeenth century Old Believers withstood assaults for eight years before immolating themselves in the crumbling defenses.

97. In 1754 Empress Elizabeth formally abolished the death penalty, although it was employed selectively thereafter, as in the case of Vasily Mirovich, who tried to free Ivan VI in 1764 and make him tsar once again, or Pugachev in 1775.

98. The Guardianship Council was the body that ran the Foundling Home. It was formally set up by decrees of Catherine II.

99. The Neglinnaia river flowed through central Moscow, rising near Kuznetsky bridge, then flowing through a meadow where the Bolshoy Theater now stands, across the modern Karl Marx Square, and finally below the northern wall of the Kremlin, where it emptied into the Moscow river next to the Kremlin's Water Tower. In the 1790s the river was converted into an open canal. After many unfulfilled projects it was enclosed in pipes in 1817–1819. The former course of the river under the Kremlin wall was transformed into the Alexandrovsky garden in the early 1820s.

100. Prince Mikhail Nikitich Volkonsky (1713–1788) was rescued from an enforced obscurity by Empress Anna following the political disgrace of his parents. He attended the Noble Cadet Corps and reached the rank of major during the war with Turkey that ended in 1739. For most of Elizabeth's reign he was favored because his uncle was the leading minister and eventual vice chancellor, Andrei Petrovich Bestuzhev-Riumin. Volkonsky's diplomatic career began in Constantinople in 1742; he moved to Warsaw in 1746, where he made a favorable impression on the Czartoryskis. He served in Livonia before the Seven Years War, in which he saw action and was promoted to major general. The disgrace of his uncle in 1758 temporarily ended his own career. He participated actively in Catherine's coup (she and his uncle were friends), for which service she made him a senator. In 1764 he commanded the Russian troops sent to Poland in support of Poniatowski's candidacy for the throne. Back in Russia by 1767, he represented the Senate at the legislative commission. With the situation deteriorating in Poland he was sent there a third time in 1769 as ambassador to replace the heavy-handed Prince Nikolai Repnin. In early fall 1771 Saldern replaced Volkonsky. That November Catherine chose Volkonsky to replace Peter Saltykov as governor general of Moscow following the plague riot. In late 1774 Catherine entrusted him with the special commission to prepare the trial of Pugachev and his lieutenants. As an experienced provincial administrator, Volkonsky gave Catherine concrete proposals in 1775 in anticipation of her reform of provinces in that year. Volkonsky held his post in Moscow until his retirement in 1780.

101. The Order of the Holy Apostle Andrew the First-Called was one of three existing at the time when Catherine acceded to the throne. It took precedence over the other two, the Order of the Holy Great Martyr Catherine, and the Order of Holy Lord and Master Alexander Nevsky.

102. According to Soloviev, this excerpt, housed in the State Archive, had been copied in the empress' own hand, but the author undoubtedly was Orlov.

The following remark, he wrote, was of particular interest: "When I prepare to return to Petersburg, I can stop there (Tver) for two or three days." For this reason the author must have been Orlov, Soloviev concluded.

103. The issue of the danger of factories in towns, the fears that they might contribute to overpopulation, and related problems are dealt with in John T. Alexander, "St. Petersburg and Moscow in Early Urban Policy," *Journal of Urban History*, VIII (1982), 145–169.

104. Ivan Ivanovich Betskoy (1704?–1795) was born in Sweden, where his father, General Ivan Yurevich Trubetskoy, was a Swedish prisoner, having been captured at Narva in 1700. Traditionally bastard sons of Russian aristocrats received only part of their fathers' surnames—hence Betskoy instead of Trubetskoy. Educated in Sweden, Betskoy went to Paris in 1722. While there he entered Russian diplomatic service. He saw Russia for the first time in 1726. He remained in military service throughout the 1730s. In the 1740s Empress Elizabeth named him a gentleman of the chamber to the future Peter III, which permitted him also to meet the future Catherine II when she came to Russia in 1744. After 1747 Betskoy travelled abroad for a decade and a half, studying European public health institutions. He also participated in salon life, eventually becoming a convinced Rousseauian. Peter recalled him to Russia in 1762. He became head of the chancellery on construction and the following year president of the Academy of Fine Arts and the Noble Cadet Corps. In 1764 with Catherine's patronage he established the Moscow Foundling Home; a sister institution was formed in Petersburg in 1770. The foundlings were to be brought up as good citizens and hard workers, having been taught trades. Unfortunately the new urban class could not be based on an institution where more than 80–90 percent of the residents died. Betskoy also helped inspire the school for noble girls at Smolny. After 1775 Catherine played increasingly less attention to his ideas. Betskoy was laughed at by many for his programs of education; he rejected corporal punishment and emphasized developing the whole person.

105. The conspirators were arguing over which party at court should be predominant under the reign of Paul Petrovich, the Panins or the Orlovs—or still another. The competition between these factions is referred to in Chapter I, Note 2.

106. The transit of Venus across the sun occurred twice during the 1760s. It was used to compute the earth's distance from the sun, the basic astronomical unit of measure. In 1761 the French astronomer Abbé Chappe d'Auteroche travelled overland from Petersburg to Tobolsk to view it, reading a paper at the Academy of Sciences the following year on his results. The second transit occurred in 1769. Chappe's book *Voyage en Sibirie* was published in 1768 and achieved some notoriety for its comments about Russian life and mores. The book infuriated Catherine, who responded by writing her own *Antidote* refuting Chappe. Still, the *Voyage* went through four editions, including an English translation. Undoubtedly the stir created by Chappe's book drew greater attention to the second transit than it would have drawn otherwise.

107. Aleksei Grigorevich Razumovsky (1709–1771) was brought to Petersburg in 1731 to sing in the Ukrainian à capella choir at court. His tenor voice
pleased Elizabeth Petrovna, and after her coup in November 1741 he became a
gentleman-in-waiting to her. They were married secretly in 1742, a union never
recognized publicly. He rose through the ranks until reaching field marshal in
1756. Upon Elizabeth's death he retired. His younger brother Kirill (see Note
107 below) had a much richer career in public service.

   Ivan Ivanovich Shuvalov (1727–1797), another favorite of Elizabeth, attended court from 1742. He was a patron of the arts, helping to found the Academy of
Fine Arts and serving as its first president in 1757–1763. He also co-founded the
University of Moscow, together with Mikhail Lomonosov, and served as its first
curator. When Catherine came to power in 1762 the Shuvalovs lost influence,
and Ivan Ivanovich went abroad. For the next fourteen years he travelled in Europe, collecting works of art, many of which were destined for the Academy of
Fine Arts and for Catherine's Hermitage. Following his return to Russia in 1777,
he remained out of politics.

108. Kirill Grigorevich (here shortened to Grigorich) Razumovsky (1728–
1803) was sent abroad in 1743 to finish his education. After returning to Russia
he served from 1746–1765 as president of the Academy of Sciences in Petersburg, although not terribly involved in its activities. In 1750 he was made hetman
(viceroy) of the Ukraine (Little Russia), which post he held until its dissolution
in 1764. He participated in Catherine's coup in 1762, for which exploit he was
named a senator. In 1764 he was promoted to field marshal. Razumovsky served
on the Council from 1769–1771.

109. Fedor Matveevich Voeikov (1703–1778) held the post of governor general of Kiev from 1767–1775 and governor of New Russia from 1768–1774; he
was active earlier, under Elizabeth, as a diplomat in Courland and Poland.

110. The Summer Palace referred to here was a large wooden structure standing just north (towards the Neva river) of where Emperor Paul later built his palace (Engineers Castle). It sat at the rear of the Summer Garden adjacent to the
Fontanka river. The Winter Palace was the immense building designed by Rastrelli which now houses the main part of the Hermitage Museum.

111. Gendarme General Nikolai Ivanovich Chicherin (1724–1782) headed
the Petersburg police in 1764–1777. Raised to the post of senator in 1766, he
was promoted to general-in-chief in 1773. He was dismissed from his post because Catherine blamed him for the poor state of readiness for the flood that
struck Petersburg in September 1777. Ivan Perfilevich Elagin (1725–1794) was
arrested in 1758 in the Bestuzhev affair but his career was restored when Catherine became empress. He served 1762–1768 as one of her personal secretaries, helping draft legislation. He also assisted Catherine then and later in her romantic
entanglements.

112. Kamchatka, the volcanic peninsula thrusting into the Pacific Ocean in
easternmost Siberia, already was being used in the eighteenth century as a dumping
ground for dangerous convicts, especially political prisoners. It became even more
infamous for that purpose in the nineteenth century.

113. Moric August Benevsky (1746–1786) signed his name several ways, including Moric Anader Benev. Soloviev relates briefly his biography until 1774. He did return to Madagascar the same year with French forces, but left in 1776. Maria Theresa restored his Hungarian citizenship in time for him to participate in the War of the Bavarian Succession in 1778–1779. He could not get Madagascar out of his head, though. In 1779 he went to America to try to persuade the new republic to support his projects. When questions arose about his credentials, he sailed back to France to acquire better papers. In America again in 1782, he failed once more to gain financial support for his cause. Undaunted, he showed up next in England in 1783. Finally, in October 1784 he sailed again for Madagascar, but the French did not want him there. He was killed fighting the French in Madagascar in 1786. His story can be found in David M. Griffiths, "Beniovsky, Morits Avgust," MERSH, Vol. 4, pp. 11–16.

114. Alexander Turchaninov tried to replace Empress Elizabeth on the throne with Anna Leopoldovna, the mother of young Ivan VI, in 1742. Semen Gurev, his brothers Ivan and Alexander, and Peter Khrushchov were officers in the Izmailovsky Guards Regiment who failed in a quixotic plot to put Ivan VI on the throne in October 1762. Eventually Khrushchov entered French service and the Gurevs returned to their European Russian estates after refusing to join in Benevsky's escape. Doctor Meider's identity and crime remain unknown to the editor.

115. The proclamation thus addressed numerous issues of the day. To mention them individually: (1) Paul's claim to the throne was indeed stronger than his mother's. (2) Russian intervention in Poland could be seen as aiding Catherine's erstwhile favorite Poniatowski, now King Stanislaw. (3) The tax-farming of both vodka and salt could be extremely lucrative; governors had the right to approve contracts up to a certain value without approval by higher bodies, a situation that led to considerable graft and bribery. (4) The foundling homes could be seen as encouraging sexual license. (5) Church lands had been taken from them in the 1760s. (6) Catherine's Great Nakaz placed limits on the political discussion by the commission to compose a new law code. Finally, (7) the temporary taxes imposed at the start of the Turkish war were considerably higher than those existing previously.

116. In the Orthodox church calendar June 29 is the feast day of Sts. Peter and Paul the Apostles and the end of the Fast of the Holy Apostles. It follows immediately after the day of Catherine's own coup d'état, June 28.

117. Master of Heraldry Prince Mikhail Mikhailovich Shcherbatov (1733–1790) came from a distinguished family. His father was governor of Moscow and governor general of Archangel. He himself had a scholarly bent, translating Pope, Montesquieu and Voltaire into Russian. Although registered in the Semenovsky Guards while a teenager, he saw no action in the Seven Years War. He retired in 1762 but was elected a delegate to the legislative commission in 1767. In that role he was an outspoken defender of the old nobility. In 1768 Catherine named him official historiographer, in which post he began to write a universal history.

He held the position of master of heraldry from 1771–1777. The master of heraldry had administrative responsibility for the Office of Heraldry which registered the sons of hereditary nobles.

118. In the early years of the Roman republic a spring near the western end of the Forum could not be drained. Legend has it that the oracle was consulted and replied that the spring's source would be blocked only when the Romans threw their greatest treasure into it. Heeding these words, a proud young soldier named Curtius girded himself for battle and rode his horse into the water. This effectively dammed the spring, leaving the small pool bearing his name which exists to this day.

119. The preceding lines were written as Soloviev lay on his death bed. He dictated the remaining text to one of his sons in several sessions on September 21–22 and 24, 1879. He wanted to close this volume with the execution of Pugachev, but his labor of many years was ended abruptly by his death at 7:00 p.m. on October 4, 1879. His last thoughts were about his monumental survey of Russian history. (Soviet editor's note)

120. The discrepancies between this quotation and the same passage found earlier (Chapter I, p. 9) may be explained by Soloviev's extreme ill health when quoting it here.

121. Orlov was sent to Focsani, not Bucharest; Obreskov represented Russia at the Bucharest peace talks.

122. Alexander Sergeevich Vasilchikov (1744–1803), a lieutenant in the Horse Guards, became Catherine's favorite in August 1772, replacing the absent Orlov, who was in Focsani. He was supplanted in turn by Potemkin early in 1774 and retired to Moscow on a rich pension to the house provided him there. Of all Catherine's favorites, Vasilchikov seems to have been the least interested in learning, the arts, or culture—things that mattered greatly to Catherine. She later noted that of her several liaisons this one alone embarrassed her.

123. Soloviev apparently refers here to Denmark's minister to Russia, although that has not been confirmed. Because Panin spent his youth in Denmark (he was born in Copenhagen), Struisberg may have been a friend since childhood.

INDEX

Abdul-Hamid I, Turkish sultan, 162-163, 171, 268, 292.
Abdul-Rezak-effendi, Turkish envoy at Bucharest conference, 83.
Academy of Fine Arts, 312-313.
Academy of Sciences, 298, 312.
Admiralty College, 246-247, 297.
"Admonition to Schismatics" (pamphlet), 199.
Adolphus Frederick, Swedish king, 268, 280.
Adrianople, 137, 143.
Adriatic Sea, 22.
Adyge people, 267.
Aegean islands, 102-103, 277. See also Greek islands.
Aegean Sea, 103, 262, 277, 285, 287.
Afanasiev, guards officer, 249.
Afanasiev, Ilia, factory worker, 243-244.
Africa, 289.
Ahmet III, Turkish sultan, 266, 269.
Aiguillon, Emmanuel-Armand de Vigneret, duke d', French foreign minister, xvi, 30, 47-54, 59, 144, 149, 151, 186, 272, 277; conversations with Khotinsky, 47-50, 52-54.
Aix-la-Chapelle, Peace of, 141, 278, 290.
Akutin, soldier, 240.
Alexander, John T., 292, 305, 312.
Alexander Nevsky monastery, 283, 298.
Alexandrovsky gardens (Moscow), 311.
Alexeev, Pimen, Old Believer, 226.
Alexis Mikhailovich, Russian tsar, 76, 283.
Ali Bey, Egyptian pasha, 102.
Ali Bey, seraskir pasha, 168.
Alps mountains, 21.
Altona, 282.
Ambrose (Zertis-Kamensky), archbishop of Moscow, 218-219, 227, 239, 308-309; murder of, 227-233, 239, 241-244.
America, 314.
American colonies, 272, 279, 283.

Anatolia, 283.
Andrei Nikolaich, prince, 170, 293.
Andrei Yurevich, prince of Vladimir-Suzdal, 309.
Andrusovo armistice, 283.
Anglo-Russian Commercial Treaty (1766), 271, 298.
Anna Ioannovna, Russian empress, 251, 306, 311.
Anna Leopoldovna, duchess of Brunswick, mother of Ivan VI, 314.
Andreev, Vasily, house servant, 241.
Ansbach, margravate of, 3, 5, 20, 272.
Apraksin, Count Peter Fedorovich, Russian general, 61.
Archangel, 190-191, 287, 314.
Archipelago islands. See Aegean islands.
Areopagus, 94.
Armed Neutrality, 291.
Armenia, Armenians, 267.
Armenian church, 270.
Arneth, Alfred, Ritter von, 266, 271, 273, 278, 294.
Arnim, Baron, Prussian envoy to Denmark, 157.
Artisan and armory office, 199.
Asch, Egor Fedotovich (Georg von), army doctor, 170, 216, 293, 306.
Asia, 285.
Assignat Bank. See Bank of State Assignats.
Assigned peasants. See Peasantry.
Assyria, 166.
Astrakhan government, 284.
Augustus II, king of Poland, 288.
Augustus III, king of Poland, 134, 275, 288.
Austria, Austrians, xii-xiv, xvi, 2-4, 6, 8, 12, 28, 45-46, 49, 52, 54, 65, 72, 75, 97, 99, 126, 138-139, 141, 143, 176, 178, 180-184, 186, 262-263, 265, 267, 271-272, 274, 276, 278-279, 289-290, 293; foreign policy, 2, 19-27, 81, 136, 150, 263, 266, 268, 272; convention with Turkey,

INDEX 335

Shamanism, 296.
Shatsk, 215.
Shcherbak, Tikhon Ivanovich. See Timothy, metropolitan of Mosow.
Shcherbatov, Prince Mikhail Mikhailovich, master of Heraldry, 254, 256, 314-315.
Shcherbinin, Evdokim Alexeevich, general, 14-16, 170, 173-175.
Shemiakin, tax farmer, 197.
Shkiadan, Grigory, doctor, 216, 306.
Shmelev, guards grenadier, 255-257.
Shuisky settlement, 210.
Shumla, 89, 99-101, 164, 166-167.
Shushchov, nobleman, 204.
Shuvalov, Count Andrei Petrovich, director of assignat bank, 194.
Shuvalov, Count Ivan Ivanovich, Elizabethan favorite, 249, 313.
Siberia, 190, 202, 204-205, 211-212, 214, 253, 256-257, 287, 300, 303, 313.
Sievers, Jakob Johann, 191, 206, 208-209, 211-212, 296, 302, 307; correspondence with Catherine II, 211.
Silesia, 3, 5, 20, 24, 31, 35, 37, 136, 141, 150, 265. See also Lower Silesia.
Silistra, 88-89, 99-100, 143, 162-163, 166, 286.
Simbirsk, 207.
Simbirsky, ensign, 205.
Simolin, Ivan Matveevich, Russian minister to Denmark, 156-159, 291; correspondence with Panin, 156, 157.
Simonov, lieutenant, 205.
Simonov monastery, 221, 238, 307.
Single homestead holders (odnodvortsy), 204, 213-214, 301.
Sixth Department of the Senate. See Governing Senate.
Skopchestvo (Skoptsy), heresy, 200-201, 300. See also Castration heresy.
Skrypitsyn, ensign, 205.
Slobodsk Ukraine. See Settlement Ukraine.
Slobodzeia, 87.
Smolensk, 213, 219, 260, 283, 298.
Smolny Convent, 17.
Smolny Institute, 270, 312.
Smuggling, 198.
Smyrna, 103.

Sobakin, Mikhail Grigorevich, senator, 222, 225, 307-308.
Sobolev, Kliment, 302-303.
Solms, Count Victor Friedrich, Prussian ambassador to Russia, 21, 24, 27, 29-30, 33-36, 61-63, 67, 136, 140, 144, 180-181, 183-185; correspondence with Panin, 33.
Solomon, Western Georgian king, 267.
Solovetsk monastery, 243, 310-311.
Soloveytchik, George, 284.
Soloviev, Sergei Mikhailovich, viii-xix, 266, 268, 270-274, 276-278, 280-281, 283-285, 290, 294-297, 299, 302, 306, 308-309, 311-312, 314-315.
Sołtyk, Cajetan, bishop of Cracow, 116, 118, 288.
Sophia Magdalena, queen of Sweden, 268.
Sorcery, 190-191, 296.
Soroka village, 308.
Soul tax, soul tax lists, 48, 196, 198, 298, 301-302.
Souls (serfs), 194, 196, 207-208, 210-211.
Sound tolls, 281.
South Slavs, 102.
Southern alliance, 50, 262.
Spain, xii, 35, 46, 50, 53, 71, 75, 138, 144, 150, 272, 276-277.
Spassky crossing (crossroads), 228, 308.
Spassky gates. See Savior (Spassky) gates.
Spencer, lord, 276.
Spics. See Zips.
Spiridov, Grigory Andreevich, admiral, 102, 287.
Sprengtporten, Jacob Magnus, Swedish nobleman, 279.
Stackelberg, Baron Otto Magnus von, Russian minister to Poland, 42-45, 112-113, 115-118, 120-121, 123-134, 162, 177-179, 276, 288, 294; instructions to, 42-43; conversations with Stanislaw Augustus, 44-45; correspondence with Panin, 119-120, 121, 122, 131-132, 175-179.
Stakhiev, Alexander Stakhievich, Russian resident in Sweden, 187, 294-295.
Stanislaw Augustus (Poniatowski), king of Poland, xiv, 4, 30-31, 34, 36-40, 43-46,

THE EDITOR AND TRANSLATOR

George E. Munro was born in 1944 in Ohio and grew up in South Carolina. He discovered Russian history while an undergraduate history major at Wheaton College in Illinois, where he received his bachelor's degree with Honor in 1965. He began learning Russian at the University of North Carolina at Chapel Hill as a graduate student in history, supplementing his language study with two summers in the Slavic Workshop at Indiana University. He spent ten months in Leningrad in 1969–1970 researching a dissertation on the history of St. Petersburg in the reign of Catherine II. He received his doctoral degree from the University of North Carolina in 1973. Since 1971 he has been a member of the history faculty at Virginia Commonwealth University in Richmond, Virginia. He spent an additional five months in the Soviet Union in 1977 continuing research toward a still-forthcoming book on the development of St. Petersburg. He travels in the Soviet Union regularly as tour leader and lecturer for student groups and for the Smithsonian Associates travel/study program. In 1988 he was Visiting Professor at the University of Virginia. Besides grants to study in the Soviet Union he has received fellowships from the Woodrow Wilson Foundation, the Fulbright program, and the National Endowment for the Humanities. The author of numerous articles in professional journals and a major contributor to the *Modern Encyclopedia of Russian and Soviet History*, he is co-editor and translator (with David Griffiths) of *Catherine the Great's Charters of 1785 to the Nobility and the Towns* (1991). He is a frequent speaker in central Virginia on Russian and Soviet topics.

FROM ACADEMIC INTERNATIONAL PRESS*

*Request catalogs **OP–out of print